Entebbe Decl

The Untold First-Hand Stories of the Legendary Rescue Operation

Authors: Sayeret Matkal Operators

Entebbe Declassified
The Untold First-Hand Stories of the Legendary Rescue Operation

Authors:
Sayeret Matkal Operators

Editors:
Yiftach Reicher Atir, Shlomi Reisman, Aviram Halevi

Cover design by Peleg Michaeli

Translated from the Hebrew by Mitch Ginsburg

Published by BooxAi
ISBN: 978-965-577-906-6

Originally published in Hebrew by Effi Melzer LTD, Israel.

ENTEBBE DECLASSIFIED

THE UNTOLD FIRST-HAND STORIES OF
THE LEGENDARY RESCUE OPERATION

ISRAEL INTELLIGENCE HERITAGE
& COMMEMORATION CENTER (IICC)

The Israel Intelligence Heritage and Commemoration Center (IICC) is a non-profit organization dedicated to commemorating the fallen from all branches of Israel's intelligence community and perpetuating the values and heritage of the community through research and educational programs.

"THE OPPOSITE OF TO WRITE IS TO FORGET."

Maj.-Gen. Nehemia Tamari (died in a helicopter crash in the line of duty in 1994), Sayeret Matkal commander 1978-1980

WRITERS

INTRO TO THE ENGLISH EDITION

Forty years after the hostage-rescue operation in Entebbe, we published the Hebrew edition of "Operation Yonatan in First Person: Sayeret Matkal Operators Tell the Tales of Battle at Entebbe."

Over the ensuing five years, we've come to realize that the world at large, too, ought to be exposed to these first-person accounts of one of the most unique operations ever pulled off, and that is why we decided to have the book translated and to make it accessible to a far wider audience in English.

All proceeds from the sale of this book will be used for social programming that, like the operation in which we took part, benefits the entirety of Israeli society.

The English edition includes the accounts of 33 soldiers and operators, whose voices, at times with their own help, were skillfully and devotedly brought into English by our translator, Mitch Ginsburg.

TO THE READERS

Yonatan Netanyahu, killed at age thirty, never had the chance to tell his tale.

On Sunday, when the plane was hijacked, Yoni was in command of a covert Sayeret Matkal operation in the south. He instructed the Unit's officers to participate in all preparations and planning sessions regarding the hijacked aircraft and asked to be kept abreast of all developments.

On Thursday Yoni returned from the Egyptian border. He received from Brig.-Gen. Dan Shomron, the commander of the whole operation, the mission orders for Sayeret Matkal, was updated by his staff officers on the situation, and planned, along with them and the Unit officers and operators, the takeover of the old terminal and the rescue of the hostages.

Yoni determined the shape of the force and its personnel, authorized the plans of each and every squad leader, and presented the operational orders. The force was formed and organized, outfitted and trained, its operational plans adjusted in real time - all under his command.

On Friday Yoni presented the operational plan to Dan Shomron and to the IDF Chief of Staff Lt.-Gen. Motta Gur and Defense Minister Shimon Peres, and instilled in them the confidence that the Unit could accomplish its goal of killing the terrorists and freeing the hostages. That faith in the Unit and its commander had a pivotal role in the government's decision to authorize the mission.

On Saturday we headed out under Yoni's command. We trusted in him. We considered him to be an outstanding combat officer and, despite the difference in age and in background, a friend.

He led the force to the terminal and decided - rightly, in most of our opinions - to eliminate the Ugandan guards blocking our path. Yoni led the force to the building, gave the order to charge, spurred the troops on when he noticed a blockage, had the chance to see the first of his operators storming through the door, and charged ahead until he himself was felled.

The story of his abruptly severed life is woven in the story of our lives. We were given the opportunity to return from Entebbe, garlanded in glory. Our lives continued. We matured, formed families, crossed the border of middle age.

Our stories are devoted to him, our commander. May his memory be a blessing.

Operation Yonatan was a multifaceted, long-distance raid conducted on the night of 3-4 July 1976. Forces from the ground, air, and sea took part in the operation, during which passengers from the Air France flight were freed after being taken hostage and brought to Entebbe by members of Wadia Haddad's organization.

During the planning and execution of the mission it was known as Operation Thunderball, and the name was subsequently changed to Operation Yonatan, in memory of Lt.-Col. Yonatan Netanyahu (may he rest in peace), the commander of the force that liberated the hostages, who fell in battle during the operation.

Excerpted from: Operation Yonatan (Thunderball), Operations Directorate, History Department, IDF, November 1977

INTRODUCTION

Sayeret Matkal's role in the hostage-rescue operation at Entebbe was to kill the terrorists, neutralize the Ugandan soldiers aiding the terrorists, and free the hostages. We, together with combatants and pilots from the Israel Air Force, troops from the Paratroop and Golani brigades, doctors and medical personnel from the IDF Medical Corps (over 250 soldiers in total), accomplished our mission and returned to Israel, carrying the body of our commander, Yonatan Netanyahu, who was killed in battle. After the funeral, the operators and staff officers and the entire personnel of the Unit returned to the routine of clandestine operational activity; Operation Yonatan - the most dramatic hostage-rescue in history - became just another chapter in our operational record.

Maj. Amiram Levin, who was appointed commander of Sayeret Matkal after Yoni's death, sent the post-operation report to the IDF General Staff. Amiram began his summation with a single sentence: **"All forces accomplished their mission."**

The entire report, including the commander's summation, is but 14 pages-long. Only 11 of the 65 Sayeret Matkal soldiers sent to Entebbe participated in it, having sent in their written version of events. Looking back across the decades, this is something one can only regret.

Over the years, only the most vociferous voices have been heard, providing differing accounts and generally obscuring what a wealth of voices would have made clear. This volume, a collection of thirty-three first-person accounts, affords freedom of expression to each writer. It gives each individual the choice of deciding what to include, what to exclude, what to underscore. In this it is unique. We have not written a historical account with a single driving narrative; that is why we did not touch the texts submitted to us, aside from copy editing and proofreading. The many accounts and the repetition of certain facts, always from a fresh perspective, allow the reader to follow the trail of preparations, the unfolding of the mission, and to construct his or her own analysis of what took place. He or she must choose what to believe, which version to cling to. And despite all, despite the individual points of view, the discrepancies are not vast.

Yoni Didn't Write

We've asked ourselves what Yoni would have done had he returned from the mission, taken his place behind the commander's desk, and looked ahead. We have no doubt that he would have conducted a rigorous internal debriefing and given each and every one of the operators and support staff an appropriate platform to speak his mind. That is how an operational review is conducted in the Unit. You get on the stage and you report, without cutting any corners and without burnishing the facts, precisely what occurred from your perspective - to ensure that the lessons are learnt and that, next time around, the troops arrive better prepared. Yoni would have stated his role in the operation and analyzed in detail the process that began with the order he received from Brig.-Gen. Dan Shomron (may he rest in peace), who was - it bears recalling - the commander of Operation Yonatan and the ranking officer on the ground at the airport in Entebbe.

Sayeret Matkal's soldiers and officers needn't be reminded of the way in which the Unit's unique operational activity demands an uncompromising effort in pursuit of perfection. The operation in the south - headed by Yoni until the Thursday before departure - prevented him from being personally involved in the creation of the operational framework; nevertheless, he trusted that the Unit's officers would do their utmost to ensure that the Unit was given the mission's central role, which they did. It stands to reason, then, that Yoni would have reported that, on his way back from Beit Ha'tzanchan (the Paratroopers' House), where he first touched base with his staff officers, he found the troops organized and ready, set to begin planning and preparing for their role in the operation.

He would have thanked his staff and administrators for their work during the preparation stage, praised the operators for their actions, and been unsparing, where necessary, in his operational critique. That is who he was - a combat officer with vast experience, a demanding and precise field commander who threw himself in his entirety into the mission at hand, and led his soldiers from the fore, until he was stopped cold by an enemy bullet.

Most of the people who submitted testimony to this collection recall Yoni's final briefing on the ground in Sharm el-Sheikh before takeoff; his faith in the Unit's capabilities, in the justness of the action, the likelihood of the mission being inscribed upon the pages of history. One of the soldiers who submitted an account for this volume even described the personal briefing he received from Yoni after his operational role was changed at the last minute and he was posted to the assault team's lead squad. Yoni, the commander of the Unit, briefed him personally, along with his squad commander. Before landing, Yoni walked through the crowded plane and shook soldiers' hands, slapped men on the back, offered encouragement with a glance and a kind word. On the ground, facing the terminal, he spurred the force forward at the critical moment.

We thought that upon return, after the debriefing, which in no way resembled the standard operational debriefings that were conducted in the Unit, and after the elation and exultance at having pulled off the mission, and once we'd internalized (according to the customs of the time) the loss of our commander, there would be nothing left to say.

We were wrong. We found ourselves not just bereft of our commander but also lacking a comprehensive report detailing the Unit's actions in full. Together we decided that rather than writing yet another book that depicts the single narrative of its author, no matter how esteemed a historian that person may be, we would do well to have the operators who were there, forty-five years ago, put their stories at long last to paper.

And there's another reason. The world's reaction to Operation Yonatan - and not just that of the Jewish People, the State of Israel, and the Israel Defense Forces - exceeded and continues to exceed that of similar military missions. The documentary and feature films, the books and countless articles, are testament to this. Additionally, the many items in the media have contributed to the image of the operation as one that was unprecedented, never to be surpassed. It has become synonymous with success and daring.

Not only the operation was made public. The individual stories of several of the soldiers were widely heard. But not all. Not remotely. There were sixty-five operators from Sayeret Matkal on the ground in Entebbe. Many staff officers and hundreds of soldiers back at the base helped with preparations. Their voices have not been heard until now.

This book is being brought into the world for them, the silent voices.

This book is a collection of first-person testimonies written by soldiers who took part in the mission. The Unit's code, signed by us, the veterans, states that secrets are not to be revealed and the operational activity of the Unit is not to be publicly discussed; this agreement was adhered to during the compilation of the book. The accounts herein include the testimony of three people who did not land at Entebbe. Their written account sheds light on elements that have up until now been shrouded.

Thirty-three soldiers and officers submitted their stories to us (we asked all of the participants to submit their recollections and hope that one day we will be given the opportunity to read their stories,) and we believe that the diversity of perspectives will shed light on the roles played and the actions taken by those who opted not to write.

Not all were given the opportunity to write. Zvi Chibutro, Yoel Tzibulski, Tzachi Fuchs, and Uri Ben Ner have all passed away. May their memories be a blessing.

Let us also remember the hostages who were killed during and after the mission. Jean-Jacques Meimoni, Pasco Cohen, Ida Borochovich, and Dora Bloch, who was in the hospital in Kampala at the time of the mission and was subsequently murdered on orders from Idi Amin.

This is also the space to thank the dozens and hundreds of soldiers and civilians, Africa hands, Mossad combatants, and unnamed people who did their best to ensure the success of the mission and to adequately prepare the soldiers for the task at hand.

Aside from myself, none of the participants are writers. They are not historians or journalists. They are former Sayeret Matkal operators and staff officers, who concluded their service with ranks ranging from staff-sergeant to lieutenant-general (the IDF Chief of Staff), and one former head of the Mossad, all of whom today work in an array of different professions. Many of the accounts are enriched by the crucial and fascinating retrospective that was lacking in the days immediately following the operation. The passage of time and the trajectory of each different life enrich the text and add diversity, and that is why we added a short bio at the end of each account.

The personal accounts appear in chronological order. First, several participants who helped with the planning but were not on the ground in Entebbe: The Unit's chief intelligence officer, followed by Yoni's personal secretary, and then a reserves soldier from the Unit, who was working in Kenya at the time. Next are the recollections of the two soldiers in Yoni's command formation - his radio operator, (who happened to go on to head the Mossad) and the doctor. After them come the testimonies of those who charged into the terminal and fought there, each in order of his actions. Let us not forget that the battle waged by the entry team was curt and compressed, and therefore, though the texts are delivered chronologically, much of the action happened nearly simultaneously. From seventeen different accounts, we receive deeply personal perspectives and a vivid collective portrait.

One account details the actions of the Land Rover and Mercedes drivers; these operators drove the assault team to the terminal, provided suppressive fire at the control tower and prevented the enemy from mowing down our forces from above, before driving the hostages and the assault team back to the waiting planes.

Finally, we have the accounts of the soldiers on the armored personnel carriers. Their role was to create a perimeter around the old terminal, to make sure that the Ugandan army was not able to intervene, and to destroy the Ugandan planes on the ground. The twelve accounts detail that force's actions and include the recollections of the last soldier to board the final homeward-bound plane.

Secrecy and security. After the mission we returned to the blessed anonymity of the Unit and there was hardly a one of us who thought about revealing his experiences during this and other missions. We believe that the Unit's actions ought to remain in the shadows and not the limelight, and, in the past, have felt that even the Unit's very existence was best left unstated. But after over forty years and ample deliberations, we've reached the conclusion that actually there are some things that are best left said. For example, delving into the details of the operation in Entebbe, in pursuit of truth.

Operation Yonatan exceeds all that we have known. It is the most famous rescue operation in the world and our soldiers and others lecture about it regularly, and factually we are not revealing anything that has not yet been revealed. We are instead offering the first-person testimonies upon which the books were based, the movies made, the analyses written -the unfiltered perspective of those who took part. We hope that this diversity of voices, each independently written, will fix, in the historical record, that which needs fixing.

We've done our thing. We've written our truth. Thirty-five truths. We hope that the readers will reach the same conclusion that we have: we took part in a bold mission that encompasses the very essence of Zionism. We succeeded. There's enough fame to go around. For us too.

Who dares wins.

In the name of the editors: Yiftach Reicher-Atir Brig. Gen. (ret.)

Deputy commander of Sayeret Matkal at the time of the mission, commander of the entry force assigned to the Ugandan soldiers' hall.

1

STAFF OFFICERS AND NCOS

AUTHORS:
Avi Weiss (Livne)
Yael Zangen Taterka
Michael Aaronson

Captain Avi Weiss (Livne), Sayeret Matkal Intelligence Officer
Unit Intelligence Officer for Operation Yonatan

––––––––

AVI'S STORY

Background

Several days before the Yom Kippur War, I, a young officer, was sent to the Suez Canal to compile the reconnaissance reports from the southern sector. I set up camp at an outpost called Mefatzeach. During the days before the war, we relayed multiple reports about Egyptian Army actions, which, to my dismay, were not treated appropriately, to say the least; in fact, they were ignored! The Yom Kippur War came and I - like all of Israel - greeted its onset with complete surprise as the roar of the jets and the artillery violated the serenity that had preceded it. After three days of war, our ammunition ran out and all of the soldiers stationed at the outpost surrendered and submitted to captivity. The forty days I spent in Egyptian captivity were for me a foundational period in my life, and upon returning to Israel I realized the severity of the national intelligence failure to which I had been part.

After a period of rehabilitation, I requested to return to the Sinai as an intelligence officer and was posted as the 401st Armored Brigade's intel officer, serving under brigade commander Ehud Barak. The decision to return to the Sinai and serve there was, among other things, rooted in my desire to contribute to the revival of the intelligence corps' image, and to lend a hand, so as to ensure that the disgrace of the Yom Kippur War, from an intelligence perspective, would not recur.

Brigade commander Barak demanded, from the start, a high professional level. I would later learn that his intelligence expectations - the height of the bar - were in accordance with the norms of the Unit. In the spring of 1975, he summoned me to his office. "I've decided that it's important that you be transferred," he said. "Your next post is as intel officer for Sayeret Matkal. You can pack your things and report for duty at Sayeret Matkal."

Surprised on the one hand and pleased on the other, I reported for duty with no preparation whatsoever. That is how I arrived at the covert unit, which I had hardly heard of beforehand. I showed up at the base during the transition period between the command of Giora Zorea and Yoni Netanyahu. It worked out, then, that I accompanied Yoni from his first day as commander of the Unit. Only with the passing of the years did I realize what a major impact my service in Sayeret Matkal had on the course of my life, and how lucky I was to have been a partner to one of the more significant episodes in the history of the State of Israel.

Quickly upon arrival, I discovered that whatever I had done up to that point, whatever I had learnt, was unlike what was expected of me in the Unit. The commander's demands were higher, the concepts were utterly new, the professionalism was at another plain altogether. The time given me for acclimation was short, the grace period nonexistent.

———

Sunday 06.27.76 - roughly a year after Yoni had taken the reins - started as just another week of operational activity, this time down in the Sinai. Yoni and some of the Unit's staff, along with a group of operators, headed down to the Sinai for a week of operational action. Already on the way south we received word of the hijacking of an Air France flight, en route from Athens to Paris. Later in the day the plane was reported to have landed in Libya and, after a short layover there, to have continued south to the airport at Entebbe in Uganda. According to Unit protocol, the operators on base remained on alert for the eventuality that the plane would circle back and land at Lod. But as soon as the plane touched down at Entebbe, some 4,000 kilometers from Israel's border, the state of readiness was called off, the assumption being that we'd done our part and that, from here on in, the matter was in the hands of the politicians, who would commence with negotiations.

On Monday, Tuesday, Wednesday - while engaged in operational action in the Sinai - we followed the developments, like all of Israel, and received updates from Muki Betser (who was on the base) to Yoni (who was in the Sinai) regarding the IDF General Staff discussions on the various hostage-rescue options.

The reports that reached us, regarding the IDF's plans to carry out a mission beyond the mountains of darkness, brought smiles to our lips and at times sparked outright derision.

Comment: By this point the Unit had acquired vast experience with hostage-rescue operations in Israel, including the Savoy Hotel, Ma'alot, Sabena Airlines and more. However, Israel had carried out no such operation beyond its borders, and the implications of that were significant.

On Thursday, 07.01.76, early in the morning, once the operational activity had come to a close, we hustled back in Yoni's car, driving from the Sinai to the base in 6-7 hours. The previous evening Yoni and Muki had agreed that, immediately upon return to the base, we would get our things together and head out to Beit Ha'tzanchan for a meeting with Brig.-Gen. Dan Shomron, where the various IDF operational plans, already under consideration, would be presented to us. I got ready quickly and set out for the scheduled meeting with Yoni and several staff officers. There I met Muki Betser, who had, up until that point, been the Unit's representative in all Chief Paratroop and Infantry Officer and General Staff forums. Dan Shomron, at this stage, presented to us the two central ideas that had been considered thus far.

A) Parachuting a force into Lake Victoria, from which it would reach the shore and launch an assault on the terminal in Entebbe, freeing the hostages and taking them, by (commandeered) vehicle overland to Kenya.

B) A large military force, arriving on eight Hercules C-130s, would seize control of the airport, free the hostages, and fly them back to Israel.

At this stage, at least as far as I was concerned, these ideas seemed to me to be on the cusp of the surreal, and I was in doubt as to whether the options were even operationally feasible. At the close of the meeting, Dan Shomron charged the Unit with planning the assault on the old terminal at Entebbe and rescuing the hostages therein. We were not surprised by Dan Shomron's decision to assign the mission to the Unit, as Sayeret Matkal had, by then, amassed plenty of experience in hostage-rescue scenarios. Toward evening, upon arrival back at the base, an initial meeting was convened in Yoni's office. The following people were present: Yoni, Muki Betser, Ehud Barak, Avraham Arnan (the founder of the Unit), and Avi the intel officer (me).

Comment: By Wednesday evening, once the foreign hostages had been freed and flown to Paris, we learned that, in Entebbe, the hostages had been taken off the plane and led to the old terminal, where they were put through a selection, separating the Israelis from the rest of the passengers. This incident, reminiscent of the Holocaust, brought home the significance of the term selection in the historic memory of the Jews.

From open sources (news and TV) we learnt that Idi Amin himself had paid a visit to the hostages in the old terminal. Additionally, we received information regarding the release of the remaining foreign passengers on Thursday morning, at which point they were flown to Paris. In light of this information it was decided to dispatch Amiram Levin to the French capital to question the released hostages, as per a prioritized set of intelligence requirements.

Significantly, we learned that Idi Amin and the hijackers were collaborating with one another and that dozens or perhaps hundreds of Ugandan troops were deployed to guard the old terminal.

During the first part of the meeting, Muki, the Unit representative earlier in the week, updated the forum in a detailed fashion about the discussions and ideas that had surfaced in and around the General Staff during the previous days, where they had sought an acceptable operational format, and not yet a detailed plan. During the second half of the meeting, Yoni, knowing that Muki had spent years in Uganda training the Ugandan armed forces, asked Muki for a tour d'horizon of the country and its army, and insight into the conduct and leadership of Idi Amin. During the third part of that meeting we discussed how to surprise the terrorists and the Ugandan troops. The matter of surprise is central and deeply significant to a mission of this sort; it has a decisive influence on the chances of success and a lack thereof.

Aware that Idi Amin had personally come to visit the hostages in his presidential vehicle (a Mercedes), we discussed the idea of using a similar vehicle to lead the convoy of operators from the aircraft to the terminal. Our initial premise was that traveling in this way would enable a 'quiet' arrival at the terminal, using to our advantage the guards' hesitancy to open fire. Muki provided detail on the sort of Mercedes used by Amin, including the Ugandan flag ornaments typically resting on the front of the hood. TV footage helped us fill in the rest of the blanks. During the course of the meeting we were informed that the General Staff and the Chief Paratroop and Infantry Officer had determined the IDF force structure for the mission: four Hercules aircraft and a specified number of operators from the Unit along with a maximum number of vehicles.

Yoni, in summation, instructed the relevant staff officers to procure a black Mercedes sedan and tasked the intel officer (me) with, among other things, the job of making a Ugandan flag that could flutter on the hood of the Mercedes. Once the room was cleared, Yoni called in some of the staff officers and team leaders.

As the intelligence officer of the Unit, I presented there for the first time an architectural sketch of the old terminal. Amnon Manki, Muki's intelligence officer, had given it to me. The sketch had been made by Military Intelligence Directorate personnel, who'd used old photos and video footage that had poured in from private individuals and Israeli army officers who had been stationed in Uganda during the heyday of the Israel-Uganda relationship.

On the basis of that sketch and the additional information that had come in, we began to discuss and form an operational plan, and to delineate forces and objectives.

During that meeting Yoni determined the force formation as based on the primary objectives:

A) Five strike squads, delivered to the terminal by vehicle, to storm through the four entrances and to secure the halls and the second floor, where the Ugandan soldiers were housed.

B) A vehicular force to provide perimeter security around the old terminal, preventing the arrival of backup.

C) A Mercedes sedan to lead the strike force convoy.

D) A command-and-control squad led by Yoni.

E) A suppressive fire force to zero in on the control tower along-side the terminal.

During the meeting, Yoni debated which teams ought to take part in the mission. On the one hand, it was important to take veteran troops with ample experience; on the other, some of those operators were slated to participate in a pending mission of great importance.

Furthermore, in keeping with Unit tradition - everyone wanted in and no one was willing to relent. As is common, and again happened here - the rumors reached the ears of the reserves operators and they began calling Yoni and staff officers and demanding to be included in the operational roster. By Thursday night (at around midnight), and in the wake of internal "battles" between the team leaders and groups of reservists in the know, Yoni finalized the list of participants for the mission.

The staff and team leaders dispersed and Yoni remained secluded in his office late into the night, thoroughly planning the operation in his typical way, writing down in his notebook all the gaps that still needed to be bridged and the operational points that still needed to be underscored. Staff officers came in every now and again with an update or a request for further instructions.

I - as the intel officer - tried via military intelligence and the Chief Paratroop and Infantry Officer to attain further information regarding the terminal and its surroundings. In the meanwhile, I acquired an atlas and familiarized myself with the pattern and colors of the Ugandan flag. The staff in our bureau, using a bed sheet taken from one of the rooms, started sewing it together.

From that moment until Friday morning - the staff personnel, the team leaders, and the operators, all focused on their respective assignments.

During the night on Thursday - Yoni sent word that at 08:00 on Friday morning there would be a formal, force-wide briefing for all mission participants.

Comment: It bears noting that, from the Thursday meeting with Dan Shomron, in which the Unit was effectively assigned the hostage-rescue mission, until the Friday morning briefing, the Unit, under Yoni's leadership, and by the force of his personal example and his devotion to the goal and belief in the right- eousness of the mission, managed to present a detailed opera- tional plan - this in the span of 12 hours. From my perspective, that is a noteworthy achievement.

On Friday morning - at around 08:00 - the entire force was briefed, in a formal and organized manner, on the operational plan.

As is customary, after an introduction by Yoni, I gave a detailed intelligence snapshot of the target. The data at my disposal that morning included, among other things:

A) An architectural sketch prepared by the Military Intelligence Directorate on the basis of photos and video footage.

B) Partial information, still incoherent and unorganized, relayed to us from Paris on the basis of an initial questioning of the released hostages.

First, I presented a 1:500,000 scale map of Uganda and its neigh- boring countries and began the briefing by stating the country's geographic location. From there I segued into the surrounding coun- tries, and provided some facts about the Ugandan armed forces. All of this was information that I'd managed to glean during the previous night. Carrying on, I presented the contours of the terminal on the basis of the sketch and conveyed that there were reportedly ten armed terrorists and dozens, or perhaps hundreds, of Ugandan soldiers ringing the perimeter of the terminal; furthermore, explosive devices had allegedly been placed within the terminal where the hostages were being held.

Comment: In this type of operation the majority of the operable intelligence is collected on-site, in real time, as the troops prepare for action; this is done by the intel officer and the troops on hand and the timing of the counter-strike is based on this real-time information. It was clear to me that in this case, based on the conditions on the ground, that would be impossible. This served to underscore one of the primary weak points of the operation: the lack of constant contact with the target area. A consequence of that given situation was our inability to monitor the actions and changes on the ground, which could prove critical to the success of the mission and to our ability to mitigate casualties among our forces.

In light of this, I felt uncomfortable - to put it mildly - with our intelligence picture of the terminal. The physical details were based on old materials and the snapshot of the situation on the ground was far from complete. At the close of the intelligence presentation, the other staff personnel presented their relevant areas of expertise and Yoni summed up. As soon as the briefing was over, I rode with other staff officers to the Chief Paratroop and Infantry Officer's central bureau in Ramla, where formal operational orders were issued. Brig.-Gen. Dan Shomron presented the general outline of the operation and introduced the forces taking part in it. After his address, an Israel Air Force representative presented the IAF's role in the mission, followed by Golani and Paratroop Brigade officers, whose role was revealed to us for the first time.

At the same time, Yoni was summoned urgently to IDF headquarters in Tel Aviv for a meeting with the IDF Chief of Staff and the Defense Minister. They wanted to hear directly from him about the Unit's readiness for such a mission and his opinion regarding its feasibility. Yoni expressed to them his feeling that the mission could be accomplished and that the Unit was fully equipped to pull it off successfully. There's no doubt that Yoni's stance was important to the decision-makers and helped the leaders form a positive opinion of the mission.

After receiving our operational orders, we returned to the base, which hummed like a swarm of bees. Inside, staff officers and force commanders were running around, acquiring the necessary gear and preparing for the mission; outside, the other forces, the troops from the Golani and Paratroop Brigades, gathered for briefings and simulations in advance of the mission. During the day on Friday, information continued to trickle in from Israelis who had spent time in Uganda. This information was amassed by Amnon Biran, the Chief Paratroop and Infantry Officer's intelligence officer. It consisted mostly of photos and old videos collected by intel officers of various army units.

Up until that point - due to security clearance restrictions - the Unit's base was closed to all military and other personnel not directly affiliated with the Unit. But on that Friday, each time new information arrived, be it photos or films, the rumor circulated, the gates to the base were opened, and we all huddled in one of the rooms to study the incoming material. Personnel quartered in a neighboring base came freely in and out of the Unit gates.

On Friday evening, after a tense waiting period, Amiram Levin, who'd flown to Paris to interview the released foreign hostages, sent a detailed and updated intelligence dossier. In effect, this was the only current report we had, and it included crucial details that assisted us in buttressing the plan.

Comment: It should be noted that this dossier was current as of Thursday morning, the day that the foreign hostages were released and flown out of Uganda. In essence, it was the first and last updated report that we had at our disposal until the H-hour for departure. It was clear that the chances of receiving additional information, covering the period between Thursday and Saturday night - when the mission was to be launched - were slim to none. The meaning of this was that we were going to embark on a mission with a three-day gap in intelligence, wherein we had

no chance of receiving updates about the hostages and the activity around the terminal in Entebbe. All this in a dynamic operation in which the variables are in constant motion. Accordingly, we had to hope there would be scant changes on the ground and, at the same time, be ready for changes that we had not foreseen.

The dossier's main points were as follows:

A) Further information about the old terminal, which, luckily, largely supported the information we had already gleaned from the sketch. The Amiram Levin dossier confirmed that there was no need for a rehaul of the plan, but merely refinements.

B) The Israelis were being held in the large hall in the old terminal.

C) The Israelis were being guarded by approximately ten terrorists armed with personal firearms.

D) Ugandan army personnel were cooperating with the terrorists, and 50-100 soldiers were deployed in and around the old terminal.

E) The dossier refuted the information about the passenger hall being booby-trapped with explosive devices.

Upon receiving the dossier, I reported to Yoni's office and he called in the relevant personnel and the force leaders. Together we went over the report. The dossier did not necessitate changes to the plan, but rather pointers that were given by Yoni. At the close of that meeting, I felt a degree of relief in light of the fact that the old information, upon which we had based our planning, largely dovetailed with the reality on the ground. Our central concern revolved around the dozens of Ugandan soldiers stationed at the terminal, and the understanding that their positioning and number could change by the time we arrived.

In effect, after receiving Amiram's dossier, I finished the intelligence planning in advance of the operation. There was little chance of receiving additional updated material and I understood that, with the information we had at our disposal, the troops would depart for Entebbe.

Comment: There can be no doubt that the information made available to me and placed at the disposal of the operational

forces during the planning stage was far from the customary high standard of the Unit. That said, it was clear we were operating under pressure applied by the terrorists and the ultimatum they had issued. Therefore, throughout the planning stage I felt that I was not able to provide the operational force with the high quality, up-to-date intelligence so fundamentally necessary for the success of such a mission; information that is inextricably linked to the minimization, if possible, of casualties. Truly, Amiram Levin's dossier lightened that feeling, but the fact remained that there was a three-day window between Amiram's report and the date of the operation, which, in this sort of an operation, created an unacceptable intelligence gap. When I expressed these feelings to Yoni he noted, in a soothing manner, that when all was said and done, we would be the superior force in the field and we'd know how to address whatever events and surprises came our way.

At this stage there was a brief intermezzo, and for the first time I was able to take a moment and consider what I'd done in the past two days, the events I'd been partner to, and to consider if, what had seemed to us, several days ago, to be nearly imaginary, would become reality. I admit that even at this stage, with all of us awaiting the government's decision, I was very much in doubt about the mission being authorized.

On Friday evening, after completing the model drill, the feeling among some of the force commanders and operators was that the operation, with all of its many variables, carried a risk factor that was unacceptably high. In light of this sentiment, which reached the ears of the Unit commander, a meeting was called for all force commanders at 08:00 on Saturday morning, in the Unit's memorial room.

Saturday, 08:00

At the meeting, some of the force commanders raised qualms about the risks inherent in the mission. They made plain their feelings about the degree of readiness for such a mission, the acceptable threat level, and the existing information gaps. All were well below the norm in the Unit. Yoni listened carefully to what the commanders had to say, and though he agreed with some of their points, he addressed the underlying significance of the mission. He emphasized the importance of carrying out this mission, and his faith that, despite the unknowns, and despite the fact that the preparations were beneath Unit standards of readiness, the risk was reasonable and the chances of success were high; come what may, he said, we would be the superior force in the terminal at Entebbe. Hovering above all of the participants at the meeting (including Yoni) was the history-stained vision of Israelis/Jews being separated from the pack and executed. This feeling, and the fact that the terrorists' final ultimatum was to expire on Sunday afternoon, at which point the first round of executions was to begin, fortified the feeling and the belief that this was far more than just another run of the mill operation. Raising the bar on risk, therefore, was justified. The commanders left the meeting strengthened and full of faith.

Comment: I'd like to highlight that this complex operation was prepared in a mere 36 hours. From Thursday evening, when the Unit was given its directives, till Saturday, when the planes took off. For that, all who took part in the planning of the mission are worthy of special appreciation.

At nine in the morning, I drove with Yoni in his Rom Carmel car to the Lod Airbase, where there was to be a final briefing before departure. On the way we talked about the mission, and I felt that Yoni was confident, determined, and very much aware of the significance of the success of this mission. In the squadron's briefing room there was a final briefing for the commanders while the soldiers loaded the gear and the vehicles onto the planes. During the course of the briefing we expected to receive word of authorization of the mission from the political echelon, yet confirmation was slow in coming. The military leadership, therefore, decided to depart without authorization, making a pitstop in Sharm el-Sheikh, in hopes that, in the interim, the long-awaited authorization would be given.

I left the squadron briefing room with Yoni and accompanied him to his car. He withdrew his battle vest and personal gear; we parted with a handshake, a slap on the back, and I wished him luck. While standing there outside Yoni's car, with the roar of the plane engines in our ears, a representative of the Chief Paratroop and Intelligence Officer's bureau arrived with new photos taken by a Mossad combatant. I snatched the photos and ran toward the runway, where the Hercules C-130s, some of which had already taken off, were waiting. I managed to flag down the last of the planes, which was already in motion. It stopped, and the door opened. I threw the photos in and asked that they be given to Yoni upon arrival at Sharm al-Sheikh. Those photos, taken by a Mossad combatant who had flown from Kenya to Entebbe in a light aircraft and then circled overhead and landed at the airport before finally departing, were the first and last up-to-date photos that we had at our disposal in advance of the operation.

The photos were given to Yoni in Sharm and distributed among the operators for study and reflection. There's no doubt that those photos, even though they were delivered as is, with no intelligence processing, greatly improved the operators' feelings about the mission. Afterwards I drove Yoni's car back to the base, to the quiet in the eye of the storm. I received word that the political echelon had authorized the mission and that all systems were go. Additionally, I was told that Prime Minister Yitzhak Rabin's main concern, in weighing whether or not to authorize the mission, had revolved around the number of Ugandan troops stationed at the airfield. The information we initially had at our disposal, put the number at dozens to hundreds of Ugandan soldiers.

The Mossad man, besides managing to photograph the airfield and deliver up-to-date photos, reported seeing only dozens of Ugandan soldiers around the old terminal. That information, along with the similar report relayed by Amiram Levin from Paris, held considerable weight in Prime Minister Rabin's decision to authorize the mission.

On Saturday night I drove to the IDF headquarters in Tel Aviv, where there was a command-and-control room that operated alongside the airborne war room run by Deputy IDF Chief of Staff Kuti

Adam. I need not detail the excitement in the room as the planes landed at Entebbe, the tension and the anticipation, the relief we all felt with word of the last plane lifting off. I returned to the base and, finally, after three days with hardly any sleep, went to bed.

On Sunday at 05:00 I was woken by the ring of the phone (I don't remember who was on the other end of the line) and informed that Yoni, the commander of the Unit, had been killed during the operation. The satisfaction that had coursed through me since the last of the planes had taken off from Entebbe, curdled at once into sorrow and deep pain over the loss of my esteemed, brave, and daring commander, Yoni.

Epilogue

I cannot complete this story without a personal note about Yoni, the man and the commander. It was a great privilege to serve under him as his intel officer. Despite his introverted nature, we forged ties of mutual trust, appreciation, and friendship. I got to know a man and an officer for whom the love of the land and the fate of its people were always a guiding light.

Our intense year of work together was a continuum of days and nights, one-on-one meetings and plans and war rooms and more… and what we weren't able to accomplish in six days of work we routinely finished on Shabbat at Yoni's house in Ramat HaSharon.

During this period Yoni led the Unit on groundbreaking operations that continued to contribute significantly to the security of the State of Israel for many years after his death. Getting to know Yoni during this year exposed me to the eclectic nature of his personality. On one hand - a brave commander, level-headed and daring, a thorough professional who knew how to make a decision. And on the other hand - a lover of the written word, who utilized every pause in the action to read a few more pages in his book or write a few more lines in his notebook. These characteristics came to the fore during the lead up to Operation Entebbe, both within the Unit and beyond. Despite the doubts about the ability to implement the mission, Yoni, from Thursday evening on, harnessed himself with great determination to the mission and towed the staff and the operators behind him.

Yoni organized all stages of mission planning. He assigned staff and commanders and personally built the roster of operators filling the ranks. With the passing of the hours, I felt his faith in the feasibility of the mission grow.

Beyond that - in his meeting with the Chief of Staff and the Defense Minister, Yoni projected great confidence in the Unit's ability to carry out the mission. His firm and level-headed position carried a lot of weight with the political leadership in their eventual decision to authorize the mission. I appreciated and valued Yoni. His death left me with a wound that to this day has not healed.

Personally, I feel, even today, some forty-five years after the fact, that I was lucky to have lent a hand in one of the most significant episodes that the State of Israel has ever had to face.

Maj. (res) Avi (Weiss) Livne is from Moshav Kerem Maharal; during the Yom Kippur War he served as an intelligence officer at the Mefatzeach outpost along the Suez Canal and was taken captive by Egyptian armed forces. Upon return from captivity, he returned to the IDF and to the Sinai as the intelligence officer of the 401st Armored Brigade under the command of Ehud Barak. From 1975-1979 he served as the intelligence officer of Sayeret Matkal, under the command of Yoni Netanyahu (may he rest in peace), Amiram Levin, and Nehemiah Tamari (may he rest in peace). He was discharged from the IDF in 1979 and began to work for the Mossad, where he served for more than two decades, rising to the rank of deputy department head before retiring in 2002.

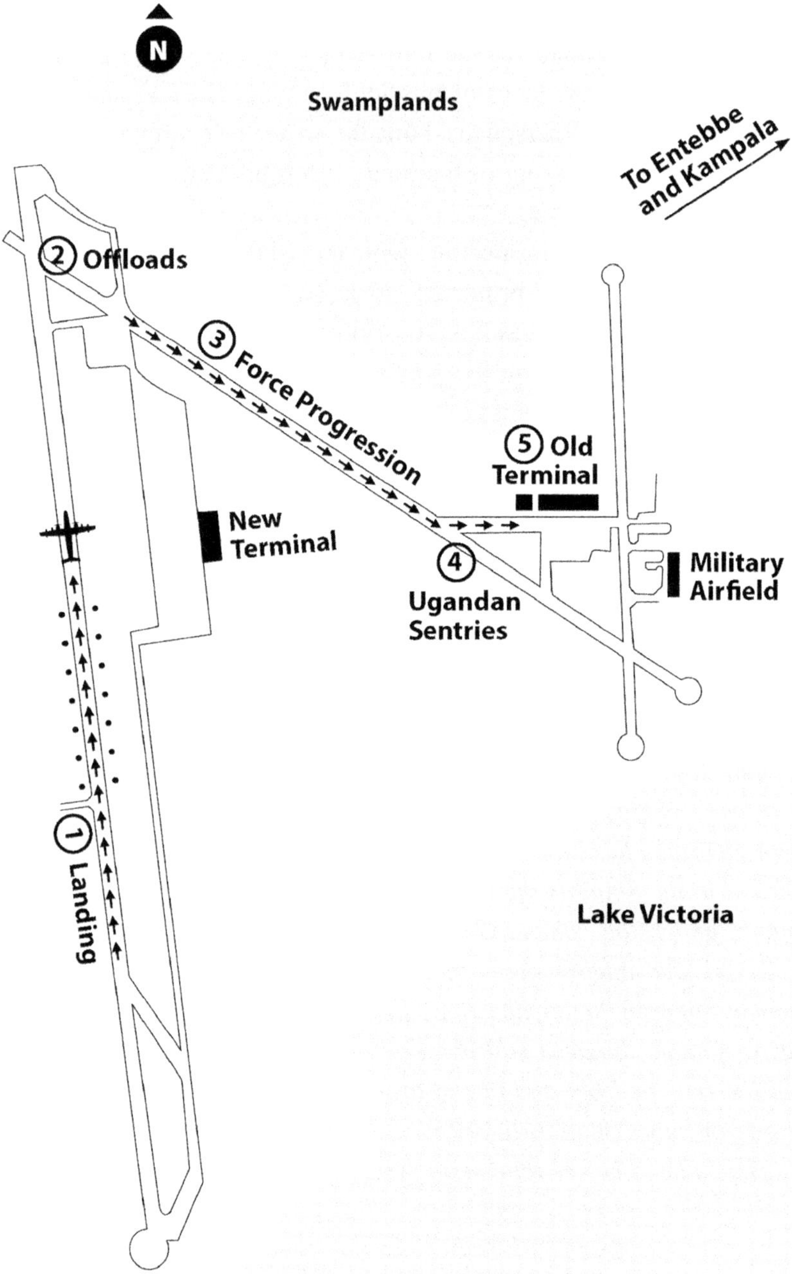

Swamplands

To Entebbe
and Kampala

② Offloads

③ Force Progression

⑤ Old
Terminal

New
Terminal

④

Military
Airfield

Ugandan
Sentries

① Landing

Lake Victoria

Schematic Diagram – Entebbe Airport

An aerial photo of the old terminal at Entebbe, provided by the Mossad at the very last moment, while the final plane was revving its engines for take-off for the mission.

Sgt. Yael Zangen Taterka

Administrative Bureau Chief to Unit Commander Yoni Netanyahu

YAEL'S STORY

The commander's bureau, the nerve center of the Unit, was run by Eilat Kantor and me, two of around five or six female soldiers on the base. We were not a "team." The ties between us were not tight. Each of us came to her post in a different way. I was not the "daughter of" nor the "sister of" anyone...no family ties nor friends in high places brought me to the Unit. I started my army service in the IDF Operations Directorate (in "the Pit") as a bureau clerk in the office of Moshe "Moishe-and-a-half" Levi, the commander of the directorate. After a year of service, I felt I wanted a change and I made contact with the Unit. Right around then they were looking for an administrative bureau chief and that's how I transferred to the Unit. I must say that it's a bit difficult for me to dredge up memories from this period. I've never examined my memories from then, and yet the impressions remain powerful, likely never to be forgotten.

Before the hijacking there was a rather intense period of general and specific assignments, the usual grind of operational activity. An intense period of plans, actions, preparations, model simulation drills. Around one week before the hijacking I returned from a pre-discharge trip to Sinai with one of the teams.

After the hijacking, our role as bureau directors didn't notably change. During the preparation and planning stage of the mission we wrote up gear lists, made schedules, did intense office work into the wee hours of the night. The soldiers conducted model drills all through the day and night. Afterwards, once they were done training, meetings were held in the bureau: discussions, conclusions, future plans. A string of nights with no sleep and intense work. Officers of all rank and from all branches of the armed services milled around the base, along with enlisted soldiers and reservists and others involved in the planning and organizing of the mission.

The sensation was that something major was afoot. I recall that one of the people very much involved in the planning was Muki Betser, who had knowledge of Uganda and of the airport. We, the girls, worked really hard. I don't remember anyone talking to us, or inviting us to a meeting or explaining the ongoing activity or the possible future scenarios. Dr. Arik Shalev was a reservist in the Unit. One night, shortly before the mission, he invited me to join him on the rooftop of one of the hangars. From up there we watched the preparations. Only then did the nickel drop.

On Saturday, before takeoff to Entebbe and before leaving the bureau, Yoni called me in. As usual, he was taciturn and task-oriented. I can't really remember the words that were said, but the feeling I got from him was that we were headed towards a large mission. Alongside his confidence in the planning and preparations, there was the unspoken understanding that something could go wrong. A single picture stands clear and sharp in my memory: in Yoni's office, on his desk, there was a copy of Alistair MacLean's novel *The Way to Dusty Death*. I have no idea what happened to that book. I can't remember.

The soldiers left the base and took off for Sharm. Those who remained behind were on edge about whether the mission would be authorized, and concerned and scared about the results. The tension was hard to bear. The soldiers that stayed behind on the base were also tormented with a feeling of having missed out. Some walked around "in mourning, heads covered" and tried to come to terms with their exclusion. Looking to change the mood a bit, I went with one of the other girls to my parents' house in Hod HaSharon. A hot shower and a good meal soothed us a bit. A short while later we returned to the base. We, the girls, did not talk amongst ourselves about what was happening.

On Saturday, once the prime minister's authorization had been given, the forces took off from Sharm and embarked on the mission. Avi Weiss offered me a ride to the Operations Directorate, to "the

Pit," a place I knew well from my previous post, to follow the mission from there. We arrived and found vigorous activity and tension in the air, but also a lot of hugging and mutual support. We were there till very late. We returned to the Unit and grabbed a few hours of sleep.

Only on Sunday morning did I learn that Yoni had been killed. Amiram Levin replaced Yoni immediately. He arrived at the bureau in the morning. It was a strange sensation. We waited for the arrival of the troops. Mixed feelings. A euphoric happiness for the success of the mission, mixed with sadness over Yoni having fallen. But there was no choice. We knew that life goes on, and that we had to get back to routine. Around the world and around Israel, among the families and friends of the operators - celebrations; on the news, on TV, in get-togethers and all around. Word was that there were cakes and other goodies left at the gates to the base. The world rejoiced. Only we were sad and marked by loss. I don't remember anyone gathering us, the female soldiers, to speak, to listen, to process our feelings. Each of us was left with her own baggage. If my memory serves, the first funeral I ever attended in my life was that of Yoni Netanyahu. Even at that stage there was no preparation of any sort besides technical! The only warm embraces were given by officers and others not from the Unit. In the Unit, emotions are shielded.

The Shiva visit at the Netanyahu family home was difficult. The meeting with Bruria, Yoni's girlfriend, was powerful and significant. Bruria asked me to come with her and speak in private. The only available room - the bathroom. I was afraid…I wondered: what is it that she wants? What sort of answers can I provide? And then Bruria put me in front of the mirror and asked: "What do you see in the mirror?" I replied: "Myself." And she asked that I look again, and tell her: "Is this what a twenty-year-old girl looks like? Is there anyone looking out for you, for all of you, the girls? Is there someone around to help you cope, to talk with you and take care of you?" I didn't let my guard down. I replied: "Everything's fine!" After all, in the Unit, emotions are not to be revealed. Those questions have endured. They've stayed with me all these years. I hope it is no longer like that in the army today. For several more months Yoni's driver and I stayed in touch with Bruria.

Personally, this was one of the more significant events of my life. For more than ten years after my discharge from the military, I veiled my service in the Unit and the fact that I had been administrative bureau chief to Yoni Netanyahu. I wanted to be appreciated for who I was and not for a certain role I'd filled. I'm grateful for the opportunity to put these thoughts to paper and to process them.

Sgt. (res) Yael Tsengen Tatarka was born and raised in Hod HaSharon. For 22 years she lived in Kibbutz Givat Haim Ichud. She is a mother to a wonderful daughter and son.

Staff-Sgt. Michael Aaronson, Operator Shai-Sussmann Squad

Newly Discharged; Military Instructor in Kenya During the Mission

---

BEHIND THE SCENES OF OPERATION YONATAN

In early 1976 the Israeli intelligence community learned of a plot to attack an El-Al airplane at Nairobi's international airport. The Kenyan authorities arrested the Black September terror cell in advance of the attack and covertly turned the terrorists over to Israel. In return, the Kenyan government asked Israel to establish, train, and arm an anti-terror unit that could serve as President Jomo Kenyatta's presidential guard force. Israeli authorities offered this assignment, as a bonus, to officers from the Unit at the end of their service.

A Mossad unit was chosen to run the operation and four officers from the Unit were selected as candidates for the mission: Shai Avital, the commander of the delegation; Amnon Peled, Yochai Yazdi (Rotem), and Rami Sherman. Three kibbutzniks and one moshavnik. The Mossad officers inquired: who among this group spoke English well. Well? None of them. They instructed Shai to find someone who had a strong command of the language. Shai asked Dani Avnon, but he had a prior obligation. Then he turned to me, as someone who was born in London and was presumably well acquainted with this "strange" language. I agreed immediately. It was decided that as a first stage Shai and I would depart for Kenya and establish a commanders' course for the presidential guard officers. Later, Amnon and Yochai would join us and together we'd train the entire unit. The task would take four more months, with the final two weeks devoted to anti-terror skills.

The following day we were summoned to a meeting with the Mossad officers in charge of the project, including the commander of that geographic region (Nahum Admoni, who would later go on to head the spy agency). Much of the details relating to our stay in

Kenya were decided at that meeting, including the type of gear we would be traveling with, and, no less importantly, the decision that, during the second part of the course, once the rest of the guys had showed up eight weeks later, our girlfriends would be allowed to join us.

Shai and I were flown to Nairobi in May 1976. After several days of acclimatization (Nairobi is situated at roughly 5800 feet) we were introduced to the soldiers of the unit. Finally, we'd start assembling a team of commandos. Only we were in for a surprise. Some of the soldiers were middle-aged. Their equipment was mostly British and out of date and not well kept; it was quite clear they had little enthusiasm for the task at hand. I can only imagine that the soldiers were also duly surprised by the look of us, two white guys, who, for the first time in their lives, were dressed in suits, jacket sleeves flopping down to their knees. In our conversations with the soldiers, we learned that their primary motivation for service in the GSU (General Service Unit) was the prospect of a job that enabled them to support their families, securing stable and long-term employment.

We also learned that beyond the security detail provided by the force in and around Nairobi, the GSU was charged with ground security for El-Al planes on the way to and from South Africa. This later proved significant.

―――――

In late June, an Air France plane was hijacked and forced to land at Entebbe. As soon as we learned of the hijacking, we ceased training and convened at the home of a man named Eli, the Mossad representative in Nairobi. (At the time there were no diplomatic ties between Kenya and Israel; relations were severed after the Yom Kippur War and the Mossad representative, though known, was not in an officially recognized position).

Several ideas arose, including checking to see which post-army Israelis were by chance in Nairobi at the time and could perhaps serve as an immediate intervention force. At the time there were two other operators from the Unit in Nairobi, both serving as El-Al onboard security officers (Doron Linik and Beni Bilitzer) and a few other young discharged infantrymen working in other capacities in the city. The idea, even at the time, seemed totally surreal and in fact it was taken off the table quite fast.

The next day Shai and I were called to a meeting at the office of Benjamin Gethi, the supreme commander of the unit. He presented us with a tourist map, on a scale of 1:1,000,000 and, with his large palm covering half the surface of the map, laid out his plan to rescue the hostages. We were clearly taken aback and immediately forwarded on the man's dangerous ideas. As far as I know calls from Israel were patched through to Kenya in an attempt to calm the situation and deter local forces from intervening in the hostage crisis. It was clear to us that back in Israel something was coming through the pipeline, but we had no idea what it was. Shai was agitated, and he repeatedly asked to be allowed to return to Israel so that he could be included in whatever was being assembled, both in terms of planning and execution. His requests were denied.

Ehud Barak arrived in Kenya early on Friday. I assumed that part of his mission was to soothe the Kenyans. For his part, he offered us not a morsel of information. We received word, though, that the hostage-rescue plan under consideration was to parachute a Naval Commando force into Lake Victoria along with rubber rafts, and then, once ashore, the force would storm the nearby Entebbe airport and free the hostages. Concurrently, larger boats would be brought to shore (led by us?) and those crafts would deliver all passengers across the lake to safety in Kenya and from there by plane to Israel.

While discussing this bold plan, a question emerged: were there crocodiles in and around Lake Victoria? It turned out that no one in the planning department in Israel knew definitively. I was told that there were two Naval Commandos coming to Nairobi and that I was to rent a car and take them to the lake (some 400 kilometers from Nairobi on dirt roads). They would scan the shores for crocs and size up the lake and the harbor and the available boats and gauge the overall suitability of the locale for such a mission.

I rented the only car I could find (a tiny Fiat 127) and drove to the airport to pick up the pair of frogmen. One of them was Haninah Amishav, the deputy commander of the Naval Commandos at the time, and the other was an officer whose name I can't remember. Both of the guys, like most Naval Commandos, were tall and broad-shouldered and were barely able to fold themselves into the back of the Fiat. But without much in the way of discussion we set out and drove for several long hours till we reached the shores of Lake Victoria. The answer was evident as soon as we arrived. Yes, there are crocodiles in Lake Victoria, and they're giant Nile crocodiles lying in nearly endless rows all along the shore as far as the eye can see. The Naval Commandos were instructed to refrain from speaking English so as not to reveal their nationality and to allow me to do all the talking with the locals. We milled around the village of Kisumu. We snapped photos and they checked whatever it was that they checked and after a few hours we got back in the car and returned to Nairobi. I remember well the discomfort that those two guys felt during the long trip, but they didn't utter a word of complaint.

We got back to Nairobi at night and promptly presented ourselves before those handling the operational affairs, ready to report on our findings. We were told, instead, to head straight for the airport, where the planes, returning from Entebbe, were due to land at any moment. Turned out that no one had been waiting for our reports; the Unit had cooked up a different plan, along with roughly half the officers in the army, and it had been authorized and executed. We drove straight to the airport and I continued driving right to the foot of the plane (thanks to our ties with the unit that provided the ground security for Israeli aircraft). There I met the forces that had participated in the operation - especially the wounded, who were taken off the plane for immediate treatment in Nairobi, along with some of the medics.

The Jewish community in Nairobi immediately mobilized to accompany the wounded to a private hospital in Nairobi and to protect them, particularly from reporters. At that stage the two Naval Commandos boarded the IDF Medical Corps plane and headed back to Israel. I stayed behind and accompanied those being treated in

Kenya and only later came back and heard, for the first time, the full chain of events.

Later on, I brought the medics back to the airport and loaded them up on a civilian flight to Israel. It goes without saying that they had no passports or travel documents of any sort. They were clad in flight coveralls and only due to our special relationship with the GSU were we able to take them straight to the plane without having to go through any sort of passport control.

The epilogue of this tale relates to a slightly wider circle and to the dear people who helped secure the special cooperation we had with the Kenyan authorities, thereby guaranteeing the success of the mission. This includes a certain Bruce McKenzie, who was then the minister of livestock, fisheries, and agriculture in Kenya and a great friend of Israel's. His assistance was pivotal in allowing the C-130s to land in Kenya and also helped a great deal in soothing the spirits of the Kenyan government, because the authorization allowing the planes to land was given without the knowledge of President Kenyatta, who was furious after the fact.

Bruce McKenzie, a popular figure throughout east Africa, was also a known friend of Idi Amin's. The Ugandan leader invited him several weeks after the operation to a feast of reconciliation in Kampala, held in his honor. Amin presented him with a gift: a stuffed lion head. On his way back to Kenya, flying in his private plane, the taxidermized lion head, laded with explosives, blew up and killed McKenzie (and two other passengers on board the plane). A forest in Israel, near Kibbutz Beit Rimon, in the lower Galilee, was planted in his honor and in memory of his accomplishments and as a testament to his friendship.

Roughly one week after the operation we returned to training the presidential guard and within several months our assignment was complete. The resonance of the mission in Kenya is hard to describe and it offered Israel a special status that, I would not be surprised to learn, endures to this very day.

St.-Sgt. Michael Aaronson is from Moshav Regba. He was inducted into the Unit in November 1972, a member of Team Giora Sussmann; he was discharged in 1975 and continued his service in reserves in the Unit and in Shaldag as part of Galili Company, until he was discharged from service at the age of fifty. He lives in Regba and is a father of four.

2

YONI'S COMMAND SQUAD

AUTHORS:
Tamir Pardo
David Hassin

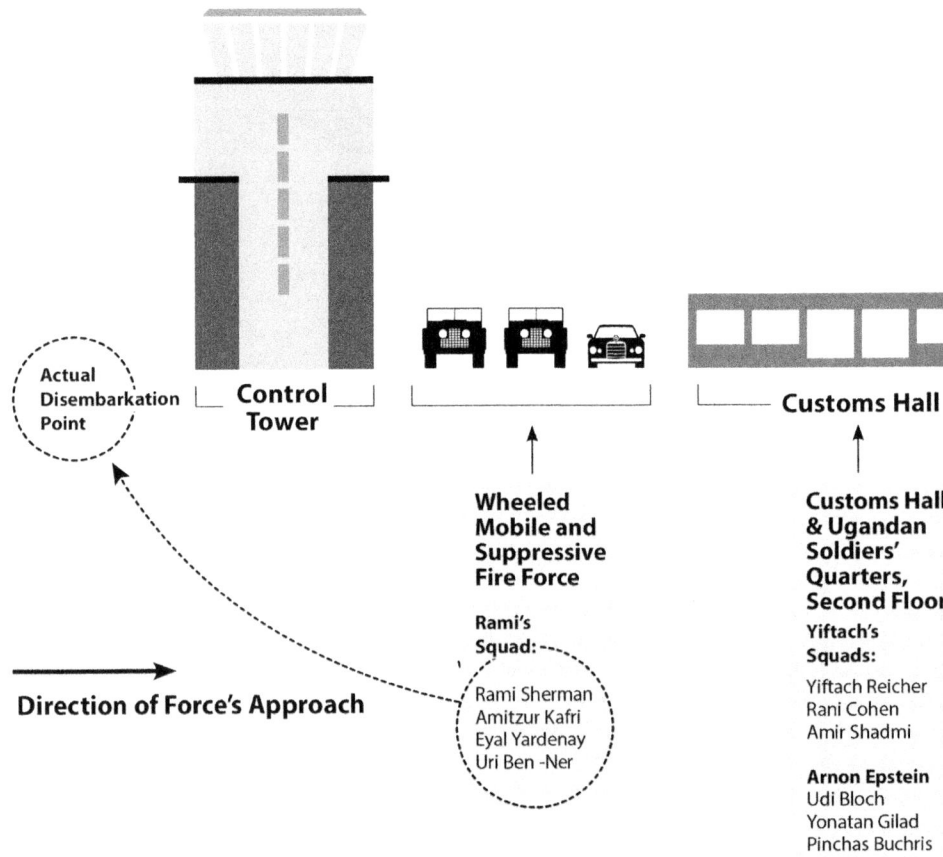

Actual Disembarkation Point

Control Tower

Customs Hall

Direction of Force's Approach

Wheeled Mobile and Suppressive Fire Force

Rami's Squad:
Rami Sherman
Amitzur Kafri
Eyal Yardenay
Uri Ben -Ner

Customs Hall & Ugandan Soldiers' Quarters, Second Floor

Yiftach's Squads:

Yiftach Reicher
Rani Cohen
Amir Shadmi

Arnon Epstein
Udi Bloch
Yonatan Gilad
Pinchas Buchris

Assault Force Under Yoni's Command: Old Terminal assault - Squads & Tasks

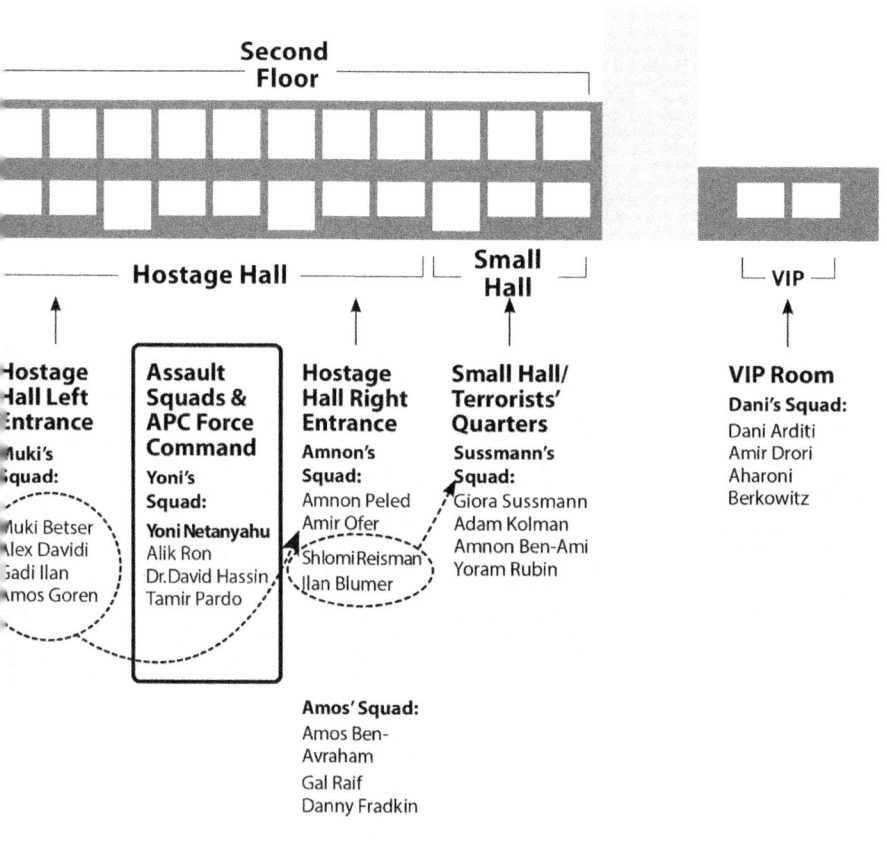

Second Floor

Hostage Hall | **Small Hall** | **VIP**

Hostage Hall Left Entrance
Muki's Squad:
Muki Betser
Alex Davidi
Gadi Ilan
Amos Goren

Assault Squads & APC Force Command
Yoni's Squad:
Yoni Netanyahu
Alik Ron
Dr. David Hassin
Tamir Pardo

Hostage Hall Right Entrance
Amnon's Squad:
Amnon Peled
Amir Ofer
Shlomi Reisman
Ilan Blumer

Small Hall/ Terrorists' Quarters
Sussmann's Squad:
Giora Sussmann
Adam Kolman
Amnon Ben-Ami
Yoram Rubin

VIP Room
Dani's Squad:
Dani Arditi
Amir Drori
Aharoni
Berkowitz

Amos' Squad:
Amos Ben-Avraham
Gal Raif
Danny Fradkin

Plan
Actual -------

Lt. Tamir Pardo, Unit Communications Officer
Communications Officer-Operator; Yoni's Command Squad

ENTEBBE—MYTH, RESPONSIBILITY, AND FAME

Afternoon. Descending through clear skies, the plane starts to dip low over Lake Victoria. My first visit to Uganda. Beside me, Yuval Fein, a team commander in the Unit at the time of the operation. We look out the window as the plane touches down on the black tarmac at the Entebbe airport, near the capital city of Kampala. Our hosts are excited, so it seems to me. The head of the Ugandan delegation stands at the foot of the rear ramp of the plane. His introduction is in English: "Welcome to Uganda, this time as a guest. From here we will depart to the place you arrived at many years ago as part of the effort to free the hostages whom a Ugandan dictator allowed to be held here while shielding the terrorists. From there we will conduct a helicopter tour of the area." After a short ride by car, we reach the old control tower. It seems that aside from a memorial plaque, nothing at all has changed, though back then it was dark. The place seems small and crowded and the distance between the tower and the hall so very short. Yuval Fein and I exchange looks. In the blinding light of day, the gap between victory and disaster appears very narrow…

Today, forty some-odd years after the fact, I'll try to paint a picture that combines the recollections of a twenty-three-year-old soldier and those of a retired head of Mossad with thirty-five years of diverse operational service under his belt.

As a junior officer, a veteran of the Yom Kippur War, I served as the head of communications in the Unit. At the time, between operations and amid frequent terror attacks, we were in the midst of feverish preparation for a mission that was the first of its kind, entailing an array of complex techno-operational challenges. On the eve of our 1:1 dry run, an Air France plane was hijacked. The Unit was spread across several operational focal points, and during the early days of the hijacking, after the initial call to readiness, I continued to work on the pre-operation model while remaining only partially and incoherently aware of the exploration of several operational responses to the situation in Entebbe. I admit that during those first three or four days, many ideas seemed to me to be unrealistic, their objective, apparently, to exhaust all options before the inevitable capitulation to the terrorists' demands. Throughout the period of Yoni's absence, Muki was the Unit's representative at the IDF planning forums. Familiar with Uganda and the sub-par skill-level of the Ugandan armed forces, he believed it was possible to arrive undetected at the airport. Once Yoni returned to the base, on Thursday, as far as I recall, the preparations swung into high gear. As the communications officer, I was in charge of planning the internal radio connection between the different forces from the Unit and the integration of our radio plan into the wider communication plan that was being handled under the auspices of the IDF's Chief Paratroop and Infantry Officer. The internal plan, despite the lack of time, was relatively simple and not fundamentally different from the one we used for local hostage-rescue situations. The more complex element of the radio plan was the contingency in the event of complications, a scenario that, in this case, the IDF wasn't familiar with and had never been tested. Our experience maintaining operational radio contact across thousands of kilometers, including an eventuality in which the forces were dispersed into small bands, without a dry run or careful preparation, was meager and rather amateurish, certainly in retrospect. The commanders of the secondary forces, who usually tried their best to avoid carrying too much radio equipment, were eager to take every last bit of gear that was offered; the working assumption being that if we found ourselves in a situation in which the planes were no longer an option, the only way home was going to be a very, very long trek and, at minimum, it would be a good idea to be in touch along the way.

I'll admit that during the preparation stage I never believed that the operation would be executed: the distance from Israel, Uganda's standing as a hostile country, the lack of familiarity with the theater of operations and the understanding that success rested on the preservation of the element of surprise until the moment the force burst into the hostage hall—all seemed to me to be unreconcilable and yet fascinating, good kindling for the imagination. The preparations, starting on Thursday, neutralized much of my skepticism, or, to be precise, left me with no time to ponder, to consider if the plan made sense or was doable. Friday ended with a dry run that did not resemble anything I had previously known. An operational order, a briefing, an inspection, and it was time for take-off.

The flight to Sharm was horrible. I don't know if it was the low altitude or the stormy weather, but I felt sick. Luckily, we landed before I was sidelined. One of the other operators was not so lucky and he was forced to step aside. Then a final briefing and a look at aerial photos taken by a Mossad combatant the previous day, an action that I'll detail a bit later on.

We took off. Most of the time I dozed in the jeep, my body in an impossible position. Shortly before landing Yoni came over and reminded me to link up with him as soon as the vehicles stopped. He was going to ride in the Mercedes and I was in the jeep right behind him. The Hercules C-130 descended and landed; the rear ramp opened; the runway lights glowed, just like on the tarmac in Tel Nof. Within seconds we were in motion. The plan was for us to reach the edge of the terminal in silence, the first volley of fire coming only as we charged through the door…

Life does not go according to plan, though, and the first exchange of fire came on the tarmac, while still rolling to the terminal. It was from the lead car, the Mercedes carrying Yoni and Muki. I got out and started to run, glued to Yoni's side. There was fire from the control tower and to the best of my recollection a Ugandan soldier alongside the tower also opened fire…Yoni was hit…an arm's length away from me, a half-turn with his body and he fell…I remember saying over the radio: "Yoni's hit." David the doctor went to Yoni and I joined Sussmann's squad. On the way I shot at that soldier who, I believed, was the one who had shot at Yoni. Bursts of fire from the control tower sent chunks of asphalt flying into the air, scratching my arm. In motion, as the last man in Sussmann's squad, I passed a terrorist sprawled out on the ground. I didn't know if he was dead or wounded and I shot him…and then it was all over…I radioed Muki and the command was passed on to him.

To the best of my recollection, within less than ten minutes the hostages were in our hands and the process of preparing them for evacuation had begun.

One hour after we'd touched down, we were on board the last plane home from Entebbe. We stopped in Nairobi to re-fuel and I heard that Yoni was dead. Another hour passed and we were back in the air for the long flight to Tel Nof. The camo print uniform was stained with blood from the chunks of asphalt…all sorts of thoughts passed through my head. I'd been three feet from Yoni, how had he been wounded, why him…the success of the mission, as I recall it, brought no sense of exultation. I felt like a deflated balloon. Back at the base, there was a debriefing in the mess hall…a few hours later Amiram was made the commander of the Unit. Evening came and Amiram asked me to go to Jerusalem, to tell Yoni's brother, Iddo, what had happened…

———

The days passed, the years followed. The operation has become part of the Israeli ethos of the unwavering fight against terrorism. As in every operation, each person departed with his own story. There's a reason why the term Rashomon is used to describe this and other military operations. Taking an example from soccer, where, even today, with cameras perched over and around the field, covering it from every angle, there are countless unresolved arguments about events and calls made by the referee. Disagreements about what did or did not happen are frequent and at times cameras are incapable of delivering a clear and incontrovertible verdict, because each angle provides a different version of events and this is the case even when the event is replayed ad nauseum. Human nature allows us to see and experience only that which we have seen and experienced. Time, and the perspective it provides, isn't much of a help, as we tend to hunker down in our positions.

Before presenting my own understanding of the operation, I'd like to note the contribution made by a single combatant, unknown to any of the participants. In 1976, Israel did not have the ability to take satellite photos. The only way to get current aerial photos was with a plane and a pilot. The Mossad was asked to deliver to the planners and the decision-makers and operators a series of up-to-date aerial shots of the airport. A Mossad combatant, a licensed pilot, rented a plane, equipped himself with a camera, and executed a surveillance sortie over the airfield. With no back-up, no escape route, a lumpy cover story, and very little time to prepare, the combatant carried out the mission to perfection. He faked engine troubles and landed at the airport and managed to have the film delivered to the commanders of the mission moments before take-off from Sharm el-Sheikh; the shots confirmed the basic working assumptions upon which the plan was based. The Mossad also played a role in convincing Kenya to allow the planes to refuel on its soil, as necessary, and to deploy IDF troops at the airport in Nairobi. In advance of the mission it also fulfilled several intelligence tasks related to the questioning of hostages released in Paris.

Today, more than forty years after the fact, I've decided to present and highlight several essential issues regarding the operation:

Taking Responsibility

An operation is measured first and foremost by the question of responsibility for potential failure. As regards the operation in

Entebbe, the matter was completely clear. The prime minister, Yitzhak Rabin, was directly and indivisibly responsible for the mission. Any mishap or development that led to failure, whether it be a simple tactical error like the unintentional discharge of a weapon leading to the premature detection of the assault force or the collapse of the undercarriage on the tarmac, was his direct responsibility, for the prime minister, when signing off on a mission, must address eventualities that have not been adequately considered. Before reaching a decision, he is supposed to have decided whether eventualities of this sort nonetheless enable the operation to proceed. In Entebbe, the number of eventualities for which there was no practical response was very, very large. As opposed to a war, which is often forced upon the country, in this case the prime minister had another option: to negotiate with the terrorists. The support and backing that he received from the members of the government and from the parliamentary opposition were of no significance in the event of failure and disaster. In descending order, the people beneath Rabin in the chain of command were: Defense Minister Shimon Peres, IDF Chief of Staff Motta Gur, Israel Air Force Commander Benny Peled, ground operation commander Dan Shomron, and commander of the hostage rescue operation Yoni Netanyahu.

I recall a meeting with Shlomo Gal, one of my commanders in the clandestine service. This was just before I was entrusted with the command of an operational unit in the Mossad. "Remember," he said, "you'll never be able to justify a major operational failure. Not the justness of the act, not the bravery shown, and not a track record of success…your courage as a commander is measured in your understanding of the price of failure, your decision to go ahead with an operation once you're certain of your capacity to succeed and once you've come to terms with the price of non-success!!"

Responsibility for Old Terminal and Hostage Rescue

This segment of the operation, the very heart of the mission and its central purpose, was given to the Unit. The commander of the Unit was Lt. Col. Yoni Netanyahu, and so the responsibility of fulfilling this part of the mission was his. He bore responsibility up and down the chain of command; he was the sole bearer of responsibility to his direct superior officer and he was responsible for the actions taken by the officers serving under his command. Those are the basic rules of command and control in any and all operational situations. In this sort of operation, in which the force would have but a few minutes to accomplish its mission once on the ground, he was charged with constructing the force so that—no matter who was wounded or incapacitated—the mission could be completed without a single additional command issued over the radio. In reality, though Yoni was hit at the start of the operation, the transfer of command occurred only once the hostages had been freed, the battle completed. The Unit's ability to see the mission through stems from the wellspring of talent serving in its ranks: capable and talented planners, creative and groundbreaking thinkers, courageous, steadfast professionals of the first order. Muki Betser, in my opinion, played an important role in the entire affair, from the day of the hijacking to the takeoff from Entebbe. He, as Yoni's second-in-command within the assault force, is party to the success, but he who bore responsibility for the mission within the Unit was its commander.

The Key to the Success of the Mission

The success of the mission depended on the IAF's ability to deliver the troops from Israel to the runway in Uganda and to enable the assault force to reach the terminal without being detected by the terrorists or the Ugandan soldiers. Perfect planning, the majority of which, if my memory serves, was conducted by Lt. Col. Iddo Imbar, plotted the delivery of four planes to Uganda completely undetected and veiled as commercial jets, traveling along a largely hostile and inhospitable route, with full knowledge that the arrival of the first plane was absolutely crucial to the success of the mission. As I said, perfect planning and brilliant execution by the airmen, as led by squadron commander, Lt. Col. Shani, the formation leader, and orchestrated by IAF commander Benny Peled. In my eyes, their achievement is the crown jewel, the act that enabled the execution of the mission. The confidence that Peled, the IAF commander, was able to instill in the chief of staff, the defense minister, and predominantly the prime minister, as pertained to operational capacities that were riddled with more question marks than answers, was remarkable. Parenthetically, it is worth noting that three years later the United States launched a hostage-rescue mission of its own, in Tehran. After months of training and preparation, flawed planning led to an operational and political disaster. There are no guarantees of success in such a complex aerial mission, but careful planning is a key, if albeit not sole, condition for success.

There were many partners to the mission's success, from the prime minister to the operators and commanders who took part in it. The planning officers, the intelligence teams, the staff, the logistics troops, all played a crucial role in the mission's success. Operational excellence is measured by "the strength of the weakest link in the chain." Today, in retrospect, we can but regret the unnecessary differences of opinion, for a Rashomon is a foundation in the soul of man, and there is room for everyone in this "hall of fame."

A former head of the Mossad, Tamir Pardo was the Unit's communications officer during the hostage rescue at Entebbe. In late 1976 he was discharged from the army and joined the Unit's reserves. He later went on to serve as the first communications officer of the IAF's elite unit, Shaldag, and later returned to the Unit as a reservist, until 1980, when he was inducted into the ranks of the Mossad.

1980-2003: served in the Mossad in an array of operational roles, from field agent to head of the operational division.

2003-2006: deputy head of the Mossad.

2006-2008: Israel Defense Forces, General Staff

2008-2009: deputy head of the Mossad

2011-2016: head of the Mossad.

Captain Dr. David Hassin—Unit Doctor
Doctor-Operator, Yoni's Command Squad

OPERATION ENTEBBE—IN MEMORY OF YONI

My medic, Nir Giladi, and I were part of the 33-man force from the Unit charged with raiding and asserting control over the old terminal at Entebbe International Airport, in Uganda, where the passengers of an Air France flight, from Tel Aviv via Athens to Paris, were being held hostage. We were assigned to the second Land Rover, as drilled during the model simulation.

Before boarding the planes to Sharm el-Shiekh, at Lod Airbase, Yoni came over and told me that he was cutting Nir Giladi (the medic) from the roster and adding an additional operator instead—Alik Ron; that meant that I would be the only medical personnel in the immediate vicinity of the hostages, the hijackers, and the Ugandan troops. I told Yoni that it was a mistake to leave me without a medic, as it limited my ability to function as a doctor; he was resolute, however, in his decision.

On the way to Sharm, the planes flew low in an attempt to evade enemy radar, a tactic that caused harsh turbulence, inducing motion sickness in most of the operators. At Sharm, before getting onto the second leg of the flight to the operation, we distributed antiemetic pills to the entire force; the medication leads to drowsiness and most of the operators fell asleep during the seven-hour flight to Entebbe. I remember waking up to get organized and feeling refreshed thanks to that. Before landing, Yoni went from man to man and shook hands and wished each operator good luck.

A total of four Hercules C-130s landed at Entebbe. The fourth plane, an Israel Air Force (IAF) tanker (the only one capable of flying back without refueling) was to take the hostages straight back to Israel. Ten senior medical personnel were on board that plane, including a trauma specialist, Dr. Eran Dolev, a surgeon, Dr. Menachem Ophir, an anesthesiologist, Dr. Meir Silverstone, the head physician of the IAF, Dr. Yossi Factor, and several IAF medics. The plane was to park 300 meters from the site of the assault on the old terminal and to receive all of the hostages, both harmed and unharmed, and the wounded personnel from the force.

The vehicles rolled out of the first plane at midnight and into pleasant weather and complete silence. We drove toward the old terminal, the Mercedes in the lead and the two Land Rovers trailing behind; I was in the second Land Rover, on the right side of the formation. Approaching, I saw two Ugandan soldiers. The one on the right was shot with a silenced weapon and then with audible fire; the one on the left disappeared from my line of sight. I saw a burst of tracers pass in front of the Mercedes.

The square in front of the terminal was illuminated. Contrary to what was planned, Yoni made the decision to stop the vehicles before the control tower in a concealed part of the lit square, and the operators disembarked from the vehicles and ran along the walls of the control tower and the terminal, shielded from the fore of the building. In my opinion, that decision saved the mission.

I was practically last in the line of soldiers and, while running, I saw flashes of fire from the control tower, gunfire that I later presumed killed Yoni. When I reached the entrance to the main hall, the room where the hostages were being held, the gunfire inside was still ongoing. A soldier kneeling at the entrance to the terminal told me there was a man down behind me and I turned in that direction.

I recognized Yoni, who lay there, unconscious, eight meters from the wall of the terminal, in front of the entrance to the hall. I grabbed him by the battle vest and pulled him out of the control tower's line of fire, flush against the wall of the terminal. He was unconscious and pale—evidence of significant blood loss. I cut his shirt with scissors and removed his battle vest and undershirt. I identified a small bullet entrance hole, an incision one-centimeter long, on the upper right section of his chest cavity, beneath his collarbone, with no signs of blood, and a clear exit hole, carved by the bullet in a cylindrical downward trajectory toward his lower right lumbar spine. After bandaging the wounds in order to assist the medical team aboard the plane to locate the points of injury, Arnon Epstein and I placed Yoni on a stretcher and transferred him to the Land Rover. On the stretcher, for a fraction of a second, Yoni tried to sit up. The vehicle took him to the evac plane, which was already in place 300 meters from the terminal. There, on board the plane, after a failed resuscitation attempt, the medical team pronounced Yoni Netanyahu's death.

The injured hostages were brought to the same spot where I had treated Yoni. Pasco Cohen, hit by a bullet that penetrated from one side of his pelvis and exited on the other side, was bandaged and given intravenous fluids through two IV lines. He was conscious during treatment but died later in the operation room in Nairobi as a result of an internal pelvic hemorrhage that couldn't be stopped. Jean-Jacques Meimoni, who jumped up when the operators burst into the hall, was mistakenly shot and killed by our soldiers. I saw three entry wounds in the center of his chest. Ida Borochovich arrived lifeless at the treatment point and the cause of her death was not identified. Additionally, an operator from the Unit had a shrapnel wound in the leg.

Throughout this stage, suppressive fire (machineguns, RPGs, etc.) from the vehicles and the APCs was directed at the control tower and the roof of the terminal. Dr. Giora Martinovich and I loaded the wounded and the dead on a Peugeot pick-up truck (manned by Golani Brigade soldiers). We drove them to the evac plane and transferred them onto the plane, which shut its doors and taxied over toward the runway. The Peugeot drove off to its plane.

I remained alone on the tarmac and the assault team vehicles picked me up and took me to the first plane. Surin Hershko, accompanied by Dr. Gadi Sedovsky was evacuated to that plane. Surin, a soldier from the Paratroop Brigade, was wounded during the assault on the new terminal; a bullet penetrated through his mouth and damaged his cervical spinal cord. He became paralyzed from the neck down. We diagnosed the devastating nature of the injury only on board the plane, en route to Nairobi, and treated him accordingly.

Lt.-Col. (res.) Dr. David Hassin transferred to the Unit in 1976 after serving in the Golani Brigade. He served in the Unit, as a reservist, until the age of 45. He is a specialist in internal medicine, infectious diseases, and HIV/AIDS medicine and *director of an Internal Medicine department at Tel-Aviv Medical Center (Ichilov).*

3

ASSAULT FORCE

AUTHORS:
Amir Ofer
Amnon Peled
Giora Sussmann
Shlomi Reisman
Ilan Blumer
Adam Kolman
Yiftach Reicher
Rani Cohen
Yonatan Gilad
Pinchas Buchris
Amos Goren
Alex Davidi
Gadi Ilan
Dani Arditi
Amos Ben Avraham

Staff-Sgt. Amir Ofer, Member of Team Amnon
Operator in Amnon's Squad; Member of Yoni's Assault Force;
Hostage Hall

PERSONAL RECOLLECTIONS FROM ENTEBBE

Intro

The rescue mission at Entebbe is well-situated in any top-five list of "best commando missions of all time," and a quick online search offers dozens of such lists. Nonetheless, the public seems to have adopted Muki Betser's version of events, which describes the mission as a "lucky-duck" op that "went totally off the rails," was "lost" and was "facing a catastrophe" (all Muki's terms). The commander of the assault force (Yoni Netanyahu), he has said, made a terrible mistake. I categorically deny this (as do all my friends) and submit that the performance—of the commander and of the vast majority of soldiers and officers—was stellar. That peak performance—and not luck—is the reason for the incredible success. That's why I've decided, after all these years, to put my story to writing in an orderly way.

Thursday, 23:30: "Return to Base ASAP"

Our team, Team Amnon, was the most veteran in the Unit, and a few days before the operation we were sent home for some pre-discharge R and R. At around midnight, somewhere between Thursday and Friday, we were called up on the phone and told to return to the base. I was asleep when the phone rang. My parents picked up, knocked on my door, and said: "It's for you." Yael, the commander's secretary, was on the line. "Be back by eight tomorrow morning," she said. I immediately connected the dots to the hijacking. I asked her, "We going far?" and she said, "Very far." My mother was a witness to the conversation, and she heard my question and she put one and one together, understood what was happening, and started to change color. Her eyes said everything. I told her to not dare reveal a word about the conversation she'd just heard. Doing so would put me in danger. That was the strongest argument I could come up with to plug-up a possible security leak. Much later she fessed up to me that on the following Saturday night, the night on which we left for the mission, after not hearing from me for forty-eight hours, she broke, and while speaking to a friend she said she feared that I was on the way to Uganda. Her friend told her, "You're crazy, that's not possible," and that was the end of the matter and the information was not leaked any further. She dared tell me this only many years after the mission, fearing that our relationship would be harmed if I found out that she had revealed the secret.

The mission seemed impossible. I lay in my bed in the dark and thought how it might be carried out. Suddenly I had an idea that seemed to be the only feasible option: the Mossad had bribed Idi Amin, and the whole thing was just a big show. We would be flown to Uganda as a sort of bonus prize after a long term of service. We'd fly over there, shoot a few rounds into the air, bring back the passengers, and he'd pretend that he had had no choice in the matter. In retrospect, not such a bad idea—too bad no one considered implementing it…

"There's an IDF mission; the Unit is the Spear and We're the Tip"

When I arrived at our base on Friday morning, nothing looked like my imagined scenario. Soldiers scurried around, signed off on gear; outside the perimeter of the base, other units, from the Golani and the Paratroop brigades, were mobilizing. It looked more like preparations for WWIII than an end-of-service, bonus-prize trip to Africa. In the square outside our quarters, I bumped into Amnon, our team leader, and asked him what was happening. He told me this: "There's a big IDF mission to rescue the hostages; the Unit is the spear and we're the tip." At that stage I had mixed feelings: on the one hand, appreciation of the audacity of the mission, the enormous distance, the unique setting, and our central role in the whole thing, and on the other hand, a very serious concern regarding the level of risk, especially for the entry assault team. At the Savoy Hotel [in Tel Aviv] our team had led the hostage-rescue mission and we'd lost Itamar in the assault, and nearly lost Shlomi, who was wounded, and I had no reason to think that this time it would be any easier. On the contrary. It seemed like an operation that entailed far more risk than any hostage situation we'd even been in—both for the hostages and the rescue force. Even the slightest blunder could lead to systemic disruption (or in less academic terms—dozens of dead, perhaps more); a security breach could trigger an ambush on the ground at the airport; Russian intelligence ships or hostile states' ground radars could detect us en route; the blind landing could go awry; we could be discovered on the way to the terminal; the planes could be debilitated on the tarmac while waiting for the arrival of the hostages; hostile fighter jets could engage us during the evacuation; there could be difficulty re-fueling for the return leg of the trip; Ugandan reinforcements could show up at the airport; the intelligence info regarding the way the hostages were being guarded and the location at which they were being held could be faulty—and this was but a partial list of the unique dangers associated with the mission. And that's without even relating to the battle itself, the elimination of the terrorists directly guarding the hostages, in a hall in which there were expected to be more than a hundred people and a good likelihood that the assault squads, both in the hall and all around the terminal, would be severely outnumbered by hijackers and Ugandan soldiers. The mission seemed highly dangerous, but my concern was tempered by my sense that there was no way the mission would be authorized and so there was no reason to get all worked up. I figured we'd waste a day or two doing drills and getting ready and then we'd turn back and head home. At around nine in the morning, we gathered in the briefing room and Yoni told us about the Unit's role in general and our role specifically. The briefing was not very detailed but I do remember that we were informed that there were between two-hundred and one-thousand enemy soldiers on the ground (I definitely recall that the minimum number was set at two-hundred and I'm nearly certain that the maximum number was given at one-thousand, though I can't swear to it), somewhere between eight and fifteen terrorists guarding the hostages, along with fighter jets and Ugandan air force ground crews. The general plan was presented. It was based on surprise, deception, and our professional capabilities: the first wave (Plane One) would consist of roughly thirty operators on three Land Rovers, dressed up as Ugandan soldiers (the famous Mercedes had not yet been discussed), we'd take out the terrorists guarding the hostages and all of the Ugandan soldiers in all halls of the terminal, and in that way eliminate the threat of a massacre of the hostages. We'd deploy defensively around the terminal and then, ten minutes later, Planes Two and Three would land, delivering the perimeter force, borne on four BTR-40s. We'd evacuate the hostages and high-tail it out of there. The assault force, flying in on Plane One, I learned from the briefing, would be utterly outnumbered during the first minutes on the ground, at a ratio of at least 10:1.

We were told that the hostages were either in the first or second hall: Hall A (designated by the direction of our arrival) had two doors and Hall B had one. A three-man squad led by an officer was assigned to each door. I was slated to be part of a back-up squad, thrust into the action in the event of trouble. At that point we knew that the commander of the Unit's assault force was Ehud Barak, but after a short while we were told it would be Yoni. Swaps were then made in the assignments, and our squad (Amnon—commander; Shlomi, Ilan, and me—soldiers), was moved up and assigned the second entrance to Hall A. The soldiers posted to the first door, under Muki's command, were also from our team (Gadi, Alex, and Nir). We felt that they trusted us—our team would be at the crux of the opera-tion, manning the two lead squads. On the other hand, the risk was only rising…

I ran to the combat supply office to sign out an operational kit—a special mirror and a HiD flashlight—two items that were used back then to signal a rescue helicopter in case you were left alone in the field. Suddenly I caught myself saying: "You're an idiot. No heli-copter's making it all the way out there. There'll be no rescue. No one's coming to get you. There's no need for this gear." The feeling of danger only rose. As far as I know this was the first (and last) time that an IDF force was sent on a mission with no rescue troops ready to mobilize in the event of complications.

Friday morning was devoted to gear-acquisition and weapons-and-ammunition testing as well as other technical drills. We scrambled to complete our gear kit, studied the intelligence dossiers, practiced strapping the jeeps down in the center of the plane, and so on. The drill for attacking a building in which hostages were being held was something we all knew well and had practiced dozens of times. Our team was very experienced: we'd taken part in other hostage-rescue missions and in more than a few operations on enemy soil—some very complex and very physically demanding—so that when Entebbe came along we were at the peak of our professional and operational capacity, backed by plenty of experience.

In the afternoon, the commander of each squad conducted a pre-combat inspection. Amnon had to go to a funeral and was absent for a few hours, so we joined the first-entrance squad and were inspected by its commander, Muki. At this stage, it was decided that each squad would carry explosive door-breaching devices, in case the doors were locked, and in the lottery we held, I won the dubious honor of carrying several kilograms worth of explosive devices on my back and a handful of blasting caps, which I stuffed into my shirt pocket, ready for quick removal, the fuses already attached. One more thing was added to my pack, a megaphone, which I was to use to relay messages to the hostages.

It was around then that the Mercedes arrived. It was decided that we'd use it instead of one of the Land Rovers, as part of an attempt to deceive the ground forces and pretend that we were part of the presidential motorcade. It was a genuine Mercedes, but in dreadfully bad shape: bald tires, poor mechanical condition, white (and made black with a coat of spray-paint), etc. We all gathered around it and angled for a spot in it. In the end, the officers made order and determined a final line formation. I was unlucky enough to land the worst seating arrangement of all: in the back of the second jeep, next to the radio.

The seat itself wasn't too bad but I had a serious personality clash with my neighbor, seated on the radio to my left: a giant and aggressive dog, trained to spot and attack gun-wielding terrorists. Throughout the training runs and the model drills I prayed that the dog would not have a political change of heart and decide to turn his teeth on me rather than the enemy. After the fact, it turned out that we were all afraid of him but each of us kept his thoughts to himself.

I'll return to the order of events: after the inspection, a delivery from the IDF sewing unit arrived, containing a bundle of camo-stripe uniforms meant to resemble the ones worn by the Ugandan armed forces. I imagine that those uniforms confused the Ugandan soldiers a bit during the battle. For example, a Ugandan soldier passed just a few centimeters from Pinchas but mistook him for one of his own. Additionally, two of the terrorists had good reason to shoot me in the back (as will be described later) and they hesitated for a fraction of a second because of the uniform I wore and in that way my life was spared, though of course I have no proof of this.

Night fell and we waited for the IDF Chief of Staff on the runway near the base for the start of a model drill. He showed up several hours late, which caused a lot of anger because we were on a tight time schedule (weapons-and-gear testing, further gear acquisition, studying of the intelligence material etc.). Years later I learned that while we were "stranded" on the airstrip, he was in flight with the pilots, testing to see if they could land in a darkened airfield with no navigational instruments, and that was the reason for the delay.

Once he arrived, we did two very simple simulations. For some reason it was said after the fact that those drills convinced the brass that we could pull it off. The drills were totally schematic, with no element of flight. Using burlap cloth, the Unit built a sort of mock-up of the terminal and our role was to come bounding out of the vehicles and "clear" the "building." The first drill was completed without a hitch. Then we were told to get back on board the planes. We loaded the vehicles up and strapped them down. The rear ramp of the plane was shut and we waited two minutes in the belly of the plane in order to mimic flight and then we "landed" and the rear ramp opened up again. We rolled out with the cars and redid the same drill. This time there was a surprise. They'd placed several soldiers off to the side of the burlap structure. Those soldiers "fired" at us and we hopped out of the vehicles before the planned stopping point, and charged the shooters, "eliminating" them before charging into the terminal itself. I'm underscoring this point because it was very similar to the scenario that we faced one day later, four-thousand kilometers away, at the Entebbe airport, and because it was this drill that convinced the Chief of Staff that we were operationally able and that the mission was feasible. All this talk of having "opened fire prematurely" or having not "acted in accordance with the original plan," is a complete lie. During the operation we did exactly what we'd practiced during the model drill, in the presence of the entire leadership of the Israel Defense Forces.

During the model drills, late Friday night, the Chief of Staff ordered several soldiers removed from the assault-force vehicles on account of excess weight and lack of room. An argument ensued. In the end, the CoS made do with the removal of one soldier and the dog. This was to have been the first time an attack dog was used in a combat situation. As for me, I was plenty happy with the decision; the jaws of that monster—my seatmate for the entire day of training —were scarier than the terrorists' rifles. Additionally, I did not feel that there was much in the way of chemistry between us during our first date. The dog looked at me the whole time like he was wondering whether or not my ear was delicious. How was I to know what might go through the mind of that monster during eight hours of flying, or what its reaction might be to some turbulence. One bite from that dog and you could be left missing half your head, walking around for the rest of your life with the face of a chimpanzee.

The rest of the night was spent checking weapons and preparing gear. During the few hours we had left before departure, I relayed to Ilan the following prophecy: "This is either going to be the IDF's worst failure or its greatest success. There's no middle ground." A prophet indeed.

After the weapons testing, in the small hours of the night, I drained my magazine of regular bullets and started snapping in incendiary armor-piercing rounds. We were under the impression that if the planes were taken out of commission we might well have to escape to Kenya. If so, there was a good chance we'd face armored vehicles, in which case it'd be a good idea to have armor-piercing bullets.

Saturday Morning: Bumpy Ride

Early on Saturday morning we left the base and headed to the military airfield in Lod, where we boarded Hercules planes bound for Sharm. A bit earlier, on Saturday morning, I'd had a moment to peek at the mission folder and look over a few photos that proved very helpful later on in identifying the right entrance. I found another interesting thing there: during training, the operation was called Operation Stanley. A short while before the mission I'd read these books about the search for the headwaters of the Nile. One of the main characters in those books was this guy Stanley (the American reporter who found Livingstone—the famous Africa explorer). I was sure that since the operation was taking place on the banks of Lake Victoria, someone had given the matter some thought and had decided to call it Operation Stanley, since the lake is one of the sources of the Nile and one of the places where Stanley looked for Livingstone. I'd built up a whole theory that collapsed that Saturday morning when I looked at the file: the title, Operation Stanley, had been crossed out with a thick marker and instead was written Operation Thunderball. I'd read a book by that name, too—one of the James Bond novels. Truly, a great name, uniquely fitting for this sort of operation. Years later Dan Shomron revealed that a computer had spit out automatically generated names for the mission and that he'd kept on going until it finally came up with Operation Thunderball, which he decided was fitting. He was certainly right.

The flight to Sharm was awful. I (and others) vomited the entire time in the turbulence and the heavy heat. We got off at Sharm and I asked Arik the doctor to give me some pills to help with motion sickness—otherwise I'd just collapse. He gave me a box of Travamin tablets and during the second leg of the flight I took a pill every hour until landing. I arrived at Entebbe with six doses of Travamin in my stomach. One of the soldiers in the first assault squad (Muki's squad) vomited so much he just collapsed on the ground at Sharm and had to be switched by one of the soldiers from the back-up force—Amos Goren. Though he filled an entirely different role in the model drill, and though he hadn't gone over the relevant intelligence dossiers, Amos fit smoothly into the assault force and was excellent during the op itself.

At Sharm [at the southern edge of the Sinai Peninsula] Yoni delivered a final briefing—a stellar address. Focused, concise, keenly foreseeing the eventualities that did in fact occur. I was especially moved by the way he was able to ignore any and all notions of personal risk and brief us calmly as though he was a staff officer staying behind and not the man who, in several hours' time, would be leading a small, isolated force in a faraway land on a singularly complex mission at great personal risk. The performance that he "threw down" on the taxiway there seriously boosted my confidence in our ability to prevail. I no longer remember the exact wording of what he said but one line remains lodged in my memory: "I'm sure that you are better and better trained than they are and in a one-on-one situation we will always beat them." That sentence gave me a lot of confidence. He was one hundred percent right—literally. During the operation there were many one-on-one clashes—both with the terrorists and the Ugandan soldiers on the second floor and in other parts of the terminal—and in each instance, without exception, we prevailed. He also made a point of emphasizing that reality would not conform to plan—people may be wounded, the line formation may get screwed up, etc.—but the important thing is the main goal. We must all strive to get to the hostages' hall as fast as possible, elimi-nate the terrorists guarding them within the inner circle, neutralize the explosive devices if the hall is booby-trapped, and only then take care of the wounded.

In Sharm I made a bet with one of my friends from the Paratroop Recon Unit (which shared the first plane with us) that the operation would be called off. Even then I was sure that the government would get cold feet and turn us around somewhere along the way. In the oppressive heat of a July-third afternoon in Sharm el-Sheikh the thing we wanted most was a popsicle, so I bet him a popsicle (which, by the way, I still owe him).

Since there wasn't enough fuel to fly there and back, it was decided that while we fought for control of the terminal, the air force would pump jet fuel from the Ugandan storage tanks and fill-up for the return leg.

Saturday night: Approaching the Target

We changed out of our regular uniforms and put on the fake Ugandan army fatigues and packed up our clothes and our wallets and ID cards and stuffed them into duffels that were later picked up by a truck and taken back to the base. At one point I noticed that everyone was already on the plane and that only Shlomi and I were still on the tarmac. [Brig. Gen.] Dan Shomron showed up and spurred us along. I didn't see what the fuss was all about. A minute here, a minute there—what did it matter? The mission wouldn't get the green light anyway. We took off. At some point I looked down at my watch and realized that there'd be no turning around—there was not enough fuel. It was a one-way ticket. I realized that the government had signed off on the mission and that I'd lost the bet. I seriously hoped that my losses for that day would end there. Next time—if I lost again—I'd forfeit more than a popsicle…

Some of the guys slept on the flight. I didn't sleep a wink. The plane was packed and I was afraid that someone would step on my weapon or drop something on it and it would be taken out of alignment. Once every few minutes I picked it up and shined the Yaror tactical flashlight on the plane wall, making sure that the sights were lined up with the beam of light. Then I started to worry that the repeated flashlight checks were draining the battery so I reduced the frequency of that drill. During the flight I was very focused on the approaching operation and thought of nothing else. Dozens of times in a row I played and replayed and played again the actions I was to take as soon as I burst into the hall and I thought of the last photos I'd seen and of the ways I would identify "my" entrance. Getting the entry point right is the most problematic part of any takeover operation, so I made myself two special signs: I counted, from our angle of attack, the number of metal frames dividing the glass panels of the outer wall and decided that during the assault I'd count them while in motion so that I'd know when I was at the glass panel that was actually the entrance. Another sign I made for myself was the little rain canopy over the entrance. It protruded a bit. That roof wasn't visible in the first photos we'd received, but it was clearly visible in the ones we got on the morning of the mission, as taken by a Mossad combatant.

During the flight, Muki approached me and asked what I thought about the idea of changing the orders we were to give the hostages. My job was to call to them on the megaphone and tell them to stay down and not move. Muki said that maybe it would be better to order them out of the hall as fast as possible because the whole thing might be booby-trapped and they shouldn't remain there. He asked for my opinion and I told him that I thought there was no way to change that drill now, in mid-flight, since there was no way to inform all the warriors and since we hadn't practiced it that way in the model drills. I added that as far as I was concerned the original drill is the better option because the chance of the terrorists harming them as they scurried out toward the door was greater that the possible good that could come from the change in plan. In the end, we stuck to the original drill, calling out to them to lie down and not move.

Saturday, 23:00: Landing and Engagement

As soon as the wheels of the plane touched the ground, I flipped the safety catch off and chambered a round. Ilan, who was sitting next to me, yelled at me: "You don't load a weapon on a plane!!" He was right, of course, but I replied: "Shut up! This is a real war!"

The ramp dropped open. I knew we were on the equator and I expected to see the Africa of my imagination—lions, giraffes, and jungle. Instead we saw a standard airport runway with edge lights flanking it on either side, like at every international airport around the world. We turned on the headlights and started to drive. The plane disappeared into the darkness behind us, and the farther away we got the more alone I felt. I was at the tail end of the convoy—in the back of the rear vehicle—and I thought to myself here I am watching the shadows of 32 soldiers headed to inevitable confrontation and who knows how many of them will be on their feet in another five minutes. We rode along the tarmac, marked with lights on either side. We hit a junction and turned left toward the lit terminal, and then, a few hundred meters from the terminal, we saw two soldiers standing guard; one stood on the right side of the taxiway, on the edge lights, and the other was at first by his side and then he crossed over the road and stood on the lights there. There were several other soldiers standing around them (some of whom we later clashed with on the way to the terminal), but we did not see them and saw only those standing alongside the taxiway lights.

From my seated position I saw the one on the right raise his weapon and aim it at the lead Mercedes. A few shots were fired, some silenced and some loud, and the soldier on the right fell. Immediately afterward the soldier on the left started to run toward us and was shot by Pinchas.

This action was without any shadow of a doubt the right thing to do. From where I was sitting there wasn't even a question of, "Should we open fire?" The only feasible question was, "Who would seize the advantage and open fire first?" Without question the soldiers standing guard recognized us and had we not shot them they would have opened fire from point blank range and gunned us down like sitting ducks. We were tightly packed into the vehicles, with no possibility of responding. What's more, it was the exact eventuality that we had drilled during the final exercise. Later on, some people contended that the force had been briefed about a drill done by Ugandan army soldiers whereby they raise their weapons as though ready to shoot at approaching vehicles but that the gesture is not to be taken seriously and the action is to be treated as an empty threat. I can testify first hand that I never once heard any such directive before the mission, nor did any of my friends. From my vantage point—as a passive spectator seated in the rear vehicle—there was no doubt that shooting the soldiers standing guard was the right thing to do, and the intent of the guard on the right was unequivocal.

One Minute

The vehicles sped up and stopped fifty meters short of the designated spot. The original plan was to park between the control tower and the passenger hall, but since we'd been detected it was very important that we get out of the tightly packed vehicles and spread out and start to move. Jumping out of the jeep, I felt my knee tighten and I grabbed the side of the Land Rover so as not to fall. I looked up, and in the darkness did not see the commander of my squad (Amnon). I figured he was already on the way to the terminal and so I took off at a sprint and tried to catch him so as to have his back. In fact, he was right beside me, but in the darkness and commotion I didn't see him. From around fifty yards out I saw that canopy over the entrance that we were supposed to use (second entrance to the passenger terminal), and I cut a diagonal line straight toward it. At the same time, the rest of the force—as planned—ran from the vehicles to the control tower and from there to the side of the terminal and along the glass outer wall of the terminal to the doors. I didn't join the main force because I was sure that I was late and that Amnon was already on his way to the building, and so I ran along the fastest route I could find and passed the rest of the force on the right. In general, you could describe the rest of the formation as moving along the two right-angle legs of a triangle, with Muki at the head, as planned, and the rest of the guys in two lines behind him, while I ran alone, a few dozen meters apart from them, along the hypotenuse side of the triangle. My route was shorter and so I passed them all and made it to the passenger hall before the rest of the force.

A Ugandan soldier or two popped out in front of the formation and they shot them without breaking stride. At this stage, with me just about even with "my" door and about twenty or thirty meters from it, the leader of the main assault force (Muki), who was at the corner of the terminal building (in other words off slightly to my left and a few dozen meters away), stopped for no discernable reason. To this day it isn't clear why he stopped. Off to my left I heard Yoni call twice, a few seconds apart, "Betser, forward!" Officers and soldiers immediately swung past the immobile Muki and carried on with their tasks without waiting for someone to lead. Seconds later, out of the corner of my eye, I saw Yoni fall and then heard someone yell, "Yoni's hit."

I saw all of this out of the corner of my eye and from a distance of a few dozen meters, while running as fast as I possibly could to get to the building. When I was about 10-15 meters away, the wall of glass shattered; a prone terrorist, lying about five meters into the hall, aimed a very long volley of fire right at me. The bullets whistled past either side of my head but thankfully missed their mark. Later on, I counted how many bullets he had left in his magazine and assuming it had been full he'd fired a 17-round barrage at me. I returned fire. We were both shooting at the same time, with him on automatic in a prone position and me on semi-automatic, running and closing the gap to him. Through the shattered glass, I fired four quick shots. Two of the bullets were tracers and I saw them hit their mark; his head dropped and his fire stopped. I went in, took two or three steps into the room and shot him again from point blank range. I looked right— where I thought I'd find Amnon—and saw that there was no one else from our force in the hall. That's when I realized that I was first in the terminal, and in a flash, I realized that I was in grave danger. I was completely alone, in a large hall, which eight soldiers were supposed to have burst into at the same time from two separate doors, and around me there were more than a hundred hostages with several terrorists in their midst, and it was practically certain that a few of their guns were trained in my direction from a few different points in the hall. I'd taken one out, but with any shadow of a doubt there were more. It was completely clear to me that I couldn't afford to stay still for even another tenth of a second, as a volley of fire was about to be shot in my direction. Looking to move and change silhouette, I jumped back and pressed myself against the wall and crouched as I turned to the left, to the other end of the hall, where, I assumed, there were other terrorists. At that instant, a few meters behind me, a true drama unfolded. Amnon had been a few meters behind me and he'd run as fast as he could to catch up. I'd run as fast as I could to catch him (by mistake) while he'd run as fast as he could to catch me (for real). Once I'd taken two or three steps into the hall and turned toward the terrorist who had shot me, I failed to notice two other terrorists who were crouched down three feet to the left of the entrance that I'd used. They were facing the main force, which approached along the glass wall (while I entered at an angle closer to perpendicular). I entered behind them, their backs to me, and shot the terrorist, but since they were crouched down alongside the wall and I was in the middle of a firefight and looking through rifle sights, my field of vision was narrow and I didn't see them. As soon as they heard me fire, they turned toward me, swiveling their weapons in my direction, just as I thought might happen in that snap-quick analysis I'd made, and they were, in fact, about to shoot me in the back from two-to-three meters away. At that second, Amnon charged in. He told me later he saw them as they swiveled toward me, leading with their rifles, which were already trained on my back, and that's when he eliminated them. Even today, more than forty years later, my hair still stands up on edge when I talk about this. Twice I was asked (by the Israel Broadcasting Authority and *Yedioth Ahronoth*) to go to Entebbe and talk about my experiences in the terminal as "the first guy through the door" and both times I insisted that I'm not going anywhere without Amnon and that they have to pay for his airfare and hotel, too. He deserves it. He saved my life (and the lives of many hostages) and I set him up with two free trips abroad.

As I jumped straight back and "glued" myself to the wall, I yelled to Amnon "Don't advance!" so that he wouldn't cross my line of fire. The initial plan was to get into a row and clear the hall as soon as the first two assault squads had entered, but Muki's squad, which was supposed to have come in through the first door, hadn't yet arrived and so I thought it was too soon to start sweeping the room. The hall was around twenty-five meters across and within it there were approximately one-hundred hostages and several hijackers, and there's no way for two soldiers to effectively clear a room that size when filled with that number of hostages. I saw no other terrorists within view so I kept my right hand on the trigger and with my left hand I squeezed the PTT on the megaphone mic, which was fixed onto my battle vest, and called out twice, once in Hebrew and once in English, "Everyone lie down." The tension and excitement were so great that I was hardly able to get the words out of my mouth. Luckily I had a megaphone to increase the volume. I remember exactly what I was thinking at that moment: "Get this announcement over with and get your left hand back on that Kalashnikov so you can shoot with two hands if a terrorist pops up." The megaphone itself was tucked into my backpack and only the mic was threaded through the opening of my pack and fixed to my battle vest. After the operation there were a lot of pictures of a soldier carrying a megaphone and calling out to the hostages and some of the hostages themselves described in great detail how a soldier burst into the hall holding a megaphone and calling out to them. In the movie "Operation Thunderbolt" there's a hot blond soldier clutching a megaphone and calling out to all the hostages to stay down.

As I said, it was in my pack…

A few other curios related to the believability of the hostages' reports about the moment of entry: one of them was asked what the first soldier through the door looked like and he said that the picture of him was forever etched in his mind: blond hair, blue eyes, very tall. It flattered me to be described as Clint Eastwood, the ultimate movie hero. On the other hand, another hostage, a woman, said that the first guy into the hall was a short Yemenite with black hair. Well, if we take the average of those two descriptions, then, all in all, the eyewitness reports were pretty accurate. I'm 5'9", brown eyes, brown hair. When they asked the guy who described me as blond and tall how he knew the force had come to save them and not kill them, he said: "It was very simple. I saw the I [of the IDF insignia] on the B [fatigue] uniforms they wore and I knew our forces had arrived"— but we were dressed in fake Ugandan army uniforms…when he was given that information he went into shock, realizing that he had built himself an entire imaginary world. A third hostage has insisted that the terrorists tossed a grenade into the room and that his pillow had stopped the shrapnel…in my opinion, not one of them witnessed the entry into the room. They were sure their time had come, they were down on the floor, their heads buried behind whatever sort of shelter they could find, their eyes shut, waiting for the bitter end.

A few more seconds ticked past. Amnon and I were the only ones in the room, our backs pressed against the shattered glass wall, feverishly scanning the large hall for more terrorists and trying to locate them before they could do harm. Our eyes moved with the muzzles of the Kalashnikovs, racing from one prone person to the next, trying to figure out who among the hundred people on the ground was a hostage and who a hijacker. The hostages were all "glued to the ground" lying without movement. They were sure that people had come to slay them. Some hid under blankets and mattresses that were scattered across the room. That's when Amos, Muki, and Gadi entered the crowded hall. Their squad was supposed to enter through the first door but for reasons unknown Muki came in through the second entrance (the one we'd used), his soldiers behind him. It's worth recalling that the entrances were very hard to find because both the doors and the outside wall were made of glass and it was hard to tell the difference between the walls and the doors, especially when the doors were shut. Muki's mistake had a ripple effect. Several of the soldiers had learned their entry point based on the leader. In other words: "If Muki goes in here, I go into the next one." But since Muki had made a mistake and gone into the second door (instead of the first one) two soldiers from our squad (Shlomi and Ilan), who were supposed to go in through the second opening, went in through the third door and popped into Hall B instead of Hall A. Nonetheless, they got their bearings, quickly joined one of the officers (Giora) and took out three terrorists and several Ugandan soldiers in that hall. Afterward Ilan came into the main hall and Amnon and I greeted him with a great sense of relief. He was part of the second pair in our squad and since we hadn't seen them for a few moments we figured that, like Yoni, they'd been hit while moving toward the terminal and were lying wounded or dead on the tarmac. When I saw him, it was a real resurrection as far as I was concerned. The first sentence I said to him was: "Ilan, I got a brand-new Kalashnikov." Years later he was still talking about how of all the things in the world that was the first thing I said when I realized that he was alive.

I saw Muki standing over the bodies of the terrorists that Amnon had eliminated and shooting them; I remember a thought flashed through my mind: "Unnecessary, they're already completely dead," and then I turned to the right and heard shots fired to my left. I did not see the actual occurrence but the result, to my chagrin, was evident: one of the hostages had jumped up—despite the clear warning I had given—and was mistaken for a terrorist and shot.

On the left side of the hall another terrorist rose to his feet and was shot by Amos, perhaps by Muki, too. Amos told me later that he checked the terrorist's weapon. The terrorist had already squeezed the trigger but Amos had been a fraction of a second quicker and one of his rounds had hit the terrorist's Kalashnikov, bent the cylinder and blocked the bolt from closing and the bullet from firing.

From the moment the first hijacker opened fire on me to the moment that Amos neutralized the fourth terrorist, I'd say that some 15-20 seconds had passed, with the first three terrorists, eliminated by me and Amnon, dropped within five seconds.

In the hostage hall we were by now six soldiers (Amnon, Amos, Muki, Gadi, Alex, and I)—a force large enough to scan the big hall. We spread out across the width of the 25-meter hall and combed it in a row, just as we'd practiced during the simulation. We knew that five of the terrorists in the hall had already been eliminated (we later realized that the fifth one was actually a hostage) but we still didn't know if there might be others and our nerves were stretched to the point of snapping. At any given moment a terrorist could pop up out of the corner of the hall, from one of the side rooms or from under one of the mattresses, release a burst of fire, throw a grenade, flip a detonator switch, and kill dozens of people. The tension was so great that one of us spotted a suspicious figure and then, while squeezing the trigger, realized that it was a hostage. He could not stop the motion of the trigger so he jerked the rifle upwards and the volley hit the wall above him. We were advancing in a row when an African man three feet away from me popped up. My rifle was aimed right at him and my finger was curled around the trigger when I saw that he was unarmed. I stopped myself at the last, but really the very last, possible instant before pulling the trigger. Today I know that he was one of the Ugandan workers who cleaned the hall and the bathrooms, but then he seemed to me to be one-hundred percent part of the enemy force—but unarmed. For some reason at that moment the thing that popped into my head was that he mustn't be allowed to see our Ugandan uniforms, our special radios, and the rest of our classified gear. I yelled at him in English: "Lie down, face down!!" He was sure I was going to shoot him in the back of the head and so he turned toward me. I pressed his face down and he raised his head again and started speaking in Swahili, fast and hysterical. I don't speak Swahili and the misunderstanding nearly cost him his life as I kept pushing his head down and he kept raising it up, time after time, and begging in Swahili. I was but a short step away from shooting him. That was the only time in my life that I saw what it means to be scared to death—literally. His eyes nearly popped out of their sockets, he spoke quickly and hysterically even though he knew I was not understanding him, and the blood had drained from his face so that although he was black he seemed nearly white with fear. In the end he realized what I wanted him to do and he kept his face down to the floor and stayed that way until we left. Amnon came over to me, checked him out, and said something like, "Leave him be." He was remarkably composed and utterly in control of himself—far more than I was—and functioned there in that terminal in a way that was remarkable and worthy of all praise. The fact that I owe him my life, I've already noted, but not merely in this episode but throughout the sixty minutes of our presence there (and if I may say—throughout the years of our compulsory service and the dozens of years of reserves) his operational comportment has always been remarkable. In retrospect I'm very glad I did not kill that Ugandan and that I had enough self-control and enough training to discern, even in that extreme-pressure situation, between an enemy and an element that represents no threat.

At that stage—tens of seconds since the first shots had been fired at the first terrorist in the hall—the hostages were still certain that a force had come to kill them. Not one of them imagined that a rescue force had arrived. One of the hostages later described the mass execution in these words: "We heard gunshots from far away. The shots came closer, got stronger and stronger. It was clear that the time of our execution had come. I lay down and prayed that the death would be fast and without pain. I was sure the end had come. Bullets flew around the room to our left and right and the noise was deafening. And then suddenly there was quiet. I didn't dare get up but I turned my head to the side and saw a soldier, with a big gun, who called to us in Hebrew. I didn't know if I was alive or dead in heaven and if the soldier had a pair of wings, I was sure he was an angel." The person who called out to them was me. That woman was referring to me. I think that to have a person ponder whether you are a human or an angel is the greatest compliment one can get in his life.

The main hall was cleared of terrorists but all through the terminal rooms the battle raged on, gun shots ringing out and grenades exploding. Four separate squads of ours operated on the second floor, in the terrorists' resting quarters and in the remainder of the terminal. Another squad kept heavy suppressive fire on the control tower. Those squads, operating in areas without hostages, were able to fight with less restrictions (using grenades and automatic fire and not having to conclusively confirm the identity of their targets before opening fire). All acted professionally, with determination and bravery, and barred terrorist reinforcements from arriving in the hostage hall and shielded the freed hostages as they were taken back to the planes. Within roughly one minute, seven terrorists and fifteen Ugandan soldiers were eliminated in close-quarter battle, with our forces emerging victorious in every single encounter, without exception. Dozens of others ran away and dispersed in all directions. Yoni had it right in Sharm el-Sheikh. For the umpteenth time it was proven that quality trumps quantity. In the midst of the maelstrom that lashed the old terminal in Entebbe, during those fateful few seconds of combat, a group of 105 terrified hostages was left largely unscathed. Both professionally speaking and in terms of the end result it was an incredible achievement that no other army in the world has managed to attain—not before and not since.

At this point Amnon sent me outside to provide suppressing fire at the control tower. I set up right next to the door that I had entered through and fired up at the tower. Here I saw how the doctor (Dr. David Hassin) treated Yoni alongside the edge of the terminal building, outside, around where the first door was located or a bit further on. The treatment was administered under occasional bursts of fire from the tower and David exhibited considerable bravery.

While firing, I saw two armored personnel carriers from Mofaz's force arrive in the area and I felt a true and great sense of relief: the second plane had also landed safely—we were no longer alone. Their fire power, both toward the tower and other enemy forces in the area, was far greater than what I could provide with my Kalashnikov and rendered my small-arms fire redundant. I went back into the main hall to help with the hostages.

Saturday 24:00—Evac of Hostages and Return to Planes

The interaction with the hostages was one of the most interesting and unique elements of the mission. Two of the more compelling scenarios I found myself in were with a French pilot and a stewardess.

The French pilot: The Air France crew was situated in the far end of the hall, near the first door. I told them in English that they should go straight to the main door, where Gadi was standing, and that he would direct them out. The flight engineer could not find his shoes under the mounds of blankets and mattresses. He looked for his shoes madly, as though his life depended on it. At the same time, I got word over our Motorola that the hostage-evacuation plane was rolling forward and I figured he could make the few-hundred-meter dash to the plane barefoot. I told him to call off the search and to move

toward Gadi. He walked toward Gadi—who had no Motorola and
didn't know the plane was being brought closer—and he sent him
straight back to get his shoes. He came back to me like a child talking
to his kindergarten teacher and said: "But he told me to put on my
shoes…"and he pointed at Gadi. I said: "Okay, okay, find them," and
I smiled. Already in real time, while under pressure and with the need
to get out of there as fast as possible, I realized that I was witnessing
an incredibly comic situation that could only happen in this sort of
unique situation. A flight technician, a mature man responsible for
the lives of hundreds of people, was talking to Gadi and me—two 21-
22-year-old phishers who hadn't done anything yet in life—in total
submission and utter dependence. He found his shoes, put them on,
and only then remembered that he was in his pajamas and tried to
pull his pants on over the pajamas but the slacks got stuck on his
shoes…In the end, once he was finally organized, he also wanted to
grab his suitcase, but of course I didn't let him. There's a famous
picture in which you see him getting off the Hercules in Israel,
standing behind the pilot, still wearing the checkered pajamas that
he'd gone to sleep in and which he was wearing while speaking
to me.

The stewardess: most of the hostages had already been led out
toward the planes and only the wounded and the dead remained in the
hall. At this stage I was given the honor of carrying a very lightly
wounded French stewardess, clad only in her underthings, a few
hundred yards to the evacuation vehicle. She was really lightly
wounded and could have walked out on her own. I asked her to get
up and leave but she was so panicked she nearly passed out and
Amnon ordered me to carry her out on my back. When doing the
buddy-carry, you usually fill your chest with air, get the whole 90-
kilo mass of soldier, battle vest, and rifle over your shoulder, bounce
it up to distribute the weight, lock your knees and start hauling. I did
the same drill, expecting the same weight, and nearly flew up into the
air. She was light as a feather. I forgot that French stewardesses, who
eat one croissant and a few leaves of lettuce a day, weigh around fifty
kilos, not ninety, and that their primary weapon (though lethal, to be

sure…) is not made of steel. While running with her across the tarmac, I heard a few bullets whistle past my ears. I heard—for the second time that night—the terrifying whoosh that, if you've ever heard it, stays with you forever, and I thought to myself that this was really too much, and that it had happened too many times over the past twenty minutes. In my heart, I cursed her and thought: "I've used up every ounce of luck I have. I've lived through the barrage of fire that the terrorist shot at me from ten meters out, and the two characters that nearly shot me in the back from two meters away, I'm not about to die on account of some spoiled French stewardess who's refusing to walk because of a few scratches." This situation recurs in hundreds of war movies: the tough soldier, sweating and dirty, hauls the half-naked, beautiful, wounded woman over his shoulder, weaving through the whistling bullets. On screen it works really well and it happens a lot but in life it's far less frequent. As far as I know I'm the only IDF soldier to have ever had the privilege of carrying, under fire, a beautiful woman dressed only in her undergarments— and a French stewardess at that. Only we were not married at the end of the movie and we did not get ourselves a room at a hotel in Entebbe. It goes without saying that all the guys asked me later, "Hey, we lost you there for five minutes, didn't we?" and "Which alley did you take her to?" and the rest of the lame jokes of that genre. Now that I think about it, though, all of the James Bond movies end in just that way—including the original Thunderball, in which he does it with a gorgeous Frenchwoman (the actress Claudine Auger—a stunning woman who was runner up to Miss Universe— who is called Domino in the movie): James Bond engages in a lost-cause battle against the bad guys, completely outnumbered. Against all odds he emerges victorious, rescues her, manages to escape a last second explosion along with her and then a transport plane swoops down and picks them up, in an embrace, from sea. Well, in our Thunderball she was also saved at the last second and was picked up by a transport plane (though, to her likely regret, with no embrace from Sean Connery…) Naturally, she was the prettiest of the those wounded in the operation and so she was given a starring role on

Sunday's nightly news. From her bed in Tel Hashomer hospital she said in French something that went like this: "Everyone had already left, and I was afraid they'd forget me there, and only this one soldier remembered me and took me." That of course is not true—everything was under control, we did not leave anyone behind and I did not take her on my own initiative but rather on direct orders from Amnon—but what does it matter. The important thing was that she complimented me…she was full of praise for me but she had no way of knowing that while running with her on the tarmac I'd cursed her stridently in my heart.

After escorting the hostages to the planes, we got back on our vehicles, counted off, and saw we were missing a soldier. He hadn't heard the order to fall in around the vehicles and had remained at his guard post. Once he joined the group we did a roll call, this time by name, with Shlomi holding a piece of carton on which he'd written every operator's name. We rode back to where the plane was parked, boarded it, and flew to Nairobi. While rolling toward the plane I remembered the blasting caps that I had in my shirt pocket, to be used in case we needed to blow the door open. On the flight over I was really not happy about flying with those things in my shirt pocket—not to mention charging the enemy with explosives strapped to my back and the sort of blasting caps in my shirt that could be activated by any random knock or fall—and the thought of flying back home with them was even more abhorrent. They were no longer needed. Very carefully, I pulled them out of my pocket and tossed them as far away from the Land Rover as possible. They exploded with a loud bang, but after all the shooting, the grenades, the heavy machine guns and the RPG rounds, it sounded like a cap gun.

During the operation there was reams of suppressive fire aimed at the control tower (RPGs, heavy machine guns, grenade launchers etc.). The heavy machine guns fired incessantly, till their barrels turned red and nearly exploded—all with the goal of putting an end to the incoming fire from there, and yet, every once in a while, the fire started up again. Dozens of years later I returned to Entebbe, this time during daylight. The tower itself was riddled with bullet holes, the glass windows shattered, and there was not an inch of the upper barricade that wasn't harmed. All along the roof, the impact marks of the rocket-propelled grenades were visible. It was clear the suppressing-fire force had done its job well. The reason why the gunfire from the tower was never fully stopped became clear to me only once I climbed up to the top level: I found a ring, about five-feet thick, of reinforced concrete and the shooters had taken cover behind it and remained unharmed despite the inferno of fire rained down on them. Every so often they raised their heads, fired off a few shots, and ducked back down beneath the concrete balustrade. That was a piece of data we hadn't had during the planning stage.

An Improvised Debrief on the Plane

The flight to Nairobi was tense, since we (the soldiers) didn't know if the stopover had been coordinated with the local authorities. We remained strapped into our battle vests, ready for more combat. The plane landed, the door opened, and on walked Ehud Barak and Shai Avital. That's when I realized that the stop had been coordinated with the Kenyan government. There was a burst of joy and then Ehud told us that Yoni had died of his wounds. It was a moment of transition from great joy to deep sadness.

On the flight from Entebbe to Nairobi we clashed with Muki about the entrance used by both squads. He said we'd used the first one, while everyone else said he was wrong; it had been the second entrance, and that was why Shlomi and Ilan had been led astray and had charged in through the third entrance (to Hall B) and similarly the reason why Amnon and I were left to fight alone for several seconds with no one bounding in through the left side of the hall. Muki insisted that he'd come in through the correct entrance. Only then did I realize why I'd found myself alone in the room and how lucky I'd been with Amnon's improvisation; he saw that no one had gone in through the first, left-most door and then rather than pivoting right (as had been planned) he pivoted left and killed the two terrorists who were about to shoot me. At some point during the flight to Nairobi, Muki admitted that he'd made a mistake but during the following years he's changed his version of events and said that the first door simply hadn't existed. When multiple photos of that entrance were shown to him—by people who were there before and after the mission—he changed his version of events yet again and said that there was a door but it was bolted or locked. And yet hostages have confirmed that both doors were used and that the Ugandan workers who brought them food and other things came and went through both, and I too saw the first door when I spoke to the French cabin crew in the far-left corner of the hall. By the way: in his own operational report—written several hours after the mission—he admits the mistake ("...I mistakenly skipped over my entrance and reached Amnon's entrance...") So it remains unclear why he has found reason to change this during all subsequent public interviews.

Another matter that came up during the improvised debriefing on the plane—and in a loud tone of voice, at that—was Muki's halt during the charge, which put me, and Amnon (and of course a lot of hostages) in grave danger. He was asked why he'd stopped, and said: "I had a firearm malfunction in the Kalashnikov." His response seemed mystifying as the Kalashnikov is a remarkably reliable rifle, nearly always free of malfunction, and each one of us had tested his weapon and every single one of his magazines before the mission. We did not conceal our skepticism about the reason he had given for his stop. Once we landed in Israel, and during the following years, the reason changed to an "empty magazine"—even though it was not clear to us how or why his magazine would have been empty at that stage with all of us firing on single fire and with no target yet to have appeared that would have justified emptying an entire magazine before charging into a hall full of hostages. Additionally, it is not clear how an officer as experienced as Muki could have neglected to keep rounds in his magazine before the crucial stage of charging into the hostage hall, a charge that he was to lead. In short, the explanations given about the stop have not been convincing and it remains unsolved.

Sunday Afternoon: The Return Home

We took off from Nairobi and the tension snapped and the stories started to flow. Each person recounted his role and there was a feeling of exultation. It was an incredible accomplishment and our team, it turned out, was—not just in planning but also in action—"the tip" of the spear. We'd met all expectations and then some. Additionally, despite our grave concerns in light of the assault on the Savoy, in which Itamar had been killed and Shlomi wounded, no one from our team was harmed. On board the plane I heard about the battle that Shlomi and Sussmann had waged in the hall next to ours, and about Yiftach and Rani's exploits up on the second floor, and about the action carried out by Dani's squad on the far end of the terminal. Only one of the guys on our team did not take part in the swirl of the conversation. He sat there with a fixed expression on his face. I came over to him, smiling from ear to ear, and said: "What execution!! We were amazing!!" And he turned to me and said in a very sad voice: "I killed a hostage." I'd seen the dead hostage, of course, but not the shooting itself. At the time I was looking the other way and didn't know which of the other five warriors in the room had shot him. I told him right away that he had done the right thing, that he had acted according to protocol and that the hostage had not followed clear orders to stay down, which I'd called out twice over the megaphone before his squad had entered the hall. Had I seen the hostage pop up, I added, I would have shot him, too; a terrorist, acting in that way, could easily have activated an explosive device and killed fifty people. No one had the luxury of taking a chance. Later I learned that the hostage was young and dark-skinned and had jumped up in an intimidating way, and since he had been lying alongside the terrorist that I'd killed earlier, he was also stained with blood. Two warriors, one of whom was from our team, recognized him as a terrorist and shot him at the same time. Both were absolutely certain that he was one of the hijackers and only at the end of the battle did one of the hostages identify him as one of their own. It was a tragic mistake, but one that was categorically unavoidable. It's a wonder, in a room filled with so many terrorists and so many hostages, that there was only once such case. I've already mentioned how close I was to shooting an innocent Ugandan and how another hostage had nearly been shot.

A few hours into the flight, by the time we were already thousands of kilometers from Uganda, the pilots put the BBC radio on over the loudspeakers and we heard Idi Amin's statement about having just repelled the force that had landed at Entebbe and how his forces had reclaimed control over the airport. I burst out laughing. Turned out that the time-delay bombs that Mofaz's force had left behind had worked quite well and had waylaid the Ugandans for a while.

We landed at Tel Nof. I was completely drained. Two straight nights without sleep, the vomiting and the pills, the stress in advance of the mission, and above all, the string of hair-raising incidents at the terminal, events from which I escaped by the skin of my teeth, sapped me of all my energy reserves. I was done. When the rear door of the plane opened and I saw dozens of photographers waiting outside, I opted for the side door. That's why there's not a single picture of me from the mission. I stepped out of the dim plane and into the blinding, searing light of the fourth of July. Dizzy and starting to blackout, I was forced to sit down on the tarmac and tried to get my bearings. I sat there for the better part of a minute, alone, eyes closed, slowly digesting the experience of the past forty-eight hours. A woman soldier approached and asked to talk to me. I opened my eyes and said: "Please, not now, I don't have the strength to talk," but she insisted and seemed genuinely upset. I overcame the urge to tell her to get lost and asked how I could be of help. She said that her boyfriend serves in the Unit and that he wasn't among the operators getting off the plane and that she was worried he might have been killed. I saw that she was serious and asked for his name. She gave it to me. I told her that I swear by all that I hold dear that there is no such soldier in the Unit, that he hadn't flown to Entebbe, hadn't been killed, and that she could relax. Then I saw a spark of rage flash in her eyes and she mumbled through her lips: "Son of a b....!! He's been lying to me for a year and a half!!"

As the entire country went bonkers, we rode from Tel Nof to the base. By the time we'd landed at Tel Nof the second or third edition of the papers had been released and they handed them out for free. On the bus we saw the photos of the celebrations at the military airfield in Lod, where the hostages were received, and we heard Kaveret's "Medina Ktana Mitchameket Mitzara" and Ariel Zilber's "Rutzi Shmulik," which starts a little bit sad and ends very glad and I felt that those two songs were very fitting indeed. Till today, whenever I hear those songs I think of the ride on the bus and the euphoric feeling that engulfed me throughout. Back at the base, I got off the bus, went to my duffel, which had already arrived from Sharm el-Sheikh, and saw that my wallet (in which I had my national ID card) had been stolen. On the ground in Sharm someone had decided to utilize the time between our departure and the arrival of the truck from the base to make a few quick bucks. That's how it is in Israel. There's a division of labor. Some people fly to Entebbe and some people steal the wallets of those who fly to Entebbe. A few days later, I went to the Ministry of the Interior building in Jerusalem to get a new identity card. There was a long line and I was wearing civilian clothing. I waited in line like everyone else when all of a sudden a pretty young woman walked in. The clerk rose from behind her desk and said: "Come on in, come on in, you go straight in without waiting on line," and everyone clapped for her. I got upset and said: "What's that supposed to mean? Why doesn't she have to wait on line?" The clerk replied: "What do you mean? She was in Entebbe, her passport was left behind and she's continuing to travel and needs a new passport and so o-f-c-o-u-r-s-e she is going to go in without waiting on line!!" She walked in and started filling out the forms while I remained on line. I could feel everyone's contemptuous stares, glaring at my pettiness at growing upset that one of the heroes of Entebbe was being asked to go in before me. I shut my mouth and didn't say a word to the dozens of people beside me, but I was unable to restrain myself entirely and I eventually asked her to step aside a moment. We stood there a few dozen meters away from the crowd, at the end of the hallway, and spoke in private while everyone watched us—or rather her—the celebrity from Entebbe. I didn't tell her my name but I did tell her that I'd been at Entebbe and asked her what they saw from their perspective and at what point she realized we were coming to save them and not kill them. She gave me a condescending look and said: "I have two things to say to you: One, they told us not to say anything to anyone, because it was a top-secret operation. And two, you're already the fifth guy who's tried to tell me that he was in Uganda." I said to her: "The French flight crew was at the far-left end of the hall, near the small door, there were two couches over there, the German terrorist was here and the pillars were the color of…" At once she realized that not only was I at Entebbe but that I was one of the few soldiers that had stormed into the hostages' hall. She was shocked, burst into tears, and then embraced me hysterically, hugging me in a way that no one ever had before and no one has since. All of a sudden there was a very different look on the faces of the people in the line and I realized that I had made a grave breach of security. I told her: "I have to leave," I pushed her off of me and ran for my life as she called out after me in a loud voice: "You were wonderful," and I berated myself for the way I'd violated the code of secrecy. I returned home and told my mother (who of course knew that I had taken part in the mission) about what had just happened at the Ministry of the Interior. It turned out that she had been that girl's teacher for several years. Five years later she sat for a long, one-hour interview on Galei Tzahal radio, talking about the hijacking and the rescue and among other things she also mentioned our meeting and said that, to her, I looked like a smiley seventeen-year-old boy. I've kept the identity card that I got that day, even though it's completely faded. I met her again thirty years after the operation, when the *Yedioth Ahronoth* daily invited me and Amnon to return to Entebbe and she too had been invited to talk about the events from the perspective of the hostages. Thirty years later she remembered every detail of that meeting in the Ministry of the Interior.

Yoni

I can't wrap this up without a few words about Yoni. We were the most veteran operational team in the Unit for the duration of his command. Occasionally we clashed over certain issues, but all that is insignificant and irrelevant to the operation in Entebbe. There, during that operation, he made no mistakes. Not one of us has even the slightest contention regarding his role during, and while preparing for, the mission. From my vantage point his operational comportment during the mission, which, to my great dismay in the end bore his name, was stellar. From the moment that I was involved, I saw him leading the process of preparation, and it was he who briefed us, he who shouldered the burden of responsibility by saying to both the higher command and the officers under his command that "we'll do this," while all around him there were more than a few who were not so certain. The briefing he delivered at Sharm el-Sheikh was artistry —the best pre-op briefing I've ever heard. The instructions I received there were what guided me when I lost eye contact with Amnon. His operational comportment during the mission was also superb. He made the right decision in shooting the soldiers on guard; he made the right decision in instructing the vehicles to speed up; he made the right decision in having us disembark sooner than planned; and he spotted Muki's stoppage and issued the right orders to solve the problem. In terms of the results, that might have been the most dramatic single minute in the history of the IDF. The lives of one-hundred hostages were hanging in the balance and there were but a few seconds left in the hourglass—and all this in a foreign, faraway, and hostile land. In addition, the result of failure was more than the sum of the lives of the hostages and the soldiers. Rabin, we know today, had already prepared a letter of resignation, and in the event of failure the diplomatic damage and the damage to Israel's deterrence are beyond what we can gauge. Facing all this stood a small force, significantly outnumbered by the enemy, a force that was supposed to resolve the hostage situation with the help of surprise and qualitative advantage. And Yoni—who had all of that dreadful responsibility resting on his shoulders and his alone, under the most extreme pressure imaginable—was, in that one minute, focused, purposeful, capable of accurately reading the situation and reacting precisely as necessary. A true commander. He has been horribly wronged in some of the depictions of the operation. I must emphasize that this paragraph has nothing to do with him having died and the custom of speaking well of those that are no longer. No and no. It is meant to right a historic wrong as pertains to this operation and as an expression of deep gratitude for a man who was killed in the service of the state of Israel, in a distant land, on a mission that was unassailably just, while handling himself at the highest possible level, making the right decisions, and serving as a significant factor in the overall success.

Personal Remark

On 30 August 1939 (one day before the outbreak of World War Two) my mother endured a Judgement of Solomon—from the perspective of the child. In the Biblical version there were two mothers and one child—here there was one mother and two children. She was a nine-year-old girl living in Poland. Her mother (my grandmother) understood that war was upon them and decided to save at least one of her children by splitting up the family. Just thinking of the tragedy that Grandma must have experienced when forced to choose between her two children drives me mad. She chose to keep her young son beside her and to send her daughter, my mother, to the faraway house of an aunt. Her hope was that in this way at least one of them would survive. The next day my mother was witness to the beginning of the German bombardments—a nine-year-old girl, without parents. That was the opening chord of a six-year period of survival, a daily battle, during which nearly her entire extended family was murdered—courtesy of the Germans. The fact that at Entebbe we hit two German terrorists in the main hall—both arch-bastards who didn't hesitate to perform a selection even among women and children and those who still bore numbers tattooed on their forearms and had already been through one German selection, and all this just thirty years after the Holocaust—this, as far as I was concerned, was a most significant event and the closing of a circle. I think that my mother was happy about that too but since she's a restrained person she never told me so explicitly.

And another little story linking Entebbe and the Holocaust: a few years ago a Hollywood producer came to Israel to work on a movie about the operation. He interviewed all the VIPs—Shimon Peres, Benjamin Netanyahu, Ehud Barak and a few of the soldiers who'd operated on the ground. At the end of the joint interview with me and Shlomi, he asked us what the significance of the operation was for us. Shlomi told him that his parents were Holocaust survivors and that for him preventing Jews from being led once again like lambs to the slaughter was his main motive in serving in the Unit. I told him that I too had a little story from the Holocaust: a Jewish woman with two little children fled Belgrade in 1941, on the last train out of the city before the arrival of the Germans. The train stopped before a bombed-out bridge. They got off utterly helpless. Suddenly a man whom they didn't know showed up and asked, "Jews?" The danger in answering in the affirmative was great—Jews were killed like roaches in those parts—but the woman had no choice and so she confirmed that they were. He said quietly: "My name's Cohen, come with me." He hid them and without any doubt saved them, at great personal risk, and without asking for a thing in return. That woman was my grandmother and the two kids were my father and his sister. I told the producer that I would like to think that for the hostages in Entebbe we were like that Cohen character on the bombed-out bridge, and in both cases it was proven that, as the saying goes, all Israel are responsible for one another. A few weeks later the producer gave me a call and said that he'd decided that the main motif of the Entebbe movie would be the linkage between the operation and the Holocaust as told through that tale. The movie is called "Cohen on the Bridge" and it is an animation movie that begins and ends with my father and grandmother's story in Yugoslavia in 1941, while the middle of the movie depicts the raid on the terminal. The movie was shown at the Cinematheque here and has won prizes as a documentary film in festivals around the world. It was shown dozens of times as part of the Mossad exhibit about the operation, and is one of the main features of the Entebbe exhibit on display now at the Rabin Center.

Two days after the operation we all went to Mount Herzl to take part in Yoni's funeral. We met Aryeh Ben-David, Itamar's father, whose son had been a member of our team and was killed on the night of 5-6 March 1975 during the hostage-rescue raid at the Savoy Hotel in Tel Aviv. That wonderful and unique man worked in the fields at the age of eighty as though he was still twenty and could tell endlessly fascinating and funny tales about the British Mandate and the Second World War and the pre-state days of the Yishuv. He was for me an object of unmitigated admiration. Eyes shining, Aryeh hugged me and said that at Entebbe we'd settled some of his personal score. I felt like I was floating on a cloud. Years later he told whoever would listen—and there were many such people—that "Itamar's team were the ones who'd eliminated the terrorists at Entebbe." Nothing can ever fully settle the score, but the fact that we were able to give him and Hadassah a smidgen of *naches,* and were able to ease, if only for just a bit, their terrible and interminable pain, has been for me over the years the peak of this special event.

Several Professional Comments

I've added a few technical comments of my own for readers who are not familiar with hostage-rescue drills and a few comments regarding the force's operational capacity (from my subjective point of view, of course):

1. A general comment: the operation was an extraordinary success, attained amidst near-impossible circumstances. It was the result of excellent planning, prior experience with hostage terror attacks, skilled comportment from the soldiers of the Unit (and the IDF in general and the IAF specifically) and the brave and fine soldierly conduct exhibited there.

2. Level of execution: the media has repeatedly broadcast Muki's version of events regarding the assault force, and the picture that is painted is one of a luck-struck operation that had gone totally awry

and was on the cusp of mayhem and catastrophe, saved only by a miracle. ("Awry," "adrift," and "catastrophe" were the terms he used to describe the stage before the charge into the terminal). I categorically reject this (as do my friends). The operation went down almost exactly as planned; nothing went awry and nothing was adrift (other than Muki's mistake, passing over the first entrance) and nearly all of the soldiers fulfilled their roles as planned—and at a high level at that.

3. Determination: Despite the live-fire engagement far from the building, the force managed to reach the terminal and engage the terrorists and the Ugandan soldiers within seconds and to eliminate both elements in close-quarters combat without giving them the opportunity to kill the hostages. That is testament to the force's determination, professionalism, and daring.

4. Selective fire and professionalism in the vicinity of hostages: The force fired dozens of bullets in a passenger terminal that contained one-hundred-and-five hostages and four terrorists, who did not show restraint with fire. Despite the immense density of the crowd we only confirmedly hit—to our deep sorrow—one hostage, who was mistaken for a terrorist—Jean-Jacques Meimoni—while the other two (Pasco Cohen and Ida Borochovich) were hit by what might well have been terrorist bullets or ricochets. In terms of the force's operational skill within the hall that is an incredible display of selective fire at the highest possible level.

5. Initiative and improvisation as needed: During the course of events many soldiers found themselves in unplanned-for situations: Amos, who was moved from the perimeter security to the assault force without having drilled that role at all; Shlomi and Ilan, who found themselves in an unfamiliar hall; I, who found myself unaccompanied by my commander; Amnon, who decided in a fraction of a second to turn left rather than right once he noted that Muki had not gone into the first entrance; Yiftach, who immediately passed Muki as soon as he stopped; Yoni, who called out the correct orders, and many others. The functioning of everyone throughout the battle was extraordinary and testament to a high degree of faith in one another, a

capacity for improvisation, initiative, quick orientation, and the ability to keep a cool head under pressure.

6. Overcoming mishaps: Every hostage-rescue mission entails a high degree of risk. From the outset it was clear to the planners that the main card they had to play was the high level of soldiering, improvisational ability, and initiative, and Yoni said that plainly during his final briefing in Sharm. An operation of this sort never goes down exactly as planned, and every plan is but the basis for change. The question is, how does the force react when it is met with something unforeseen. In Entebbe, despite the inherent difficulty of dealing with two rings of guards (the outer ring comprised of Ugandan soldiers and the inner ring of terrorists), and despite the premature live-fire engagement, despite the halt imposed by the force leader and his subsequent entry through the wrong door, despite the commander of the Unit being shot even before the entry—events that, individually, had the potential to break up an assault in certain conditions—despite all of this, the force managed—while sticking nearly precisely to the initial plan—to eliminate the terrorists within seconds and take out a few dozen Ugandan soldiers in and around the terminal while causing almost no harm to the hostages.

7. The believability of the IDF debrief: Not one single soldier from the assault force and not (to the best of my knowledge) one single officer from the force, aside from Muki Betser, was questioned after the mission by the IDF History Department. It is unclear to me how the IDF History Department could issue its report on such a significant operation without questioning us. I've read the report in question, and the part that relates to us is distorted and perverted in a most biased way.

In summation, a final sentence: I have described here what I saw with my own eyes. I have tried very hard to be as precise as possible and not note any fact of which I am not one-hundred-percent certain.

Staff Sergeant (res) Amir Ofer, a resident of Jerusalem, is married and a father of three. He was drafted to the Naval Commandos in August 1972. Late in the training stage of his service, he was injured in a diving accident, lost consciousness, drowned, and was saved by his steadfast diving partner, Ami Weinberg, who died several months later in a different accident. As a result of the accident, Amir was incapable of diving and was transferred to the Unit in June 1974. He was integrated into Team Amnon and completed his training with that platoon. Several years ago, at the age of 61, he finished serving with the Unit in reserves. He holds a masters in computer science and is a founding partner of three start-up companies.

Cpt. Amnon Peled, Team Leader

Amnon Squad Commander; Yoni's Assault Force; Hostage Hall

BACK TO ENTEBBE

A few days after returning from Entebbe on the morning of July 4, 1976, we were discharged from the army, and after the army, we went on with our lives. We traveled, we studied, we worked, we had families. It's true that we had heard, on the plane ride home, that the BBC was reporting that the operation was a present from Israel to the United States in honor of its bicentennial anniversary, and we were, of course, aware of the joy sweeping across Israel, but we, for our parts, didn't delve into it. Hardly any of us so much as owned a television set at the time, and I don't remember being overly impressed by the mission. Maybe because sometime before the rescue mission at Entebbe we'd pulled off an operation that was, as far as I was concerned, far more special and far more dangerous, only it was covert and couldn't be spoke of and so it was as though it hadn't happened.

In essence, we didn't speak of Entebbe for ten years. We showed up for reserves duty, as necessary, and didn't treat Entebbe as the peak of our military careers. When all's said and done, everyone simply did his job. No one did anything extraordinary or anything beyond what was expected of him. No one was decorated for valor. Everything went more or less according to plan and the elimination of the terrorists was not technically complex. The difficulty of the assignment was only in that it was situated in Entebbe, some four-thousand kilometers from Israel.

I remember the first time it dawned on me just how significant the operation was in the eyes of the public. At the time, quite a few years after Entebbe, I was doing reserves duty, serving in the Israel Air Force's commando unit, Shaldag. A new commander, whom we didn't know, had been appointed. He asked that I assemble the company and he introduced himself, first and foremost, as someone who had participated in Operation Entebbe. In other words, he spoke of the operation as the most significant thing he had done in his military service. This coming from someone who had been in charge of the guys who'd lit the torches on the runway. We knew of course that there had been other IDF forces operating in Entebbe. Some of them had even flown with us on the same plane, but we weren't very much aware of their roles; we were focused on our own task.

Forty-five years have passed, and I see how the operation has only been amplified by time. In the Israeli psyche the mission is seen as a Sayeret Matkal operation under the command of Yoni Netanyahu, but that is inaccurate. Many other troops took part: from the Golani and Paratroop Brigades, from the Israel Air Force and the IDF Medical Corps. Yoni was the commander of the Unit and the commander of the assault force. The commander on the ground in Entebbe was Chief Paratroop and Infantry Officer Brig.-Gen. Dan Shomron. At the very top of the chain were Prime Minister Yitzhak Rabin and Defense Minister Shimon Peres. Maj.-Gen. Benny Peled, the commander of the IAF, is said to be the one who pushed for the operation, and it's rumored that the IDF Chief of Staff, Lt.-Gen. Motta Gur, showed responsibility and wasn't overly enthusiastic.

The participants' stories can be sorted into six categories. One is the operators from the Unit, who flew, shot, rescued, and flew back. Two is the hostages, who were put through a harsh ordeal and carry the memories of that experience for life. Three is the terrorists. When we embarked on the mission, we were told there were a total of ten terrorists, but we only killed six or seven of them. Perhaps some managed to escape, and if so, they truly have a special story to tell. Four are the airmen of the IAF. Their story is heroic: they did something unprecedented. They took apart the interior of the plane and reassembled it so that it could carry the necessary number of troops and quantity of fuel. It's the sort of project that takes six months just to get authorized, and they did it in the span of three days, while planning the route and assembling the flight crews and drafting reserves pilots who were familiar with international civilian aviation procedures. One of the pilots once told me: "You guys, what did it matter to you guys: any airfield we would have put you down on, you would have run, shot whoever needed shooting, and brought back whoever was in the terminal. The fact that we put you down on the right airfield, that's the operation right there." There's some truth to that, because the IAF didn't have a protocol for a mission like this; they invented it in a week. There was no plane in our possession that could fly that distance with that weight and return home. Five is the Mossad combatants and the intelligence officers. And six is the French flight crew, as led by Michel Bacos. Their decision to remain behind with the hostages in Uganda—that, to my mind, is heroism.

Each time I tell the story of Operation Yonatan, I tell it a bit differently, depending on the audience. When I speak before a combat unit, I tell it in a way that will motivate them to train hard. When I tell it to school kids, I tell it in a way that's age-appropriate. When I tell it to twelfth-graders, I tell it in a way that will increase their motivation to serve in a combat unit. And when I tell it to a general audience, I tell the known story of Entebbe. But there's always the matter of background and the chain of events, and of course the experience from a personal point of view. There is always the matter of where we'd come from and where we were going.

In June 1976 my team and I were on the cusp of pre-discharge vacation. I'd already gotten clearance from the Foreign Ministry, along with three other friends, to go to Kenya as soon as we were released from service and train President Jomo Kenyatta's bodyguards. Sometime before then the Kenyans had caught a cell of terrorists planning to shoot a shoulder-held, LAW missile at an El-Al passenger plane, and turned them over to Israel. As a token of its gratitude, Israel offered to send to Kenya some of its commandos to train the presidential guard. Traveling to Africa right after my military service seemed to me, at the time, to be a unique opportunity.

When the Air France plane was hijacked, we were in the middle of preparations for a different operation, in the Sinai Peninsula. The Unit was put on readiness alert for the possibility that the plane would be landed at Israel's international airport in Lod, as had happened four years earlier, in May 1972, when a Sabena Airways plane was hijacked and forced down in Israel.

The rescue of the passengers on board the Sabena flight was one of the Unit's first overt operations and it stirred up a great deal of publicity. The assault force managed to free the hostages and disable the hijackers within two minutes and with hardly any casualties; using a sophisticated ruse, in which the operators, in white coveralls, were disguised as mechanics allegedly tending to the aircraft, the force burst into the plane and asserted control, killing two hijackers and capturing two others. As it says in Bible: "...by wise counsel thou shalt make thy war." Two years later came the terror attack in the city of Ma'alot, which turned into a hostage crisis once a class school trip from Safed was caught up in the attack. We were deployed to rescue them. In the end we did rescue the hostages that remained alive, but the operation itself was a failure, as far as we were concerned. Twenty-two school children and one soldier were killed and many more were wounded. Few emerged unscathed, certainly from a mental health perspective, and we too felt that our souls had been "scratched." I remember that Motta Gur came to console us. The troops were rounded up and he said: "Guys, don't look at those who were killed, look at those who were saved." Later, in June 1974, there was a terror strike on the coastal city of Nahariya, and in March 1975 terrorists took over the Savoy Hotel in Tel Aviv, and we, during the course of the rescue operation, lost one of the operators from our team, Itamar Ben-David. In advance of Entebbe, which at that stage was still called Operation Thunderbolt or Operation Stanley, my team was the most senior platoon in the Unit, and we already knew we were not immune.

Once the hijacked Air France plane had been landed at Entebbe, we were taken off alert and sent down to the Sinai. We were there for two days, and on Tuesday, when we returned to the Unit, we were told that we still had to be on readiness alert. I spoke with Yoni and told him that my team wanted to start its pre-discharge vacation, and he authorized the request but said that we should leave contact details at the office, so that they'd know where to find us. We arranged our gear, left it in order, and went our separate ways.

On Thursday I was over at Hagar's place. She didn't have a phone. At eleven at night a D-400 truck driver started knocking on doors and asking for the paratroops officer. By midnight I was back at the Unit. There was not yet any talk of a detailed plan, only that we'd been ordered to prepare a rescue operation to free the hostages from the old terminal. The officers received a general briefing and then we went to sleep.

The next day, Friday, at nine in the morning, Yoni briefed the team leaders, detailing our placement in the force and our roles. The briefing was meant to give us a general picture of what was happening, to let us know what still needed to be organized, and to familiarize us with the force formation. At this stage, they still didn't know where the hostages were being kept. In the meantime, someone drove off to a local travel agency to buy some road maps of Africa. "If the 'nutters' actually decide to go for it," he said, "at least we'll have a road atlas so we can get back, or to Kenya by car."

During the early stages of preparation, we had intelligence materials that had been garnered in two different ways: from the Israeli construction company Solel Boneh, which had built the terminal in Uganda and had provided some basic facts about it and the runways, which were once used, during better times, by Israeli pilots when aiding and training Idi Amin's military forces; and far more precise information gleaned from the passengers who had passed the selection and been released. The selection, separating the Jews and Israelis from the rest of the passengers, was awful for everyone, but for the planners of the rescue operation it was a savior. As soon as the passengers were released, Amiram Levin was sent to France; he isn't a French speaker, but he knows what to ask. He interviewed the passengers and found out the hijackers' daily schedule, the sum total number of hijackers on the ground, what they looked like, the weapons they carried, whether they had explosive devices, etc. Most of the passengers were rather confused, but there was, among them, a retired French major who knew all the answers: He knew where they slept, the guard duty rotation schedule…and when he was asked about explosive devices, he replied: "Don't worry, the cartons are empty." Turned out that someone had bumped into one of the cartons and it, being weightless, moved easily.

While preparing for the mission—boarding the vehicles, performing live-fire encounters, deboarding the vehicles, running through some drills on a mock terminal made of burlap—the Mercedes appeared from who knows where, as did the idea of dressing up like Idi Amin's soldiers, in tiger-stripe uniforms and Kalashnikovs. We signed off on whatever gear we needed at the supply store, and acquired white hats so that the difference between them and us would be clear, especially in a situation in which we'd be bursting in from every possible entrance.

Anyone who's ever served in an army knows that when you go to the quartermaster's supply store, the clerk is always ready with many different versions of the word no: "We're out…we're closed today… come back in a few hours." This time, though, even the clerks seemed to realize that something was afoot. The windows were wide open and they actually asked how they could be of help and what else we might need. This was a surprise, considering the usual balance of power between combat soldiers and clerks.

The pre-operation simulation drill was set for seven in the evening and IDF Chief of Staff Lt.-Gen. Motta Gur came in person to oversee it.

Generally, in the Unit, you train for a mission for three months and each soldier, as in an operating room, knows his role precisely. We were used to long and highly organized battle procedures that moved along with the efficiency of a pharmacy, and here we were heading out on a big mission for which we'd trained a total of one day, a battle procedure of twenty-four hours. But we were well-trained soldiers and we knew our tasks. We boarded the Hercules, tied down the vehicles, untied them, went up and down the ramp a

few times, and ran through the model drill. At the end of it, Motta
Gur huddled with the team leaders and said to Yoni: "The Land
Rovers are packed, you've got too many soldiers loaded up on them;
you won't be able to fire like that while in motion. I want you to drop
two from each vehicle." I was squad commander of a strike force that
was to storm into the main hall of hostages, an officer under Yoni's
direct command. Yoni looked over at me, and I said right away:
"Drop the dog and the handler." The canine unit was new in those
days and we had a Doberman Pinscher and a handler in our vehicle.
I, for one, was rather scared of the dog. He didn't appear at ease and
who knew what he might do with that set of teeth in all sorts of
shifting situations, like a jolt of turbulence in mid-flight or in the
midst of the charge on the terminal—would he be on our side or
theirs?   .

We finished the mock drill on Friday night at around midnight.
We drew conclusions from the havoc of the drill, especially regarding
the counting of our men after the operation. We each added the gear
we realized we were lacking, and I gave Shlomi Reisman, a particularly precise soldier of mine, the task of ensuring that everyone was
accounted for at the end of the mission. Goes without saying that on
the night before the operation, we did not get much sleep...

On Saturday morning we drove to Lod and from there we flew to
Sharm. In Sharm, at the southern tip of the Sinai Peninsula, we got a
final briefing from Dan Shomron and were shown some intelligence
material and photos of the terminal and the airport in Entebbe; these
materials, the product of gritty on the ground intelligence gathering,
had travelled a long way to Sharm. My squad, I then realized, was set
to storm into the hall where the hostages were being kept! Yoni gave
a final briefing, tailored to the assault teams, emphasizing several
different scenarios and responses. Government authorization for the
mission had not yet come through, but still we tookoff, with the
knowledge that if the government did not grant authorization we
would simply turn around. The decision had to come no later than the
halfway point, so that there'd be enough fuel to return to Israel.

In so far as our return from Entebbe was concerned, we knew that there was an IAF squad with us, armed with a pump, and their role was to fill the planes with Ugandan flight fuel while we operated on the ground. We studied the layout of the airport, too, and the escape routes, so that if some of the planes were disabled or something else happened, we'd be able to ride the roads, burst through checkpoints, and make it to Kenya.

The flight to Sharm was rough, as the planes had to fly low over the sea to evade Egyptian radar. The flight from Sharm was mostly smooth, and I must have fallen asleep, because I awoke to the sound of a bell in the cabin. The lights glowed red and someone said we had twenty minutes to landing and then it was all happening for real. Everyone strapped themselves into their battle vests, checked they had all their gear, and then we were landing, galloping out, the mission clear and well-known. The Mercedes was in the lead, followed by two Land Rovers, with me in the front of the second one. As we charged ahead toward the terminal, two Ugandans pointed their rifles at us. Yoni shot them with a silenced pistol, then came Kalashnikov rounds from the first Land Rover and then from our vehicle, too. Pinchas Buchris, seated in my Land Rover, fired from the hip with the MAG machinegun, hitting the Ugandan soldiers around the terminal. The operation was now loud and out in the open, and there was nothing to do but race to the entrances, each to his own task.

We hopped out of the vehicles. It was a bit chaotic, as thirty guys disembarked at the same time. Just as planned, I charged toward the door leading to the hostage hall. Because the operation was now overt, it was clear to me that we had to run as fast as possible. I saw Amir sprinting ahead and I tried to catch him. While running, I saw that the officer leading the troops to the first door of the hostage hall (Muki), was stopped and not advancing. Yoni yelled "Forward, Betser" or "Betser, forward"; everyone remembers it a bit differently. While running I heard someone yell that Yoni was hit.

Amir was first to the hall. One of the terrorists engaged him through the glass door, shattering it with gunfire as he approached. Amir responded perfectly: semi-automatic fire, as in the manual, and then he sprinted ahead to close the gap physically to the terrorist. I charged in behind him and saw two terrorists, a man and a woman, aiming rifles at Amir's back. I shot each of them with two bullets, and toed their Kalashnikovs out of reach. Later it turned out that they were the German terrorists. Amir called out over the megaphone in Hebrew and in English: "Everyone get down, we're here to take you home." Several long seconds passed in which it was just me and Amir in the hall. Then Amos Goren, Gadi Ilan, and Muki Betser came in. I couldn't understand why they'd decided to enter through our door and not theirs, which was closer to them in the direction in which they'd been running. They spotted another terrorist and shot him. A hostage rose to his feet and was also, mistakenly, shot. Later we learnt that the man was Jean-Jacques Meimoni.

We started to scan the hall, making sure there were no more live terrorists amid the hostages. We heard the constant rattle of fire coming from the control tower. Giora Sussmann's squad was operating in the other room along with Shlomi Reisman, handling the VIP lounge, where apparently the terrorists had slept while off duty. The elimination stage was over. I popped out of the hall; saw they were treating Yoni. I popped back in and told Muki Betser, the most senior officer in our immediate vicinity, that Yoni had been hit and that he should assume command. Then Dan Shomron arrived at the terminal and gave the order to evacuate the hostages and returned to his command post, where he presided over all of the forces involved in the operation.

He ordered us to wrap it up and get the hostages on board the plane. We had some wounded and the fire from the control tower had never really stopped, despite the rocket-propelled grenades and the heavy machinegun fire that Rami Sherman's squad directed at the tower.

I led some of the hostages on foot to the plane, which was around 300 meters away. Rami managed the evacuation of the wounded and the rest of the hostages. Once they reached the plane, I returned to the terminal and made sure that all soldiers under my command were accounted for, a task that we knew was not so simple to accomplish.

The combat stage had taken roughly twenty minutes; the organization afterward—another twenty minutes, and so, along with the evacuation of the hostages and the forces on the ground, we were, in total, in Uganda for roughly an hour. Then we took off, all four planes rising to the sky.

Immediately afterward, in the loud belly of the plane, on the hood of the Land Rover, we conducted the first and only probing debrief of the assault on the terminal. Muki approached me and we tried to put together all that had happened. We were a group of squad leaders, officers all, and every now and again we summoned one of the operators to come and share his version of events. Muki submitted that my squad had stormed in through his entrance, and that had confused the rest of the force. But that wasn't right and from the debriefing of the other soldiers it was clear that he had gotten confused and not us. When we asked him where he'd been and why he hadn't charged forward, for his role had been to lead the assault force into the terminal, he said that his rifle had jammed, and that once he'd cleared the jam, the door had been locked. I, not put at ease by his responses, felt that the matter would be clarified back at the base, in the full debriefing that was sure to come. But without Yoni, the Unit commander, there never was a true debriefing of the mission. What happened instead was a show put on for VIPs and for all of the Unit's soldiers, including the non-combat troops, in which we were not, as is only logical in such public circumstances, asked to submit our official version of events. Afterwards, once we were discharged from the army, Amiram Levin took over as commander of the Unit and he was extremely busy and life just went on. To this day we've heard nothing of the official IDF protocol of the mission.

Taking off from Entebbe we had no idea where we were flying to, nor did we realize that the planes had not been re-fueled at the airport in Entebbe. After around forty minutes, perhaps more, we landed again. I looked out and saw a belt of armed African soldiers surrounding the plane, pointing their weapons at us. For several long, unsettling moments I had no idea what was going on, until Shai Avital and Michael Aaronson boarded the plane. They were friends from the Unit and were in Kenya training the presidential guard. They promptly said that everything was alright, that we'd landed in Kenya to refuel and to evacuate the wounded for treatment in a Nairobi hospital. We'd be taking off again soon, they said, and the armed soldiers surrounding the plane were there to protect us.

Several days later, once we'd been discharged from service, Yochai Yazdi and I flew back to Kenya and joined Shai Avital and Michael Aaronson in Nairobi, where we lived at the presidential guard base and trained the very same soldiers.

Since the operation I've been back to Entebbe twice, marking the 20th and 30th anniversaries of the operation. I went there with Amir, with some of the hostages, and with members of the media—Micah Shagrir of the Israel Broadcasting Authority and Nehama Dwek of *Yedioth Aharonoth.*

At times I run through the old memories: how we had no idea who made the plans or what they had planned and only later did we realize that the plans had shifted continuously. How the control tower seemed so tall in comparison to what I'd been expecting based on the intelligence photos. I recall one of the hostages, a kid at the time of the operation, who, years later, when we met again at Entebbe, looked disappointed. When we inquired why, he said: "I thought you were giants, but you're actually just like me…"

I think of how much the world has changed in the ensuing years. For those who weren't yet been born at the time, the operation is to them the way World War One seemed to me: a distant history. Back then, in order to remain in contact, each one of the forces carried a fifty-five-pound radio and still the connection was patchy. Back in those days, telephones were not mobile and field intelligence security consisted of a female clerk who sat beside the only outgoing tele-phone in the Unit and didn't let anyone make calls.

So, if we ask ourselves what has changed over the years—not very much. The Arabs are here and so are we, the cycles of violence continue. And yet I think that in the wake of the operation, aside from the specific cases of Misgav Am and Nachson Wachsman, there were no further hostage-taking attacks by terrorists. It seems that after Entebbe the terrorists reached the conclusion that the hostage trick isn't so great after all, that the crazy Jews won't give up and that they'll go for it anywhere, under any circumstance.

For years after the operation I rebuffed the operators' requests to publicize our story of the assault on the terminal. I asserted that the mission had been to free the hostages, we'd done it well, and the technical details weren't of interest to the citizens of the world. Of late, after having seen the official IDF debriefing, I realize that forty-five years is a long time, and that even if it isn't really important to the citizens of the world, or even of Israel, it is important to my friends, the operators of old, to relay what happened in reality.

Maj. (res) Amnon Peled is a native of Kibbutz Ma'agan Michael. He was drafted into the Unit in August 1971 and was a soldier in Rami Lapidot's team. Ehud Barak, the commander of the Unit at the time, sent him to officers' candidate school, and he returned to the Unit to lead a team of his own in August 1973, serving under Giora Zore'a and Yoni Netanyahu, may he rest in peace. Immediately after Opera-tion Yonatan, he was honorably discharged from service. He is married to Hagar and is a banana and mango farmer in Moshav Ma'ale Gamla on the Golan Heights.

Cpt. Giora Sussmann, Operational Company Commander
Sussmann Squad Commander; Yoni's Assault Force; Small Hall

Entebbe—Personal Story

Years after the operation was over, I happened to take part in an evening of battle heritage on an army base in Judea and Samaria. Up until that point I had not met a single one of the hostages and had no real sense of the experience they'd been put through. Aside from the footage of them landing at Ben-Gurion Airport, I had not seen them and did not know a thing about them.

I sat among a group of shiny-eyed soldiers who waited to hear about the famous mission and the army's great moment of glory. But then I listened, along with them, as Ruth Gross told her story. Only then, during the course of that night, did I begin to realize the breadth of the solidarity and the strength of the bond that this operation had forged.

I understood then that the hostages' ordeal—swinging from the bliss of vacation to the abyss of Entebbe, where they were corralled and incapacitated by their captors, and then thrust again to the elation of the rescue and the arrival home—well, it far surpassed our experience, and, at the same time, it adds a special significance to the operation.

The story of how one-hundred people were led like sheep to the slaughter; the way in which, in captivity, they were subjected to a selection process, a separation of Jews and Israelis from the rest of the pack, took me back to my mother's past and the way she and her family were put through a similar selection at Auschwitz. It underscored for me how, as the Passover Haggadah puts it, "in each and every generation they rise up to destroy us," and in this case it was us who were fortunate enough to save them "from their hands."

During the week that the Air France plane was hijacked, we were engaged in intense operational activity in the Sinai Peninsula. That year, 1976, I served as the commander of the Unit's operational company. It was a year packed with a wide variety of action. The number of terror attacks was down from the previous year, but still loomed large in our training and in our urgent calls to action. On Sunday we headed down to the Sinai Peninsula and had two special-ops lined up for the week, the first on Sunday night and the second on Wednesday night.

On the way down south, we heard of the hijacking. An Air France plane had been seized by terrorists and yet somehow it seemed clear that, this time at least, it wasn't on us. It was far away and looked like it would just get rolled to the government's door. Israel, denied any feasible military option, would have to negotiate with the hijackers. We were focused on the mission before us. The first night went well. We prepared avidly for the next operation and even managed to rest a bit before Wednesday. Like all the rest of the citizens of Israel, we followed the developments—the landing at Entebbe etc.—and hoped for the best.

On Thursday, after successfully completing the mission, we flew back to the center of the country. Tired and satisfied, we got ready for the debriefs and the gear inspections. After that we were homeward bound. We felt like we'd done our thing and were deserving of a weekend of R&R with our friends and girlfriends.

I was the commander of the operational company but didn't have the slightest idea that an operational plan was in the works. Yoni was with us in the desert for most of the week and I didn't hear a word about a plan being assembled. Even when the debriefs were done and the soldiers were wearing their dress uniforms, we didn't for a second think that there would be any sudden change to our weekend plans.

The team leaders approached and asked me if they could send the guys home. I checked with the Unit's headquarters and, surprisingly, I was told that leave was cancelled until further notice. This news was delivered on Thursday, at five or six in the evening, with all the soldiers in dress uniform and ready to be let out for the weekend; in such situations, soldiers "smell" home and their reserves of patience are easily tapped. As officers, we heard loud and clear what they thought of us. And the truth is, we also didn't know what to make of the mysterious hold that had been imposed on us all well into the night.

At some point, we were summoned to Yoni's office for a meeting. And still we had no idea where this was going.

All the staff officers and commanders were seated around the table—Yoni, Muki, Mofaz, Yiftach, Yohai and all of the company and team leaders—as Yoni, for the first time, presented us with the operational plan. We heard what he said but it didn't sink in—it seemed illogical, impractical, the sort of drill that the army only does because that's what it's supposed to do, the sort of thing that's never going to be authorized upstairs. Someone, somewhere, it seemed, had gotten a little "unhinged." The longer the briefing went on, the clearer it was that leave was cancelled, and that we, tired, eyelids heavy, were heading for another night without sleep.

In advance of a mission there is always a process of determining the size of the force and the number of participants. Often some of the soldiers are not given a slot. It was always a wonder to me the way that commanders and soldiers fought for the honor of participating, especially when a live-fire operation seemed likely. Some of my best friends from the peace movement strived, openly and secretly, to get themselves in the lineup, which only goes to show that the test of a personal challenge trumps ideology: Peace Now!, my foot. But maybe that's the duality of our lives—Crying and Shooting…

Friday morning the commanders huddled in a tent on a nearby base for a briefing by Brig. Gen. Dan Shomron. I met buddies from other units, commanders in the Paratroop Brigade who were in the same draft as me—Nali Packer from Battalion 202 and Giora Eiland from Battalion 890. Amid the commotion and the mounting excitement, we traded personal stories, as old friends do, and shared quiet moments in which we felt we were in this unique operation together…I also met Nehemiah Tamari, may he rest in peace, who had recently served as the deputy commander of the Unit, and Matan Vilnai and Uri Sagie, who were idolized by those of our generation, and others.

The IDF's ability to gather disparate units, from the Paratroop and Golani Brigades, the Unit, the Air Force and a host of staff officers, and assemble a complex plan and drill it on such short notice seemed to me, both then and now, incredible and unique. And perhaps, besides the sense of a calling that we all seemed to share, the lack of time also worked in our favor: it spared us months of coordination and hours of pleading with the logistical branch, which, for a brief window of time, forgot the words "no" and "we're all out."

The commanders—Yoni, Muki, Mofaz and Yiftach—stayed behind to tie up loose ends. I went with the team leaders and their soldiers to an open stretch of field next to the workout area and laid out a white marking ribbon. Behind that, with the help of a blueprint, we built a model of the old terminal at Entebbe. For the better part of an hour we drilled the raid and the takeover of the terminal, emphasizing a synchronized charge through all entrances. We ran through a few different eventualities and some scenarios and responses. The commanders started to find a common language and the first questions started to rise to the surface: what if it happens this way, what if it happens like that?

Time flew. We went back to our quarters and started to carefully organize gear, as always, and especially the items that were unique to this mission—American jungle fatigues as used by the Ugandan army, white kibbutz-style hats for identification and all sorts of other things. We worked on the vehicles that were going to be used during the mission—the Mercedes, the two Land Rovers, and the four BTR-40 armored personnel carriers.

Toward evening the entire force gathered for a model drill: four Hercules C-130s descended in silence on the runway nearby and all the forces gathered—the Paratroops, the Golani recon guys, the Unit, the re-fueling force under the command of Ran Bag and the medical team. Dan Shomron gave a short briefing and then we rolled up onto the planes and strapped down the vehicles. The plane taxied very briefly and then according to the plan we rolled out, drove for a bit, drilled the takeover of the terminal, and promptly returned to the aircraft. Then we drilled the evac and fell in around the tent where Dan Shomron's staff officers were running the drill. Our feeling was that, okay, nice, we did a cute little model drill and now we'll do a few more and run through a whole lot of scenarios and responses etc., as we usually did.

The IDF Chief of Staff, Lt.-Gen. Motta Gur, who was present throughout, had but a few brief comments. He offered his impression of the mock raid, and we were, rather surprisingly, dismissed back to our tents for final preparations. My sense was that the training was done in an offhand manner, and that feeling only contributed to my sense that this was just a perfunctory exercise, conducted solely so that a box could be checked, and that, at any moment now, the responsible adults would show up and excuse us from this categorically unreasonable operation.

Once again, though, we stood for more gear inspections, staggered throughout the night, and on this night too we went without sleep…though we did manage to steal an hour or two.

On Saturday morning Yoni briefed the whole force and we dispersed for final preparations before departure. Team leaders approached me and complained: not all of the details were sufficiently nailed down. I passed the message on to Yoni. He assembled a final officers' meeting, in which we ran through all the remaining what-ifs and the appropriate scenarios and responses. With time dwindling down, he summarized the protocol, and managed, as usual, to instill in me the feeling that we'd get it done and get it done well.

The room was full of officers, many of whom went on to climb high up the command ladder: Shaul Mofaz, who went on to become the IDF Chief of Staff; Yiftach and Dani, who both rose to the rank of Brig.-Gen. and served as commanders of the army's special ops command; Udi Salvi and Alik Ron, who both later served as commanders of the Air Force's Shaldag unit; Tamir Pardo, the communications officer, who later served for years in the Mossad and eventually headed the clandestine service; and the rest of the Unit's staff officers. On top of the pyramid, in that room, were Yoni and Muki—both veterans of the Paratroop Brigade who joined the Unit as officers and, each in his own way, were pivotal influences on generations of operators. They were brothers in arms and friends in every way, and both of them brought with them the tradition of a fighting spirit from the Paratroops.

Yoni was our first company commander. He walked our two teams (Dudik and Zvika) through the paces in the Paratroop Brigade Basic Training base, Sanur, and taught us all of the soldiering essentials. A warrior in every fiber of his being, he was a courageous and nearly flawless soldier blessed with an unflappable prudence under fire. He led us during the 1973 Yom Kippur War in the Golan Heights and in a string of operations against terrorists. A lover of the written word, a true intellectual, a man of action. Besides his natural ambition to climb the chain of command, he also carried deep within him a calling, a devotedness that he passed on to us, in word and in deed. During his year at the helm of the Unit he went through a sort of personal crisis and at times he was not at his best, but whenever we were called to arms, he emerged as a true leader, emitting a sense of confidence and serving as a stable source of authority.

Muki—we matured under his command. He led my platoon, Team Sussmann, and others during our advanced training. A remarkable man blessed with natural leadership qualities, courage, original thinking and a unique sense of humor that never marred the sincerity of his actions. He and Yoni led us into battle in the Golan Heights and the Sinai desert during the Yom Kippur War and later into a variety of missions. Like Yoni, he saw the military as a calling and at the time of the operation was up to his eyeballs in drawing lessons from the Yom Kippur War, trying to figure out appropriate war-time missions for the Unit. He did this with the reservists of the Unit, who went on to form the spine of Shaldag, the Israel Air Force's commando unit.

Muki was the one who led and represented the Unit during the early stages of the Entebbe planning. He and several of the Unit's staff officers prepared the skeleton of the operational plan until Yoni returned to the base on Thursday and took command. Besides leading the strike force at Entebbe, Muki was also Yoni's deputy during the mission.

Over the years a rivalry has broken out, a sort of factional feud between the Netanyahu family and Muki. Personally, it pains me, because this relationship does not reflect reality nor the friendship that Yoni and Muki shared, and we, the operators, knowingly and at times unknowingly, have poured fuel on the fire, and that's a shame.

———————

We headed out to the airfield, where the C-130s waited for us on the runway. The vehicles were restrained and ratcheted down to the floor of the plane. Fully loaded and dressed in our Ugandan army uniforms, we strode toward the aircraft. On the way I saw Yanush Ben-Gal heading straight for us. Serving at the time as the head of the operations division in the IDF Operations Directorate, he had come to see us off. He also had a special relationship with Yoni. But I, in ordinary times, would have made a big detour to avoid coming face to face with that tough man. On that Saturday morning, though, Yanush was more emotional than us, and since he knew me from previous missions, he came over, shook my hand firmly, and wished me luck. And I, suckling that I was, offered him this: "Looks like the government's really going to authorize this, huh?" and Yanush replied in a serious tone: "They'll authorize alright." Nonetheless, at that moment, I didn't believe him.

The flight to the Sharm el-Sheikh airbase took an hour. The planes hugged the ground to avoid enemy radar. The desert landscape of the Negev, so familiar to us from months of nightly orienteering drills, seemed to be waving at us, wishing us well.

In Sharm, we waited for the green light from the government. Brand new photos from Entebbe, taken by a Mossad combatant, arrived at the airbase and confirmed the intelligence information and gave us the feeling that the information we'd been given about the airfield, the terminal, and the control tower was complete and exact.

One of the unique elements of this mission was the intelligence. Surprisingly, even though Uganda was not an enemy state and therefore not a target of our intelligence branches, and even though it's located far from Israel's shores, the information we received was more detailed and more precise than that which we were given before nearly all of our previous anti-terror ops, including those in Israel proper. The intelligence poured in from Israelis who had worked in Uganda, including, among others, Muki Betser and Amnon Halivni, who piloted one of the C-130s. The hostages who were released and sent to Paris were debriefed by Amiram Levin and Mossad officers and provided additional information.

The H-hour arrived and we set off. Slowly the planes took to the air and clung to the Red Sea as we flew south. The view out the window was incredible—the Egyptian coast to our right and the Arabian coast off to our left as we skimmed over the face of the water. I still felt that we'd be turned around at some point, but the flight continued in a southerly direction and with each kilometer away from Israel's coast it became clearer and clearer that we were really doing this!

As we pulled away from the borders of Egypt and Saudi Arabia, the planes ascended to a cruising altitude and the week without sleep came crashing down on me. I fell asleep in the Mercedes. For me the flight to Entebbe was a dream…

Yoni shook me awake a few minutes before landing. He made the rounds, checked that everyone was suited up and ready, offered a few words of encouragement and sat down in the front seat of the car alongside Muki. Behind the wheel was Amitzur, of course, who'd gotten the Mercedes ready and was its designated driver. There were six other operators in the car, members of Muki's squad and of mine.

The plane touched down serenely on the lit tarmac, slowed, and then the rear door was opened and the paratroop force jumped out. The paratroopers from the recon unit, under the command of Doron Avrutzki, secured the runway and lit torches to mark it for the following planes. Nehemiah Tamari and Giora Eiland led a force from Battalion 890 to secure the new terminal along with Matan Vilnai, the brigade commander. The plane reached the junction between the old and new runways, turned, and dropped the cargo door for us. The Unit's entire force, thirty operators borne on two Land Rovers and one Mercedes, sailed down the ramp and drove quickly toward the old terminal.

The drive was made in silence. Each of us was focused on the mission ahead, tense, our stomachs sending signals of fear on the way to battle. Thinking of our loved ones and our beloveds at home, we gripped our rifles hard, the rocks of our salvation.

The plan was to maintain cover and to get as close as possible to the entrances and then to charge through them as one. The concern was that a Ugandan perimeter force would engage us on the way and we hoped that we would be able to dispatch them with silencers and maintain the element of surprise. That's exactly what happened. Two Ugandan sentries stood guard several dozen meters before the old terminal, cocked their weapons, and seemed to be about to open fire. Yoni gave the order to shoot them, and we both, apparently with no success, tried to take them out with the silenced handguns. At the split second in which the order was issued, Muki screamed not to fire, because he estimated that the Ugandans weren't really going to fire, but he was too late. The guys in the jeep behind us were the ones who hit the Ugandan soldiers and it was their fire that changed the ride from an exercise in deception to an open battle.

After the exchange of fire, Yoni ordered us to stop opposite the old control tower. We dismounted in the agreed-upon order, with Muki's squad in the lead. A German terrorist popped out and came toward us, causing the force to momentarily stop. Once he saw us, he scurried back into the main hall. Yoni issued a command: "Forward!"

and right after that the squads took off at a sprint, each squad to its entrance and its goal.

I was first into the small hall. I slipped through the side of the door frame, as we'd been taught, and fired at a bed in which the terrorists slept when they were off duty; for a second it seemed there someone was lying in it. I discovered that off to the right there was a hallway that we hadn't known about. I fired down the length of it, too. Having emptied my clip, I stepped out and re-loaded. Meanwhile, Adam Kolman and Ben-Ami arrived and cut through to the rear of the small hall, which was blocked off with a partition, and took out two Ugandan soldiers.

Dani Arditi and his squad were supposed to charge into the VIP area but contrary to our plan, there was no door leading into that space. Additionally, two of his soldiers were wounded. Turned out that the hallway I'd fired into was the way to get into the VIP Lounge. I called out to Dani and told him that I'd clear those rooms. Shlomi, a member of Amnon's squad, popped out of nowhere and together we headed into the labyrinth of the VIP lounge, firing into open rooms and bathrooms, alternating the lead between us.

Two people came out of the last room. They had their hands in the air. For an instant Shlomi wasn't sure if they were hostages or hijackers. To me it was clear that they were hijackers, and since we'd been told that the hijackers might be wearing explosive vests, I gave Shlomi an order to shoot them. I was at an angle that opening fire might have meant hitting Shlomi. Shlomi fired and hit them. A grenade that one of the terrorists had been holding exploded and luckily didn't impact us. At the end of the day, my squad killed three terrorists and two Ugandan soldiers. The strike, from the moment the vehicles stopped till then, had taken around one or two minutes.

At the same time, Amir Ofer, and behind him Amnon and the rest of the squad, killed the terrorists in the main hall. The hostages stayed down, hugged the floor. Muki's door was barred, so he joined Amnon and Amir. All told they killed four terrorists in the main hall. Most regrettably, three hostages also lost their lives. Yiftach and his squad went up to the second floor and eliminated several Ugandan soldiers.

Meanwhile, outside, all hell was breaking loose: Mofaz and Omer arrived with the armored personnel carriers and were firing into the second floor and the control tower. Omer and his men, in a matter of minutes, destroyed the Ugandan air force, reducing their fighter jets to balls of fire. Once we'd finished our task, we joined the force in the main hall; the feeling that greeted us is hard to describe. In silence, as though they still didn't believe what had happened, the hostages were led out of the hall. A Golani force under the command of Uri Sagie arrived to lead them to the airplanes. The Main Hall was empty aside from three Ugandan service providers, whose dark faces were white with fear. They didn't believe that we would not harm them, and we had to put them at ease.

Dan Shomron arrived at the terminal and urged us to speed up the evacuation. It was crucial that we wrap it up and depart before the Ugandan forces came to their senses and tried to attack us from the rear.

Once the hostages were evacuated, we received the order to pack it in. The assault force withdrew first toward a plane waiting outside the new terminal. The operators in the APCs laid down cover fire and after a heavy blast they too turned toward their planes. The first plane off the ground was the one carrying the hostages and the wounded. The assault force was second and after us the other two planes. Till I reached the plane, I had no idea that Yoni had been wounded. Back on board, rumor had it that Yoni had been hit and that he'd been evacuated on the first plane.

As soon as the wheels lifted off the runway, a feeling of relief swept over us. Like every warrior at the end of the battle, we touched our bodies and confirmed physically that we'd emerged intact and that we'd "striven with God and man" and prevailed. The recognition that you've had the privilege of participating in an extraordinary operation trickles into your mind, and also the gratitude that you are homeward bound.

We stopped in Nairobi to refuel. Shai Avital, a close friend who was like a brother to me, was stationed in Nairobi at the time. He'd been posted there as part of the training crew of the president's armed guard. It was clear to me that once we landed and the door opened, he'd be waiting for us on the ground and I yearned for that meeting. The plane touched down in Nairobi and stopped. I was first at the side door. It opened and Shai stood there. I was so happy to see him and then he said: "Yoni was killed," and for a moment I stood there thunderstruck. The joy of our meeting curdled into a profound feeling of loss.

Shai questioned me about the course of events. We caught each other up and then parted once the plane was ready for departure. From that moment on, I felt a confluence of emotions: on the one hand, we'd lost Yoni; on the other, we'd taken part in an extraordinary and successful mission, which would clearly lead news cycles all over the world.

On the way home, I sat in the cockpit. Matan Vilnai and Nali Packer, my buddy from boarding school, were up there with the pilots. We filled each other in and also discussed the events of the previous night. The euphoric crew scanned the radio channels. Somewhere over Ethiopia they found a French broadcast that reported the operation, and the crew broke out in a joyous Hallelujah and from who knows where they drew a bottle of Champagne.

———

Upon landing at Tel Nof, a feeling of excitement and relief prevailed. Ran Packer, the base commander, called a few of us over and informally interviewed us. We returned to the Unit, showered, and showed up at the mess hall for a debrief with the commander of military intelligence and with Amiram, who was made commander of the Unit during the course of the previous night, immediately after receiving word of Yoni's death.

In those days, there were no cellphones. The guys stood on line at the payphones to talk to their loved ones. I, as one of the officers, was busy managing the post-operation process and didn't find time to call my girlfriend, Anat, whom I was to marry in a month. Anat, I later learned, had heard about the operation from a friend who then served as a security agent at the Lod Airport (known today as Ben Gurion International); he'd called her and told her that the operation had been a success, but that the Unit had lost an officer in battle. And I hadn't called. Anat was sick with worry. Only in the afternoon did I find time to put in a call and set her mind at ease, but to this day, she, my wife of 43 years, does not let me forget the nerve-wracking ordeal I put her through.

Yoni was buried at a mass funeral on Mount Herzl's military cemetery. Immediately afterwards we threw ourselves into the preparations for the next mission, which was already in the works pre-Entebbe.

I had several sit-downs with Yoni's parents, Zila and Benzion Netanyahu. Benzion, pained by the loss of his son, sat with me for many long hours and asked, both as a historian and a bereaved father, for me to walk him through his son's final days and hours. I understood the unquenchable need to relive a beloved son's last moments. Iddo, his youngest brother, interviewed me at length for his book on Yoni's last battle.

This glorious battle, which enabled many to rightly claim paternity on the planning and execution, became, over the years, a hard road to travel, laced with bitter rivalry and the settling of personal scores, and that's too bad.

Out of respect for Yoni and Muki and the rest of my brothers in arms in the Unit and the Paratroop and Golani Brigades and the Air Force, all of whom took part in this mission, I hope that this book will offer the personal perspectives of the participants and not serve as a tool with which we bludgeon one another in pursuit of the alleged truths, which, immediately after the mission, were already in dispute.

A few years after the operation I got a call from Gadi Ilan, a reserves operator in Amnon Peled's platoon. He was working at the time as an onboard security agent with El-Al. A random chat with one of the pilots revealed that both of them had taken part in Operation Yonatan. The pilot told Gadi: 'I've got a picture of one of your guys. He sat up in the cockpit on the way home.' Gadi gave me a copy of that photo, and I've kept it to this day.

———

The story of Operation Yonatan is not complete without a few words about Yoni. I spent most of my time in the Unit under his command and under his influence. This book, which commemorates the crown jewel of his operational activity, is unfinished without a rendering of him, the man and the commander.

December 1970

A bunch of cadets, nervous and kitted out in simple vests and FN rifles, stood outside the barracks and waited for the arrival of the commander from the Unit.

Giora in the cockpit, between two pilots, on the way home.
Photo: air crew member Ram Levi

For the majority of us, the battle vests didn't fit right. They were loose in some spots and overly snug in others, our bodies seemingly resisting the organ transplant that would, with time, be like a second skin. A handsome man with a strong, solid face and a field uniform that fit well and a battle vest that was tailor-made for him in the Unit, received us at attention. We raised our eyes in endless admiration and listened closely to what seemed to us like the words of a living God. That was our first encounter with Yoni—the Basic Training company commander of the new draftees of the November 1970 draft to Sayeret Matkal.

Yoni introduced himself briefly and took off on what was known then as a battle vest-acquaintance march. Half walking and half running, we scurried after him, hiking up the hill toward the sheikh's grave that marked the top of the ridge looming over the Sanur Valley. The path was steep and rocky and we reached the top bathed in sweat and short of breath. The company commander, Yoni, looked like he'd been out on a morning stroll. And there, above the stunning valley, like Moses atop Mount Nebo, he delivered a speech that became the formative address of our service; a speech saturated in praise for the land and its people and studded with a sense of mission. It conveyed the need to defend the country and to train hard; there would be no compromise on excellence and on devotion to the mission. And we, young wild boys that we were, drank in his every word.

June-July 1971

Some of our pilots were being held as POWs in Syria. An opportunity to seize Syrian officers near the Lebanon-Israel-Syria border presented itself—a mission known as Operation Argaz. The plan was to abduct Syrian officers which we could then exchange for our captive airmen. The Unit tried to execute the mission three times. The first two attempts were aborted, each time for a different reason. Only on the third try, near Zarit, was the mission accomplished. The Maestro, Ehud [Barak], conducted the symphony from a war room, while the concertmaster, Yoni, waited with a small force on the ground. Yoni, the commander in the field, was a brave and determined operator, blessed with unflappable judgement. His leadership in battle was naturally accepted by soldiers and officers alike. Our platoon arrived on a half-track during the final stages of the abduction. We helped shackle the Syrian officers and evacuate our wounded troops. When we received word that one of the Syrian officers may have fled to a Lebanese village east of our position, Yoni took a few soldiers from our team, myself included, and tore through the fields toward the Lebanese town. Other than a Lebanese policeman, whom we promptly disarmed, we found nothing and Yoni led us back to the theater of operations and presided over the wrap-up of all of the forces.

October 1973

Nine months into my tenure as a platoon commander, seemingly out of nowhere, like the rumble of thunder on a perfectly clear day, the Yom Kippur War broke out.

We spent the first two days on the base getting organized, listening to the dreadful reports from the fronts and growing frustrated to the point of horror that we were not being deployed. Only on Sunday evening, some thirty-six hours after the outbreak of war, did we, under the command of Yoni and Muki, head up to Rosh Pina, west of the sloping plateau of the Golan Heights. We gazed at the fire and the smoke and knew that we could not come to their salvation. Yoni and Muki pleaded for a combat assignment and on Monday night the half-tracks arrived and we rode up to the Golan Heights in a column with Yoni in command. Two other forces from the Unit, under the command of Giora Zore'a and Yuri, operated in other sectors.

For the next eight or nine days we got a taste of infantry warfare, absorbing endless bombardments, during which you learn that all you can do is keep your head down and pray for a miracle. Yoni was cool and collected; his quiet and authoritative voice over the radio instilled a sense of confidence in us. As Ben-Gurion said, "May every Hebrew mother know that she has entrusted her son in the care of commanders worthy of the task."

The highlight, which I missed, was the face-to-face battle against the Syrian commando troops, which had been airlifted into Nafah, just a few miles north of our position. Yoni and Muki led the force, aside from my platoon which "lost" its half-track and arrived at the scene once the battle had quieted. In combat, the Unit lost Baruch Zuckerman, a reservist from the desert moshav of Hatzeva, and Gidoni Avidov from Nahalal, who was wounded and evacuated in worse condition than we realized at the time. We learned of his death only later on, while operating in what was known as the enclave within Syria. According to my friend Shai's eyewitness account, Yoni was again exemplary in battle, a cool-headed and brave commander who charged at the head of his troops and pulled the other commanders and soldiers in his wake. He would later be awarded the Medal of Distinguished Service for his role in that battle and the rescue of Yossi Ben-Hanan.

As part of Raful's division, we were situated deep within Syria. A force under the command of Yossi Ben-Hanan had launched a frontal attack on a Syrian position atop Tel Shams; many of their tanks were hit and the treads of many tanks were thrown, but a determined Yossi Ben-Hanan continued to advance with the intent of storming the position. The Syrians fired heavy bursts of anti-tank missiles and within minutes all four of the tanks, including Yossi's, were on fire. Most of the tankers were killed; Yossi, badly wounded in his leg, took cover in a small trench along with his radio operator and another soldier. Speaking over the brigade frequency, Yossi radioed the commander of the Seventh Brigade, Yanush Ben-Gal, in a desperate voice asking for a rescue operation, and Yanush was largely at a loss. There seemed to be no way to get to Yossi and rescue him. The Syrians dominated the area and pummeled it with fire. Any attempt to get close was clearly very dangerous.

Yoni and Muki huddled with Yanush and took on the assignment. Shai, the leader of our parallel platoon, heard from a friend of his, who was the commander of Yanush's APC war room, a very pessimistic estimation of our chances for success. You're committing suicide, he told Shai before we headed out. We, Team Shai and Team

Sussmann, got on board the APCs and set out with Yoni in the lead and Muki riding second; we passed blazing and smoldering tanks hunched amid formations of black basalt rock. The going was brutally slow and the air smelled of corpses and of war.

With gathering darkness, we arrived at the foot of Tel Shams. Yoni stopped the force and ordered us to proceed on foot to avoid missile strikes. We moved swiftly, stumbling over thickets of missile-guidance wires, evidence of the barrage that the tanks had faced, and finally reached Yossi and his men.

We mounted the tanks and searched for more survivors but found none and retreated with Yossi on a stretcher, carrying him to the APCs and from there into the heart of the lava fields of the Lajat, where we landed a helicopter. At the hospital they were able to save his leg. Yossi owed Yoni his life, and for years afterward they maintained close contact.

1974

In the wake of the war and the losses inflicted on the armored corps' command structure, Yoni stepped forward and volunteered for the corps. He went through training and was given the command of Battalion 71 in the Golan Heights. Soon enough he invited me and Shai and our platoons to join his battalion in a training drill.

It was strange to see him in a tanker's coverall and mindset, giving off a demand for order and discipline, demands that were foreign to us in the Unit, where excellence was expected and formal discipline did not exist. Yoni was visibly proud of his platoon. Eyes alight, he told us about the crucial role of armor in battle, the firepower of the tank, and the need for steel-rigid discipline in the armored corps, and yet he was visibly happy to be working with us again.

July 1975 and Onward—Commanding the Unit

Despite the respect we had for Yoni, he was still, in the eyes of many, an outsider in the Unit and his appointment was greeted by some with a chill and a notable lack of applause. By the way—it's very typical of operators from the Unit to want someone who's "one of our own," someone who'd come up through the ranks, and the way that Yoni was treated was not unusual. He replaced Giora Zore'a and, as is always the case, he had to contend with his predecessor's legacy. The officers beneath him chafed under the new commander's ethos, testing limits and conducting ongoing comparisons and so forth. In September 1975, I was appointed the commander of the operational company, and was, with Yoni, a partner to all of the wide array of operational activity launched during his year as commander of the Unit. Yoni—an introvert, a man apart from the people, a thorough, deep thinker with sky-high demands of himself and of others, was by nature inclined toward combat leadership; the details of the covert operational activity in the Unit were less close to his heart.

During that year Yoni went through some soul searching and inner struggles, as reflected in his posthumous book of letters, but nonetheless managed to lead the Unit on many successful missions and headed several counterstrikes against terror attacks. During what came to be known as Operation Yonatan, he was immersed almost in his entirety in ground-breaking operational activity that he was not able to fully see through, but was, surely, one of its progenitors.

Epilogue

Yoni was a young man, blessed with talent and full of promise. The song of his life was cut short. He had a bright future ahead of him. The family's grief knows no cure, but in death, he, quite rightly, earned the glory of the world. The rescue operation was named after him. Many of the cities in Israel have a street that carries his name. Year after year as the anniversary of the operation approaches his name is spoken by the youth that are raised on the legacy of this special operation. His name is known around the world as a symbol of the determined fight against terror and as part of the Israeli people's rise to independence.

To me, Yoni was a commander who influenced me greatly and stood as a symbol of courage, composure, and responsible leadership in battle. A rare blend of a true intellectual, a man of letters, who clung devotedly to his military calling and then paid for his devotion in blood.

Over the years we had together, as I matured along with him and learnt of his human weaknesses alongside his strengths, my admiration for him and his personality did not waver in the slightest, and I, as a disciple of Rabbi Nachman, am reminded of his teaching, "There is nothing more whole than a broken heart."

May his memory be a blessing.

Lt.-Col. (res) Giora Sussmann is a native of Moshav Bnei Zion in the Sharon Plain. He was drafted into the Unit in November 1970 as a soldier in Team Dudik and went on to serve as a team leader, an operational company commander during Yoni's tenure, and as deputy commander of the Unit—under both Shai Avital and Omer Bar Lev. He is an electronic engineer and has served in the IDF Military Intelligence Directorate's technological unit, where he was a joint recipient of the Israel Defense Prize. An active entrepreneur who works in technology start-ups, he's married to Anat and a father to Yonatan, who served in an elite unit in the late nineties. He and his wife Roni have four adorable children.

Staff-Sgt. Shlomi Reisman, Team Amnon

Operator in Amnon's Squad; Yoni's Assault Force; Hostage Hall

---

OPERATION YONATAN: MY 45-YEAR-OLD NOTES COME TO LIGHT

Initial Surprises

The phone rang before dawn on Friday: "Return to base immediately." Was this the Unit, yet again, calling up the guys who live close by to fill out the readiness ranks? I didn't feel like ending an intense, fulfilling, nerve-wracking three years of service in this way. I'd just finished a final operational deployment and my long-awaited pre-discharge leave had begun with a few days of chilling at home. The news had sailed past. I'd heard talk about a French plane that had taken off from Israel, been hijacked by terrorists during a stopover in Greece, and then flown to some African backwater and hoped it would all end well. Luckily, this time at least, there was no chance it was on us.

Listlessly, I grabbed my rifle and stuffed some uniforms into my duffel bag. On the way back to the base I picked up the redhead from my team. As we drove in, I saw the place was abuzz, but still had no idea about the source of the commotion. I pulled into the parking lot next to the Unit's HQ. Ilan, another member of our team, stood on the opposite side of the fence. No pleasantries, just: "We're on the assault force, the hostage hall."

A flock of butterflies took flight in my stomach. My feet felt heavy. I knew the price. Just over a year ago we'd lost Itamar, a dear friend and a central member of our team, in a battle with terrorists in the Savoy Hotel in Tel Aviv. I'd been shot. There, too, our team had been given the honor of being first through the main door. As we burst in, the terrorists detonated an explosive device. This time, too, if the terrorists rigged or booby-trapped anything at all it would be, first and foremost, in and around the hostage hall.

Itamar Ben-David, may he rest in peace, was a dear friend and a central character on team Amnon. Killed in action during the Savoy Hotel rescue mission.
Photo: Itamar's camera

Getting Ready

Yoni stood beside the blackboard in our modest and ascetic briefing room, a refurbished old plane hangar from the days of the British Mandate, before Israel's birth, a space from which dozens of audacious operations had been launched. The operation that Yoni described in general terms sounded, without any doubt, like one of the craziest endeavors ever cooked up in the Unit. Much less complicated operations were usually worked on for months before being approved, and here, "we have twenty-four hours to get ready." Entebbe. I'd never even heard of the place. Turned out it was the international airport in Uganda. I'd heard something about their president who was trained to skydive here and had turned into a dictator who tossed humans into crocodile-filled rivers. Around one hundred Jews and Israelis were now in that man's custody. The terminal in which the terrorists were holding the hostages was surrounded by a ring of Ugandan soldiers collaborating with the hijackers. We'd storm in and they'd shoot us in the back. It was going to end badly.

Team Amnon Peled – Sport Day, around the time of the operation.
Photo: Shlomi's album

True, not one of us believed that a mission this insane would ever be authorized, but we knew there was no getting around the preparations. Earlier that morning there were rumors circulating that Ehud Barak [former commander of the Unit and a rising star in the IDF] was going to command the mission. We caught up with Yoni on the lawn outside his office. He said that if that turned out to be the case, he and his squad would slide over and take our role—storming into the hostage hall. We argued and tried to convince him we'd do a better job. From my perch here, at age sixty-five, it sounds silly, but back then, as a twenty-year-old soldier, I viewed the thirty-year-old Yoni and the other officers in his squad as a group of rusty old men. With considerable chutzpah, I argued with him, but deep in my heart I appreciated his leadership and courage, his willingness to assign himself the most dangerous task. The matter was quickly removed from the docket. Yoni was the leader and the commander of the operation and we retained the honorable role.

Most any person from outside the orbit of the Unit might expect us to have drilled close-quarter combat and firearms handling in the scant time remaining before the mission. But the truth is, it takes many months and years to construct a trained operator. Many hundreds of boring firearm drills and combat simulations were imprinted in us like instinct. There was no way and no need to make us proficient at that, and so instead we spent the precious little time at our disposal on the specific technical drills needed for this mission. None of us, for example, had ever practiced securing two Land Rovers and a luxury Mercedes in the body of a Hercules C-130 aircraft, and Sussmann, our company commander, timed us again and again, without letting up. We paid special attention to the offloading of the vehicles after landing. We needed to cut down the time from the moment the rear door opened until we arrived at the old terminal where the hostages were being kept. Speed and surprise were essential ingredients of success.

We were not alone. The IDF assembled a task force including the Air Force, parts of the Paratroop and Golani Brigades and others. During the repetitive drills, I met up with Lt.-Col. Nehemiah Tamari, (who died, as a two-star general, in a helicopter crash in 1994, may his memory be a blessing) a former deputy commander of the unit, the brave leader of our assault team at the Savoy hostage-rescue operation and now a participant in the mission as a Paratroop Brigade battalion commander. Yoni Lior, a childhood friend from my old neighborhood and for the ensuing fifty years, a combat soldier in the Paratroop recon unit. Soon we'd be taking off together in the lead plane: a social network of the kind only found in Israel.

Later in the day, between drills, I found time to peek at the thin study dossiers issued for Operation Thunderball, then the official name of the operation. Intelligence material was scant, light years from the Unit's normal standard in advance of an operation. We'd been taught that prior to every operation we had to be ready to escape and evade capture in the event that things went awry or one of us was left alone on the field of battle. In this case there was no choice but to improvise. No one had yet dreamed up Google or the internet. The digital camera didn't exist. I hadn't even yet heard of the fax machine. Someone went out to the nearby town and bought an atlas from a school supplier. From one of those geography-class maps, I learnt where Uganda was located, and on it we planned how, if necessary, we'd seize vehicles and avoid capture and escape to the neighboring state of Kenya.

As part of our specific training for the mission we simulated storming into an installation made of rusty metal bars and burlap cloth. We did it to drill the line formation and to work out how we'd operate within the confines of the hostage hall. It was decided that our team, eight operators in all, would enter the hall simultaneously through two doors. The hall was expected to contain around one-hundred hostages and up to ten terrorists, and once inside our job was to kill the terrorists as fast as possible. And if that wasn't sufficiently challenging, it was noted there was a good chance the whole thing was going to take place in complete darkness, while under fire. During one of the practice drills, Yoni surprised us and stationed "enemy troops" before the simulated terminal, on guard as we approached with the vehicles, apparently in order to simulate the ring of Ugandan soldiers protecting the terminal building. Part of the assault force's task was to deal with them.

On Friday night we waited in the dark for the arrival of the Chief of Staff, Lt.-Gen. Motta Gur. He was supposed to watch us conduct a model simulation, but was late due to his participation in an Air Force drill related to the mission. The delay was aggravating because we still had a lot of tinkering and improvising to do before dawn: The Mercedes was a jalopy, with an engine that barely started and tires that were newspaper-sheet thin. Worse, someone had seen a news report that showed Idi Amin rolling around in a black Mercedes, while ours was still white. But the CoS's visit wasn't a complete waste of time: Once he'd seen us driving, hopping out, charging ahead, and shouting "Boom-boom! Boom-boom!" and in that way easily asserting control over the burlap sacks, he noted that our two jeeps were too crowded. That was entirely true. We sat on the jeep like a *horde,* unruly, with legs sprawled every which way, even dangling over the bumper. On one hand, the need for surprise and the limited amount of space on the plane dictated a small formation of one Mercedes and two jeeps. On the other hand, the sheer number of terrorists and Ugandan soldiers waiting for us in and around the terminal sparked in us a desire to fill the three vehicles with as many operators as possible. As it was, we were a very reduced force. And still I was delighted that thanks to Motta we got rid of the assault dog handler on our jeep and, better yet, the Giant Schnauzer with the foot-long fangs. It could've been fun flying for eight hours in each direction stuck next to that monster. Who knows what a dog like that might decide to do when suspended in mid-air, especially if hungry.

Early Saturday morning – after oiling my weapon and loading my magazines, after gearing up with some "mini" grenades and equipping my rifle with a bore-sighted tactical flashlight, after deciding that we'd call out in Hebrew and English for all the hostages to lie down as soon as we burst in, after being fitted for and issued camo-striped uniforms and green berets of the sort the Ugandans wore (though we still hardly looked like Ugandan army regulars), and after we'd grabbed white, kibbutz-style workers hats so that we could easily identify one another as soon as we opened fire; after all that and a thousand-and-one other things – I finally went to sleep for whatever time was left: around an hour.

I lay down and considered the tight time schedule and the limited and incomplete intelligence information. During the pre-battle preparations some of the puzzle had been filled in but large chunks became clear only during the operation itself and over the subsequent years. The clock of the terrorists' ultimatum was ticking and we had to stick to a tight schedule.

I was intimately familiar with hostage-based terror attacks. At the school in the town of Ma'alot there were "only" three terrorists and yet they had managed to hit the lead squad of the assault force and had found the time to butcher the children. I remembered all too well how they'd fired wildly and tossed grenade after grenade. At the Savoy Hotel, there were eight terrorists and they'd managed to detonate an explosive device, blowing up the hostages' room so it collapsed on us during the assault. One of the terrorists put up a fight and killed Itamar Ben David and Uzi Yairi (may their memories be a blessing) and shot me as well. The results were painful and grave. At Entebbe we were supposed to face more terrorists (ten) and many more Ugandan soldiers. This time, despite the increase in the size of the enemy force, we would arrive with fewer soldiers than we'd had during those previous battles. These were far and away the worst and most daunting opening numbers I'd ever encountered and my feeling about it all was grim. During previous hostage-rescue operations, we, the assault force, had at least been able to see the many parked ambulances waiting close by as we approached the target. This time we'd be at the other end of the world. Was this how the Japanese WW2 Kamikaze pilots felt? Only I, unlike them, wanted to live.

The Plan

The plan that Yoni presented to us, a plan that continued to be shaped by the officers and soldiers until the moment we left the ground, hinged on the need to surprise the terrorists, to reach them fast, to eliminate them and at the same time to protect the hostages. According to the plan, the first Hercules, ours, would land alone, in the dark, in the middle of the night. Dressed in jungle-camouflage uniforms, we would try to pretend to be local forces. We would drive to the old terminal, stop in the space between the terminal and the control tower, and then each squad would charge out and fulfill its mission. We hoped that all of us operating together, seven small squads bursting in through five terminal doors, would allow us to simultaneously kill all terrorists and colaborating Ugandan soldiers, hitting them before they could kill us and the hostages.

Sounds simple. But the entire plan—hung by a thread.

There were so many of them that if they chose to deploye explosives it would only take one press on a button, to tear the hostages and us into pieces and bring down the terminal on our heads.

It was them or us.

All squads of the assault force would be under Yoni's close and personal command. His squad was manned by Alik [an officer in the Unit], Tamir the radio operator, and David the Unit's doctor. Yoni would position himself in the middle, right in front of the doors to the main hall, the crucial spot from which he could best control the many squads operating throughout the giant terminal. Our team, the most experienced and veteran in the Unit, got the "cherry on top"—the hostage hall. One squad from our team was under the command of Muki, who was supposed to be at the head of the first trio into the hall. Alex, Gadi, and Nir (subsequently swapped by Amos Goren) filled out Muki's squad and were slated to charge through the first door on the left, leading into the hall where the hostages were reportedly being kept. Their door was the one closest to the point where the vehicles were to stop (coming from our direction of arrival, the second entrance to the terminal along the terminal wall). Amir, Ilan, and I, under the command of our team leader, Amnon, were to charge through the next door, an entrance leading to the righthand side of the hostage hall. Amos Ben-Avraham's squad, manned by Gal and Fradkin, were to be on our heels.

Yiftach, the deputy commander of the Unit, was to lead two squads through the first entrance, into the customs hall. From there one squad would sprint to the second floor, where dozens of Ugandan soldiers were quartered. He was to race through the customs hall before clearing it, and on his way to the second floor, head for a door that supposedly led straight to the rear of the passenger hall. Rani and Shadmi filled out his squad and they were linked to Arnon, who was in command of Yiftach's second squad, manned by Udi, Yonatan, and Buchris.

Sussmann, the company commander, would lead Adam, Ben-Ami and Yoram through the terminal's fourth entrance, to a small hall to which the Jewish passengers had been moved after their selection, and which, we were told, was being used either by the terrorists as a lounge or as a room housing some of the hostages. Dani Arditi, a team leader, would lead Drori and Aharoni to the VIP room at the far end of the terminal, which was apparently being used by the terrorists as their living space. Rami, the operations officer, along with

Amitzur, Eyal, and Uri, the drivers, were stationed near the vehicles and charged with providing close suppressive fire, as needed. That was it. A handful of operators, 33 in total. That was the entire assault force.

Assuming we would manage to preserve the element of surprise, two more Hercules C-130 aircraft would land while we were in the heat of battle, seven minutes after us, and deliver two pairs of armored personnel carriers, carrying around thirty more operators from the Unit, who would link up with us. They'd spread out around the terminal and provide perimeter security for the freed hostages and us.

The notion of flying such a small force to the middle of Africa, in planes that held fuel for only one leg of the journey, with incomplete and out of date intelligence information, based mostly on the questioning of foreign hostages who had been released two days earlier and supplemented by TV reports and a few ancient photos, seemed to me to be unrealistic. We didn't even have any way of knowing if the hostages would still be in the terminal when we arrived or whether they'd been moved to a nearby city or flown elsewhere in the meantime. We'd already done the leg work for far less dangerous operations that were not given the go-ahead and so I took solace in the knowledge that the "big boys" upstairs would never authorize this operation.

Taking Off

We drove to Lod airport on Saturday morning, loaded the vehicles on the plane, and took-off. Time limitations forced us to depart without knowing if the operation was to be given the go-ahead. I hoped that the Cabinet, scheduled to meet later in the day, would not approve the fantastical mission and we'd all be turned around and sent home. Our vehicles were positioned in the center of the plane, along the length of the aircraft. The Mercedes, nose facing out, was at the rear of the plane, so that it would be first down the ramp and behind it the two Land Rovers. On either side of the vehicles, sprawled out on the floor, were a few dozen paratroopers. We had no choice but to seat ourselves in the vehicles. Our squad sat in the very back of the last Land Rover.

There were no seats and of course no bathrooms on the plane. If you had to urinate—it was in the jerry can. The C-130s flew low, practically scraping the ground. Four cargo planes flying south on a Saturday morning was not a common occurrence and we had to make sure the formation was not picked up by enemy radar. Nice that someone thought of that, but the decision came at a price. It was a boiling hot summer day, full of air pockets, and the plane, more than surging forward, bucked up and down like a mustang. We sat on the vehicles and the suspension only increased the intensity of the movement. Every now and again our heads met the ceiling. Green faces all around. It seemed like I was the only one not vomiting on board. Eight more hours of this and the terrorists, once we'd landed at Entebbe, wouldn't have any work left to do.

Landing at Sharm

The plane landed at Sharm to re-fuel. We huddled around Yoni for a final briefing. We should expect the battle to veer off course, he said, to run counter to what we planned. Yoni drilled into us the central elements of the operation and did not neglect to note the great significance of the historic moment. After twenty-four hours of intense preparation, little sleep and the acquisition of a ton of confusing details, he did a good job of instilling order in our minds. We used the break in Sharm to tend to the important things that every soldier and general need to do before a battle sandwiched between two, eight-hour flights. Eating and defecating.

On the runway, in the fiery desert heat, engulfed in the fumes left by the tankers, the roar of the C-130s' turbines in our ears, we took out of our duffels the jungle camouflage uniforms that had been kept a deep secret and pulled them on. I transferred my camera to my battle vest, too, but decided not to take a photo pre-combat. I'm not really superstitious, but decided not to tempt fate. Maybe a final photo before combat would give me the evil eye. I was still getting the new uniform on when someone yelled at me to get moving and get on board pronto. We had to take off.

Another Surprise

The plane raced along the runway forever. It seemed like it was having a hard time getting airborne. Seemed like it was going to roll all the way to Entebbe. But at the far end of the runway, it managed to rise heavily and fly low over the water. I shoved my face into the little window, saw the blue waters of the Red Sea and the island of Tiran and recalled the vacation that I'd had a year earlier on the nearby beach of Nuwieba, where I'd fallen in love with Irit, the beginning of an affair that has been going strong ever since.

We ascended to a cruising altitude and surprisingly the flight was smooth and pleasant. We could make use of the time for a little nap. We still hadn't reached the point of no return. I still thought that there was no way the mission would be given the go-ahead. I woke up from my nap and saw Yoni emerge from the cockpit behind us with a little smile on his face: "The government has authorized the operation."

The plane was silent. The tired, cramped people on board kept sleeping, sprawled out over one another on the vehicles, as though this was not a suicide mission. Time passed slowly; night fell. Nothing could be seen through the dark window. I worked through different scenarios in my mind; I checked again and again that the bulky flashlight and the Kalashnikov's gun sights were in alignment. In a few hours, in the dark, my life might depend on it.

Landing at Entebbe

Half an hour before landing a warning buzzer went off and red lights came on, illuminating the dark cargo cabin. We woke those who'd managed to doze and store up sleep.

Packed close to one another, we strapped ourselves into our battle vests and sat down in formation in the vehicles. The pleasant ride ended over Lake Victoria and the plane again started to buck. The weather was stormy outside. I saw Yoni get out of the Mercedes on the far end of the plane. On either side of the cars the Paratroop Brigade soldiers were busy with their own preparations. Yoni climbed from car to car, traveling the full length of the plane, touching base with the whole assault force as we readied for battle, offering words of encouragement and slaps on the back, soothing some and readying others, all the way to our Land Rover which was backed up against the cockpit. He smiled at us and warmly shook the hand of Buchris, who was the youngest soldier, and then turned around and picked his way back to the Mercedes that would a few minutes later slide out the rear of the plane. It would head the formation, with Yoni leading us from the front seat, beside Amitzur, the driver. Combat leadership by a veteran commander. The Hercules began its descent, sliding low and smooth toward the ground. The three other planes parted from us, hanging back and circling over Lake Victoria.

We sat in the vehicles, taut and ready for battle. The pilots opened the plane's rear ramp while we were still in the air, gliding toward the tarmac and then running along it for what seemed to me like ages. What awaited us outside? The drivers started their engines. The paratroopers began hopping off with the Hercules still in motion, their role being to mark the runway with lights for the following planes. The plane taxied along the tarmac. We undid the restraining straps and took the chocks out from under the wheels. The Hercules reached the end of the runway, turned a bit, and stopped. Engines still thundering, the back door opened a bit further and rested on the tarmac.

Seconds later the Mercedes rolled off, followed by the pair of Land Rovers. The vehicles made a bit of a U-turn, headlights on, and stopped for a moment. In total silence and without saying a word to one another, we loaded our Kalashnikov rifles, snapping a first round into the chamber, and the convoy took off fast in the dark in the direction of the old terminal.

I was surprised by the warmth of the tropical weather. Before the flight I'd wondered if it would be cold, if I should wear a thermal shirt or not. Africa. All around, a deep pitch dark. I wondered how Yoni was able to handle the navigation. We pulled away from the lone Hercules. I knew it had only enough fuel to get us to Entebbe but not back. Far ahead in the distance, maybe a kilometer or two away, I saw a smattering of weak lights. That must be the old terminal, I figured, and there, as far as I knew, were ten terrorists and between eighty and one-hundred Ugandan soldiers waiting for us.

We Were but Thirty

It's accepted that the assault force should be three-times bigger than the defending force. This time the ratio was inverted. Just one year earlier, aided by very much luck, I emerged wounded but alive from battle. I looked over at my friends sitting beside me in the moving vehicle. In five minutes, who among us would be alive and who dead? I listened hard for the sound of gunfire. Had the terrorists heard us and started to butcher the hostages? For the time being there was nothing but complete silence.

Engagement

A few minutes passed and the Mercedes slowed and the Land Rovers followed suit. Coming from the forward-right side of our formation, I heard the rattle of a rifle being armed. The headlights revealed two Ugandan soldiers getting into position to fire. The precise scenario that Yoni had drilled during the simulation the day before. I sat there like a sardine, wedged into the back seat of the last Land Rover on the right side, my back facing out, pointing in the direction of the soldiers. We would have to pass right by them. I was completely exposed, with no protection whatsoever, and felt like a sitting duck. An industrious Ugandan soldier could take aim and slowly, leisurely, skewer four of us with a single bullet. The operation could end before it had even started.

A few seconds later one of the guards skipped over and scurried left, crossing our lane of travel. I heard, from the direction of the lead Land Rover, a few shots fired from an Uzi, but the Ugandan soldier kept on running. We kept driving and a few shots were fired from the front seat of our vehicle, too, but to no avail. We called out to Buchris, who was seated far left in the back and armed with a heavy machine gun, pointing out. He opened fire and was on target.

Only in the morning, on the homeward-bound plane, did I find out that Yoni and Giora had opened fire first, from within the Mercedes, with the silenced pistols they'd taken for this sort of scenario, but apparently had not been able to take down the guards. At any rate, the incident, which was identical to what we'd practiced twenty-four hours earlier, did not change the results of the battle.

At the time, I thought it was all over and that the terrorists, made aware of our arrival, would start shooting the hostages. But to my surprise, the airfield remained perfectly silent and still. We drove on for a few hundred more meters, I'm not sure how many. The plan was for the vehicles to continue to the space between the control tower and the terminal and stop there, allowing us to get out and charge toward the entrance doors. Surprisingly, the convoy stopped alongside the control tower, around twenty meters before the planned spot, perhaps because it was darker there. We jumped out of the vehicles as one, thirty people together, and huddled as planned, on the righthand side of the cars. Around us was complete quiet. No one fired at us. No one shot the hostages. A thought passed through my mind: maybe the hijackers and the hostages aren't even here, maybe they've moved?

Charge

We started walking fast toward the terminal building, which loomed up ahead. In his briefing Yoni had stressed not to run, not to reveal our intentions to the guards who were supposed to be outside the terminal. We strode forward, a single bulk of around twenty operators, walking and approaching the entrances to the terminal, a few dozen meters away from us, forward left. And still, a strange quiet all around.

The façade of the terminal was made of large glass plates. Some of the openings were marked by canopies and low walls. I was concerned about finding the right entrance along the wall. The low light and the side angle of our approach made the task even more difficult.

Muki led the force, as planned. I was glued to his right. Yoni had assigned him what is considered to be the most crucial role in a hostage-rescue mission: to be the first officer at the head of the first squad through the first door of the hostage hall. The terminal's entrances were on our left. Amnon's squad, of which I was part, was to take the next entrance, slightly further along, a door that opened onto the righthand side of the hostage hall. Muki had already been to the terminal and knew it from his time training Ugandan soldiers. That's why I had made him my left-hand marker.

We moved fast, totally exposed, still without fire, toward a battle with terrorists and Ugandan soldiers who outnumbered us and could surprise us from anywhere and could even detonate part of the building and bring it down on us. I looked left and right and was filled with a sense of confidence. Still today, in my mind's eye, I can see us striding widely and determinedly, in our jungle stripe uniforms and green berets, Kalashnikov's raised and pointing forward, Motorola radios tucked into the battle vests of the commanders, the little red ball at the tip of the antennas lending it the look of an alien device. The thought that passed through my mind then, and I am not saying this only after the fact—I wouldn't want to be on the other side.

I was attentive and very focused. It was totally silent around us. The silence was violated by a short burst of fire. A Ugandan soldier appeared out of nowhere on our left, in the space between the tower and the terminal and before he knew what had happened, he was shot, I think by Muki. And still there was no fire within the terminal and no one fired out at us.

A Surprising Stop

We continued on at a faster clip. We had already passed the control tower, which loomed over us on our left. Up ahead the large terminal building was revealed. There were big boxes out in front of the terminal. The walls and the square were lit with weak yellow

light. We were just a few paces shy of the edge of the terminal building. The most critical point in the mission. A few steps away were the
entrances—the heart of the operation. All that remained to be done
was to charge ahead, get into the hall where the hostages were kept,
and hit the terrorists before they had the chance to raise their
weapons.

And then, one second before the charge, something happened,
something inexplicable that was never properly probed in the Unit
and has raised questions for many of the members of the assault
force, from then to this day. Completely by surprise, and in contrast
to the plan and the drill, Muki, who was supposed to lead the charge,
broke left and stopped. At the corner, just where the terminal building
started, Muki stopped, raised his weapon, and started shooting ahead.

It's a moment I will never forget. The lead squads, myself among
them, had to stop behind him and stand still. I looked ahead to see a
source of fire. No one was firing at us. The only gunfire we heard
was coming from Muki's weapon.

After a few seconds of confusion, we heard, from very close by,
a few meters away, Yoni's sharp voice: "Betser, forward." But
Muki remained in place, firing. I looked and saw no target, and at
any rate, no one firing back at us. Those moments, in which the
whole lead force stood stock still in front of the openings, not
charging as planned but watching Muki shoot, seemed to me like
an eternity. I heard Yoni yell a second time and this time in a
louder voice: "Betser, forward." Not many seconds passed before
soldiers and officers stopped dawdling. They acted as expected in
this unforeseen situation, passing Muki and charging ahead. In an
instant the square in front of the terminal was filled with charging
soldiers, each man to his opening, like a wasp nest that had been
kicked. The silence was broken by gunfire. There was no need to
call out orders. Everyone knew his role and what needed to be
done.

Only after the operation, on the plane ride home, did I find out
that Amir and Amnon had charged in ahead of everyone and saved
the day, and perhaps prevented the entire operation from ending in

the sort of massacre that we'd seen at Ma'alot. The force surged forward behind them.

Amir, so I later learned, had landed badly while dismounting from the vehicle. Briefly waylaid, he feared that the charge had already begun and that Amnon would be left alone in the hall, and so he sprinted ahead and passed everyone on the right. Arriving at the door at a dead run, he spotted a terrorist who had opened fire at him from within the hall. Amir fired bursts of semi-automatic fire while in motion, kept charging through the door and into the hall and closed the gap between him and the terrorist in order to finish off the job. Only then did he realize that he was the first man through the door and that he was alone in the hall. Amnon, our team leader and squad commander, hopped off the Land Rover and charged straight for the hostage hall. He chased after Amir and tried to catch up with him, burst in right after him and took out a male-female pair of German terrorists an instant before they managed to shoot Amir in the back. Over the ensuing years Amnon has steadfastly played down his role in the battle, saying that throughout the operation he only fired a total of four shots. Later, a few long seconds later, other operators came pouring in, including Muki, Gadi, Goren, Alex, Amos, and more. The key terrorists in the hostage hall were killed seconds after they realized that the shots heard outside the terminal weren't loosed by "crazy Ugandan soldiers" (as one hostage witness said of their last conversation) but by crazy Israelis who'd made a midnight trip to Entebbe.

But all that I learnt only on the plane ride home.

A Failed Operation?

At that stage I joined the fray and charged ahead with the rest of the operators. While running forward I kept flashing glances up to the second floor, where a few dozen Ugandan soldiers were supposedly quartered and any one of them, at any point, could slip a rifle barrel out of the dark windows above us and mow us down. Every now and again I also stole a glance to the right, to the large boxes, trying to make sure that nothing popped out from behind there and caught us from the rear. And in fact, though I was waiting for a surprise from the right flank, I was surprised. A Ugandan soldier popped up with great speed. He didn't opt to run away or hide. Before I had even registered what I was seeing, he had raised his weapon and gotten into a firing stance. I charged toward him and began squeezing off rounds of single fire. From the lit path of the tracers, I could see that I was missing the mark. Other operators and to the best of my recollection, Alik among them, hit him. He rose up into the air and fell.

Far off to my right I saw the hijacked French aircraft. I recalled that Irit and I had already bought flight tickets for an end-of-service trip. Departure date was a month away. Just don't die now.

I kept running forward, trying to find the door through which I was supposed to enter. I saw two entrances close together. I managed to see Muki's tall silhouette swallowed by the entrance nearest to me. That was then the first opening leading to the hostage hall. According to the plan, I was supposed to take the next one down.

I sprinted in and stopped.

The hall was empty, no trace of the hostages. Mattresses on the floor and off to the right a table loaded with radios and electronics and a pile of passports. Aside from Ilan, who was trailing close behind me, no one else from our squad was in the hall. I was sure the operation had failed. Maybe the hostages had been transferred to the city or to the airport's new terminal?

Sussmann, standing to the right of the door and firing intensively down the hall that branched off to the right, yelled to me: "Terrorists down there." Adam and another operator charged in and passed us, heading for the far end of the hall, toward an opening that led somewhere unknown, and yelled to me that he saw a soldier or two beyond the opening. I tore a few mini fragmentation grenades off the front of my battle vest and rolled them across the floor to him, on the other end of the hall. He and his partner picked them up and used them, taking out two Ugandan soldiers in the adjacent room.

What were Sussmann and the rest of his squad doing in our hall? Where was my squad? I remembered that during a previous battle there was also no firm link between the planning and the intel we'd received about the interior of the building and what we'd seen on the ground. I dropped the green beret and pulled out the white kibbutznik hat tucked beneath my camo shirt and put it on. I buddied up with Sussmann and we started to advance down the hallway, providing cover for one another and rolling mini grenades down the unfamiliar corridor.

While Sussmann and I fought our way forward, during one of the breaks in firing, a pair of Middle Eastern-looking people suddenly appeared in civilian clothes, rounding the corner of the hallway into which we'd been firing. They passed Sussmann and walked, single file, toward me, their stride clipped and quick. The one in the back looked like a woman, with black curly hair and a big behind. As they passed Sussmann, he yelled to me: "Reisman, shoot them, shoot them." He couldn't fire at them without hitting me. The two were advancing toward me fast, arms beside their bodies, neither raised nor lowered, as though they had yet to decide if they wanted to surrender or not. I moved out of the way, letting them pass. Despite Giora's order, I hesitated and didn't open fire. I wasn't convinced they were terrorists. Maybe they were frightened hostages?

I ordered them to stop in Hebrew, English, and Arabic. They completely ignored my yelled-out calls and my raised rifle aimed at them, and continued walking toward the hall's exit door, trying to slip out into the dark. Only then did I spot the grenade hung on the belt of the lead terrorist. Because of the tricky angle and the fear of hitting one of my buddies, I approached rapidly from behind and shot them both, one through the other, with the more distant terrorist serving as an impact barrier. My burst of fire pinned the two of them together and they collapsed as one to the floor.

Under the bodies there was a flicker of blue. I knew exactly what it was. During the Ma'alot school massacre the kids had tried to run away and jump out the classroom window and had fallen to the ground right beside us. The terrorists threw Russian fragmentation grenades out after them. Same blue flicker, seconds before explosion.

I yelled, "Grenade!" but there wasn't a good place to take cover. I pulled Tamir, who was standing next to me, into a little nook alongside the hallway. Luckily, the grenade exploded beneath the terrorists. Even nowadays, every time I go to the dentist I get asked after the x-ray about the little lump of metal in my face. This description is lengthy, but the pace of events was quick and the decision to open fire was made in less time than it takes to read one of these sentences. Looking back, I sometimes wonder what would have happened had they made it out of the hallway and managed to throw the grenade into the adjacent room, filled with hostages and soldiers.

In a nearby room someone had thrown a phosphorous grenade and a thick suffocating cloud of smoke spread through the area and sat heavily in the toilet that Giora and I had found at the end of the hall and from which the pair of terrorists had likely emerged. I didn't want to go in there and clear the room physically. The ceiling was made of rotten, hole-filled boards. Who knew what the floor was made of. That's all I needed, to fall through the floor and get forgotten in a deep hole of feces in Entebbe. I made do with a grenade and some rifle fire from the outside. Adam, having finished up at the far end of the room, joined us and dared to clear the bathroom physically. The shooting stopped. All of a sudden, the terminal was silent. I still hadn't seen a single hostage. I quickly cleared the hall and the rooms branching off from it. There, too, I saw not a single hostage. At that point I was certain that the operation had been a complete failure.

Twenty-five years later I returned to the old terminal. This time as an invited guest, in the light of day. I looked closely at the bullet marks along the walls and particularly in the hall in which I had fought. I was surprised to find an enormous amount of impact holes at the bend in the hallway. In the intensity of battle, we hadn't noticed the massive amount of fire from the two terrorists, who I later eliminated with a single burst of fire.

Organizing for Evacuation

Once the hall was clear, I stepped out into the square in front of the terminal. Bursts of gunfire were coming from the control tower. When we'd arrived, all was quiet in the tower but now it was manned by someone brave and determined, who fired incessantly. The operators in one of our armored personnel carriers sprayed the tower with heavy machine gun fire, but each time they let up, the fire from the tower resumed. The other APCs drove around the terminal area and fired aggressively at the MiG fighter jets parked on the tarmac of the nearby Ugandan Air Force base. Someone hammered the utility pole transformer and the lights in the terminal went out. It was then easier to see the MiG fighter jets bursting, one after another, into balls of fire. At least they would not be able to chase after our planes and shoot us down. A few guys on an APC had just taken out a country's entire air force.

I examined and bandaged Amir Drori, a soldier in Dani's squad, who'd taken shrapnel from what seemed to be a grenade that his squad had thrown. Taking cover so as not to get hit by the gunfire from the tower, we ducked, somewhat theatrically, behind a wall that was at best knee-high. But that's all we had. In the dark in front of the terminal I saw a tight cluster of civilians. I was glad. At least we'd managed to rescue a few of the hostages, I thought.

Later on, I helped carry a woman's body and laid it on the Golani recon unit's flat-bed Peugeot pickup truck, which had arrived in the interim. The Ugandan soldier's body was sprawled out nearby, behind the boxes. He was the guy who'd popped up at me as we'd charged in. I couldn't resist. I bent down and took a souvenir, the brand-new bayonet that he had tucked into his battle vest and I put it into an open box on the Peugeot. I had no time to deal with that. Back home, I figured, I'd retrieve it from the Peugeot. Big mistake. The sort of strategic error made by a green paratrooper who thinks he'll leave booty on a Golani Brigade vehicle. It's been over forty years now, but it's not too late for the honest individual who found that bayonet to come forward and return it.

Don't Leave Buddies in Entebbe

The fighting over, we, Yoni's assault force, re-grouped around the three vehicles we had ridden to the terminal. During the preparation stage Amnon had ordered me to make a list of names of each operator in the assault force so that we could read off the names at the end, before heading home, and make sure no one had been forgotten behind. Forgetting a wounded mate, a corpse, a soldier buried under some rubble, or just some soldier stationed at a far corner of the giant terminal and left behind in Africa was one of the nightmare scenarios in this sort of mission. To prevent that, I'd written out each name on a white piece of carton, in a way that was legible in the dark. I told my buddies in advance that I had the carton hanging around my neck and was wearing it beneath my shirt. If I was shot, I told them, someone else should use the list.

We sat on the vehicles in the dark. Every now and again there were exchanges of fire between the tower and the APCs. I called out the names of the operators, one after another. Everyone answered. Until I got to Yoni's name. I called it again and again until someone said in the dark that Yoni had been wounded and evacuated to the fourth plane, with the hostages.

Done with my role as the company clerk, we set off for the faraway new terminal. There we picked up a wounded paratrooper and placed him and his gurney on the hood of the jeep. Later on, I learnt that the soldier was Surin Hershko, who has dealt with his injury admirably over the years. We drove the vehicles carefully into the aircraft, this time headfirst.

Actually, It Was a Success

An hour had passed since our landing and the start of the assault. Up until that moment I'd seen things only through my narrow field of vision. I had no idea whether or not the operation had failed or been a success.

Visit to Old Terminal in Entebbe- 25 Years Later

Control Tower

Ugandan Soldiers' Quarters

Hostage Hall

Customs Hall

The first exchange with my buddies from the team revealed that the cluster of civilians I'd seen outside the terminal was actually around one-hundred freed hostages. The operation had succeeded! All that was left to do was to get home, and fast. But we still weren't given the order to take-off.

Amnon, my team leader, motioned me over to him and Muki. The two were engaged in a very heated argument. Amnon wanted my opinion. It became clear to me that the two of them, counter to the plan, had entered the main hall through the same entrance rather than from either side of the hall. With considerable stubbornness Muki insisted that Amnon was wrong; he, Muki, had gone in through the first opening on the left, precisely as planned, and Amnon had made a mistake and gone in through the same opening rather using the second one, the next one down. But Amnon stood his ground and said that it was just the opposite; he, Amnon, had gone into the hostage hall via the second door, the righthand side, just as planned, and Muki, who'd gone in after him, had mistakenly used the same door.

To a bystander the argument may seem trivial, but in a hostage-rescue situation the entry of the assault force through two separate entrances simultaneously is of crucial importance. The argument between the two grew white-hot. In one corner, Amnon, my team leader throughout my service, a man who I, like a chick that has been marked, saw as my superior officer even when, many years later, I outranked him and served as his commander in the reserves. In the other corner, Muki, the officer who had realized that at the end of the tryout for the Unit they had mistakenly put my name in the rejection column and to whom I owed my service in the Unit.

As they argued, everything fell into place in my mind. I realized why I hadn't seen a single hostage in the hall in which I'd fought and how it was that I had found Sussmann and his squad fighting in "our hall." I'd simply made a mistake and gone into the small hall, the terrorists' quarters, which was where Sussmann and his squad were supposed to go. I'd made a mistake and gone in through an entrance further along, one hall down, the one after the hostage hall. I told them that I'd seen Muki go in through an entrance and so I'd gone in through the next one, which was actually Sussmann's hall. Amnon was right.

It was one hour after the battle had ended and Muki was still disorientated. Later on, Muki changed his version of events and said that actually there was no first door to the hostage hall and that was why he had gone through Amnon's door. But some of the guys insisted that the first left hand-side door did exist. (And in fact, all those who went back to Entebbe over the years clearly saw two doors to the hall and one of the hostages reported that the Ugandans used both doors to bring water to the hostages.) After that Muki changed his mind again and said that there was a first door, but he'd passed it because it was shut. When asked by one of the operators why he had stopped, and started firing in a standing position, instead of storming ahead, he said it was because he'd spotted a terrorist. We looked at one another in surprise and said we had not seen a terrorist, and certainly not one who was firing at us and barring us from charging in. Later on, he said he had stopped because he'd had a firearm malfunction. Later still, Muki said it was because his magazine had been empty.

Impatiently, we waited for take-off. After several long moments on the ground the order was given and the plane started to accelerate along the runway. I prayed that some determined Ugandan soldier, armed with a heavy machine gun, would not skewer us now as we labored up into the air. Once the wheels lifted off the runway and we climbed into the sky my heart felt liberated and the entire plane was filled with happiness. What a difference from when we'd landed.

Pitstop in Kenya

We stopped to refuel in Nairobi. The entire plane was in high spirits. I was delighted that the hostages had been freed and that I was alive. As soon as we landed, I hopped out to relieve my full bladder. This time without worrying that I might get shot.

In the dark, familiar figures approached: Ehud Barak and Shai Avital, both of whom had been in Kenya. They informed us that Yoni had died of his wounds. The happiness and the merriment were extinguished at once, replaced with an oppressive silence.

I remembered that I'd last seen Yoni for an instant outside the terminal, in front, a few meters from the doors to the hostage hall. Maybe next to the door that Muki had skipped and maybe alongside the first opening. I'd seen him near that low stone wall, turning, pivoting to the left, toward the force, his arm outstretched as though he was dropping to a crouch. Perhaps that was the moment he was wounded. I don't know for sure and never will. What's clear though is that Yoni was hit just as the assault was unleashed, once all the squads had stormed through the doors and the fate of the battle had been decided in our favor.

Like every person, Yoni had his virtues and his faults. But in the commander's ultimate test, the true test of battle—he was at his best. As a leader and combat commander he was head and shoulders above everyone else. During the Yom Kippur War his reputation preceded him among the operators of the Unit as a cool-headed and brave commander. At Entebbe I had the privilege of serving under his command and witnessing it with my own eyes.

Home

In the dark, the plane took off from Nairobi toward home. As the sky lightened, I shoved my face back into the windowpane and saw patches of jungle and a mighty river. Africa by day. I noted that this was actually my first time flying abroad. The pilots piped the morning news in on over the loudspeakers: foreign sources were reporting a military operation at Entebbe. That bit of news annoyed and worried us. All we needed now was for a few Egyptian fighter planes to rise up and shoot us out of the sky. A few hours passed and outside the window I saw an Israel Air Force fighter jet take up a position by our wing. At last I felt safe.

On the runway at the IAF's Tel Nof airbase, as soon as we got off the plane, I finally took the camera out of my battle vest and snapped some pictures as mementos. No more evil eye to worry about. After the mayhem and the thank-you speeches and the flashes of the cameras, we went back to the base. Normally after a battle the commander of the Unit would lead a piercing and in-depth debriefing of the troops in the intimacy of the briefing room, with representatives of the IDF History Department listening and recording all of the soldiers and officers. But this time, we sat in the mess hall, in front of the entire Unit, and mostly just told stories. I learnt that the body of a third terrorist was apparently found in the hall where Giora and I had fought. During the firefight I hadn't even noticed that or the fact that we had cleared part of the VIP lounge, which was the responsibility of a different squad, but its front door had been locked and most of it was actually linked to our hall via the corridor. Feeling euphoric, we each went our own way. Some to preparations for a next major clandestine mission and some, like me, to the discharge base. Today I know that we made an error in leaving the documentation of history to others. The IDF History Department's report is studded with many errors in all matters concerning Sayeret Matkal's role in the mission.

The Secret Sauce

I came full circle with the operation that also marked the end of my compulsory service. Already as a child, as a son of Holocaust survivors whose helpless grandparents had all been wiped out, I had decided to become a Jewish warrior in the Israel Defense Forces. That is how I wound up on the path that started at the IDF induction center and ended at Entebbe. And yet again, at Entebbe, too, there was a selection done among the hostages, separating the Jews and the non-Jews, and at the head of the hijacking force stood a pair of German terrorists. The plane was French, it was hijacked from Greece, and had landed in Uganda. And yet once again in the hour of truth there was no other state willing to lift a finger. Only this time the state of Israel and the IDF showed up in all their glory to deliver salvation.

I returned home safely and thought, despite the country-wide euphoria and the unusual glare of the spotlights, that when all was said and done this was just another mission, just like any other hostage rescue, just like any other battle fought by IDF soldiers. Only now, looking back across the years, I realize the enormity of the mission and what was achieved.

An operation that began with a feeling of helplessness—with an assumption that all was lost, that there was no choice but to accept defeat and surrender—ended with tremendous success, a marvel and a source of inspiration not merely for the state of Israel but for the world. It was, for me, a free lesson that I've kept with me my entire life—just how far one can go.

Anyone looking for the secret of success in the perfection of the plan or its execution, though both excellent, will be disappointed. An operation this complex, involving hundreds of people, thrust into a dynamic and shifting situation, laced with question marks, uncertainty and intelligence gaps, further stressed by a tight time schedule, will never be free of mistakes and failures. This would have been the case even if we'd have been given months to prepare and carried out countless simulations.

Yoni, may he rest in peace, handing Shlomi a trophy during a 1976 sports day.
Photo: Shlomi's album.

So what is the secret of success? The people and the spirit. Lady luck was working overtime for Israel that night, for certain, but there was also a rousing spirit. It started with Prime Minister Yitzhak Rabin, who opted not to surrender to terror but to authorize an operation despite the many risks, of which he was well aware. It continued to the commanders and every last one of the pilots and soldiers. Everyone took initiative, thought big, assumed responsibility and showed determination and resourcefulness in achieving the goal. It was this spirit that delivered us to the doors of the terminal in the heart of Africa, over the mountains of darkness, and in the end led to the elimination of the terrorists and many Ugandan guards in a matter of seconds, defeated by squads of operators operating independently and with unflinching determination. Alongside the very painful price that was paid, more than one-hundred hostages were brought home unharmed.

That is how, together, the impossible is accomplished.

Lt.-Col. Shlomi Reisman, a son of Holocaust survivors, is married and a father to three IDF combat soldiers. He was drafted into Sayeret Matkal in 1973, to Team Amnon, and served for 27 years as an operator and commander in compulsory service, and in reserves up until his discharge. An engineer by training, he is a technology entrepreneur and industrialist.

Staff-Sgt. Ilan Blumer, Operator Team Amnon
Amnon's Squad, Yoni's Assault Force
Hostage Hall

OPERATION YONATAN

My Operation Yonatan started in the small hours of the night, early Friday morning, the third of July, with a call from the Unit. The message: come to the base urgently! At that moment the only possibility that crossed my mind was that we would be sent to operate against terror targets in Lebanon. I didn't for a second consider that we would soon be deployed to the heart of Africa….To this day, I remember the silence and the restraint in the house as I departed. Nowadays, as a parent to a combat soldier, I understand precisely what my late parents were feeling.

I arrived at the base and saw some unusual activity, jeeps rolling around alongside small "Bambino" armored personnel carriers. In response to my question of what was going on, I was told that we were flying to Entebbe. At that moment, I thought to myself: it won't happen, it isn't serious, and it, like previous, less dangerous missions, will be denied authorization.

Our very first briefing changed my mindset. I realized that it was dead serious and that the risk factor was very high, especially for our team, Team Amnon. Of the eight operators slated to storm the main hall, housing the hijackers and hostages, seven were from Team Amnon (all aside from Muki).

Already during that first briefing there were questions raised about how an eight-man assault team was supposed to counter a group of ten terrorists. The other forces were to assert control over the terminal building, including the second floor and the VIP rooms, and provide perimeter security and suppressive fire around the terminal. Additionally, we were told that a full company of Ugandan soldiers was being quartered on the second floor.

We were also told that Team Omer, the team directly below us, was forbidden from taking part in the assault force because at the time they were in the final stages of training for an important mission. I felt that Team Amnon, which was already on pre-discharge leave, was shouldering all of the heavy responsibility.

During the preparations stage I tried to memorize an escape route so that if something went wrong, or if one of the planes was damaged, I'd know how to get out of Entebbe. What I remember most of all was the way we kept piling more and more ammunition on the jeeps, far more than the gear list required, so that if we were stranded in Uganda and had to make our way overland to Kenya, we'd be able to fight our way out. Of course, this weighed the planes down even more and we barely were able to lift off.

The flight to Sharm was a nightmare. The low-altitude flight in the middle of the day caused awful turbulence. Most of the guys vomited (I personally didn't vomit but I did feel unwell). I thought that if this was how it was going to be all the way to Entebbe, we'd be wrecked on arrival and there'd be no one capable of combatting the terrorists…

In Sharm, we were given the tiger-stripe uniforms, which felt like canvas and were really hot. We also got final briefings from Yoni and from Dan Shomron. We took off without knowing if we were really going to go all the way to Entebbe, and only after some time, while in midair, were we given word that the operation was a go.

I was in the second Land Rover. There were ten of us in that jeep; we sat folded up in the seats while the paratroopers, mostly high-ranking officers from the brigade, lay alongside us on the floor. In my opinion the composition of that force was a mistake, because had we been engaged in battle—I'm not sure that a random group of high-ranking officers would have functioned well as a combat outfit. For this reason, though, for years after the operation, there was hardly a single senior infantry officer in the IDF who did not claim to have participated in Operation Entebbe…

During the flight I couldn't help but think about who among us might not make it back, as, statistically speaking, it was highly unlikely that none of the seven operators on the assault force would be hit, and we, as a team, had already suffered losses during a hostage-rescue operation.

Upon landing, we released the jeep from its cargo restraints. It was positioned closest to the nose of the plane and so all of the force of landing was exerted on it. We landed on a lit runway and drove in a convoy, headlights on, toward the terminal. The paratroopers who hopped off the plane marked the runway with torches for the following planes, which turned out to be a good idea because, after the first live-fire engagement, the lights on the runway were shut off.

From a distance that's hard for me to gauge today, the Ugandan soldiers indicated for us to stop and could be seen cocking their weapons. I did not hear the silenced fire that was directed at them, but loud fire from our jeep soon followed and the sentries fell. This was drilled during one of the simulations; we had been briefed and prepared for such a scenario.

We carried on, driving rather fast, and stopped around 50 meters short of the planned spot. We jumped out of the vehicles and ran toward the terminal and the staging point between the control tower and the left corner of the building. Then I heard Yoni yell: "Betser, forward!" I saw Muki start to run right and I ran after him.

While running I saw a Ugandan soldier off to our right. Several operators shot him while in motion. I held my fire because I couldn't draw even with the force in front. I saw Muki go into the terminal. At that stage I didn't realize that Muki had skipped over one of the entrances and I continued running along with Shlomi toward the next entrance.

I burst into the room and was pretty shocked: it was empty. In the corner I saw a pile of passports and I thought that maybe the hostages had been moved and we'd missed them. Then I heard Amir calling out over the megaphone and saw Giora and realized that I was in the wrong room.

I left the room and while outside I saw Giora and Shlomi firing down the corridor; I later learned that they killed three terrorists during that stage. When I came into the large hall, I saw Amir standing near the door, with the body of a terrorist a few feet in front of him and the two dead German terrorists, a man and woman, off to the left. Amir's first words were: "I shot the terrorist and he's got a new Kalchka (which was how we referred to the Kalashnikov on our team)!" He shoved the rifle sideways out of the way so that no one would take it from him…

The hostages were still prone on the floor. I saw an injured person and called "Medic!" but Muki silenced me and said that first we had to finish clearing the area and only then treat the wounded. We called out to the hostages to go outside and as soon as they reached the door, there was fire from the control tower and they came pouring back in.

At this stage Alik [Ron] called me over to accompany him to the hostage-evacuation plane, which was parked a few hundred meters away from the terminal and needed to be brought closer. That was a slightly scary assignment as the Golani Brigade soldiers, who were lying in position around the plane, could have mistaken us for Ugandan soldiers and shot us. While walking over, I had time to look around. The APCs ringed the terminal and shot at everything that moved. They lit up the MiGs and a few Ugandan trucks and the whole scene looked like something from a Hollywood movie…

All told, we were on the ground for 35 minutes. We were on the first plane to land and the first plane to leave…

Several times, when speaking to soldiers about the operation, I've been asked who was the commander of the mission. My answer is, Yoni Netanyahu. But the soldiers generally persist: wasn't he killed in the early stage of the mission? I reply that such is the character of the Unit: as soon as the bullets start to fly—there are no commanders. Everyone knows his role, and in our case, we all ran to our assigned entrances and knew how to improvise in the face of confusion.

Having read the stories of the rest of my friends from the team, I hope that our story will truly be published without any of the wars of the generals and the pointless arguments not befitting the Unit and its legacy. This was without doubt one of the IDF's boldest missions and perhaps even one of the bolder ones in the annals of military history. The majority of the credit, in my opinion, goes to the political echelon and the Air Force, which was given the most difficult assignment: delivering us to the target and bringing us home safely.

And we, we did what was expected of us, with a bit of luck and a lot of fortitude from the operators. The mission was a success and the rest's history.

Personally, I've come full circle in another way: For the past twenty-five years I've been working in east Africa and have been landing, at least once a month, at the airport in Entebbe. The old terminal was demolished years ago and only the restored control tower now stands as a reminder of the mission and as a memorial to Yoni Netanyahu.

———————

Staff-Sgt. Ilan Blumer, born and raised in Bethlehem of Galilee, a moshav in the Jezreel Valley, was drafted in August 1973 and became a soldier on Team Amnon. After his army service he grew greenhouse roses on his farm and raised wildlife. Since 1990 he has been living on-and-off in east Africa (Kenya, Uganda, Ethiopia, and Tanzania) where he works as an advisor on rose cultivation. A farm owner, he is married to Carmel and a father to Shira, Shahar, and Ron, who, as a combat soldier in the Paratroop Brigade, was chosen to represent his IDF regiment and to read the memorial Yizkor prayer during the 2016 ceremony in Entebbe, marking 40 years since the operation and commemorating those who fell during Operation Yonatan.

Staff-Sgt. Adam Kolman, Team Dani
Operator in Sussmann Squad; Yoni's Assault Force
Small Hall (Hijackers and Hostages)

ENTEBBE: A QUEST

This story is told from my personal perspective as a soldier on Team Dani, a veteran team with less than a year left to serve at the time. It is told after years of silence and forgetfulness and life; a memory scoured by time.

The Way Back

In the plane, on the return leg, we were all in a psycho state of "Wow, we did it," in elation over having pulled it off. Who even thought it could have been any other way? It was crowded in there, very crowded; no one cared. We sat in the cargo hold of the plane, on either side of the vehicles. Not much room to move. Those who could, grabbed a spot in the cars. Best spot was in the Mercedes.

A jumble of endless conversations, in clusters and in pairs. Everyone relayed what he did, what he saw, what happened, how it happened. Conversations leapfrogged from one group to another; stories started but didn't end and morphed into other stories, other experiences. What a release! What intensity! What noise and commotion in the warm belly of that Hercules! And there may have also been a body, covered, on a stretcher…

Amid the laughter and the noise, Amnon Ben-Ami was very quiet. He'd taken shrapnel, the wound apparently superficial because he was with us, and I asked him why he was quiet. I didn't know he'd been wounded. Last time I'd seen him he was in the entry hall. And then he told me he was hit by a grenade that a terrorist had released when they were ushered out of the hall. He said that after the terrorists had surrendered, they were taken to the entry hall and then suddenly there was a flash in one of the terrorist's hands and the soldiers understood that they had activated a grenade. We shot them (Amnon said) but the grenade still went off and I was wounded.

With great pride we pulled out the spoils that we'd taken from the Ugandans. Gal Raif produced a pistol and I displayed a German G3 service rifle that I'd taken from the Ugandan soldier that I'd killed, and a magazine from a Tokarev mini-gun, a very new Russian weapon at the time with a curved, full magazine that had been lying alongside a Ugandan in a black suit at the entrance to the VIP lounge. I'd looked for the mini-gun but hadn't found it. I figured the guy was lying on top of it, but I couldn't flip him over. He was dead and large and heavy, so I just took the magazine.

After a short while we landed in Kenya. They didn't let us off, we just filled up on fuel. The side doors opened and I remember the sight of armed Kenyan soldiers. It was very strange and disturbing, as roughly one hour earlier I'd killed Ugandan soldiers with very similar uniforms and a somewhat similar appearance, and the shift from war to safety, from being cocooned in the warm belly of an airplane, surrounded by friends and on the way home, to landing in an airport that looked like the one we'd left and in which we'd just fought, was jarring.

Confusing matters further, we were told that Yoni was dead. It was a strange situation, because we were very happy, very proud, and the entire plane was wrapped in an atmosphere of excitement and laughter and then all of a sudden we were informed that Yoni was dead. Surprisingly, news of his death did not completely douse the excitement. The adrenalin levels were too high; it took time to calm down. Only later was there space made for the fact that Yoni was no longer.

I had, and still have, many positive feelings for Yoni. He lived in Ramat Ha'sharon with his girlfriend Bruria, who was a good friend of a high school friend of mine. The girls, my friend and Bruria, served together in the armored brigade in which Yoni served before coming back to the Unit. We, a group of friends from Neve Magen, hung out with Bruria several times during that period and I was surprised that a woman who was around my age, back when I was still in conscripted service, was already sharing her life with a guy who was, as it happened, the commander of my unit.

Yoni occasionally gave me a ride back from Neve Magen to the base. We were already a veteran team at the time and occasionally got nights off. There was no problem checking in with him and asking if he could give me a ride in the morning. He'd pick me up near the on-ramp to the main road. The vibe in the car was friendly, the two of us sharing eye-level conversations about random subjects and about the Unit. Yoni was wonderfully articulate and clear. He gave off the feeling of a responsible adult who knew what he wanted and what was right. It took me a long time to realize that when Yoni was killed, Bruria, too, was part of the story; they were a couple in every way and there had been a great love between them and an enormous and deep mourning in his wake.

We took off from Kenya to Israel. The plane got drowsy; the tide of adrenalin subsided and the sadness swelled. It was hard to find a good spot to drift off. The pop-up seats in the cockpit were taken—by Dan Shomron and someone else. Slowly the sky lightened into morning. And then we heard the Voice of Israel broadcast at 7 a.m. The news was about us, about the operation, and it became clear that we were on the way home. It was the Fourth of July, American Independence Day, the broadcaster said, and who even remembered that. The fear of God. We were halfway back, in the middle of nowhere, over the Red Sea, crossing opposite Somalia or Sudan or Egypt, and we realized we might yet be shot down. Air escort arrived; we calmed down quick. Everything was okay. Soon enough the Sinai Peninsula came into view and all was quiet. Two or three more hours and we'd be home.

There was a large reception. Loads of people on the runway, soldiers and civilians. And I met my neighbor, Hadas, a young female soldier in the air force. Everything was garbled and scattered and full of emotion. People milling around, meeting up, buddies, hi-fives, hugs; where do we go from here? What do we do? There was a ceremony, a reception, the prime minister, the president, the chief of staff, everyone. And there was also a car that needed to get driven out of the plane and a pair of Land Rovers that needed to be brought back to the Unit. Yardenay convinced me to join him and to drive the second Land Rover back to the base, skipping the ceremony; who needs that whole mess? We drove back from Tel Nof to the Unit. On the way, we crossed through towns and villages, still dressed in Ugandan military fatigues and driving uncommon vehicles and it seemed to me that everyone was standing and staring.

Back at the base we assembled at the mess hall in the afternoon. The hall was packed to the gills, all the Unit's personnel in attendance, gathered to hear battle stories from the operators. An alleged debriefing. Each of us relayed what he did. I remember Muki critiquing me for throwing a phosphorous grenade in a closed space, saying it could have started a fire and that it cut visibility to nothing. As far as I was concerned, of course, I'd done the best with what I had. But the memory of the critique has not faded.

We were given a night off and sent home and I let my family know I was on the way. Great excitement. My mother and father, my brother and sister, Modi, Dalia, and a lot of friends and neighbors were all waiting for me on the balcony. They all wanted to hear stories, to see, to touch, to hug, to bask in the fame and the legend that had been created at Entebbe, and here was someone who had been part of it. My mother and father were emotional. They'd been very worried. Two days earlier, when I told them I wasn't coming home for Shabbat, they'd guessed that something was up. In our neighborhood there was always someone who knew what was happening, someone who could clarify the situation. Our neighbors Aharale Yariv and Avraham Yaffe—generals both—came by and offered congratulations and hugs. Uri Yarom, a neighbor friend of my parents', a legendary pilot, collector, and weapons expert whom I looked up to as a child, looked over the spoils and praised them and, atypically, added no stories of his own. It took a while for my father to calm down; he trusted me and was proud of me and was worried, but not in a way that was visible; struggling, as always, with emotions. And mom was worried and trusting and proud, bursting with happiness, joy, and tears.

Since then the operation has been with me, accompanying my life.

The Way There

The route was straight forward. We boarded the planes at Airbase 27 at Lod Airport and flew down to Sharm, to cut the distance to Entebbe. The gear and vehicles were all loaded onboard. A standard flight. At the airbase in Sharm there were long runways, well-suited to heavy planes. The C-130s were especially heavy—laden with fuel and gear to the very edge of their carrying capacity. The government hadn't given the go-ahead, but we carried on as usual. The mission was formally presented to us in a large hangar stuffed with soldiers and lined with Bristol boards. There were flow charts and blueprints, intelligence briefings, a radio and communications briefing, commanders milling around with walkie-talkies and earpieces, operators, hand signals and screaming, separation of forces, delegation of responsibilities, commanders, warriors, division of sectors. The usual.

Then Yoni spoke. He delivered an address that I can't recall verbatim, but its essence rings in my ears to this day. He spoke of the spirit of the Jewish People and the People of Israel, the duty to not forsake those in captivity, the unwavering confidence he had in us to accomplish the mission. It was a speech of faith and of belief in our chosen path; it was a speech that underscored our role in the historical moment at which we stood, undertaking an operation the likes of which the world had never seen. It was a speech laden with values and with Zionism, a speech mindful of the beating of the wings of history above us; a sensation that we all felt. It was a speech addressed to us, the believers.

And I believed in our success. I don't remember fear or concern or a lack of confidence upon departure. From the hangar we walked to the planes and got ready for takeoff. Still no green light. Nir, an operator from Team Amnon, was left behind, scratched from the roster. He'd vomited the whole way down, and was deemed physically incapable of going. It was sad to see him like that.

The view from the airbase was of late afternoon summer light in beautiful Sharm el-Sheikh. A view of the desert and the sea and nothing else. The engines were fired up and we started to move. The plane was heavy. It accelerated and accelerated and accelerated, and still didn't lift off. The runway was practically finished and beyond it —the sea. What was going on? One more breath, and we detached. The liftoff seemed almost eternal.

In the Hercules there was a black Mercedes, nose facing out, and behind it two open Land Rovers, modified for military use, with extra foldout seats for additional personnel. We, the operators, were on the jeep seats or against the walls of the plane. It was crowded back there. Darkness fell and the plane quieted. We traveled inward, chatted, napped. The warmth and the monotonous noise of the aircraft were calming and lulling. A long flight, some seven hours.

I made a spin through the cockpit, had a chat with the pilots. Brig.-Gen. Dan Shomron, the commander of the operation, was with us on the plane, his uniform clean, neat, his battle vest in mint condition, all polished. I found a free stool, took a load off.

Entebbe loomed. Time moved slow. We approached and the tension rose. Soldiers were woken up. Noise and talk and conversations. Tension rose further. Yoni made the rounds, chatted, checked in. I spoke with Muki, Dani, Amnon and Sussmann. Commanders, soldiers: we were all in this flying lump together, united behind a single mission. We talked, chatted, took the edge off the stress. The feeling was: get it done, go home.

Battle vests were laced up. The Ugandan tiger-stripe uniforms looked sharp, combat-ready. We managed to get the sizes right so that the uniforms were comfortable and not sloppy. Still it felt strange. Battle vests were packed with gear, full and heavy. White hats for everyone and for me a megaphone too. I wanted to take a camera. I thought it was only fitting and important that there be documentation. I suggested to Amitzur, our R&D officer, that we bring an infrared camera with no flash. He seemed nonplussed. I didn't demand it;

during preparations the matter was dropped. In the plane, I remembered again.

We boarded the vehicles; got ready to land. The working assumption was that the runways might not be lit and we'd need to mark them with torches. That role was given to the Golani or Paratroop Recon Unit, who were on the first plane, our plane, so that the three trailing planes could land safely. In actuality, the lights were on, at least some of the time. Others can say how that happened. The wheels pounded the tarmac; my diaphragm clenched; a hard landing, stable, just as it ought to be with all that weight and stress. Ace pilots.

The plane taxied and stopped; the cargo ramp started to open and we saw sky and lights. The bottom fell out of my stomach like when a helicopter starts to rapidly ascend or you drop down a daredevil slide. A deep swallow. First time I felt fear. We were in the Mercedes; first in line. The cargo ramp came down and we started to drive out onto the runway and into the dark, into battle.

The Battle

We're in the Mercedes. Three rows of seats, new black paint job. Snazzy. Two days earlier it was white. A pair of flags, one on either side of the hood; manual gear shift alongside the steering wheel; bench seat upfront with room for three. Middle row has a fold-down seat that allows the guys in the back row to wiggle out. Two years later, as a student at the Bezalel Academy of Art and Design, I'd take these same cars from Jerusalem to Tel Aviv. Seven passengers and a driver in those share-taxis, the flat rate for each passenger passed up front from hand to hand. In Entebbe the ride's free. And there are ten of us in the Mercedes. Up front, behind the wheel, Amitzur Kafri, and to his right, Muki Betser, and next to the door, Yoni. Middle row's filled with operators from Team Amnon: Gadi, Alex, and Amos Goren, who replaced Nir. In the back row, I'm on the far right, Amnon's next to me and Yoram Rubin's on the far left. Giora Sussmann sits down, squeezes in on top of us, between me and Amnon. Nowhere to move. Battle vests full. In a bench designed for three, there are four fully loaded soldiers. The Kalashnikov is on the floor and the megaphone's in the back. Crowded. Can't see well. To the left, can't see a thing. Sussmann fills the frame. No access to my firearm. Good thing it isn't a long drive.

Muki and Yoni navigate very confidently amid the sea of asphalt. They know the route cold. The Mercedes rolls on through the weak airport lights. We're Idi Amin in a presidential convoy, in the middle of the night, a shiny black Mercedes with two flags on the hood accompanied by two Land Rovers full of soldiers.

The ride is quiet. To our left, a lit and silent building. No flights; no action; the airfield is asleep.

We're advancing towards the old terminal, which is lit in a paltry light and alongside it we see the darkened control tower. I start to get used to the situation. There's no talk in the car. We drive in silence. We're on the way, headed toward the terminal. All of a sudden there's a little hut and a coil of barbed wire across the road, with only a small lane left open. Alongside the hut a soldier suddenly stands at attention, rifle flat, barrel pointing ahead in a sort of salute.

A terse, tense discussion about what to do. Muki says the sentry is just saluting and there's no call for concern. Yoni disagrees and wants to eliminate the soldier. In the confines of the car the driver is being given different orders from Yoni and Muki. Left, Amitzur; right, Amitzur; left, Amitzur. And Amitzur responds. He drags the wheel left, drags the wheel right. In the end, he swerves right, toward the sentry, on Yoni's command. Yoni apparently doesn't want to leave armed Ugandan soldiers behind us, and he tries to take the sentry down in mid-motion with a silenced Beretta .22, but he's in an impossible position. There's no chance. The car continues slowly but doesn't stop.

The commotion and the swerving of the Mercedes doesn't upset the sentry or spur him into action. He maintains the same posture, rifle rigid at his waist, pointing right at my head. We pass him slowly. The rifle barrel is about half a yard from me and I think that if he does squeeze the trigger, he'll skewer all of us with a single bullet. Even if I try, there's no way for me to get to my rifle on the floor. Time stands still. One more second and he's going to fire and I'm stuck. The moment passes terribly slowly. The sentry is in salute mode, his rifle aimed right at me, and Yoni has his body out of the car and tries to shoot him to no avail. The car keeps going and the barrel passes; the soldier is behind me and has not issued a single shot. What a relief.

The sentry has no idea what just happened. Aside from the soft sound of the silenced Berretta the quiet persists and there's a moment to inhale, and then a long burst of fire rattles out from behind us. Someone from the Land Rover has gunned down the sentry and immediately after that there's another burst of fire.

The Party Starts

Yoni yells to Amitzur: "Punch it, straight ahead." We realize that the element of surprise is gone. The stress level rises, we're heading toward a building that's awake and waiting for us. We surge towards the terminal. Can't see a thing; just hear the sound of gunfire and the spark of bullets in the night. Stress.

The Mercedes stops about 40 meters from the building, the Land Rovers pull up next to it and behind it. The building is both like and unlike what we'd seen in the photos. A two-story building, rather large windows in front, a sort of arcade of thin pillars, with a roof and large display windows. The ground floor is only partially lit. There's weak light outside and the second floor is dark. Off to the left, the control tower sprouts up out of the ground. It too is dark. Yoni's standing by the vehicle and shouting: "Forward, charge! Forward, charge!"

The disembark is slow. We, the ones in the back row, are stuck until the guys from Team Amnon in the middle row clear, and until Sussmann gets off us and out of the car. Only then is my squad of Amnon and Yoram able to get out. Yoni's standing outside the Mercedes. He realizes that everything's stuck, that the guys aren't heading out, that the charge is stalled and the operators aren't moving. And he yells at us: "Forward, charge! Forward, charge!" and a thought flashes across my mind—it's a lot like the movies, like in the drills, and then Yoni runs ahead and charges, leads the force behind him and clears the bottleneck. A true commander; a brave man. That's the last time I see him alive.

Finally we're out and running, charging toward the terminal and our hall. I yell to Amnon and Yoram "Follow me!" and we start running in the direction of Sussmann up ahead. A big group of operators has tumbled out of the Land Rovers and they're all sprinting toward the building and the fire. While running, some 20 meters away from the Mercedes, I see Muki Betser take a knee and handling his Kalashnikov; it looks like he's trying to change magazines. He's got a new orange Bakelite magazine in his rifle. What the hell is he doing over there? He should already be in the building. Do I see right and there's already someone down alongside the control tower? No time to stop; we fly forward into the building. The bright orange glow of the Bakelite twinkles on to this very day.

Before getting on the plane, Muki relayed something very simple to us about stress and excitement. First thing, he said, is fire off a shot and then all the stress is released and you can operate by the drill.

To my right, from behind a trash receptacle, a Ugandan soldier in a dress uniform, like something an MP might wear, rises to his feet and then, as in a silent movie, I see a row of rifles swivel toward him and all of us release our first shots. And the guy falls slowly, as in a ballet, like an emptied puppet. That's my first shot. I again thank Muki Betser for the sage advice and vast experience, for the first shot amid the stress, which frees me of inhibition, frees the capabilities and instincts necessary to win this war; frees the beast.

I'm part of the assault force with Amnon Ben-Ami and Yoram Rubin under Sussmann's command. Our role is to enter the small hall, which was used by the terrorists as a rec-room and a bedroom, to clear it and kill the terrorists while keeping in mind that there may be hostages present. We reach the terminal building. We glue ourselves to the wall, which is full of showcase windows and the like, and start to advance along it to the right, in the direction of the entrance to our hall.

We enter the small hall. A large, half-lit square with two doors: one on the right, alongside the outside wall of the building, and one on the left side of the hall, on the far end, beyond which is a corridor that bends right. Sussmann sends us to the far door and he turns to the one on the right. I reach the corner and peek down the corridor, which is about 15-meters-long, and see the barrel of a rifle. The corridor itself is around two meters-wide and lined with pillars that offer good cover.

I start throwing grenades down the corridor toward the rifle barrel and advance with Amnon covering me from behind. Towards the end of the corridor, I realize that it leads to a large room full of packages and cargo. I throw one more grenade in the direction of the rifle barrel and then step around the corner and shoot the soldier who's lying there from point blank range. He looks as though he's already been hit by the grenades. Amnon closes the gap. Rubin yells that he's heading toward Sussmann.

We return to the corridor and there I see a Ugandan soldier coming from somewhere at the far end of the hall, moving towards me while taking cover among the packages. I yell to Amnon and Yoram that there's another soldier and that they should stick with the cover fire. It's a very big space, filled with packages and the like and it seems like a dangerous spot to wander into; could be full of surprises. I toss another grenade or two in his direction and then am out of grenades. All I have is the white phosphorous one. I decide I can't leave that soldier behind without knowing if he's alive or dead. I toss the WP, which flares and gives off a cloud of white smoke, and then charge under its cover through the packages toward that soldier. I close the gap, shoot him from close range, confirm the kill, and then fly out of there towards the corridor and the entry hall.

Amnon Ben-Ami, Yoram and I go into the entry hall and give word to Amnon Peled of two dead Ugandans. I'm in an unstoppable craze. We return to the small hall on our left and see that another squad has joined us—Reisman and Ilan from Team Amnon—and with Sussmann they're stuck along the wall, not passing the opening and the bursts of fire. I can't quite figure out how time passes here; I just finished waging war with two Ugandans and here they still haven't made it past the entrance. What's going on? I draw close and see a large black man in a black suit dead on the floor, blocking the path, and there's constant fire from where we're trying to get into.

There's another entry attempt with another grenade. Reisman's first. Who's got grenades? I'm out. Reisman's in the lead. A grenade is tossed and Reisman's magazine is empty. I yell that I'm taking the lead and go ahead. The fire from the hall stops and I'm letting loose with the bursts of fire ahead and the force is behind. The hall is a little darker than the one we'd just come from and it's empty, and then off to the left there's another hall, slightly darker still, and inside there are three figures with their hands up. I ask them in Hebrew if they're hostages and Sussmann yells from behind: "They're terror-ists. Shoot them, shoot them." They've got their hands up; maybe they're hostages. I can't see where they're keeping their weapons. Later I realize how they managed to not get hit by all of our grenades —they were in the hall off to the side and the grenade blasts didn't reach there. You had to get around that corner to hit them.

Sussmann sends us in to clear some bathrooms and additional rooms. We burst in, shoot, make sure it's clear. I come back and see that the room is empty; all I see are the backs of several operators moving toward the small hall. I also head out to the small hall and see the terrorists prone, shot, shuddering near the display window. I ask what happened and I'm told that they pulled a grenade and that it exploded and wounded people; then they were shot. One of them is fair-skinned, maybe a woman; it isn't clear in the gloom. I fire, the shuddering ceases. Done, over. We get a report that in the main hall the situation is under control and that the hostages are on the way out, and one more thing, Yoni's been hit, apparently badly, and is being treated by Dr. David Hassin. Yonatan Gilad from our team is the medic on the mission, paired with David the doctor. We trust in them. At this stage Amnon and Yoram disappear out of sight and Sussmann heads back with the Team Amnon squad to help load the hostages up on the vehicles.

Outside the building, to the right of the hostage hall, there's a parking area full of people and vehicular traffic and the hostages are being loaded onboard and there's fire up at the control tower, which is still harassing us and still represents a danger. Someone very determined ensconced up there. Yardenay fires an RPG up at the tower. It's a tough angle, from the ground up. Still not silenced. I look for more action. It seems to have ended too fast. Near the building I see Aharoni Berkowitz, my fellow team member from Team Dani, clutching his rifle and providing cover fire while yelling that he's been hit in the shoulder. A grenade that had been thrown at the building bounced back and exploded, wounding him and Amir Drori. I pull out a sterile personal bandage and dress the wound. It doesn't look too bad.

Then I meet Dani Arditi, my team commander, and ask him what's happening. Dani says, come on, let's keep pushing ahead. He too is still looking for action. We run along the length of the terminal to the far end, where we find a storage room and alongside it a bulldozer and some gear. We shoot what we can and burn off the rest of our adrenalin and realize that the war is nearing its end and that there isn't much left to capture.

We stand there at the edge of the field and see the whole area spread before us and from afar the new terminal, buildings, hangars, sheds, and the flaming MiGs. Team Omer and [Maj. Shaul] Mofaz are on the grenade launcher, going wild on the MiGs and making sure that none of them will be taking off and that we'll be departing in safety. The sight is spectacular, like a scene from a war movie: the tail wings of the fighter jets stand out against the backdrop of the flames, only it isn't a movie. It's a reality that we created and made, a present reality that will become a distant and unforgettable memory.

Dani and I pack it in. On the way he tells me about the radio reports regarding Yoni's injury and the grenade that the team threw and wounded our own guys. On the way back I'm not able to resist looking for spoils. I stop to take weapons or gear used by the soldiers and terrorists that we'd killed. It's the basic nature of the hunter. Skulls, scalps, or weapons. I go back into the combat zone, to the inner hall, to lay claim to the rifle of the soldier I killed. I don't notice if anyone's accompanying me or watching my back. I want to take the weapon of the first Ugandan soldier I shot, the one I killed around the first corner in the corridor with a burst to the face from half a yard out. The gun's gripped in his hands and I can't pry it loose. I run over to the second soldier, who's lying bullet-sprayed amid the packages. This time it's easier. The gun's off to his side. I check the rifle and find that the safety is still on. Miserable soldier. I grab it and run back without fear and with the perfect confidence of the victor. The vision of these Ugandan soldiers, these men I shot from close range, our bodies practically touching, will accompany me for many long years; the scars of maturity. I get on one of the last vehicles leaving. On the way I hear reports of the hostages being evacuated. We ride to the plane and once again the takeoff is rather nerve-wracking; then we're airborne and the stress dissolves.

The Preparations

Summer of 1976. Team Dani Arditi, a veteran team, was about six months before discharge. The end was in sight and there was already talk about what we'd do afterwards. We didn't have a team-wide mission; the guys were spread out on different assignments. Aharoni and I were getting ready to serve as drill sergeants for the new recruits of August 1976.

Sunday morning brought word of a hijacked airplane. We ran through the drill and the usual procedure for an aircraft takeover and rushed to Lod Airport to meet the plane upon landing. Only it didn't land at Lod. We returned to the Unit. It landed at Entebbe, in Uganda. Pretty far away.

The radio news reported a large number of Jews and Israelis on board the plane. In Uganda we had an ally or sorts. Idi Amin. He'd been in Israel, received some training, some guidance, a pair of paratrooper wings. Then something went very wrong. And the friend decided to allow the plane to land on his soil and agreed to harbor the hijackers; a turncoat. The information we had was shrouded in fog; was he really hiding and sheltering terrorists? In fact, yes; a friend became an enemy.

In the Unit, among the teams, everything was as usual, routine. We followed the news like everyone else in the country, hearing about the hostages and the negotiations. Our involvement—seemed preposterous. Thoughts, however, started to roll, ideas hummed, notions of a possible rescue were considered. It was far away, but terror could not be allowed to prevail. The Naval Commandos, some suggested, could be parachuted into Lake Victoria and from there, in their inflatable rafts, they could motor to shore and storm the airport. The lake, though, was full of crocodiles, and the Naval Commandos —what did they know about hostage rescue? The whole thing sounded farfetched. But then a different plan emerged. We, the Unit, would lead the rescue. The whispers became a buzz, momentum built, routine was ruptured; an operation was in the works. We loved it. Action, prep, briefings, gear lists; the machinery came to life.

The outline was pieced together; the intelligence poured in; the plan was alive and dynamic.

Model drill on Friday night: swaths of burlap on the runway were used to simulate rooms; it cracked us up. A Hercules landed; we went over the load-up drill for the vehicles, the weight, the number of tools taken, the headcount, what and how much was needed, what was known about Entebbe, about the hijackers. Many questions, few answers. A complex and difficult operation. The commander's bureau and the planning divisions shouldered the majority of the workload. Uncertainty everywhere, but also flexibility in the face of change and constantly emerging ideas. We, the soldiers, were living off rumors. Nothing was set in stone; every minute brought another change. During the weekend, the plan congealed. A clear outline, a division of forces.

The hijacking and the terrorists' subsequent threats led the news all day. The hijackers' demands were laid out, as were the threats to execute the hostages if the demands were not met. All across the country the pressure mounted and at our base, too, the lights in the commander's office burned all night. Weekend leave was cancelled. I told my parents that I wouldn't be coming home and offered no details; they understood.

There was a plan of action; a division into teams, into vehicles, into roles. The strike would be launched at night; Saturday, if authorized. The Unit would seize control of the old terminal, eliminating the terrorists, freeing the hostages. The most veteran teams in the operational company—Team Amnon and Team Dani—would fill the strike squads. They'd charge into the hostage halls. Arrival at the terminal, it was decided, would be in a convoy meant to look like Idi Amin coming to visit the hostages: a Mercedes and two Land Rovers.

The Ugandan soldiers in the terminal, their quarters up on the second floor, would be taken care of by squads under the command of Yiftach Reicher and Arnon Epstein. Team Omer was barred from the assault force since its operators were preparing for a very important pending mission. Instead, they would deploy with Mofaz as part of the backup and perimeter security force on the runways and on the outskirts of the terminal. They'd be riding on BTR-40 armored personnel carriers equipped with MAG machine-guns and grenade launchers.

There were other units: Paratroop Recon, Golani Recon, and the Naval Commandos were to take over the new terminal and block the entrances to the airfield. Arrival was on four Hercules C-130s, set to land even if the runway lights were darkened; soldiers on the first plane would lay out torches.

On Thursday or Friday the Ugandan army uniforms were given out. The plan seemed straight out of a movie: to masquerade as Idi Amin's presidential convoy, in a black Mercedes and a pair of Land Rovers, arriving at Entebbe to see the situation firsthand. But there are many movie-like scripts in the Unit and plenty of creativity…

Team Amnon was charged with spearheading the strike on the hostage terminal. Operational company commander Giora Sussmann was made commander of another assault team comprised of operators from Team Dani; they would take the small hall, where the terrorists slept and where hostages might be present. Team Dani Arditi was given the VIP lounge, the hall alongside the small hall farther along in the terminal. Dani chose me and two teammates—Amnon Ben-Ami and Yoram Rubin—to serve on Giora Sussmann's assault force.

Aside from the usual items on the gear list, I also equipped myself with a Beretta M9, just to be on the safe side, and a sack of mini-frag grenades, which looked like toys but were effective in close quarters. I was also given a megaphone, which was to be used as necessary but seemed cumbersome and superfluous. And, of course, a white hat for identification.

At first, I was bothered by the separation from the rest of the team. I thought we'd get a peripheral assignment, but it turned out, once the roles were distributed, that Sussmann's assault force was at the fore of the charge into the small hall, where the terrorists apparently had their quarters; as a result, we would be riding in the lead car, the Mercedes. I was pleased. No way was I going to give up that opportunity.

The Unit was abuzz. That's how it always was before a mission, a hive of activity. This time it was more noticeable and more intense than ever. Activity everywhere: in our quarters, in the yard, in the quartermaster's store, the armory, the vehicle workshop, the radio shed, the intelligence officer's desk, the commander's bureau. Everywhere. Soldiers hustling from place to place, updated gear lists in hand, responding to changes upon changes. All sorts of guys showed up and vied for a spot on the force. The rumor was out and everyone realized that it was going to happen. And so they came: newly discharged operators from veteran teams stood their ground and argued that they deserved a spot on the roster, as did the officers, who felt that without them it couldn't be carried off. We checked in every once in a while, and then learned, at some point, that Noam Melamud was not included in the force. Dani Arditi was agitated and so were we. What were we to make of the fact that one of the guys from our team was not included? Someone snagged his spot. A protest started, pressure. It seemed wrong. There was not enough room on the plane and in the vehicles. Power struggles raged behind the scenes. The team was busy though, each guy tending to his own affairs, gearing up. There was no boycott. We accepted the commanders' decree and Noam was left behind; a stain that the team has not managed to erase, and an affront that Noam carries around to this very day.

In an old loose-leaf I found a yellowed piece of paper. The words were printed on a typewriter. A short draft written by me in my freshman year at the Bezalel Academy of Art and Design, Jerusalem 1977, the year we were discharged and each went his own way and the togetherness turned solitary. After that came the painting and the silence.

"Only Ben-Ami was serious and sad; his shoulder hurt.
I've never spoken to him about it, not at all.
We all laughed and told stories, showed off; each one of us
acting more a hero than the next; nearly emotionless.
Anyone of sound mind, anyone Jewish or any pursuer of
international justice, would've joined in our happiness.
And in Israel they did just that, rejoicing like after Maccabi's
win at the European championships in '77.
And we paid the price. Gray hair, wrinkles, cracked emotions
that shattered one year later. And the choice was one that I
made without regret or remorse and with an overriding
desire to take part; I plunged myself into the fathomless
depth of blood and noise, totally animalistic and with
supreme pride in my professionalism, equipped with a desire
to live and with absolute faith in the powerlessness of death
to draw near. With no fear after the first shot, with the faith of
a blindman in his cane when trying to cross an endless,
teeming, and violent highway; carried on without hesitation
and without feeling at all.
I passed through in body. Ben-Ami was the only one who felt,
at that moment, that there were those who'd been trampled."

"Only Ben-Ami was serious and sad; his shoulder hurt. I've never spoken to him about it, not at all.

We all laughed and told stories, showed off; each one of us acting more a hero than the next; nearly emotionless. Anyone of sound mind, anyone Jewish or any pursuer of international justice, would've joined in our happiness. And in Israel they did just that, rejoicing like after Maccabi's win at the European championships in '77. And we paid the price. Gray hair, wrinkles, cracked emotions that shattered one year later. And the choice was one that I made without regret or remorse and with an overriding desire to take part; I plunged myself into the fathomless depth of blood and noise, totally animalistic and with supreme pride in my professionalism, equipped with a desire to live and with absolute faith in the powerlessness of death to draw near. With no fear after the first shot, with the faith of a blindman in his cane when trying to cross an endless, teeming, and violent highway; carried on without hesitation and without feeling at all.

I passed through in body. Ben-Ami was the only one who felt, at that moment, that there were those who'd been trampled."

Staff.-Sgt. (res) Adam Kolman was drafted to the Naval Commandos in 1973. Toward the end of the basic stage—port diving—he left, and in February 1975 was accepted into the Unit and placed into a team in the middle of its course of training; at the time, the team had no permanent commander. Dani Arditi was appointed team leader after training and ever since Adam and his friends are proud to be known as Team Dani Arditi. Michael and Gaya are his beloved children and he is an architect and urban planner.

Cpt. Yiftach Reicher, Deputy Commander of the Unit
Yiftach Squads Commander, Yoni's Assault Force
Ugandan Soldiers' Hall

REPORT

I was 27 at the time. My wife (then and now) Rivka was six months pregnant with our firstborn son. As usual, she went to sleep with the radio on, and heard, early in the morning, reports of the operation and of an officer who had been killed. A friend asked: Why don't you call in and check on the identity of the officer? She replied: "Bad tidings come on their own, no need to run after them." I can't remember when I called, but I do remember that I only heard her story after the baby was born.

In light of the years that have passed and the stories that have been told and the facts that have 'changed,' I've opted to present here the operational report that I wrote immediately after the mission. The comments in brackets are mine and current, added solely for clarity.

Mission Report

1. I was commander of a squad that included: Yiftach [Reicher], Rani [Cohen], and Amir [Shadmi] on one of the Land Rovers along with Dani's [Arditi] squad. A second squad under my command included Arnon [Epstein], Buchris [Pinchas], and Udi Bloch. They were to join me immediately after the dismount from the vehicles.

2. Right after the dismount, which took place not in the planned spot, I moved quickly, along with Yoni and Muki, towards the building. Alongside the first corner of the building, Muki stood still and started shooting ahead. I saw no target and Yoni called out to Muki to continue to advance, and even took a

step forward as though to pass him. I passed Muki and entered my room.

3. Upon entry, I noted that Rani and Amir were behind me and I spotted a Ugandan [soldier] running away. I shot him and he fell. We continued to advance through the rooms, towards the stairs, and while advancing we killed another soldier or two.

4. I barely found the staircase, because it was dark and the stairs were much narrower than we'd expected. I climbed up the stairs with Rani. At the top, I turned around and saw two Ugandan soldiers coming toward me and I shot them from around two meters out and they fell.

5. I moved along the hallway with Amir and Rani. I left Amir next to the steel partition that blocked the passage down to the hostage hall [that's how we realized that there was no passage from our hall to the hall where the hostages were being held] and continued on with Rani towards the entrance to the second floor.

6. I stationed Rani on the second floor and went out to the balcony. I checked that there was no one out there and then called Rani to come and clear the roof with me. We took the stairs up to the roof and scanned it with flashlights [during the planning stage, Yoni had not authorized personnel to go up to the roof, so as to avoid being hit by fire from the control tower. I didn't argue with him then, but decided in advance to make a decision based on my read of the situation on the ground]. We saw no one and returned to Amir.

7. I radioed Arnon and he reported not being able to find the stairs. I left Rani and Amir upstairs to provide cover and went down to meet up with Arnon. At the foot of the stairs on the right I spotted another Ugandan soldier hiding behind a counter. I shot him and he hid behind a safe for cover. I went upstairs, [swerved] around Rani, and threw a grenade that exploded near us, and again we opened fire, but I was not sure he'd been hit. I ran over to the safe and found him off to the side and shot him.

8. We returned to the main entrance and linked up with Arnon. We saw there was nothing for us to do. We made another

sweep all the way to the BTR Force [the armored personnel carriers] on the far side. During the sweep, we saw a figure reflected in the glass. Amir turned around and killed him. After meeting up with Udi [Salvi] we spotted another man. We shot him too. While in motion and while searching the complex on our way back to the main force, we spotted two more soldiers and we killed them.

9. Afterwards we linked up with the force and began evacuating as planned.

10. Summary:

A. Not a single shot was fired at us.

B. In the building we found indications that at least sixty other soldiers had slept there and managed to flee.

C. We found only one weapon (we didn't conduct a search) and brought it back with us [to the Unit's base].

D. The Yaror [tactical flashlight] proved itself despite the danger of self-exposure.

E. The pre-op intel on our hall was not precise.

F. All told, we killed around 11 soldiers, all Ugandan.

G. There was no one on the roof, despite our concerns.

H. The sweep upstairs was very quick, which made it hard for Arnon to close the gap, and left exposed areas to our rear that were not fully swept.

Brig.-Gen. (ret) Yiftach Reicher-Atir, born and raised on Kibbutz Shoval, is married and a father of four. Reicher-Atir, prior to his arrival at the Unit, served as commander of the paratroop recon unit, Sayeret Tzanchanim. In the Unit he served as commander of the training company and deputy commander of the Unit (under Yoni Netanyahu, may he rest in peace, and Amiram Levin). His last IDF post was as military attaché to Japan. After several years in the venture capital industry, he decided to change career paths and now works as an author. One of his novels, The English Teacher, *was later made into a movie.*

Second Lt. Rani Cohen, Team Leader
Yiftach Squad Operator; Yoni's Assault Force
Ugandan Soldiers Hall

MY OPERATION YONATAN (ENTEBBE)

Preparations

July 1976 found me in the midst of my service as a team commander, leading the August 1975 team through its many months of training. During the week between the plane hijacking and the rescue operation we were in the field and not truly aware of the brewing drama. On Thursday evening, once preparations in the Unit began in earnest, I was selected as a member of Yiftach's squad along with Amir Shadmi. Our role was to clear the part of the building where, according to intelligence reports, the Ugandan soldiers were stationed. We began to study the scant intelligence information and started obtaining the necessary gear. I remember debating whether I should stick with the AK (Kalashnikov) or swap it for an Uzi, which was a more effective tool in close quarters. The rationale for sticking with the AK was its superiority in the field, which could come in handy were we prevented from taking off from Entebbe and forced to retreat, over-road, to Kenya. In the end I decided that since the heart of the mission was seizing control of the building—the Uzi was best.

During the day on Friday I prepared my gear, checked my weapon, and reviewed the available intelligence information. Our squad was slated to ride in the first jeep, behind the Mercedes, and to enter through the terminal's first entrance—the customs hall—from where stairs were supposed to lead to the second floor, up to the Ugandan soldiers' quarters. Our instructions were to get up to the second floor as fast as possible because it was believed that another set of stairs led straight down to the large hall, where the hostages were being kept; at minimum, we were told, the hall could be controlled by fire from above.

On Friday night we ran through a ragtag simulation drill in which the building was marked out in white tape and burlap cloth. We rode for a very short distance, charged through the openings in the tape, and yelled "Bang! Bang!" Not for a second did I believe that this mission would be authorized. It was clear to me that the preparations were in vain, and yet, as with every operation, we treated the process with utmost sincerity and attention to detail.

The Operation

On Saturday morning we loaded our gear, and ourselves, aboard the planes headed to Sharm al-Sheikh, at the southernmost tip of the Sinai Peninsula. The flight was terrible—the planes flew at a very low altitude, jolting horribly in midair and we all vomited and felt truly awful. We landed in Sharm and were able to recuperate a little on the ground, despite the oppressive July desert heat.

In Sharm, we received photos taken by the pilot of a light aircraft who'd flown over the airfield and photographed the front of the old terminal building. In the photos I could very clearly see our entrance and the control tower, beneath which we were to park, filling in the gaps in the intelligence picture in my mind. As far as the interior of the building was concerned, though, there was still much that was unknown: the stairs, access to the hostage hall, etc.

Yoni gave a final briefing before departure and we boarded the planes for the long flight knowing that the government had yet to authorize the mission. Unperturbed, confident in the knowledge that there would be no authorization, and utterly fatigued after a week in the field followed by two sleepless nights of preparations, I slept the sleep of the dead for the entire flight. Shortly before landing, I was awoken and only then did I realize that we had not been turned back. We really were going to execute this mission.

I suited up and got organized on the jeep. As we began our descent, I remember seeing the sight of the moon reflected in the waters of Lake Victoria—a serene sight and the calm before the storm. As we approached, I caught a glimpse of the new terminal, lights blazing. The landing was perfect—soft and smooth. The plane hit the runway and started to taxi. The paratroopers jumped out the side doors to mark the runway in case the edge lights were extinguished. We reached our disembarkation point, the cargo ramp came down, and we rolled out into a warm, humid, and very quiet night.

We drove toward the old terminal in a completely ordinary manner—headlights on, normal speed. Shortly after turning onto the taxiway that led to the terminal, we encountered the two Ugandan sentries. I was on the right side of the jeep and saw only the soldier on my side. He stood in a firing position and yelled something. He was shot from within the Mercedes; I saw him fall but he kept on moving. I fired a few well-aimed semi-automatic rounds at him until we drove past.

After the live-fire clash, we accelerated and then parked more or less in the intended spot beneath the control tower. All was silent; there were no shots fired. I remember thinking to myself that the drivers had parked in a very orderly fashion—diagonal to the curb, neatly spaced, one next to the other, as though we were at a mall in Israel.

The mad dash began. We tumbled out of the vehicles and started to charge towards the building. I stuck close to Yiftach and my mind was set solely on that objective: not losing him. In mid-run, for no apparent reason, there was what seemed like a procedural stop, on account of Muki's pause. I heard Yoni yell, "Betser, forward," and then we continued to advance. We swerved around Muki, standing at the corner of the building, and charged in through our entrance.

The building was brightly lit. I found myself in the customs hall, with marked lanes and low counters on which luggage could be placed. Yiftach and I ran through the hall (I can't remember if Shadmi was with us at this stage) and hit a wide staircase off to our right, ascending to the second floor. We took it at a run and reached a long corridor that again cut right, parallel to the hall we'd just come from. I saw the entrance to the large hall, where the hostages were kept, but it was barred by a solid steel grille. I also noted that there was no advantageous position overlooking the hostage hall. On our way into the building and up the stairs we encountered several Ugandan soldiers; they were racing towards us and we shot them.

We ran through the corridor, which opened to a cafeteria on the left (with a service counter and a closed wooden shutter) and many sleeping bags laid out across the floor. There were no soldiers present; they'd all managed to run away. Off to the right, opposite the cafeteria, there was a door that opened onto the roof. Yiftach and I went out and scanned the roof (above the customs hall) and found nothing. The control tower, looming above us, was already under heavy fire.

We went back inside and began combing our way back through the cafeteria and along the corridor. Suddenly the lights went out (we later learned that one of our perimeter-security forces had shot the generator), and so we proceeded with our tactical flashlights. Suddenly I saw a Ugandan soldier right in front of me. I shot him. I heard the sound of glass shattering and he disappeared. It was a mirror…we scanned the customs hall and exited at the front of the building, near where the vehicles were parked. I saw the hostages being evacuated to the plane—a large crowd of bewildered people being led by a smattering of soldiers—slightly resembling a herd led by a bunch of cowboys. Once the hostage evacuation was complete and the plane airborne, we packed it up, turned toward the remaining planes, and took off for Nairobi, where Ehud boarded and informed us that Yoni had been killed.

Back to Israel

After the pitstop in Nairobi we took off for the long leg home. This time I did not fall asleep. The adrenalin was flowing too thick for that. We landed at Tel Nof, ravaged the food they set out for us, and sat down to listen to Rabin (the prime minister) and Peres (the defense minister) tell us how heroic we were and how grateful the entire nation was to us…

Afterwards we drove back to base I called home to let my parents know that all was okay and then, just like every other Sunday, started a new week of training with my team.

Maj. (res) Rani Cohen served in the Unit as an operator and team leader from 1973-1978 and for 25 more years as a reservist in the IAF's Shaldag unit. An engineer and a manager in the high-tech industry, he is a father of four and a grandfather to five.

Staff.-Sgt. Yonatan Gilad, Team Dani
Squad Arnon Operator, Yoni's Assault Force;
Customs Hall

ENTEBBE—THOUGHTS AND EXPERIENCES

I've spoken many times about Operation Entebbe, in front of school classes and adults. Over the years I've put together a presentation that tells the story from a variety of perspectives: that of the government, the upper echelons of the IDF command, the hostages, and the soldiers who freed them—us. I gleaned the additional material from two books: *Flight 139* by Ben Porat, Eitan Haber, and Ze'ev Schiff, and *Operation Thunderbolt* by Avigdor Shahan. In the presentation, I proceed chronologically from the day of the hijacking to the day of liberation—each day with its own specific aspects.

The myriad thoughts that emerge each time I prepare to present the matter before an audience have brought several realizations to the fore:

A. The success of the operation is the result of comprehensive military planning. With all due respect to us, the executors of the mission, we could not, in our engagement with the hijackers and the hijacked, have managed to reach that point without the creative and thorough work of the planners. Personally, in my private life and professionally, I very much value the planning stage, the predecessor to action.

B. When I tried to put myself in the shoes of the decision-makers (the government and the IDF command) I found myself fully aware of the enormous responsibility resting upon their shoulders, and of the necessity of making a decision even amid life-threatening uncertainty. I've never filled such a role, but an appraisal from afar makes it's clear that these decision-makers must have uncommon capacities and skills, which are not always adequately appreciated by the public.

C. I was surprised to find that there was no pre-existing plan or idea in place addressing such a scenario, especially in light of the numerous plane hijackings at the time and the fact that Israel was a central target of those actions.

D. If you look back and see the actual content of the hijackers' ultimatum, the list of their demands, which, if fulfilled, would secure the release of the hostages, and you weigh that against the enormous risk taken by executing the mission, it becomes clear that the decision to authorize the mission was surreal and utterly unreasonable. It's important to recognize that the legend built around the success of the mission is completely unrelated to the decision of whether or not to carry out the hostage-rescue, a goal that could have been attained at insignificant cost, and, certainly, far less than the sums paid by Israel in future years.

E. In my eyes the heroic decisions made during the planning stage are:

1. The decision to plan in separate teams so that creative and diverse ideas were given space to grow.

2. The understanding that the Israel Air Force had to lead the planning stage, with a focus on how to transport the troops to the site, rather than engaging in Hollywood-like fantasies of John Rambo coming to the rescue.

3. The decision to incorporate the accidental idea of arriving at the airport with a surprise landing as a central element of the plan, alongside the creative notion of how best to approach that landing even if confronted with a darkened runway.

4. The deployment of the squad that hopped off the lead plane and lit the runway for the following three aircraft, which enabled them to land in the dark.

5. Our ability to properly carry out our roles, which we'd drilled only one day prior.

My personal Experiences:

* During training the day before the mission (Friday) I disclosed to our team commander, Dani Arditi, that I was scared. He offered me the option of not participating and I chose to participate despite the fear. I think that having a commander with whom you can share those sorts of feelings is evidence of an unusual and extraordinary relationship.

* The fact that there were those who participated in the mission not on account of what they were able to bring to the table operationally but as a result of their ability to bring political pressure to bear on the decision-makers was a prologue to lessons learnt later in life.

* When disembarking from the jeep my foot got stuck between the body of the vehicle and the seat. It took me a few seconds to pull it free and I ran in alone, trailing my squad. I knew where to run (in other words, I knew exactly what we'd drilled and what I was supposed to do) and I joined my squad (linking up with Amir Shadmi).

* While running alone toward the building I passed a wounded soldier (I later realized—it was Yoni Netanyahu). I thought and considered the matter and decided that, though I was a medic, I had to continue into the battle and only afterwards tend to the wounded. I've thought many times about the way that the army trains you to pass by a wounded person and not stop to help him. I have no regrets because that was the right thing to do at that time and I have no information as to whether I could have done anything to save him, nor about the course of treatment he received.

* Once the shooting was over, I bandaged up the wounded hostages in the main hall. I don't know the course of treatment they received subsequently. Later on, I was informed that two of them died of their wounds. Over the years I've gone back and thought: could I have done anything that would have saved their lives?

Staff-Sgt. Yonatan Gilad was born in Kibbutz Mishmar HaEmek. He served in the Unit from 1974-1977 as a member of Team Dani Arditi. He has an MSc in civil engineering from the Technion Israel Institute of Technology and is the owner of a construction management and oversight firm in the north of Israel. Yonatan is married and a father of four and a grandfather of two.

Sgt. Pinchas Buchris, Team Arnon

Arnon Squad (Yiftach); Yoni's Assault Force; Customs Hall

THE STORY OF OPERATION ENTEBBE

On Sunday June 27, 1976 we gathered at the base after a weekend off. While getting organized for the coming week's training exercise, we heard the Unit's PA system come to life with an emergency alert about a plane hijacking. We dropped what we were doing, grabbed the relevant duffels, loaded them onto trucks, and drove to the assembly area at the international airport in Lod. We organized the gear and the vehicles and were drilled for the takeover of a hijacked plane.

Here's what happened that morning: An Air France plane, en route from Tel Aviv to Paris, stopped in Athens, and, after takeoff, terrorists hijacked the plane. There were many passengers on board, including a large number of Israelis and Jews, which triggered the counter-terror alarm at our base.

We waited a few hours at the airport assembly area, then we returned to the Unit to do some more waiting from slightly farther away. In the meanwhile, the week of training was cancelled. Monday was spent waiting; we didn't do much else on Tuesday, Wednesday, and Thursday. The truth is, we played rounds of bridge to pass the time. By Thursday, we were already joking that maybe we should just fly to Entebbe and free the hostages. Everything changed early on Friday morning. We were woken with a loud commotion: "Get up, get up, we're flying to Entebbe."

Those who were slated to participate received a gear list. Mine included the full kit of a MAG machine-gunner, and I was shocked to see, when I went to fill it, that the quartermaster's supply store and the armory had been thrown wide open; anyone could take what they needed. The most interesting items on my list were tiger-stripe fatigues and a green beret.

Five operators from my platoon were chosen to participate in the rescue mission. We were the greenest team in the operational company. We'd finished our training and joined the company only several months earlier. I felt considerable pride to have been chosen by our team leader, Arnon Epstein. He gave us an initial briefing, an overview, and informed us that later that afternoon, at 14:00 hours, we should be alongside the runways of an old, nearby airport.

A Hercules aircraft waited for us on the ground. We practiced loading and unloading the vehicles. We practiced securing the vehicles inside the plane and releasing them. We realized that this was the most crucial element and so we were asked to perform it perfectly.

While running through the drill I saw combat troops from the Golani and Paratroop Brigades approach the runway. They arrived after a week of training. I was quite surprised. I asked a few of them if they knew why they'd been called. Their response: "No. They told us to come, so we came." After drilling the quick loading and unloading of the vehicles via the cargo ramp, we returned to our rooms and continued organizing our gear.

No one filled us in on what was happening; it was all top secret. We weren't allowed to call home to let our families know we wouldn't be getting out for the weekend and certainly not to tell them that we were going to be taking part in the hostage-rescue operation at Entebbe. I think the Unit even disconnected the outgoing phone lines, making it impossible to call home.

Early on Friday evening we were given a briefing that included some of the details of the plan; it was all very vague and approximate. We didn't know much. There was a lack of intelligence information. At the same time, on the runways near the Unit's offices, soldiers built a model of the old terminal at Entebbe. The structure was made out of long metal poles, burlap cloth, and white marking tape.

The commanders of the operation and those in charge within the military decided to limit the number of operators taking part in the rescue operation. Naturally, most of the soldiers cut from the roster were from the greenest team, Team Arnon. Of the initial five, only three of us remained. We all had a bad feeling and I felt my turn on the cutting block was coming.

At around nine in the evening, we headed out on our first model simulation. We were briefed by Yoni and others. A Hercules aircraft, with the vehicles already loaded up on the plane, took part in the drill. The C-130 taxied and stopped; we released the vehicles, drove for a bit, stopped the vehicles, and each squad ran to complete its mission. I stuck close to Arnon, my team leader. The simulation was so unclear that I simply followed Arnon; whatever he did, I did. I was not able to picture the old terminal on the basis of the mock drill.

After the first run-through, we assembled on the runway for a debriefing, and afterwards Yoni (I think) said that there was no way we'd arrive at the terminal without first encountering some sort of interceptive force. Therefore, two soldiers were taken and posted as sentries outside the terminal, simulating an opposition force. We did the drill again, this time with the sentries. I think we shot and eliminated the mock enemy troops, and then each squad ran towards its task. Once again, I stuck close to Arnon, my platoon commander. Afterwards there was another debriefing; lessons were learnt and then we scattered and went back to our gear.

While getting organized, I looked over the scant auxiliary intelligence material at our disposal. There were old aerial photos of the airport at Entebbe, and I studied the location of the runways, the spot where the planes were to stop, and the drive to the old terminal.

During the course of the night, my team was forced to cut two more operators from the roster. I was the last man standing from my platoon. Once again, I grew quite concerned that I was next in line… the youngest soldier in the Unit still slated to participate. It was all too clear to me that during the next round of cuts I was likely to find myself excluded from the mission. It stressed me out as I very much wanted to take part.

Later that night I bumped into Eyal Oren, an operator I knew from before I was inducted into the Unit. I asked him when it would be my turn to be let go; he looked at me and said: "You, you're not getting cut." I breathed easier but remained on edge. I had the feeling that it still might come. I went to sleep late at night, once everything was set for the Saturday morning pre-mission inspection. In the morning, Arnon inspected our gear and made sure that everything was adequately prepared. We were briefed once again and then we got organized for the ride to the IAF base adjacent to Ben-Gurion Airport.

Once all the preparations were done, I found myself in an idle state. I sunk into thoughts about the mission. We knew we were carrying only enough fuel for one leg of the trip. What would happen if we weren't able to re-fuel? What else might happen? I thought long and hard about whether I should leave a letter for my parents in case I didn't make it back. To be honest, that was my most trying moment of the entire operation. Up until then there had not been a second to dwell on such matters; we were too busy and focused on the preparations.

On Saturday at around 11:00 hours an army bus took us to the IAF airbase at Lod; the Unit's female clerks accompanied us on the trip. At the IAF base we loaded the vehicles onto the Hercules and took off for Sharm el-Sheikh. That airbase, near the tip of the Sinai Peninsula, was the southernmost point at which we could top-off the fuel tanks before the operation. We landed there, got a final briefing, and were shown new photos that the intelligence officers had managed to procure. My squad received new orders and our point of entry was changed: instead of using a side door, we were now to use the front entrance.

After the briefing, we waited for authorization from Tel Aviv. Throughout, we were dressed in ordinary Israeli army uniforms; the tiger-stripe fatigues were in our duffels. Only with authorization were we to put them on.

The Government of Israel had announced that it would not free jailed terrorists, meaning that the hijackers' ultimatum was to expire at midnight on Saturday, 3 July 1976. Our time schedule was set so that we would land one hour before the expiry of the ultimatum. At 15:30 or so on Saturday, we were given the order to board the aircraft. It was decided that we would take off in advance of a government decision. We promptly changed our clothes and donned the tiger-stripe uniforms and the green berets. We put on our battle vests and boarded the planes.

Brig.-Gen. Dan Shomron, the commander of the operation, stood alongside us. He gave the order to board the planes and then suddenly saw us start to strip down and change uniforms. He was, to put it mildly, not pleased. The truth is, I wasn't sure he was even aware of this element of the operation. We got organized quickly and loaded ourselves onto the Hercules.

I was on the first plane, seated on the second Land Rover, on the left side of the plane.

During takeoff I felt giddy. The Hercules C-130 was packed. The soldiers from the Unit sat on the vehicles; the soldiers from the Paratroop Brigade were stuffed in on either side of the plane. Sometime after takeoff they gave us word that the operation had been approved. I felt a burst of happiness mixed with an enormous burst of adrenalin. I don't remember much else from the flight. Once the mission was authorized, I fell asleep, apparently quite exhausted. They say that at some point the aircraft hit a lightning storm. I remember no such thing.

Around half an hour before landing, an alarm went off in the cabin. We readied ourselves for landing. I remember that Yoni Netanyahu got out of the Mercedes and made the rounds among the operators from the Unit. He shook hands, wished us each good luck. When he made it over to me, I smiled. He put his hand on my head and said: "What are you smiling at, Buchris?" and then shook my hand and went back to the Mercedes.

The Hercules landed. I remember looking at my watch; it was 23:00. I thought to myself: this is the last time I'll be looking at my watch… the wheels touched down and the plane taxied on the runway. The paratroopers jumped off at a run to mark the runway with torches—to replace the edge lights in the event that the air-traffic controllers decided to darken the runway. This was something we were concerned about but prepared for. The Hercules stopped, the Mercedes rolled out, followed by the first Land Rover and the second Land Rover, in which I was sitting, back row, far left. The excitement was enormous; I remember the coolness of the air. I tried to orient myself as the vehicles headed toward the old terminal.

Then, as we approached, I saw two Ugandan guards. Their presence made it clear to me that our preparations had been done properly. For the first time, I felt that the rescue operation was going to be a success. We heard gunshots fired at the sentries. A loud burst of fire was directed at the guard on the left, who had started to flee. Then I heard someone yell: "Buchris, fire!" I shot the fleeing sentry. The third burst from the heavy machine gun eliminated him. (Later I learned that it was Amnon Peled who had given the order.)

At that moment, the operation shifted gears. It was now loud and overt and the vehicles stopped before the agreed-upon point; everyone jumped out and raced to clear their halls. My platoon commander and I were part of Yiftach Reicher's squad. Our role was to clear the terminal's first complex, alongside the large hall in which the hostages were being kept. While jumping out of the Land Rover, the strap of my MAG machine-gun got stuck on the seat bench. It took me several seconds to tear it loose, and then I found myself all alone. I tried to run, but my legs felt stuck. I said to myself, Buchris, run, and then I started to run; I felt like I was running on marbles. Apparently as a result of fear.

As I mentioned earlier, I had not been able to orient myself in the compound during the Friday drill. Instead, I had stuck close to Arnon. Only now he was nowhere to be found; he had charged ahead. I came to my senses and realized where I had to go. I went into the first complex of rooms in the terminal. As I entered, I saw, in the middle of the room, soldiers in tiger-stripe uniforms sprawled out on the floor. I thought the losses were ours. Drawing near, I saw they were Ugandan and exhaled. I continued to advance, tried to link up with the rest of my squad. I employed the usual agreed-upon signs for linking up, but was certainly concerned about friendly fire. Thankfully, the unification worked. I met the other members of the squad as they returned from the first complex of rooms.

We were supposed to head up a flight of stairs to an upper level. The stairway was locked, the door refused to give. We tried the usual drill, but it didn't work. I asked them to clear out of the way and to let me see if the MAG could coax the door open. A short burst of fire and the door gave way. Yiftach and a few other operators raced up the stairs and came back down a short while later. As we returned to the complex of rooms, I noticed a door opening to my right. I released a burst of fire and told the rest of the squad that there were people inside. The guys moved in and took care of the matter.

Once we'd completed our mission, we set off to assist other parts of the force, as necessary. We moved toward the entrance of the large hall and saw a figure face down on the ground. The Unit's doctor, David Hassin, and I approached. We flipped him over and saw that it was Yoni Netanyahu, the commander of the Unit. Hassin immediately started treating him. (This incident has a few different versions of events, but this is how I remember it.) Just then, someone in the control tower opened fire. I immediately responded with automatic fire. Everyone around me returned fire at the tower and as MAG operator I had an advantage of fire power. The angle, though, prevented us from firing effectively at the tower and we were not able to eliminate the terrorist or soldier entrenched there. A short while later Mofaz's armored force joined the fray. I must say that their arrival contributed significantly to my sense of security, knowing that there was now an appropriate amount of fire power for backup against the control tower. Eyal Yardenay, who'd arrived with the force on a jeep, was armed with an RPG, which he fired, silencing the control tower.

Once the tower had been neutralized, we were able to start scanning the area to make sure that there were no terrorists or Ugandan soldiers still hiding out. Yiftach Reicher's squad was tasked with scanning a dark corridor, a hallway that divided the complex of rooms that we'd cleared with the main hall, where the hostages had been kept. Arnon and I were stationed at the entrance to the corridor to make sure that none of our soldiers entered by mistake. After a while, I felt something or somebody touching my shoulder and mumbling in a language I didn't understand. At first I thought it was someone from Yiftach's squad; I turned my head, though, and saw that it was a huge Ugandan soldier, towering over me, the barrel of his rifle grazing my neck. I immediately realized that shooting him with the MAG would be cumbersome. I yelled to Arnon: "Someone's over me, shoot him." And he fired a shot over my head and killed him. At that moment I realized that the tiger-stripe uniform I was wearing, had probably saved my life. The Ugandan had thought I was a fellow Ugandan soldier. That incident gave me pause, with thoughts circling in my mind about what might have been.

After the terminal was fully cleared, we started evacuating the hostages. The evacuation took a long time, around half an hour. I remember that whenever the hostages went outside and heard gunfire, they promptly ducked back into the building. In the end, all of the hostages in the terminal were evacuated, including those wounded during the raid, and then they were loaded onto the fourth Hercules, which took off several minutes before midnight.

When the hostages had flown off, we started the process of making sure that everyone was accounted for. In my squad we were missing Udi Bloch (an operator from Yoni Raz's team). Someone said he had helped evacuate the hostages; later we found him. The first Hercules on the ground was the last one to leave. It was a few minutes after midnight. Once again, I looked at my watch. The feeling was stupendous, an immense sense of accomplishment. Our Hercules took off and I thought we were headed back to Israel. I didn't realize that they hadn't managed to fill up the tanks at Entebbe. Later I was told that we were going to land in Kenya to refuel.

We touched down in Nairobi and met up with Ehud Barak. He

updated us that Yoni had been killed. The news brought a great sadness to me and yet at the same time, the wonderful feeling of success remained. Those two feelings managed to coexist in me. I identified the sensation to myself; it was oil and water, two things that cannot be combined.

On the way back to Israel, the pilots tried to pick up Israeli news on the radio. They found it, but the reception was patchy. We landed at the IAF base in Tel Nof.

We returned to the Unit tired but content. Of course, we were not permitted to take part in any of the celebrations across the country marking the success of the mission.

For years I said nothing about the operation. Years later I was appointed commander of Unit 8200, the IDF's signals intelligence unit. Younger soldiers learned that I'd taken part in the Entebbe rescue mission and promptly began asking for personal stories from me.

While serving as commander of Unit 8200, I decided to promote one of my officers, Lt.-Col Ron to the rank of Colonel and to put him in command of one of the most unique centers in the unit. I interviewed him before making the decision. The officer was skilled and talented and worthy of the job, and nothing out of the ordinary came up.

The promotion ceremony took place in the IDF Chief of Staff's office. A woman came up to me and introduced herself as Ron's mother. She said there was something that I ought to know about Ron; he was one of the hostages at Entebbe. A tremor passed through me…later on I appointed him as my second-in-command. For a full year both the commander of the IDF's Unit 8200 and his deputy were a rescuer and a hostage at Entebbe! Such is life!

After I retired from the army, I joined a company: Apax Partners Private Equity. It was decided that we needed a manager in Human Resources and when I first met with the new employee she told me that she was the granddaughter of Dora Bloch the elderly hostage who had been murdered—out of sheer rage—by Idi Amin's men after the completion of the operation. She had been hospitalized a day earlier and was missing from the list of people we were able to rescue.

Lastly, I would like to refute a legend in which it's said that I was dressed up as Idi Amin...that never happened...the only thing that is true is that we arrived with a Mercedes and two Land Rovers so as to appear like a presidential delegation.

To my delight there are several pictures of our return to Israel. I'm in one of them, and I submit it as evidence of the fictional nature of the story. Only our little country is capable of coming up with such stories...

Brig.-Gen. (res) Pinchas Buchris is a brother to two operators who served in Unit. He was drafted in 1974 to Noah Kravetsky's team, then served in Arnon's team, and finally in Loni Raphaeli's. He served for three years as a soldier in the Unit, was sent to officer candidate school by Amiram Levin, and returned to the Unit as a team leader. He filled that and other command roles in the military, including serving as commander of Unit 8200. He is an engineer by training. He served as Dir.-Gen. of the Israel Defense Ministry and later as a CEO in the energy sector. He founded State of Mind Ventures, a venture capital fund that invests in cyber security and other technological start-ups.

Staff-Sgt. Amos Goren, Operator in Team Omer
Member of Muki's squad, Yoni's Assault Force, Hostage Hall

MEMORIES FROM ENTEBBE

The Entebbe story started just as our team, Team Omer, became the senior team of operators in the Unit. Several of the Unit's other teams were in the Sinai training for another mission while we were at our home base, preparing intensively for a complex and clandestine mission, the sort of thing that—unless it fails—is never made public and was to take place a couple of months after Entebbe. On Sunday, the day the Air France plane was hijacked, we rushed to Lod airport to be on high alert, anticipating that the plane might land there and a hostage-rescue operation might be required at the airport. Once the hijacked plane had left Benghazi in Libya and landed in Entebbe, it became clear that a hostage rescue operation would not be required at Lod, and we went back to our training routine. Throughout the week there was constant chatter about a variety of ways of possibly rescuing the hostages. One I recall specifically was this: Our operatives would parachute into Lake Victoria with inflatable assault boats, attack the terrorists, release the hostages, load them on the assault boats and rendezvous with a rented yacht arriving from the Kenyan side of the lake. None of the ideas, however, each of which seemed unfeasible and unreasonable in its own way, ever developed into a concrete plan. The fundamental assumption was that there was no accomplishable military solution. Only on Thursday did any sort of real activity begin and then Amnon Peled's team, which had been released on pre-discharge vacation, was called back to the base.

On Friday morning, as the operational order was read, we learnt that we were assigned to the BTR-40 force. Our role was to man the small Russian armored personnel carriers and isolate the old terminal. In other words, to secure the southeastern flank of the terminal, which faced a Ugandan military base that housed air force planes. These APCs would be equipped with heavy arms, in case we had to fight Ugandan army regulars. Stage two, once the terrorists were killed and the hostages rescued, had us maintaining the perimeter until the last of the hostages was evacuated, at which point we were to roll the APCs up the plane ramps and fly out.

Truthfully, we were a bit disappointed. We were a veteran and very experienced team. We'd been through a number of hostage-rescue operations and quite a few of the Unit's covert operations and wanted to be at the center of this mission, part of the lead assault team. At least that's what I thought. But because of the extremely important covert mission which we were planned to execute two months later, it was decided to reduce our chances of being harmed and therefore we were not in the lead assault force. The APC force also ran the risk of coming into harm's way; the entire operation entailed a high degree of risk, but it simply stood to reason that the assault team faced the greatest danger. It would land first, attack the heavily guarded terminal building and charge through the doors of the passenger terminal to eliminate the terrorists. Although I wanted to be in that critical role, I understood the considerations and reluctantly accepted them.

And in that way, we switched gears, shifting from intensive preparation for a clandestine mission to Entebbe.

The preparation stage was very brief. We had one 24-hour cycle at our disposal, and it, too, was shadowed by doubt as to whether the operation would ever be approved by the government. During the day, we prepared our gear, weapons and vehicles, sat through briefings, and conducted brief drills. Each element of the Unit's force focused on its specific role. The nighttime simulation drill gave us a sense of perspective in terms of the distances and proportions and afforded us an opportunity to study the stages and embed them in our memory. The tight time schedule made this preparatory stage utterly different from the usual, clandestine missions that the Unit executed. I'm thinking, for example, of the evasion and escape maps we were given. We were accustomed to the most detailed preparations imaginable, with constant analysis of an array of possible actions and reactions: if X happens, we'll do Y, so as to be prepared for a wide range of possible scenarios. In this case, there was something ridiculous about the evasion and escape maps. Obviously, someone thought that we needed to address an eventuality in which, for instance, the planes were hit and we weren't able to fly back home. If that happened, they said, get on the vehicles and if our vehicles are destroyed then get your hands on some others and head east, as indicated on the maps, till you reach Kenya, where there'll be people waiting for you. Or, in other words: you're on your own. But as an experienced soldier you learn to put that aside. You immerse yourself in the preparations, in the job at hand, and aren't really bothered by what's happening all around.

On Saturday, in the afternoon, we took off from Lod to Sharm. The flight was horrific. It was very hot and sticky, the planes flew at a very low altitude, under enemy radar, and we sweated and vomited, despite all the motion sickness pills we'd taken. All we could manage, once we'd landed at Sharm, was to lie still in a shaded corner trying to recuperate from the flight. The government had not yet given its approval but it was clear that the time table was such that we would soon either have to take-off for Entebbe or pack it up and go home. And then Omer Bar Lev, my team CO, approached me. "You're joining the lead assault team," he said, "you're replacing N. in Muki Betser's entry squad."

Instantly, the nausea vanished and my pulse quickened. Muki's squad was one of the two squads of 4 soldiers each that was to charge into the hall where the hostages were being held and eliminate the terrorists. I suddenly remembered the Savoy Hotel, one year prior, in March 1975. An eight-member squad of PLO terrorists had managed to land on the beach of Tel Aviv in an inflatable assault boat and stormed the Savoy Hotel, where they took hotel guests hostage. We were a relatively inexperienced team then and they put us in a location where contact with the terrorists was considered less likely. Stationed at the rear entrance of the hotel, we were to charge in along with the rest of the forces who were entering simultaneously from 3 other directions. Just as the assault was initiated, the terrorists detonated a major explosive device. My team charged in from the rear. We got stymied by a door at the entrance to the hotel and somehow I found a side entrance that led to a hallway and a flight of stairs. I sprinted up the main stairs and found myself on the third floor, one of the first to arrive outside the room where the hostages were being held, the room in which the explosive device had just been detonated.

There's nothing trivial about moving from one force to another, especially in an operation running on such a short time schedule. The drills and preparations I'd done as part of the APC perimeter force were very different from the ones done by the assault force; nor had I studied the detailed aerial photos and blueprints of the terminal building. The assault force, flying on the first plane and slated to drive in with the Mercedes and the Land Rovers, had drilled the mission on a mock-up model on which the terminal doors and the vehicle access routes were clearly marked. They'd practiced driving off the plane and arriving at the terminal, stopping outside the hostage hall and charging into the terminal building. They knew the location of the entrances, the shape of the halls, the size of the rooms. They'd practiced by day and by night, repeatedly, so that the choreography of it was etched into their memory.

With very little time at our disposal, I had to swap all my gear, including my weapon and uniform. In the APCs we were dressed in regular army fatigues, but the assault force, arriving on the Land Rovers and the Mercedes, were deceptively dressed in Ugandan military jungle camouflage fatigues. I changed uniforms and battle vests and took N.'s pack with the special explosive devices, to be used in case we needed to detonate doors or locks, and a megaphone, to call out to the hostages as we entered the hall.

Once I was geared up and had made sure that I had everything and that all was in working order, Muki came over to me and said: "During the flight Yoni and I will explain your role to you."

The Hercules C-130 was loud and crowded but the flight was relatively mellow and thankfully set at a normal cruising altitude. Twenty minutes after take-off, Yoni and Muki called me over for a briefing. We sat on the rear ramp of the Hercules, which, when closed, provided a comfortable sitting angle. Yoni took an air-sickness bag and started sketching the terminal buildings. He drew the control tower and the passenger hall, the spot where we might encounter the first Ugandan guards, the point where we'd disembark from the vehicles, and the route the assault squads would take on the way to the terminal. He went over the directions: "You run in from here; you and Muki go in through the first entrance; Amnon and his squad charge in through the second entrance…" I sat down in the Mercedes staring at the air-sickness bag with the sketches and tried to envision each stage and to commit it to memory. There's a reason why these model drills are always done on real structures. Muscle memory, exercised on the ground, is very different from cerebral memory, where you try to internalize action through your mind. But I understood my role, and Muki, who knew I hadn't been part of the training and drills, told me to stick close to him. I folded up the motion-sickness bag, put it into one of my pockets, and fell asleep.

The next thing I remember is being woken up and then putting on my battle vest and, weapon in hand, taking my spot in the Mercedes. The drowsiness of sleep and Dramamine was swapped by a feeling of tense readiness. The plane landed and the door opened. Outside there was total silence and absolute darkness. It was warm and humid and the air carried the strong smell of earth and vegetation, as in a forest or a field after a steady rain.

The drive in the Mercedes was calm, practically routine. All seemed in order. And then came the clash with the Ugandan soldiers. During the drills and preparations this moment had been noted as a nuance, a possibility. During the flight, too, Yoni had marked this spot as a possible first engagement with the Ugandans. And there I was, sitting in the back of the Mercedes, on the righthand side, watching two Ugandan sentries raise their rifles to a firing position. To me it looked like they were getting ready to fire. There was a short exchange between Yoni and Muki. Muki said: "Don't shoot." Yoni said: "Shoot," and then they were shot. At first with silenced pistols. The Ugandan on the right fell; he was hit but not eliminated. It's hard to aim from a moving car, especially with a handgun, even if the target is close, a mere five to six meters away. A burst of automatic fire from the vehicle behind us finished off the Ugandan but also violated the complete silence. Amitzur, the Mercedes driver, accelerated, as did Yardenay, the driver of the first Land Rover, and Uri Ben-Ner, the driver of the second Land Rover. The convoy stopped a few seconds after the encounter with the Ugandan sentries and the force members poured out of the three vehicles

Not having taken part in the drills, I wasn't sure what precisely was supposed to take place from that moment on, the exact order of events, who passes whom. I knew that the first entrance to the passenger hall was situated beneath a pergola on our left and that I was supposed to run there along with Muki. Off to my right, I saw Ugandan soldiers spread out in a parallel line to the building. We shot them as we ran. The transition, from the moment the Mercedes stopped to the sprint to the passenger hall, took about five or ten seconds but in my mind it seemed like an eternity. I stuck close to Muki, who ran toward the building while firing ahead, but then, for reasons that I could not discern at the time, he stopped and the force stopped behind him. I heard Yoni yell to run forward. Amnon and Amir kept on running and Muki and I ran after them. We missed the entrance that we were supposed to burst through, the first one, perhaps it was blocked. Out of the corner of my eye, while running, I saw Yoni fall. I didn't know if he'd tripped or been hit.

The passenger hall was completely illuminated. As I entered the room, I had a quick flashback from the Savoy Hotel operation. At the Savoy there were dozens of rooms spread out across three floors. The terrorists detonated a big device in the stairwell, total darkness, the building was filled with dust, screaming and shooting. And here—

silence, strong light, a single large hall with many hostages in a single room, lying on the ground and not moving – an almost ideal situation for us. I scanned the room back and forth and suddenly off to my left, behind a pillar, I saw a figure rise fast. He raised his Kalashnikov to a firing position and I immediately recognized that he was a terrorist. I fired twice. The first bullet struck his rifle, at chest level, and sent it flying from his hands. The second one hit him square in the chest. He was the last terrorist left in the room with the hostages. Even if there were explosive charges, there was no one left to detonate them.

I looked at the hostages and saw they were all in shock. They laid on their mattresses, parents clutching children, protecting them with their bodies. Amir and I walked around them with the megaphone: "We're soldiers from Israel," we told them, Amir in Hebrew and me in English. "We're here to take you home." They looked at us in amazement. Just moments earlier they had been in another world, a hellish reality in which they had no way of knowing if in the space of an hour, or a day, they would be executed; certainly, they had not imagined that there was a chance that the IDF would show up and rescue them. And then suddenly, like a hand reaching down from heaven, they were delivered from one world to another.

Some of the hostages rose to their feet, others remained prone. I walked over to a woman shielding her young son with her body, and said: "Everything's okay, we came to get you, we're going home." She looked at me with a shocked expression on her face and nodded: "Yes, yes."

It was quiet in the hall but outside the shooting continued. The fire from the control tower did not let up even as our suppressing fire at the terminal was massively increased once the APC force arrived and joined the fray. At one point, Muki informed us that Yoni had been hit and that he was heading out to take command in Yoni's place.

We told the hostages to get ready to move and to take nothing with them. They were still in shock, looking confused. The gunfire outside the building started and stopped repeatedly and then the order came to evacuate. Some of the people crawled toward the door, afraid to rise to their feet. We helped them get up and accompanied them to the entrance, where the Land Rovers and the Golani recon unit's Peugeot pick-up truck waited for them. One of the hostages headed out clutching a bag that said Duty Free. I don't know if he really had duty-free items in there, but I do remember noting his steeliness, how even amid all this he was unwilling to leave the bag behind.

We searched the hall, made sure we hadn't forgotten anyone. I took the Kalashnikov that had been used by the terrorist I'd shot and the handgun that had belonged to the German terrorist and left the hall. I got back into the Mercedes and we drove back to the Hercules and took-off from there.

———

I didn't see the hostages again. They boarded the first plane with the wounded and took off before us. We flew back in the second plane, with the Land Rovers and the Mercedes. The third and fourth planes, with the APCs, left last.

I sat down in the front seat of the Mercedes, in Yoni's spot, and went to sleep. The next thing I remember after landing in Nairobi was seeing Ehud Barak board our plane, where he told us that Yoni had been killed. Just a moment earlier Yoni had sat down beside me and briefed me; just a moment earlier he had charged alongside us toward the terrorists; just a moment earlier, after a brief battle, I'd seen with my own eyes the way the hostages had been delivered from darkness to light, from despair to life, and I felt drained and emptied and wanted only to sleep.

We landed at Tel Nof and drove to our base. We did what needed to be done. Cleaned weapons, returned gear, and were debriefed. I was surprised by the flimsiness of the debrief. Usually in the Unit there's a deep, comprehensive, and uncompromising examination of the operation. But after Entebbe we gathered in the mess hall rather than the briefing room and there was a short and superficial debrief. The whole situation was abnormal. Yoni, the commander of the Unit, the man who should have been on the stage in the room, leading the probe into all that had happened, had been killed. I don't even remember who led the debrief in his stead. Some of the things that had happened I was not even aware of and some of the things that I was aware of were not brought up at all or explored in any detail. For instance, the whole thing about the first door into the passenger hall. That was one of the critical moments of the mission. It was crucial that we charge through two doors simultaneously, Muki's squad through the first door and Amnon's squad through the second, and in the end we, Muki's squad, missed our door and both squads entered through the second door. The matter of why we hadn't gone in through the first door, what we'd seen, if there was or wasn't a door, had it been blocked (the photos show that there was a door and it was not blocked) was never raised.

After the debrief, we were sent home for a night off. We knew that upon return we'd attend Yoni's funeral and then get right back into the intensive loop of training for the other challenging mission only two months away, the one we'd been focused on, and which Yoni was supposed to participate in, as the commanding officer on the ground. We weren't even aware of the country-wide, impromptu celebrations. Entebbe, for us, was a peripheral sortie, a momentary distraction from our main task.

I drove from the base to my home in Jerusalem. I sat that evening with my parents in their living room and suddenly there was a knock at the door. Our neighbor, Eliyahu Lankin, one of the pillars of the pre-state Irgun para-military organization, and the former commander of the doomed 1948 Altalena arms ship, was at the door. He stood there, holding a bottle of whiskey. He shook my hand. For a moment it seemed like he wanted to hug me, but he just handed me the bottle of whiskey, burst into tears, pivoted, and left. And that's when I understood. If a man as tough as Eliyahu Lankin, a man in his sixties who'd already seen and done as much as he had, was incapable of saying a word…then apparently I had been part of something truly extraordinary.

A few years after being discharged from the army, I got a call from the Netanyahu family. Iddo, Bibi, and their father Benzion had decided to conduct a thorough historical study of the Entebbe mission and they asked me if I'd be willing to be interviewed for their study and to talk about the mission as I had seen it. A few days earlier, entirely by chance, I had cleaned out my storage unit and amid the boxes and crates I'd found the motion-sickness bag with Yoni's sketches on it. I didn't know whether the bag would be of importance to their study but I told them about it and promised to bring it. I remember their excitement at the sight of that item, the bag, which was in essence the last thing that Yoni had written, the last time he'd put his pen to paper.

I've not been back to Entebbe since, but every now and again Entebbe comes back to me. A few years after the operation, once I'd already gotten out of the army and was working as a ranger in southern Sinai for the Israel park service, I was visiting my parents for the weekend when once again there was a knock at the door. Two young people, a man and a woman, asked if I was Amos Soren.

A photo of the airsickness bag on which Yoni personally briefed me during the flight to Entebbe

"We've been looking for you for a long time," they said. "We just wanted to say thank you so very much." They, too, had been at Entebbe, as hostages.

These encounters take me straight back to the old terminal, to those moments when I stood there facing the people and saw them swing from the brink of death to life. A few years ago, it happened again. The Mossad curated an exhibit about the raid on Entebbe and several of the operatives who participated in the missions and several hostages were invited to attend. One of the hostages, Sarah Davidson, who'd been at Entebbe with her husband and two children, spoke about what had happened and how they had felt in the terminal and about the moment that the Israeli forces had burst in. She described how she had lay down on top of her son to protect him from the shooting and how she had raised her head and seen, "a kindly Yemenite officer with a white hat and a camouflage uniform," speaking to her in Hebrew. When she was done, I walked over to her. "I'm the kindly Yemenite," I told her, "even though I'm not an officer and I'm hardly a Yemenite…"

I look back at Entebbe today with four decades of perspective. The operation has become the stuff of legend, in Israel and abroad. Books have been written, movies made, and over the years the story has come to take on the hallmarks of a biblical tale, studded with significance and layered with meaning.

The question that is often asked is why did this operation become so legendary and meaningful. Maybe it's because from a moral and humane perspective, and in terms of our own feeling of pride and national self-worth, the Entebbe story is perfectly clear. Incontrovertible clarity and that sort of pride are something we haven't known for some time; not during the decade before Entebbe and not over the ensuing years. When I think of the legendary status of the raid on Entebbe, I think of our own desire to look in the mirror and see in ourselves a reflection of morality, humanity, and pride, and I think that we cling to those feelings to this very day.

As for me, these days, I realize that what I carry with me from Entebbe is not related to the heroism of the deed itself, but the humanity of it. The mother shielding her son with her own body; the stunned expressions; the people crawling toward the door, because they were too scared to stand. When I think of Entebbe, I think of them, of that passenger hall, of that moment in which those people moved from a world of horror and desperation to a world of hope and of freedom.

Staff- Sgt. (res) Amos Goren was born in Jerusalem. He was drafted into the Unit in November 1973 and was a soldier in Omer Bar Lev's team. He served in the Unit under the command of Giora Zore'a, Yoni Netanyahu, and Amiram Levin and later returned to the Unit to serve yet again during Omer Bar Lev's tenure as the Unit's commander. He is a graduate of the Hebrew University and the Weizmann Institute of Science, with a BS and MSc in biology and an MBA from Harvard Business School. He founded and managed a bio-tech company in the United States and upon return to Israel he joined the private equity firm Apax Partners LLP, where he co-managed the global healthcare practice. He is also one of the founders and managers of the Unit's Alumni Organization, the Le'haez Project, which leverages the Unit's alumni in a national community service program for youth.

Staff-Sgt. Alex Davidi, Team Amnon Operator
Muki's Squad, Yoni's Assault Force, Hostage Hall

OPERATION YONATAN

Forty-five years after the fact and I've been asked to stir my memories and put them to paper for the sake of a historical truth. Does such a thing exist? For the sake of future generations, for those who may, if at all, be interested, I'll try. Forty-five years is a period of time during which memories undergo processes of erosion, distillation, filtration, and self-persuasion; the result may be close to the truth or not. Everything's possible. But the result of all these processes is my truth, my history as crafted by me and my surroundings and friends over the past four decades. My story is like swiss cheese, but that which I remember is apparently that which left the deepest impression on me and was branded into my mind. Every soldier who's ever participated in a post-op debrief knows that the number of different versions of events is identical to the number of participants; every person sees and experiences the same incident in a different way; each person and his or her truth. That is the nature of man and that is reality. Here is my story:

It must start with a brief description of the period preceding the operation, a period that had a decisive impact on what happened during and after Entebbe. Me and my buddies from Team Amnon Peled were drafted about two months before the Yom Kippur War. The years after the war were marked by hostage-based terror strikes that came to be known as "bargaining attacks." A band of terrorists would infiltrate into Israel, take over a residential building, a school, a hotel, a bus…and take hostages and try to negotiate with the state about the release of their mates from Israeli prison. The government's position was that it will not surrender to terror and, time after time, the Unit was called in with one single objective: free the hostages, kill the terrorists. We were required to learn while in motion; the army did not have much experience with this sort of thing. Conclusions were drawn after each attack and new doctrines were incorporated immediately. Our lack of experience, alongside the complexity of some of these attacks, brought a string of stinging failures, such as in Ma'alot, where the school children were murdered before our eyes. Even the successes were relative and often accompanied by loss of life, for civilians and soldiers. Over the Purim holiday of 1975 we lost a great soldier and a dear friend from our team, Itamar Ben David of Kfar Yechezkel, while storming into the Savoy Hotel in Tel Aviv to free the hostages being held there. During the course of our service, we took part in many missions and became a very experienced, trained, skilled, and unified team.

I underscore these facts because in the wake of Operation Yonatan there were those who dared to cast doubt about our experience and our capabilities. Muki Betser, the man who has been shaping history to fit his personal narrative from the moment the mission ended, has placed himself at the center of the mission and its success; he has ignored simple facts that are abundantly and incontrovertibly clear to every operator who took part in the mission.

———

In late June 1976 an Air France plane en route from Tel Aviv to Paris, via Athens, was hijacked. I'll skip over all of the facts and dates that can be found in history books and on the internet.

At the time of the hijacking, my team, Team Amnon, was preparing for another mission. Later we went on short leave in advance of our discharge at the end of the month. Luckily (and in hindsight it's easy to use that word without bunny ears around it) we were the most veteran team in the Unit's operational company at the time. One month later and we would have missed out on the opportunity to take part in this glorious operation. Participation in Operation Yonatan has accompanied each and every one of us from that day forth; without doubt it has also influenced the course of our civilian lives to one extent or another.

On Thursday of that week the phones started to ring and the Unit summoned to the base all those who would clearly take part in whatever operational scenario the future held. In that way we found ourselves back at the base in no time. I do not recall the detailed chain of events during the following twenty-four hours. A general description would include a hurried operations process, briefings, gear acquisitions, model drills, force assignments for individual personnel, and then more briefings and more drills and back again, with little to no sleep. Model drills were performed on a structure erected on the runway and constructed out of metal posts and Jute fabric meant to mimic the terminal at Entebbe. We drilled boarding and deboarding the vehicles from the Hercules aircraft that landed on the nearby runway. At a certain stage I was placed in Muki Betser's squad and my designated spot was in the lead Mercedes.

At this stage I'd like to note that very few soldiers believed that this sort of operation would be green-lighted by the Government of Israel; after all, we had seen far more straightforward, less fantastic operations be denied authorization.

Immediately after the operation and over the ensuing years several men claimed paternity over the ideas, plans, and running of the operation in the field. To me and my buddies who took part in the operation, the true biological father was never in doubt: Yoni Netanyahu, may he rest in peace, who, to our sorrow, is not with us anymore to defend his own name and his role in the operation. His fingerprints and footprints were all over each and every stage that we witnessed, from beginning to end of the operation, and, to our great woe, his own end. I'll expand on his role later.

Saturday, July 3rd, the morning of the operation. After the briefest sleep we got organized and headed out to the airfield at Lod. Each man and his gear; the tiger-stripe uniforms were bundled up in our duffle bags along with the white hats and the rest of the tactical gear that each individual operator carried. We reached the IAF base and loaded our gear onto the planes. A moment before takeoff, Mossad photos from the old terminal at Entebbe arrived. We looked at them and boarded the planes. We flew to Sharm al-Sheikh at a very low altitude, scraping the valley beds so as to avoid the radars of the neighboring countries, which, in those days, were enemy states in every way. A horrible flight that caused us all to vomit up our intestines and souls. The floor of the plane, by the time we arrived, was covered with an intolerable stench.

At Sharm we made final preparations and waited for the government's decision. While waiting, and shortly before the second leg of the journey, Yoni assembled us all. His words won't be erased from the heart of anyone present that day. It was an address delivered by a mature commander to his soldiers on the cusp of a mission from which no one knew if, or how, they would return: encouragement and persuasion that we were the stronger force, better trained, alongside a clear expression of his faith in us; the kind of things that soldiers need to hear in advance of this sort of operation.

At this stage, with the Government of Israel still convened and deliberating, the time schedule forced us to depart with the understanding that there was a point of no return, after which we would carry on no matter what. At that stage, many of us, myself included, were concerned that we might be returned to Israel, the go-ahead for the operation denied. Today, forty-five years later, with a head of white hair and a bit more life experience, I still use phrases like "concerned that we might be returned," phrases that are more apt for sap-filled young men yearning for combat. Armies are built on youngsters of this sort; mature people, people of sound mind, do not look for a fight. They tussle a bit and rest a lot….

We flew to Entebbe. A plane full of fatigued operators, drained by both the days of preparations and the vomiting on the first leg. Most of us fell asleep immediately and remained that way for several straight hours, apparently sparing ourselves plenty of fretting and fear. A half-hour or so before landing, we were woken up for final preparations. Yoni made the rounds among the guys. A kind word, a pat on the shoulder. Everyone was busy with a final weapons and gear check, a last look at the Yaror tactical flashlight (sort of like the laser dot of today, only in flashlight form). Outside: thunder and lightning, the apocalypse drawing near. We came coasting in for a landing. A team from the Paratroop recon unit was with us on the plane, some of them familiar to us from a training course we'd done together (Gili, Tal Vardi and others). Their role was to deploy on the other side of the runway and mark it with torches for the following planes, in case the lights were shut by the air traffic control.

The planes glided onto the lit runway, the quiet a good sign; we hadn't been noticed and our chances of success, as a result, skyrocketed. The cargo ramp dropped open. The Mercedes slid down and, under the steady hands of Amitzur Kafri, started rolling silently along the runway, in the direction of the old terminal. The Land Rovers, carrying the rest of the assault squads, followed in our wake.

I sat in the back row of the Mercedes on the right, near the window. There were three rows of seats in that car, which came into this world as a white taxi. After a night of repairs and many layers of black spray paint, it was turned into the black luxury sedan of Dr. Fieldmarshal His Royal Excellency President Idi Amin Dada.

My gear included a Beretta 0.22 pistol with no silencer (already back then there was a constant lack of tactical counter-terror gear, even in the illustrious Unit). Amitzur Kafri was behind the wheel and alongside him were Muki and Yoni. In the middle row, on the right, was Giora Sussmann, and I was directly behind him, with Gadi Ilan to my left. He, like me, was part of Muki's squad. Other friends who were in that vehicle, please excuse my faulty memory. I can't remember who else was present. We turned left, toward the last taxiway that led to the old terminal. Up ahead, a few hundred meters of asphalt to the control tower, beside which we were supposed to jump out of the vehicles. The combat stage was about to start and with it the battle that raged after the battle about the course of events, a true Rashomon.

We were engaged by the Ugandan guard, a soldier. He raised his weapon, yelled something, and released a green tracer bullet that I saw leave his rifle and cross in front of the Mercedes. Yoni ordered Amitzur to swerve toward him. I don't recall any discourse between him and Muki at that stage. Yoni and Giora Sussmann extended their arms out of the car and shot at the Ugandan with their silenced pistols. The car kept moving, the guard still standing off to our right. As far as I was concerned the battle had begun. I stuck my arm out and opened fire with a non-silenced pistol. The guard was hit and he stumbled backwards. Loud rumbling gunfire from the Land Rover behind us eliminated him. Yoni gave Amitzur the order to hit the gas and go. The Mercedes quickly covered the distance to the tower and stopped alongside it. We hurried out. I remember that I debated what to do with the final bullet left in the barrel of my pistol. I'd counted six shots fired and knew I had one more left. I don't remember what I decided to do. I grabbed my real weapon, the Uzi (yes, yes, there was once such a thing).

We ran quickly toward the corner of the building, to a covered outdoor corridor that led to our entrances to the hall. Muki Betser was in the lead, we followed. At the corner of the building, Muki stopped, fired a few bullets at a figure that popped out along the corridor, and was waylaid swapping magazines. Yoni, who was running out in the open alongside us, yelled: "Betser, forward." The delay was unnecessary and unclear. We stood behind Muki and waited for him to finish loading his weapon. Then we continued along the corridor at a run and tried to recognize our entrances, figure out who goes where. We reached our door and burst into the room. Someone had beat us to it. Off to the right, on the floor, there was a body and the blood of the terrorist that Amir Ofer had shot from outside the hall. The firing continued; Amnon shot to the far-left corner. We looked for more targets and started to advance through the hall in a straight line. Gadi was on my right and Muki on his right. At a certain stage a young guy popped up between two operators. They both shot him at the same time. Later we learned that this was a hostage who had not heeded the warnings to stay down. Their reaction was instinctive and without doubt justified. These sorts of things happen during any battle. Other terrorists were eliminated. I want only to describe that which I saw with my own eyes and remember distinctly. After clearing the hall, I stepped out and saw a wounded soldier being treated by a doctor. A few moments later I realized that the soldier was Yoni. Torrents of fire were being directed at the control tower and I joined the fray, emptying a full magazine in quick semi-automatic fire at the control tower windows.

The proximate fire was silenced and the terrorists were eliminated. The hostage-evacuation plane drew near. With an order from Alik Ron, we started corralling the hostages along, telling them to leave everything behind and hurry toward the plane. A Peugeot pick-up truck helped ferry people to the plane. Some of the hostages didn't listen to the instructions; they tried to take their baggage with them. We didn't allow it. Once all of the people were cleared out of the hall, we conducted a head count to make sure the entire force was accounted for, then boarded the plane and took off for home, hoping with all our might that some Ugandan soldier with an RPG wouldn't rain on our parade. We knew there were those who'd been injured and wounded. There was a lot of excitement and the stories started to flow. We landed in Nairobi to re-fuel. On the ground in Kenya we were told that Yoni was gone. The shock was immense. A long gloomy silence descended. It was unviolated for some time. The price was steep. The man who'd planned and so perfectly led one of the greatest military missions in the country's history had paid the most terrible price.

During the second leg of the flight, there was an atmosphere of euphoria. The stories started to flow, each guy with his story, what he saw, what he did. Turns out we forgot to take the GoPro cameras, so most of the tales were not caught on film. Too bad...as we approached Israel, a pair of Phantom F-4s came to escort us and ensure that we arrived in peace. The pilot patched the radio news reports into the cabin and we heard over the loudspeakers what our wonderful army had accomplished.

We landed at Tel Nof Airbase. We milled around, posed for pictures, sat down and met with the VIPs who came to bask in the success. From there we went back to the base.

I could carry on and describe the hysteria and excitement in the country and the ice cream cones that I got for free for a very long while from Penguin Ice Cream in my hometown of Kfar Saba, but I choose to stop here.

Later on, the fighting started over who ought to be credited with the planning and leading of the operation; who was the rightful recipient of the worldwide fame. The vast majority of us abstained from those skirmishes. We, among ourselves, knew the truth; we knew who'd done what, when, and how. We left the field vacant for those who chose to coopt the fame. If you tell a lie often enough, it starts to grow roots, and even the teller (whose nose does not grow, contrary to the fairytales) begins to believe it himself. We, the operators, know full well who did what at Entebbe. The time has come to reveal our true story and may the intelligent reader be his or her own judge of whom to believe.

A final comment, during the First Lebanon War, while deployed as reservists in the city of Aley in Lebanon, six years after the operation in Entebbe, Alik Ron, who was our company commander, said two things that I took with me for the coming years:

First: There was enough glory for everyone at Entebbe. The whole quarrel and negative campaign over who was responsible for what, is superfluous and harmful. That was the spirit of his comment.

The second remark related to the petitions that some of the operators from the Unit had signed in protest of the Lebanon War—not just as veterans of the Unit, but as participants in Operation Yonatan. Alik said, and again this is a paraphrase, that every Golani Brigade soldier who got to his feet in the face of the Syrian snipers during the Yom Kippur War battle for Mount Hermon was more of a hero than we were. There were no heroes at Entebbe. Again, I agreed.

In closing, I must say that a hero did emerge after the operation. He's a man who few remember and few know: Surin Hershko. A paratroop recon soldier, he took a bullet and remained paralyzed from the neck down and has battled ever since, day after day, in the fight for his life.

A final anecdote: Some of us have told the story of Operation Yonatan to soldiers and civilians and school kids. One time I told the story to my son Assaf's class. I spoke as one of the rescuers. Beni Davidson, who had been held hostage at Entebbe as a 13-year-old kid on a Bar Mitzva trip with his parents, also had a child in the same class. He told the story from the perspective of a child hostage…it's a small world we have in the Jewish state.

Fortunate am I to have been blessed with the opportunity.

———

Staff-Sgt. (res) Alex Davidi, born and raised in Kfar Saba, joined the Unit in August 1973 and served as an operator on Team Amnon Peled. After Operation Yonatan, he was discharged, worked as an air marshal for El Al, studied agriculture, and attained a degree in agronomy. In 1993, he founded the company Alonim Batei Etz, and has been building wooden houses across the country ever since. He is a father of four and has two granddaughters. He lives in Moshav Sde Warburg.

Staff.-Sgt. Gadi Ilan, Team Amnon
Operator in Muki's Squad, Yoni's Assault Force;
Hostage Hall

MY ENTEBBE

Many years ago, when Bibi Netanyahu was still a deputy minister, I met him by chance in Tel Aviv. He was waiting to give an address. When I told him that I'd been in the Mercedes at Entebbe, he asked me what had really happened over there. The question, of course, was asked in the context of the feud, which already then was raging over certain aspects of the operation. ...I told him that as far as I was concerned, the whole affair and the constant probing of it was demeaning to Yoni's memory and to the operation as a whole and therefore I would not like to discuss it. I feel the same way today.

And yet, I've been asked to put down my memories of the mission "for history's sake." I admit that I deliberated long and hard before deciding to write. This is my best recollection of a night that turned out to be one of the climaxes of my life.

At the time of the hijacking, in late June 1976, we were on pre-discharge leave, hence the long hair we have in the few pictures from that night. Once the plane was hijacked, we were ordered to stay home and remain on stand-by. Two days before the operation we were called back to the base. As I drove over on my old Vespa, I remember thinking: what can we possibly do? The most imaginative plan I could come up with involved the kidnapping of some Arab countries' ambassadors, to be used as leverage and exchanged for our hostages. The idea of flying to Entebbe and physically freeing the hostages did not even cross my mind...

At the time, during our pre-discharge vacation, I was busy organizing a Scouts Movement reunion for my old high school friends, the first after three years of service. The get-together was planned for Saturday night, the precise time of the mission.

Upon arrival at the base, we were corralled into the briefing room and the daring plan was revealed to us. I remember how surprised and excited everyone was. In my opinion, praise is due to the planners of the audacious mission, who assembled it all in such a short time and under such pressure, and to the decision-makers—Prime Minister Yitzhak Rabin and Defense Minister Shimon Peres, who took the immense risk and authorized the mission.

I was surprised to read recently that one of the "points of conflict" regarding the mission was Yoni's leadership and his involvement in the lead-up to the mission. As far as we, the teams carrying out the mission, were concerned, Yoni was the dominant figure and the lifeblood of the briefings and the model simulation drills that followed, and the one whose roving attention to detail was crucial to our preparations. Although I don't know his role in planning the operation before we arrived back at the base, to us, having arrived two days before the operation, it was clear that he was very much involved in the planning and preparation of the mission that he would lead, and in which he would give his life.

Solel Boneh, an Israeli construction company, built the old terminal at Entebbe, where the hijackers and hostages were being kept. Old blueprints were fished out of the archives and a model terminal, on which we trained, was built out of white tape, fence posts, and burlap. Helpful information arrived from the non-Israeli hostages who had been released several days earlier. Muki Betser had once trained Ugandan army forces and he said there was nothing to worry about: "With the force that we're heading out with, we can conquer the whole country," he said. As long as we're able to land in one piece, he added, anything's possible…

Saturday afternoon, and the operation was about to swing into gear. Just before boarding the vehicles on our way to the airport, I made a call home (via the operator of course, as there were no cell-phones) and told my mother that we were just biding our time on base and asked her to call my friend who was organizing the event with me, and to tell him that I would not be able to make it to the reunion that evening. As soon as I hung up, I hopped on the truck…

The first leg of the flight, flown at low altitude, was a nightmare of continuous turbulence and vomiting for some of the guys. On the second leg, once we took off from Sharm el-Sheikh, I curled up on the hood of the Mercedes and went to sleep. Only during the pre-landing stage, nearly seven hours later, did I wake up. Later, I wondered how I had been able to fall asleep before this sort of operation. Apparently, several nights of little sleep and three years of service in the Unit did the trick…

───────

We landed in the dark. Seated in the vehicles with our battle vests on, we were clad in the tiger-stripe uniforms of the Ugandan army. I was in the back row of the Mercedes, in the middle; Alex was to my right, a pistol in his hand. Amos Goren, I think, was on my left. Behind us, a pair of Land Rovers. Flanking us on either side of the plane, thirty paratroopers from the 890th Battalion, under the command of the late Nehemiah Tamari. They were poised to jump out onto the tarmac and mark the runway with torches for the following Hercules C-130s. The plane stopped, the cargo ramp opened, the vehicles were freed from their restraints. We rolled out onto the dark tarmac.

We drove in a triangle formation, lights blazing: the Mercedes in the lead, the two jeeps trailing on either side. Like Idi Amin arriving for a surprise visit. Some butterflies in the belly and a full dose of adrenalin, but not fear: a balance between the feeling of a mission of historic significance and our prior experience. We'd been in similar scenarios and I was ready for the crackle of fire, the smell of gunpowder, the explosions, the wounded, and, God forbid, the dead. Ma'alot, Savoy, and dozens of drills over the years brought a sort of calm, a knowledge of what was to be expected, a certain anticipation…

The buildings took shape in the darkness, figures grew visible. Through the screen of those seated in front of me, I saw a Ugandan soldier raise his rifle toward us and stomp his foot; it looked like he was yelling something. To me it was clear that he was going to open fire. In my recollection, he even fired a shot or two, but I'm not sure about that. What I am certain of, is that he represented a clear and present threat. Amitzur, the driver, swerved left and two or three of the guys on the right opened fire with their silencer-equipped pistols. Another future point of contention: Was it necessary to open fire or was it superfluous and a danger to the mission, potentially ruining the element of surprise? As far as I'm concerned, it was completely justified. It prevented the Ugandan soldier from opening fire, which, to the best of my understanding in real time, is what he was clearly about to do.

In the wake of the gunfire, we didn't drive all the way to the point that we'd planned on during the simulation, but rather stopped slightly farther away, while angling to the left. We got out and started to run. I was part of the leftmost squad, under the command of Muki Betser. The squad was manned by Alex Davidi, Amos Goren, and myself. I was right behind Muki, carrying the radio transceiver. We were supposed to charge in through the first, leftmost entrance. While racing ahead, an armed Ugandan stepped out from behind the corner of the building, to our left, and took aim. Muki shot him and I joined in, adding a shot or two before he fell. Right after that we carried on running towards the building.

During the altercation, Amnon and Amir passed us on the right. As we resumed running, they were out ahead and arrived first at the building. They eliminated the terrorists in the hall and prevented or truncated the onset of gunfire by the terrorists, who seemed to have been asleep and caught completely off guard. "Who dares wins" – once again...

The whole affair, from jumping out of the vehicles to the elimination of the terrorists, took in my estimation a minute or two.

We entered the building. Amnon and Amir were already inside but it still wasn't clear if all of the terrorists had been killed. We anticipated another firefight. The hall was large and filled from end to end with prone hostages. There was no time; each second was

crucial. At any moment a terrorist might regain his wits and open fire
or trigger an explosive device. We advanced into the hall. The
hostages were all lying down, terrified, in shock from the experience
they'd endured during the previous days. They'd been woken at 11
p.m. by the sounds of gunfire and the noise of battle. What was going
through their minds? Probably that this was the end. Suddenly orders
were being yelled in Hebrew, "Stay down...don't move...where are
the terrorists?"...and one little boy jumped around carefree and jolly
as though he, and only he, realized what was happening in front of
their eyes.

While running towards the hostage hall, there'd been bursts of
automatic fire from the control tower, followed by screams that Yoni
had been hit. Inside the building, once it was clear that Yoni had been
incapacitated, Muki took command. Unfortunately, within the
hostage hall, there were two casualties among the hostages, innocents
who were caught in the cross fire. Then the fire died down and the
two floors of the terminal building were cleared.

The next stage began. Evacuation. The hostages were still in
shock: I asked one of them to put on his shoes and to move toward
the door. He slid the shoes on his hands and crawled forward on all
fours. One woman asked me how they would be leaving the country.
Specifically, she wanted to know, had we brought a plane? I told her
that it would be a long walk, and yes, we'd come with a plane...

The euphoria started to seep in: the IDF Medical Corps plane, a
flying ambulance filled with doctors and operating theaters, was
hardly being put to use. We'd been prepared for explosions, for many
wounded and dead. Some, of course, did pay with their lives—
several hostages, and Yoni, who at that time was still fighting for his
life. But at that point, the mission seemed a tremendous success, far
surpassing expectations...

We were the last to take off, fifty-five minutes after landing, at
23:55. Who would have believed it! Even in the best-case scenarios
this was considered too good to be true. The operation was destined
for everlasting glory. Taking off I saw the airport illuminated by the
sight of six flaming MiG fighter jets.

We landed in Nairobi and received word that Yoni had died of his wounds. The euphoria was punctured at once. We took off for Israel. Somehow, I found my way to the cockpit and grabbed a seat. The pilot listened to the news on the radio. The report stated that Idi Amin has announced that his forces had recaptured the airport and were in control of the situation. The pilot broadcast the bulletin over the loud-speaker. Laughter bloomed all around.

We landed in Israel. The hostages had already arrived long ago and were met with raucous celebration by their families. We were greeted warmly by Yitzhak Rabin and Shimon Peres, who came expressly to meet us. Some pictures were taken, the only ones from the mission. In those days, documentation in real time was far from being a priority. Not a single photo was taken during the operation itself. The few pictures that were taken, the only tangible mementos that we have, were snapped during landing. Later on, I managed to get my hands on one of those photos and I gave it to my father, who kept it fervently in his wallet till the day he died.

We returned to the Unit's base. At the gates to the base, waiting for us, was a long convoy of women carrying cakes. The country was in an ecstatic fervor. My grandmother, who lived with us at the time, got up, as usual, at five in the morning and listened to the news. She woke my parents and said that they were reporting something on the radio about Entebbe. The rest is history and hysteria. That night, after coming home, I went out to go folk dancing at the Scouts Center in Ramat Gan, just as I did every week. At first nothing special happened, but then the nickel dropped and one of the other dancers turned to me and said, 'Hold on, weren't you there?' "Yes, I was," I replied and hysteria ensued...

In the wake of the mission, Israel won both the Miss Universe beauty pageant and the Eurovision song contest in the same year. How far off that seems today, how distant from our current standing in world opinion...

By participating in the mission, we were given the opportunity to become part of a historic episode, one of the finer ones in the annals of Israel's modern history. It's a shame that this has been overshadowed by quarrels, strife, and contention over who is deserving of the glory and who is not, propagated by a small few who have chosen to focus on that to this very day. May the memories of Yoni Netanyahu and the hostage Jean Jacques Meimoni and the others who were killed during the mission be blessed. With utmost respect and love to all of the other participants in the mission and to my friends from the Unit, with blessings of a good year and with prayers for peace, for love of the Other, for patience and tolerance…

Staff.-Sgt. (res) Gadi Ilan was drafted into the Unit in 1973, to Team Amnon Peled. He worked in the hotel business after being discharged. Later on, many years ago, he was interviewed for a position in Africa. He was asked if he had any prior experience working in the region and he answered in the affirmative. He was asked how long he'd been there and he replied "for a single hour…" Ever since he's been roaming between Israel, the United States, and Africa.

Lt. Dani Arditi, Team Leader
Arditi Squad Commander, Yoni's Assault Force; VIP Room
(Hijackers' Living Quarters)

MY RECOLLECTIONS: OPERATION ENTEBBE

"In a place far away, near here
  We gathered ourselves
  And delivered our friends
  And said neither this nor that."
(From the song "Medina Ktana" (Small Country) by Danny Sanderson)

On Sunday June 27, 1976 an Air France plane, departing from Israel to Paris with a layover in Athens, was hijacked...

In July 2016 we marked the fortieth anniversary of Operation Entebbe, and now, after all these years, I feel the need to put my memories to print and to tell my personal story.

Background

Nearly forty-five years have passed since Israel launched Operation Entebbe, but time seems to have only intensified the uniqueness of the operation and its influence on us as participants, as well as on the state of Israel and the world. My memory of the operation is a stream of images that has accompanied me during various chapters of my life; their significance brought into sharp relief at crucial decision-making junctures. As is only natural, the operation seems different to me today, particularly in light of its significance in the battle against terror, its contribution to the defense of the state and the security of its citizens, and to myself.

The Preparations

We learnt of the hijacking while conducting operational training for a pending mission; this just a few days after a combat operation in the south. The team immediately shifted to a state of readiness. We prepared for the eventuality that the plane might touch down at Israel's international Ben-Gurion Airport. At the time, I was the commander of a ten-man platoon, or team. We were summoned back to the base and given an initial briefing. It's worth noting that we didn't have at our disposal the many means of communications that exist today and so we had scant knowledge of the events (a situation that would never happen today). As soon as we heard about the hijacking, we assumed a state of readiness, huddled around the commander's office, and waited...we were sent to update our passports and we thought, okay, finally, we're going to take a trip, travel, fly away...particularly they sought those who held foreign citizenship. At one point, it was understood that the plane was going to land in Lod, at Ben-Gurion Airport, and we drove there and back with our assault force. In retrospect, I feel that we did not truly internalize the enormity of the challenge and the towering obstacles we faced in addressing this sort of operation and simply "jumped into the operational waters," as would any of the Unit's trained and experienced teams.

During one of the briefings (conducted early in the week, back when we were still in a state of readiness for the plane to be landed at Ben-Gurion Airport), Shimon Peres, then the defense minister, walked into the room and said, 'Who of the operators here participated in the Sabena rescue?' I raised my hand (I think I was the only one). Back then, during Operation Sabena, I'd burst into a rear door of the plane alongside Mordechai Rahamim. At the time I was an enlisted man; by Entebbe, I was an officer. Because I'd taken part in the Sabena operation, I began, during the lead-up to the operation, to compare the two scenarios and attempted to calculate the projected number of casualties. I feared there was a chance that when all was said and done, the operation would not go according to plan, as it was much more complex, the theater of operations was far away, and the plan itself was more dangerous. During the Sabena Airlines rescue, we were tasked with seizing control of an airplane; at Entebbe, we were to raid and seize an entire terminal.

On Friday, Yoni briefed the operators. He explained the central principles of the mission, the deployment of the forces, the objectives, and the main points of difficulty. With the clock ticking fast and with a dearth of precise intelligence information, along with the given distance to the target, the nature of the briefing was starkly different from the usual pre-op routine conducted in the Unit.

From the Friday briefing till the moment of departure on Saturday we were busy preparing for the mission: We conducted weapons drills at the firing range, worked on combat fitness, and studied up on the target area. My team was scattered among the different forces, with only two of my men (Amir Drori and Aharoni Berkovitz) under my direct command. The rest of my soldiers were assigned other roles and so the team structure that we had grown used to during the previous two years was dissolved. This triggered plenty of concerns in my mind, concerns that were later proven unwarranted as, it turns out, if you train properly and professionally, the human factor, within the larger force structure, is not decisive.

Not knowing what was truly going on, I remember the atmosphere as being laced with confusion and a certain lack of focus. A junior officer at the time (a first lieutenant), I didn't know anything beyond what was happening in Yoni's office. Behind that door, Yoni, the force leader and the commander of each and every one of the operational squads in the assault force, handpicked the participants. He took into account, among other considerations, the soldiers' operational experience and time-served. Another factor was missions that were in the works. For instance, the team under the command of Omer Bar Lev was involved in training for a very important mission, and therefore, while they were sent to Entebbe, they were not included in the assault force on the terminal; instead they were tasked with destroying the Ugandan MiG fighter jets.

I distinctly remember a strong desire to take part in this mission. However, as is always the case with airborne and vehicle-based missions, weight and space limitations winnow down the number of participants. My platoon was one of the more veteran ones in the Unit and I had extensive operational experience. And yet, of my ten soldiers, one was not given a spot. When Yoni told me that one of my men was not included, I was furious and I started to argue. I really fought hard (and did things that, today, I feel were irresponsible…) to the point of "putting the keys on the table" and telling Yoni that "if he's not in…then I'm not in!" and I left the office in a huff. Charging down the stairs toward the flag pole, I bumped into Muki, who tried hard to calm me down and explained that there was no choice. That soldier of mine didn't take part, and I think he's angry with me to this very day…A few years ago I met up with my soldiers and told them the story. Not one of them knew anything about that sequence of events.

It was clear to us that this was a dangerous operation with multiple uncertainties and that some of us might be killed. I don't remember if we talked specifics, about numbers and quantities, because we were not that open with one another. I estimated dozens of dead, both from within our ranks and from among the hostages. Four years earlier, I'd taken part in the Sabena raid as a member of the assault team, in a situation that was far clearer and more "comfortable"—with the plane situated on our soil—and still a woman hostage was killed and several of our force members were wounded. I transferred some of that experience to this new situation.

During the four days following the hijacking, while maintaining a state of readiness for a possible landing at Ben-Gurion Airport, we didn't do much. As a commander, I tried to keep myself and my soldiers busy, mostly with physical fitness and navigational drills and a bit of "occupational therapy"—to keep their minds off the looming difficulties and uncertainties. We saw Yoni relatively rarely and only later in the week, on Wednesday and Thursday. By Friday everything was prepped and ready. Still, we could feel the confusion in the system. We knew that no one really knew what was going on. And Yoni's absence—engaged, as he was, in other operational duties that I didn't know about at the time—only contributed to the bewilderment and the uncertainty. I tried at all times to keep a sort of barrier between my own private feelings and the feelings and thoughts of the soldiers under my command. The only real preparation for the mission was a training drill on a runway somewhere, on which they had erected, out of burlap fabric, a mock-up of the old terminal at Entebbe. Twice we drilled the raid on the mock terminal, driving our vehicles and disembarking from the aircraft. Other than that, we conducted a few technical and intelligence drills. In the Unit we were used to working on missions for a long time, thoroughly securing all the facts and poring over all the copious intelligence information. An operation isn't usually green-lighted until almost everything is securely in place, everything clear. And here we were gearing up for a complex mission in which almost nothing was clear – to us, to me, to those serving under me, and, I knew, to those above me.

We all estimated that the chances of the mission being authorized and carried out were slim indeed. There was hardly any chance at all. It seemed fantastical and grandiose even to operators with a rich and thick record of action. I did not part with my family or my home, for no member of my family (my parents and siblings) had any idea that such an operation would be launched. Today, now that I think about it, one of my sisters served as a non-combatant in the Unit, and I'm sure she knew of my involvement, though I've never spoken to her about it.

The Wait in Sharm el-Sheikh

On Saturday morning, at our base, we stood for a full gear inspection and then flew south to Sharm el-Sheikh. The Cabinet had not yet authorized the mission and we sat there and waited for several hours, till the afternoon. Those were frustrating hours. The duration of the flight to Sharm (in the Sinai Peninsula) and the hours of waiting only served to heighten the feelings I mentioned earlier. We were on the cusp of taking off for a mission filled with no small amount of danger. We were stressed and I recall that we all receded into our shells. Each of us sat in silence and there was little talk among us. It seemed as though each one of us was making his own private reckoning.

I wondered: How would the operation unfold? Would I return alive? And what would be the fate of my soldiers? The hostages? There were no other situations (that I'm at liberty to discuss) in which I conducted such an existential reckoning regarding the coming twenty-four hours. I felt that these thoughts and reflections were something we shared. Each of us took into account the possibility that he would not return alive from the mission.

As opposed to the norm in the Unit, in which every detail of an operational plan is studied and practiced—this operation was accompanied by great uncertainty. There was much that was unknown. Many details of the plan were unclear to us, and therefore our questions and ruminations loomed here more forcefully than in other operations. But we were taut and ready and everyone knew the parameters of his own role. Mine was very clear to me. In my mind I ran through a scenario of how things might unfold and that gave me a feeling of safety, though I figured that even if all went according to plan, without any notable mishaps— we'd still suffer many casualties.

In hindsight the tactical intel on the airport and the terminal was very good. We had blueprints and sketches and photos, and even now, were I to land at Entebbe and arrive at "my room," (the old terminal has been taken down and no longer exists) I'd remember its layout and would know precisely where to go and what to do. The details—regarding the room I was to charge into, the location and the description of the door—served as anchors and helped soothe the other nagging uncertainties.

The Flight to Entebbe

In the afternoon, the Cabinet authorized the operation and there was a burst of joy diluted by a swirl of worry. When I realized I was heading off on this mission I was both nervous and excited. There was constant chatter among the officers and especially among the soldiers. Clashes over who would fill the spots on the plane and in the vehicles. The soldiers from my team were spread out among the different squads. I had only two of my own operators alongside me. Seven others were seated in different vehicles, serving under different commanders and fulfilling other roles, and I remember being concerned by the fact that they weren't under my direct command.

We took off. We left Sharm ready and alert. The flight was long and it stretched on and on and I remember thoughts popping into my mind before and during the flight: each and every one of us was very much dependent on the pilots, and we, in the Unit, were not used to relying so much on anyone else; we were used to doing it all alone and doing it well. During the flight, I wondered: what if there's a technical difficulty? Four planes, four engines per plane, all we'd need is for one engine to fail and we'd have to turn back. Technical difficulties were a constant source of anxiety.

But one could say my concerns revolved around three points: the flight and landing, which were the responsibility of the air force; the drive; and the charge into the terminal. I admit that I didn't really have full confidence in the pilots' ability to navigate and land. The navigation was very complex and had to be done under clandestine conditions. As for the landing—I didn't for a moment consider that the runway would be lit. I was sure that the Ugandans would learn of our arrival well before we came in for a landing, and that they would shut down the airport and block off the runways. Above all, I was concerned that there'd be something stationed on the runway preventing a landing or making it more hazardous, but to my surprise, that didn't happen. The landing was smooth. The drive, post-landing, from the plane to the old terminal, where the hostages were being held, was also a source of concern. Different scenarios ran through my mind, far more complex than what happened in reality. I imagined a situation in which we were discovered en route and were fired upon, and, among other eventualities, a human chain blocked our path of progress. In reality there was but a single episode, involving two Ugandan soldiers, which influenced the unfolding of the mission. In essence, we were discovered only one minute before our charge into the terminal. Additionally, I was concerned about taking fire as we approached the terminal building. In fact, we did take incoming fire, but it was scattered and not well aimed. I recall massive fire from our own forces and the sound of our own gunfire. Especially the heavy fire within the terminal. I was surprised to find that the VIP Room was locked and that we couldn't get in through the door. (By the way, it's quite surprising that the other doors weren't secured in any way. The doors to the upstairs, leading to the Ugandan soldiers' quarters and to the hostage hall— were open and unsecured.)

For most of the flight, we slept. We were very tired. Maybe there was also a sort of escape into an absence of thought. Yoni made the rounds a few times, asked how people they were doing, offered clarifications. The airplane was very noisy and uncomfortable. I slept in one of the jeeps, on one of the seats.

During the flight, the tension subsided and nearly disappeared, maybe due to the monotone of the engines and the comfort of sleep. But during the final twenty minutes, as we began to approach, the tension spiked. Everyone sat in his assigned seat. The plane was completely dark. We could not see a thing. All we could do was listen. You are in a dark blob that is meant to land somewhere and from the moment it lands and the door opens—the operation is in your hands. I remember well the transition from complete passivity and utter dependence on the pilots, the planes, and luck, to a state where the deciding factor is you and your actions. This transition (familiar to me from other airborne missions), from darkness and monotonous noise, a shuddering aircraft and a cocoon-like feeling of safety to operational action is a moment that must be focused on; it is not an automatic transition. I devoted a few minutes to internal concentration and a re-running of the operational plan in my mind, again and again, so that I'd be ready.

We landed with lights illuminated (on a runway that was still lit). The plane taxied slowly and then the lights on the tarmac were extinguished, meaning that the control tower had become aware of unsanctioned activity on the runway and perhaps our cover had been blown. A group of paratroopers, having trained for this role, jumped out of the still moving aircraft and began marking the runway with torches for the three following planes.

The Operation

The plane stopped and the door opened. Once we emerged from the Hercules, we were operating in full focus. I was in the second jeep, and as soon as we rolled out, I felt at home—I was familiar with the place, as though I'd visited it many times before...the lead cars knew the route and I too was well aware of where we needed to go. We were very focused, focused on the mission and coiled for action and we knew where we were headed and what we had come to accomplish.

There are several visuals etched in my mind: on the way to the old terminal we passed a pair of Ugandan soldiers, who stood, stomped their feet, lowered and raised their weapons. It's possible it was a salute, and it's possible it was them aiming their weapons at us. I remember that as soon as I saw them stomp their feet, I feared that our cover had been blown (we still don't know what their true intention was and there is an ongoing argument about the matter) and in fact that triggered the incident that fundamentally changed the operational plan and forced us to make the shift from covert to overt action earlier than intended. During this mission, it was our first encounter with something unscripted. But it was certainly foreseen (we'd drilled this sort of eventuality and other, more difficult ones during our preparation for the mission). From that point on, though, the mission unfolded in a way that put the force under greater stress. Order and plan-based progression had come to an end.

I heard gunfire and saw the Ugandan soldiers fall and understood that we were off script. I'd told myself the whole time: "Stick to the plan"; "stick to the drill"; and that was also one of the main things I tried to convey to my soldiers: "No matter what happens, you stick to the plan! We surge toward the doors and get in there as fast as possible."

I also remember that the first time I laid eyes on the terminal, from around one-hundred meters out, a thought popped into my mind: "It's true! What we studied is what there is. It matches!" and that gave the soldiers and me a boost of confidence. We sped up and drove to the unplanned offloading spot and rather than stop, as planned, between the terminal and the tower, we stopped about twenty meters before that, off to the side of the tower. The role assigned to the squad under my command (Team Dani) was to charge into the VIP Room. We thought there'd be hijackers present but in fact when we burst in, they were already dead. In the post-op debriefing it turned out that Sussmann's squad had eliminated them before we'd arrived. I saw someone prone, injured. I didn't know it was Yoni. He was hit before I even made it to my assigned room, and while fighting I passed by him and saw that his battle vest was being removed and someone was treating him (perhaps the doctor, perhaps Tamir his radio operator). I kept on running, in these sorts of situations you feel and know that sticking to the drill is crucial. You don't stop. Even if someone is down. Even if someone is dead. You accomplish your mission! I remember thinking that and saying it to myself as I continued to run: "Someone's been hit. I don't know who it is, but the drill is to keep on running," so I kept on running.

I do not remember being fired at (a sort of blackout to the surroundings, for you are focused on your room and your goal); it turns out that we did take fire, though, because people in my squad were hit. We reached the door to the VIP Room. I tried to open it and found it locked. I couldn't get it to open. I heard shots fired within. I decided to throw a few grenades, which was risky because it wasn't clear if there were hostages within or not, but that's the drill: if someone's firing at you from inside, better to throw a grenade. These are not full fragmentation grenades, but small ones, more like stun grenades, that neither maim nor kill, but shock and induce panic.

The firing inside died down. Later on, we learnt that those shots were apparently not fired by the hijackers or the Ugandans but by operators from our own force who had entered the room through a different door. One of our grenades went off right near my soldiers. Apparently, it had hit the door and rolled back and two of my soldiers were wounded. Not badly, but it was rather scary. We weren't able to get in through that door; in the end we made it into the VIP Room through a different entrance.

When I entered the small hall, it was already half-empty. There were only two or three dead terrorists. It later emerged that Giora Sussmann's squad had moved into the VIP Room from a nearby room and eliminated the hijackers before we'd had the chance to charge in. This action was crucial, as it made the armed hijackers defend themselves against incoming forces and denied them the opportunity to fire out as we tried to come in through the locked door. I remember feeling relief that the hard part seemed to be over and disappointment that we hadn't managed to charge in through the door. We cleared the VIP Room and then stepped outside, clearing the rest of the building and assisting in evacuating the hostages and then accompanied one of the groups to a plane that had parked around fifty meters away from us.

Returning Home

We took off from Entebbe and after landing in Nairobi I found out that Yoni had been badly wounded. During the bedlam of evacuation, we didn't know how many people had been hurt, who'd made it through and who hadn't, and I felt sure that there were many casualties. We landed in Nairobi to re-fuel, a stop we'd been informed of only several minutes before (I had no idea that we were going to land in Kenya). We remained on the plane. We didn't really know what had happened and there was thick "fog" surrounding the events. Once we took off from Nairobi, we were told that Yoni had been killed. That was a blow. A big blow. Yoni was my direct commander and I had spent many hours with him, many good and special interactions, both personal and operational.

Most of us slept on the plane ride home. I distinctly remember two things. The first is the song "Small Country" by Kaveret. At some point I went forward to the cockpit. It was daylight and we were already over Sharm (a sort of closing of the circle). For much of the way the Kaveret song had been playing in the cockpit and I remember thinking to myself: "How symbolic! And how true!" Amazing how the sight of Sharm and the song were etched together into my memory. We landed at the IAF airbase Tel Nof and were greeted by a raucous celebration. We, who were taught to operate in the shadows, who couldn't be seen and couldn't even be spoken of, were shocked to find that the doors opened to noise and commotion...I remember spotting photographers and turning my back so that I wouldn't be recognized. We returned to the unit and within days, really quite fast, we resumed our usual routines and "forgot"... truly forgot (and had they not made a little party for me in my kibbutz when I came home, I really would have just gone back to my daily routine).

Personal Reflections

At the end of the mission, once the planes had landed at Tel Nof, my operators and I stepped back into the arms of anonymity. And the media exposure about the Unit, as I remember it, grated on me. In retrospect I feel that the operation and its success contributed vastly to the Israeli people's sense of security and national pride, and that element is what should have been emphasized in the media.

Over the years, and particularly in the press, there's been an attempt to present a reality in which there is a standing argument between two camps of operators, who remain at odds regarding the assault on the terminal. Indeed? The force numbered thirty-three operators in total and as far as I can tell there is overwhelming agreement among the soldiers about what happened.

This is one of the reasons I decided to put my recollections down on paper, and one of the reasons that others—soldiers, officers, staff officers and operators—agreed to write and tell their personal stories. This group of people (roughly my own age) woke up recently and felt, like me, that they wanted their memories preserved on paper.

Today, looking back, I feel it was a mistake not to have woken up earlier. I imagine that one day, when things calm down (maybe in another fifty years) the Unit will make a movie about this, because it carefully documents its own history, in film and in print, producing both classified and un-classified works (and our story actually needn't be classified). However, for now it has just disappeared from the annals of the Unit. Perhaps on purpose…

Perhaps because Yoni was killed during the operation, the debriefings were very short and unprofessional and so very different from the detailed and exacting operational reviews generally conducted in the Unit. And the only official document that remains is one written by the history branch, which is, in my opinion, filled with imprecise information regarding the Unit's role in the operation.

Our notion here is not to produce a historical account, but rather our own individual personal stories, and to publish what we can so that it may be read. Today, looking back, I think we were naïve and we didn't understand the true dimensions of the operation. After Entebbe most of the Unit's operators simply carried on and returned to our familiar anonymity and to our daily routines and largely were just not interested in the hubbub surrounding us. We were immediately sucked into other activities and afterward hardly spoke at all of the operation. Only around a decade later did we start to recount and inquire (a decade during which I served in operational units and did not take part in conferences and the like). I personally do not know the stories of my own soldiers, and I don't know what they recall or what they tell, and that's one of the reasons that I'm writing here: I want to know the stories of my own soldiers.

A few words about my experiences: looking back I recall flash-backs and not events. Perhaps because my private history is so packed with events that are significant to me and about which I still cannot speak. I often met with Yoni's younger brother Iddo and unfortunately I had to tell him again and again: "I really don't remember" (Usually when speaking of Entebbe I open by saying that my memory is not good and therefore I use accessories), and in my opinion other participants also remember little, and since each person remembers different facts and relays them in a different way, there is good reason to record personal stories in writing.

Indeed, memory is so misleading…so inexact…and above all, so unbeholden to proof.

Hundreds of pages have been written about those few minutes during which Yoni was killed. Everyone remembers something else, and to this day we don't know who killed him or from where the fatal shot was fired. We know it was an AK-47 round that entered through his chest and existed through his lower back; we think the shot was fired from the control tower, but how did it enter and exit there? After all, he was standing. Apparently, he'd bent over, we don't really know.

By the way, the movie Operation Thunderbolt starring Yehoram Gaon is by and large on point in terms of the chronology and the atmosphere (aside from a few overly dramatic scenes). The movie accurately depicts the atmosphere and shows shots of (Prime Minister Yitzhak) Rabin and (Defense Minister Shimon) Peres going in and out of Cabinet meetings. When I tell the story of Entebbe, I use that movie.

Yoni Netanyahu

Yoni Netanyahu was my direct commander for over a year. He was a brave man and a tough and very reserved commander. Our relationship was not that of friends; he kept his distance from his underlings and talking to him face to face was not always easy. We didn't entirely know what he was thinking or what he wanted, because he kept his own company and, as his underlings, we got very little feedback from him. When Yoni spoke to us, he did not detail his orders, but rather spoke on a higher command level. The demands he made of himself were very tough, as were his demands and expectations from us. Personally, I was not close to him but I held him and his courage in very high esteem. I saw Yoni during the Yom Kippur War battle for Mount Hermon: A very brave man who conducted himself superbly under fire; calm and with a clear understanding of reality. And so he was again during the operation to free the hostages at Entebbe, even though he joined the main group relatively late on account of other operational obligations. I saw him during the preparation stage, during the training, the briefings and the flight—he was focused, determined, brave.

I remember an incident that occurred well before the operation: I had a back problem that forced me to surrender the command of my platoon for three months. When I returned, Yoni said he wasn't sure that I could resume my old command and decided to conduct a test: two nights of navigation. Just he and I. I spent a night leading him through the dark, with Yoni checking my navigational abilities and my physical fitness. Before setting out, he quizzed me on the route, but during the trek—we hardly spoke. At the end of the route, he turned to me and said: "You're perfectly fine," and I resumed my command. That memory is a gift I have from Yoni and one that remains in my heart.

Epilogue

There are two moments from the operation that are indelibly etched in my mind. The first is that moment when the doors of the plane came down on the runway at Entebbe and the second is the moment that I was told that Yoni had been killed during the operation. The first symbolizes the most critical moment of the operation —the transition from flight to ground operation, and the second symbolizes the enormous price we were forced to pay during this operation. Occasionally, during other covert operations, these moments flashed through my mind, especially when the missions were hanging by a thread and the actions of a single soldier or a single command from an officer had the power to dramatically alter the results of the mission, from shining success to harsh disaster.

Brig. Gen. (res) Dani Arditi was born in Kibbutz Yiron and drafted into the ranks of the Unit in February 1970, where he first served as a soldier in Dani Bruner's platoon. He took part in Operation

Sabena, served as a platoon commander and held other posts of command in the Unit and within the IDF Intelligence Directorate. He was honorably discharged with the rank of brigadier-general. He served as the head of the Counterterrorism Bureau in the Prime Minister's Office and as head of the National Security Council. He is married and a father of three, an expert on national security, intelligence, and anti-terror activities, and currently a strategic consultant.

Second Lieutenant Amos Ben Avraham, Team Leader
Amos Squad Commander; Yoni's Assault Force;
Hostage Hall

MY REPORT

Background
At the time of the operation I was a young team leader, 21 years-old. My small platoon of operators, Team Amos, was drafted in November 1975 and initiated into the Unit only four months prior to the operation; they did not participate in the rescue mission.

During the days leading up to the mission I was engaged in operational activity in the Sinai along with Dani Arditi's team and other parts of the operational company, including Unit commander Yoni Netanyahu. The activity ended pre-dawn on Tuesday and we made it back to the Unit and joined the operations process either on Tuesday or Wednesday.

My role was commander of the second squad, charged with storming in to the second entrance of the hostage hall, next in line after Amnon's squad.

In order to avoid mingling information that I acquired firsthand and information that was processed via outside sources (books, movies...), I'll try to stick to the facts that I experienced myself, some of which were cross-checked with my squad mates and gleaned from debrief documents (of the IDF and the Unit).

The Operations Process
I remember, from my perspective, the dramatic briefing at the start of the process in which Yoni presented the operational plan and the force structure. Everyone searched for his name...am I on the list? Where? In what role? At the end of the briefing a young commander turned to me and said he hadn't seen his name anywhere

in the formation. Eventually, that was rectified and he joined one of the forces that stormed the terminal.

I was designated a squad commander, one of five, tasked with storming the hall where the hostages were being kept. The operators in my squad were Dani Fredkin and Gal Raif, both of Team Dani Arditi. We geared up, zeroed our firearms, conducted a brief training drill, and, in the end, a simulation drill on the Unit's runways with all forces present, including a short flight and landing on the runway adjacent to the Unit's base.

There was a positive feeling during the preparations stage; all was purposeful and nimble. We classified the mission as a hostile terror action, the sort of case with which the Unit was very familiar at the time.

At the end of the operations process, Dan Shomron, may he rest in peace, briefed us.

The Operation

Once we landed in Uganda, a sudden quiet prevailed. The cargo ramp opened and the vehicles glided out of the plane. The first thing I noted was the smell; it was new to me. A sort of combination of vegetation and water. High grasses lined the runway and the ride was quiet, smooth.

We rode in one of the Land Rovers trailing the black Mercedes, down the runway and over to the taxiway. I remember the sight of the lead Mercedes slowing, signaling, and turning left toward the old terminal.

The drive was ruptured by the encounter with the Ugandan sentries.

I saw the gunfire trained at one of the sentries. The other one fled left. MAG machinegun fire from the left side of our jeep, while in motion, tracked him down.

The dismount itself was sudden, rushed, and a bit earlier than planned. Some of the guys fell as we stopped. After dismounting, my squad and I lined up behind Muki's force. A bottleneck developed at the corner of the terminal building. I remember the sight of Yoni within the formation and his call for the force to advance.

We came in through the main entrance after Amnon's squad and after Muki. The room was fully lit, the hostages lying on the floor. Upon entry I saw Muki Betser to my right; I took several steps in, beyond the entrance, and lined up adjacent to Amnon Peled. A figure popped out of a far-left corner. I, and Amnon and I think, nearly shot him, but held our fire at the last second. It was one of the hostages.

Beside me someone fired at the hostage Jean Jacques Meimoni, may he rest in peace. Seconds later, the battle in the hostage hall was over. I exited with my squad and joined Dani Arditi's squad.

During the fighting in the hostage hall, Dani Fredkin, an operator in my squad, remained outside and provided cover in the direction of the highjacked plane. From there he hit two Ugandan combatants approaching us at a run.

The role assigned to Dani Arditi's squad was to clear the remaining rooms at the fore of the terminal. Some of his squad members lay wounded (Amir Drori and Aharoni) and the squad needed reinforcement.

Dani and I entered through the window; my squad followed. We found a closed compound of rooms. We entered the compound and scanned it while firing and throwing mini-frag grenades. It turned out to be unoccupied. Within the compound we met no one and took no fire.

At the close of the battle, Muki asked me to count the hostages leaving the hall.

Additional Details

In the belly of the plane I met my classmate, Amit Milstein, of Kibbutz Metzer, who was there with Sayeret Tzanchanim, the para-troop recon unit. The pilot of the second plane was Maj. Dvir (Nati), a native, like me, of Kibbutz Ein Shemer. My classmate Gilad Gold-man, also of Ein Shemer, was there with the Golani recon unit.

Post Op

We returned Sunday afternoon. As soon as I was back on base, I was blasted with the usual issues and concerns of a young platoon commander. The team was waiting for me and we were scheduled to head out that afternoon for a series of drills in the south.

I was on my way to a training area in the Negev when my commander, Yiftach Reicher, encouraged me to stop in and visit my parents. "They're probably a little bit worried," he said. I agreed and hitched a ride with a female friend of mine to go see my parents on the kibbutz. There it turned out that they were quite worried. The initial news reports were vague. They underscored the fact that an officer had been killed and others wounded. My mother decided to "flee the tidings." She left the house and walked amid the fields on the edge of the kibbutz. "She did not want to be notified…" I imagine that many mission participants have a similar story.

My Summary

The facts I chose to note, four decades ago, in my post-operation mission report amounted to a total of several laconic lines. My squad's actions were very limited. We were not required to display a high level of combat skills, nor did we influence the sway of the battle in any significant way, if at all.

Like everyone else from the Unit and the other forces, we took part in a unique, incredible and very dangerous mission that could have ended otherwise. The country showed audacity, the army accomplished the mission, and the soldiers from all of the IDF's brigades (in those days there were only two, Golani and Paratroop) did what was expected of them and were given the privilege of partaking in a seminal national and military mission.

Operation Entebbe subsided in my consciousness, its emotional uniqueness eroded by a long service in the army and the Unit. I later experienced heights of tactical warfare that overshadowed the experience of Entebbe.

That said, in complete contrast, the historical, national, military, and Unit-wide importance of the operation has only grown. The operation's value and the lessons that should to be learned from it have been sharpened and fixed in my consciousness in a place far more central than I'd thought at the time. I do not remember a moment of euphoria, nor a moment of deep sadness. Many dry details, with nothing to do with emotion, were forgotten, but the operation, as a national and military action has endured as a milestone of great importance.

Mission Commander

Lt.-Col. Yoni Netanyahu, may he rest in peace, was the commander of the unit that performed the rescue operation. Yoni and his staff planned and presided over the Unit's role in the mission. They were there, they did it. Yoni was killed as a commander leading his troops into a battle to free the hostages at Entebbe. I believe that is how the events ought to be remembered.

I served under Yoni for two years, until he fell in the battle at Entebbe. His image is seared into my consciousness in a sharp and alive way: His appearance, his gait, his seated posture (reading a book) on Baba's bus on the way up to the Golan Heights; his voice and the contours of his face.

Brig.-Gen.(res) Amos Ben Avraham was born in 1955 on Kibbutz Ein Shemer. He was drafted into the Unit in 1973. He was commander of the November 1975 team, Team Amos. He served as commander of the Unit in 1991-1992 and later went on to serve as commander of the IDF Officers' School, the IDF Command and Staff College, and the Judea Division during Operation Defensive Shield. He was discharged from the IDF with the rank of Brigadier-General. Amos studied medicine at the Technion Institute of Technology and Tel Aviv University, and is married to Edna; the two have a daughter and son, both of whom serve in an elite unit.

4

SUPPRESSIVE FIRE FORCE

AUTHOR:
Eyal Yardenay

Staff-Sgt. Eyal Yardenay, Soldier on Team Dani
Driver-Operator on First Land Rover: Sherman Squad; Yoni's
Assault Force; Wheeled Mobile and Suppressive Fire Squad

My Story

Word of the hijacking arrived pre-noon on Sunday. I don't remember
if we'd just returned from a weekend leave or had spent Shabbat on
the base. We were called in and brought to Ben Gurion International
Airport (then known simply as Lod Airport) to be available and ready
for the arrival of the hijacked plane. The assumption was that the
terrorists would land the plane at the Tel Aviv airport (Lod) and
commence with an extortive, hostage-based attack. At the airport,
there was an Airbus plane (like the one that was hijacked) and we
used it to get to know the aircraft and practice different scenarios
before the plane's arrival. A few hours later we were notified that the
hijacked Air France plane had landed in Benghazi, Libya, and we
were sent back to our base. From that moment forward, till we
touched down at Entebbe, we were engaged in an ongoing march of
uncertainty about whether there would be a rescue operation or a
capitulation to the terrorists' demands. Throughout the week I held
firm in my belief that there would be a mission, and that, we all
understood, meant a significant role for us.

On Tuesday, Dani Arditi, my team leader, called me over and said
that Israel was going to parachute seven operators into Lake Victoria,
to serve as a bridgehead in advance of the rest of the force. He told
me that I'd been chosen as one of the seven, and that I should go and
prepare the Ruger sniper rifle. The idea seemed rather surreal—there
was no operational plan, no certainty about how and when our forces
would arrive, and a host of other issues that made it all seem unten-
able. On the other hand, I felt a deep sense of satisfaction that the
IDF had chosen seven of its best operators to send into the field and

that I could be counted among them. Moreover, the usual protocol is to take operators from the most veteran teams in the Unit and, though there were two teams above us, they still tapped me for the mission.

As expected, the parachute plan was nixed and we continued to wait. Stories about the leader of Uganda, Idi Amin, started to pour in. The brutal dictator, we were told, kidnapped and raped young women and butchered people for the fun of it. There were all sorts of tales of atrocities. Among others, we heard that he kept human organs stored in his home refrigerator. I remember my teammate, Amir Drori, hearing that and saying that he was booking a spot in the freezer.

On Thursday at midnight someone woke me and Meir Magal (Meke), the team's other driver, and sent us to fetch two wheeled BTR-40s (the armored personnel carriers used during the operation) from the large infantry base in Ramla. From that moment on we were immersed in preparations. At first, I was slated to drive one of those Soviet APCs, but was later transferred, as driver, to the first Land Rover jeep.

As part of my preparations in advance of the mission, I found myself, of my own accord, sitting in the intel bureau and studying the route overland from Entebbe to Kenya. I figured that as the driver of the Land Rover I might need that information if the operation ended in failure and we were forced to flee and evade the Ugandan forces. I decided that I'd fill an extra magazine and stash it in the back of my battle vest. That one, I told myself, would be used only in the event of an escape-and-evasion scenario.

During the on-base briefing, in which the plan was revealed, including the idea of impersonating Idi Amin's presidential convoy, I got up and said there that the roar of a Hercules C-130 landing in the middle of the night would surely tip the terrorists off to our arrival and give them plenty of time to slaughter the hostages. I was told, in response, that the pilot would cut the engines and the plane would coast down silently onto the runway. Years later, when I met the pilot of our plane, I conveyed to him what I'd been told. He had a hard time quelling his laughter. A Hercules C-130 is not a glider; if its engines are cut, it falls like a stone.

I felt fine and didn't vomit during the flight to Sharm even though it was a difficult ride because the plane flew very close to the ground and the weather was extremely hot. Before taking off for Entebbe we all gathered and sat at the foot of the plane. Yoni went from squad to squad and made sure that everyone was very familiar with all the details of the plan. I remember Dan Shomron (or maybe it was Yoni) telling us the following: "The IDF is extending its long arm 4,000 kilometers from Israel. This is the spearhead of the IDF and you are the tip of the spear, it all depends on you." With those words, we boarded the plane.

Many thoughts passed through my mind during the seven-hour flight to Entebbe. Mostly about my family and my parents and their ability to live with loss. I didn't pity myself or worry about my fate. I thought mostly about my parents.

As we prepared for landing the captain announced that we were close to our destination and we started our approach. I sat down behind the wheel of the jeep. The Land Rover was backed onto the plane so that it was nose-out, sandwiched between the Mercedes and the second jeep. While coming in for a landing, the captain partially opened the upper cargo ramp. From my perch on the driver's seat I could see the runway drawing near. I waited for the pilot to cut the engines, as promised, but instead heard the usual roar of the reverse-thrust landing. It came thundering in through the open cargo ramp. It also arrived just when I was waiting for the quiet glide of the cut engines and it shocked me. I felt a heartbeat accompanied by a sharp pain, a sort of somber skip, and I told myself that the terrorists would soon start slaughtering the hostages and that the operation was doomed to failure.

The plane came to a stop, we started up the vehicles, the pilot powered down, and we rolled out onto the tarmac. We huddled for a few seconds to get organized. That's the moment embedded deep in my memory: On the runway, 4,000 kilometers from Israel, moments before we found ourselves in the midst of the commotion of battle, surrounded by total silence, the darkness mingling with the heat and humidity of Africa.

As soon as we moved out, I was focused on the mission at hand. I felt no fear and was alert and ready. I focused on the driving and kept my eyes roving across the horizon ahead. About one-hundred meters before the disembarkation point, we encountered two Ugandan soldiers on the taxiway and they started to stomp their feet and point their weapons at us. I saw that the guys from the Mercedes were firing at them with the silenced pistols, but they missed. One of the Ugandan soldiers fled and the other stood there with his weapon still trained on us. Once I saw that he hadn't been hit, I told Dani Arditi, who sat to my right, that I was going to run him over. Dani didn't respond. I took that as an approval. I passed the Mercedes on the right and intended to hit the sentry with the left part of the front fender so as not to harm the radiator. When I was about a meter and a half away from him, a loud burst of fire hit him and he fell. Driving a jeep heavily loaded with operators, I managed to swerve around the downed soldier and not run over him and send the operators flying. At that moment, gunfire erupted from all around and once again I told myself that the operation had failed.

We reached the disembarkation point. Uri Ben-Ner, the driver of the second Land Rover, Amitzur Kafri, the driver of the Mercedes, and I stayed with Rami Sherman, the squad commander, and launched suppressive fire at the air traffic control tower. The top of the tower was lined with windows and we took heavy fire from there. A short while later word came over the radio to reposition ourselves on the other side of the tower. We boarded the vehicles and moved to face the terminal doors. The fire kept coming. I grabbed the shoulder-held RPG missile out of the trunk of the Land Rover and fired up at the glass windows at the top of the tower. The angle was very tricky, as I stood right at the foot of the tower. The rocket-propelled grenade penetrated straight into the center of the tower's control room and caused a huge explosion. A mushroom cloud of smoke and fire rose up over the tower and from that point on it fell silent, as the shooting from there stopped. I used all of my ammunition, except the magazine I'd stored in the back pocket of my vest.

At that stage, I was instructed to drive the Land Rover towards the plane. Thankfully, I hadn't had to grapple with the matter of whether or not I ought to use the magazine I'd set aside for emergency escape. When I reached the Land Rover, I saw it covered with hostages, people sitting on every available surface from the hood to the rear fender. I couldn't even get to the driver's seat. I climbed up on the hood, stepping on hostages, made it to the region of the driver's seat, opened my battle vest, lifted it up to neck-height, and plunged myself down through the mass of people. I started the vehicle up but couldn't turn the wheel; one of the hostages was standing on the outside of the jeep and clutching the steering wheel for support. I pried one of his hands off the wheel, but he held on tight with the other one. While struggling for control of the wheel, and without being able to see his face, because only his hands were threaded through the mass of people, I found myself thinking of what must be going through his mind: the IDF has come to save me and some cruel soldier is trying to wrench me off the rescue vehicle. Looking back, I'm amazed that I found the time to think of that sort of thing during the tumult of combat, especially since I knew that he could easily have walked the short distance to the plane along with the rest of the hostages. There was no way we'd leave him behind.

The pilot had taxied over to within 500 meters of the terminal and that's where I was headed with the pile of people covering the Land Rover. About halfway there, the engine started to sputter and gasp. I realized there was a problem with the fuel supply and that the engine would soon die. I dropped a hand to the floor of the vehicle, where the fuel-tank shifter is located, to try and switch over to the auxiliary tank. The valve was already shifted to the spare tank. One of the hostages must have moved it with his foot. That was why there was no fuel reaching the engine. In a split-second decision I opted not to turn the switch back to the main tank, but to pull the lever that starts the electric pump that draws the fuel from the auxiliary tank. The engine responded immediately and I continued driving. The hostages got off at the foot of the plane. A stretcher carrying a wounded person was placed on the windscreen of the Land Rover for a short while and then loaded onto the plane.

I don't remember the flight back as a celebratory jumble but rather as a long introspective period filled with the anticipation of an incoming missile and the possibility of an explosion. At the time I didn't know that our troops on the ground had destroyed the Ugandan Air Force, and I figured, judging by the stories that I'd heard about Idi Amin, that rather than face the shame he would send planes to shoot us down. Those thoughts, and the prospect of a missile impact at any moment, accompanied me throughout the flight and I only felt a wave of relief when we reached Sharm and the pilot turned our attention to a pair of Phantom F-4s that had come to accompany us home. I looked out the window on the left and saw an Israeli Phantom hugging our wing. I looked right and saw the second one glued to the other wing. That's a moment I won't forget for the rest of my days. A feeling of relief after hours of tribulation, of flying through the dark in a heavy and defenseless plane and waiting for the moment that it'll be hit and destroyed.

The planes transporting the hostages and the Golani and Para-troop Brigade troops landed at Lod (Ben Gurion Airport), where the press and the TV crews were waiting amid the joyous commotion. We landed at Tel Nof, far from the glare of the spotlights.

We drove the two Land Rovers and the Mercedes back to the base —in Ugandan army fatigues, on civilian roads, and with the blood of the wounded person still smeared on the windscreen. At nine in the evening we were given a night's leave and we hitched home.

The ceremony marking the 25th anniversary of the operation was held in the International Convention Center in Jerusalem and it was attended by the president, the prime minister, several ministers and former soldiers and hostages. It was very emotional to sit beside those who were once hostages in the same hall. A woman who had been held hostage at Entebbe turned to my son and said: 'Only thanks to your father am I here today.'

During the ceremony, each unit that had taken part in the operation sent a representative to the podium to present its role. I was granted the honor of telling my story.

Maj. (res) Eyal Yardenay, third generation in Moshav Nahalal, is a grandson of one of the founders of the agricultural community. He was drafted to the Unit in February 1974 and became an operator on Team Dani Arditi. Operation Entebbe caught him half a year before discharge. Roughly one year after discharge, the team was moved to Palmachim as part of the founding of the Israel Air Force's commando unit, Shaldag. He was commissioned as an officer in reserves and given command of Team Arnon Epstein and Team Loni in Zvika Gilad's company. Once Zvika was discharged from reserves duty he was given command of the company until they too reached the age of final discharge from reserves. Today he still serves as a reserves officer in the tactical mobility company as a scout for combat drivers. He's married to Anat, is a father of three, and lives in Nahalal.

The First Land Rover. From right to left: Yonatan Gilad, Eyal Yardenay (the driver of the first Land Rover), Shlomi Reisman and Alex Davidi.

Back in Israel on the Mercedes. From right to left: Shlomi Reisman,
Alex Davidi, Amos Goren, Amos Ben-Avraham.
In the back: Dani Dagan, Amitzur Kafri, Uri Ben Ner.
Photo: Shlomi's camera

Upon return from Entebbe, on the Mercedes. From right to left: Dani Dagan,
Shlomi Reisman, Ilan Blumer, Gadi Ilan, Alex Davidi, Uri Ben Ner.
Photo: Shlomi's camera.

On the APC back in Israel. From right to left: Itzik Kirschner, Dr. Arik Shalev.
Standing from right to left: Gadi Ilan, Alex Davidi.
Photo: Shlomi's camera.

On the Land Rover back in Israel. From right to left: Eyal Yardenay, Gadi
Ilan, Shlomi Reisman, Dani Dagan. Photo: Shlomi's camera.

5

APC FORCE

AUTHORS**:**
Shaul Mofaz
Yohai Brenner
Dani Dagan
Eldad Perkal (Dolev)
Udi Salvi
Yuval Fine
Alon Shemi
Eyal Oren
Yoni Raz
Yossi Shak
Arik Shalev
Omer Bar Lev

Alon Shemi:
Eyal Shifroni
Meke Magal
Asaf Lippman
Zeev Ronen
Yaron Asaf
Eyal Oren
Hilik Glazer

Udi Salvi
Yuval Fine
Zvi Chibutro
Tzachi Fuchs
Uri Steinmitz
Raz Gur-Arie
Maxi Katzir
Ron Gal

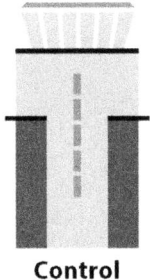

**Control
Tower**

Armored BTR-40 Force Under the Command of Shaul Mofaz (Illustrated Depiction of the Deployment)

d Terminal

Omer Bar Lev:
Yoni Raz
Yoav Wachman
Yaakov Gilenberg
Yossi Shak
Shauli Ravid
Ron Liberman
Dr. Arik Shalev

Shaul Mofaz:
Yohai Brenner
Itzik Kirschner
Arik Kamus
Eldad Dolev
Yoel Tzibulski
Dani Dagan
David Tzfira

Maj. Shaul Mofaz, (Outgoing) Deputy Commander of the Unit
APC Force Commander

YONI NETANYAHU AND OPERATION ENTEBBE

My acquaintance with Yoni dates back to when Giora Zore'a was the commander of the Unit. At the time I was deputy commander of the 890th Paratroop Battalion and a candidate for the post of deputy commander of the Unit. Giora told me that as far as he was concerned, I was a suitable candidate, but that Yoni, who was soon to take over as commander, had to make the call. I was summoned for an interview at the Petah Tikva police station; there I met Yoni Netanyahu for the first time. He was young, impressive, unassuming. Speaking eye to eye, he said he was looking for someone with combat experience who could fortify that element in the Unit operators.

Shortly afterward Yoni and Giora informed me that I'd been chosen as the incoming deputy commander of the Unit. The plan was that I'd report for duty at the base, deploy on one or two covert missions to learn about the clandestine nature of the Unit and gain an understanding of its work, and simultaneously start serving in my new role. So it was. I joined Team Omer Bar Lev on a mission and was exposed firsthand to the professional side of the Unit's work. I was impressed with the sophistication and professionalism of the soldiers, but it was clear to me that the operators lacked real combat experience. I started my service in the Unit at the tail end of Giora's term and was already serving as the deputy commander when the baton was officially passed to Yoni. That was in July 1975.

I was new to the position but, like Yoni, was a veteran of three wars, and the cooperation between us was excellent. Yoni decided that he would be nearly fully immersed in the planning and commanding of

Unit missions and I, primarily, would be charged with force buildup and training, and the administration and management of missions.

I was closest to Yoni in age. He was 29 at the time and I was 26. Yoni was reserved and introverted; he lived with Bruria in Ramat HaSharon, not far from me and my wife, Orit. I felt that he was caught in a bind—on the one hand, he was committed to the rigorous, unforgiving life of the commander of the Unit, his dream job; and on the other hand, he wanted a private life, to start a family with Bruria.

Every once in a while, during the course of the year, Yoni's internal stress bubbled to the surface, and it could not be concealed from the officers of the Unit, with whom he was in daily contact. That said, the Unit was operationally active, the missions flowing along. Occasionally, there were hitches. The most significant mishap occurred several weeks before Operation Entebbe, on a mission that for various reasons did not come to full fruition, and, by Unit standards, was riddled with problems. During the post-op process of learning the lessons of the operation, the Unit's officers were critical of the actions of those higher up the chain. I suggested reenacting the event, and Yoni voiced concern. In the end, the reenactment was done and many lessons were learned. Yoni was the commander of the Unit, situated at the top of the pyramid, but he was nevertheless attuned to the opinions of the officers serving beneath him regarding his words and actions—in every realm.

Several days before the hijacking of the Air France plane a large chunk of the Unit officer corps gathered for a meeting that was very critical of Yoni's conduct. As soon as they invited me to join, and as soon as I realized what was to be discussed, I ordered them to immediately disperse the "assembly." I asked Yoni to come to the Unit ASAP and to speak to the officers, and so it was. My feeling is that the discussion left Yoni wounded. I'm not even sure the wound had time to scab; he didn't deserve that.

The Operation and the Preparations

During the days after the hijacking, or perhaps it was the week before, I finished my stint as deputy commander of the Unit and turned the reins over to Yiftach Reicher, who, in the past, had also replaced me as commander of Sayeret Tzanchanim, the paratroop recon unit. I was up for a posting as a battalion commander, but Yoni thought I ought to study business management, perhaps even on the dime of the Military Intelligence Directorate. In fact, he set it all up, and I was, at the time, preparing for summer courses at Bar Ilan University, completing prerequisites in advance of the academic year.

During the week Yoni was engaged in operational activity in the Sinai. He called me and instructed me to be in touch with Muki Betser. I dropped everything and reported for duty at the Unit, putting myself at Muki's beck and call. Muki spent much of his time at the Operations Directorate and I mostly worked from the base, preparing the forces, the gear, etc.

From that point forward, the operation started to chug along…

Yoni was still battered by the aftereffects of the officers meeting; however, the system and the upper echelons of the command structure held him in high regard and had unwavering faith in him. Having returned from the Sinai and, afterwards, from the briefing at Beit HaTzanchan (the Paratrooper House) in Ramat Gan, Yoni, whose confidence had been shaken, told me that he was concerned that a replacement might be dropped in instead of him as commander of the burgeoning mission. He also told me that he wanted to position himself at the head of one of the assault squads. At this stage each of the force and squad commanders was focused on his mission and immersed in his own preparations. Several events, though, from that 24-hour period (and maybe a bit more) stand out in my mind:

First, the question of command. Yoni was deeply concerned and he asked me what would happen if they slotted someone in above him, appointing another officer to command all Unit forces operating in and around the old terminal. I said that such a thing was out of the question—unequivocally! You, I said, must go speak with [Brig.-Gen.] Dan Shomron on the double. He did just that, and the conversation helped him clarify his position to his superiors; namely that he, and only he, would command the Unit forces during the operation. That was agreed upon with Dan Shomron, the chief paratroop and infantry officer, and made clear to everyone. The Unit would be under Yoni's direct command during the operation.

Afterwards, on the runways, we built a mock terminal out of burlap and fence posts. Either before or during the simulation drill—I'm not sure I recall the exact chronology—Defense Minister Shimon Peres showed up at the base along with [Brig.-Gen.] Yanush Ben-Gal, an aide to the Commander of the IDF Operations Directorate. Speaking with Peres, I realized that the political decision makers felt it necessary to hear firsthand, from the operators and commanders, an assessment of the chances of success. Yoni conveyed to Peres what he felt was the heart of the matter: that the Unit knew exactly what it was doing, that it was ready for the mission, and that it would get the job done. Yoni emphasized that, so long as the first two planes were able to land, he had no doubt that the hostages would be freed and the goal of the mission accomplished. I recall that Yanush felt similarly, and his opinion held great sway with Peres, who in turn conveyed the message to Prime Minister Rabin and the Cabinet.

On Saturday afternoon we flew to Sharm al-Sheikh. There we waited for the government to authorize the mission. We knew that the Cabinet was convened in order to make a decision and that the IDF Chief of Staff Motta Gur had been hesitant during different stages of the preparations. As officers in the operational force, we knew nothing of the resignation letter that Prime Minister Rabin had penned and planned to submit should the operation fail.

I remember two important conversations in Sharm: the force-wide briefing from Dan Shomron, in which he emphasized that the operation was a serious test of our skills, that the people of Israel had faith in us, and that the essence of the operation was an unwillingness to surrender to terror—a strong briefing that I remember to this day. The second was Yoni's address: "We know how to accomplish this mission and bring the hostages home." Just then the additional pieces of the intelligence puzzle arrived; the material enabled the attack force and the APC force to update and sharpen its understanding of the target and its surroundings.

At this point I learnt of Yoni's final positioning within the force. When I heard that Yoni had placed himself at the fore of the assault force, I told him that in my opinion he should put himself in a spot from which he'd have the best overall view of all the forces, so as to be best positioned for commanding the entire operation. Yoni explained that he had to be among the lead squads, spearheading the charge. I insisted that he was wrong, and that he had to be positioned behind the lead squads, so as maintain control of all forces. The argument continued and Yoni concluded by saying that he'd think it over during the flight.

That was my last conversation with Yoni. In the end he positioned himself right after Amnon's squad, just as he'd intended. The long flight offered time to think: would the mission be authorized? And if so, what would it look like on the ground? When we were given authorization, everyone reacted in his own way. There were no bursts of joy; there was tension, and understandably so.

In the Field

The details are known, I don't think they need to be reexamined too closely. From the plane that I rode in, I saw, as we came in for a landing, the shots fired at the sentries guarding the old terminal where the hostages were being kept. In my opinion, the decision to open fire at the sentries with silenced handguns was entirely legitimate; it's unclear whether the un-muffled Kalashnikov fire was necessary.

Be that as it may, we landed several minutes after the first Hercules and charged full steam ahead toward the square outside the terminal. Udi Salvi, in command of a pair of APCs, took up his positions. While in motion I heard over the two-way radio that Yoni had been shot and that fire was being directed at the control tower. We added our firepower to the mix, trying to quell the fire from there and eliminate the threat to the forces below.

Strangely, aside from those bursts of fire, and of course our fire at the MiGs, I remember it being rather quiet for most of the time. When we spotted Ugandan back-ups heading our way from the city of Entebbe or Kampala, we opened fire and charged toward them and they retreated once and for all. Radio contact with the airborne control room was problematic. Control asked repeatedly about the MiG fighter jets on the ground. On account of poor reception, and since our advance orders were anyway in the same vein, we opened fire on the MiGs without final authorization from the command-and-control room. Quickly, the jets burst into large bonfires.

Once the hostages had been evacuated to safety, the soldiers in the APCs threw up smoke screens and dropped explosive charges on the taxiways. Just then we received word that the head count indicated that several people were missing. We were directed to go back and check the hijacked plane. My force turned around and had a look at the exterior of the plane—we did not go inside and after some time we returned to the loading zone of the Hercules C-130s. Throughout, there was a Ugandan soldier with a supply of ammunition up in the control tower, but since we fired at him every now and again, he remained down, behind cover, and just fired at the sky, the angle allowed him by the tower. I waited with Dan Shomron for the last of the APCs to be loaded up onto the plane and secured there, while the Ugandan soldier fired continuously at the heavens. We were the last ones on the plane. I sat down next to Dan and I remember saying to him that to my mind, "this is a historic operation."

In Nairobi we were told that Yoni had been killed.

Perspective

From our point of view in the Unit, Yoni was the one who gave his seal of approval as to the readiness of the force to carry out the operation, and his confidence in the Unit's ability was conveyed directly, without filtration, to the decision makers. Aside from that, in my opinion, in hindsight, the key to the mission's success was the element of surprise.

The political leadership showed true courage and determination. Their ability to make such a decision was drawn, in part, from the confidence projected by the Unit's operators and officers, our faith in our ability to accomplish the mission even though to us as well the task seemed hard to imagine. The IDF Chief of Staff, in a departure from his ordinary self-assurance, began accepting the opinions of his underlings and grew enthusiastic about the mission only as the plan progressed, and particularly once the pilots demonstrated a lights-out landing on the runways at Sharm on Friday night. Central figures who influenced both the political and military leadership were: IAF Commander Benny Peled and Commander of the IDF Operations Directorate Kuti Adam and his aide, Yanush Ben-Gal.

But the courage was first and foremost political. The decision was Nahshonian: a jump into the sea of uncertainty and a willingness to send the forces into the field, with the understanding that, so long as the first planes managed to land, the odds were that the mission would be a success. It was, by any means, a national mission; a defiant message conveying that we shall not surrender to terror, and a message to Israelis and Jews that no matter where they may be on this earth, if they are in trouble the IDF will find a way to get there. There can be no doubt that the mission improved Israel's position and its image in the eyes of the world, and also improved the national carriage, straightening the spine of an entire nation.

I felt that the weight of the mission weighed on Yoni more than on previous missions. As pertains to the fact that he positioned himself in the spot where he was hit—in my opinion he wanted to prove to everyone that he was the commander and that he was no less brave, and given the circumstances he had no choice. The message that "we can accomplish the mission" was, solely, on Yoni; it was his word and his knowledge of the capacities of the operators and officers that allowed him to say clearly: we'll get it done.

The demanding role of Unit commander clashed, inescapably, with his desire for a personal life. I felt that the story was tragic: the rocky road he traveled ever since being appointed commander of the Unit, the rupture of faith with the officers several weeks before the operation, the face-to-face meeting with the officers, his positioning within the force—it all weighed heavily on him. And yet, Yoni stiffened his lips and with a herculean effort led a historic mission that straightened the spine of Israel. I am certain that the minister of history will count that in his favor.

The details of the operation and the contribution of every one of the operators and officers is important, but more so is the knowledge that, in times of crisis, any physical distance and operational complexity can be overcome; the capacity is boundless. As someone who's seen many complex operations and has observed the balance between military and political courage: here, in Operation Yonatan, the political courage prevailed.

Yoni could have risen very high up the chain of the command were he not killed by the bullet of a Ugandan soldier. And yet we tend to say that the bullets of war are blind.

Very pleasant hast thou been unto me, my brother Yonatan.

Lt.-Gen (res) Shaul Mofaz was born in Tehran in late 1948 and immigrated to Israel at the age of nine. He studied and lived at the agricultural boarding school in Nahalal. In November 1966 he was drafted into the Paratroop Brigade and served as a soldier during the Six Day War, a platoon commander during the War of Attrition, and as the commander of Sayeret Tzanchanim during the Yom Kippur War. After his service as deputy commander of the Unit, he served as a battalion commander and later as brigade commander of the Paratroop Brigade (during the First Intifada). From July 1998 to mid-2002 he served as the IDF Chief of Staff. From 2002-2006 he served as Defense Minister and as Deputy Prime Minister, and up until 2009 as Transportation Minister. Today he is involved in the high-tech industry and in consulting.

Maj. Yohai Brenner, Operations Directorate Officer
Operator-Officer in Mofaz's APC; Armored Force

OPERATION ENTEBBE IN 54 MINUTES

For me, Operation Entebbe remains a clash of emotions. On the one hand, a tremendous success, the scope of which we had no way of evaluating in real time, and on the other, the knowledge that our commander, the man who ensured the unit's successful execution of the mission and was among its leading planners, has died.

For a year I worked closely and intensively with Yoni Netanyahu and many memories come to mind when thinking of him. But one day in particular stands out. It was the winter of 1975-76 and a friend who served in the Development HQ of the Merkava Tank phoned me and said: "Tomorrow at 5 AM at the Arik Bridge, there's going to be a trial run of the Merkava. If you'd like, you're invited." "Oh, I would very much like!" I answered, "and I'm coming with Yoni."

Before joining the Unit, Yoni served as an Armored Corps battalion commander, and he loved tanks with all his heart and soul, if such a phrase can be used to describe his fascination. So, when I told him that we're leaving at 3 AM to be at the test run, his eyes lit up. He promptly started shifting his schedule around, and for a Unit commander that's no simple task, to put it mildly.

Only the two of us drove to Arik Bridge. Once there, we downed a coffee and waited for the trial to start. When it began, I stood outside the turret, staying there for roughly two hours, while Yoni positioned himself inside the turret and stayed put for the entire trial run. I think that as the day reached its end, there was no one happier than Yoni!

I remember the Sabbaths when I stayed at base on duty, and in the afternoon my wife Talma and my kids and I would drive over to Yoni

and Bruria's home, sit with them and chat. Sometimes Ehud Barak
and his wife Nava joined us, living as they did in the same building
in Ramat HaSharon. I also remember how we all wandered around
back in those days with our "brain bag" in hand: a bag in which we
kept notebooks, pens and grease pencils. Yoni always had a book in
his bag, too: even if he had just ten minutes to spare, out it'd come
and he'd be immersed in reading.

There's a theory that describes life as a parabola. You're born, you
study, you enlist, establish a family.... That was my first parabola,
which ended at the end of the Yom Kippur War. My second parabola
began when Yoni asked me to join the Unit. That was in 1975,
shortly after Yoni received command of the Unit. He was missing a
few functionaries, among them an operations directorate officer. I
was already a civilian by then, having completed my military service
as a paratroop commander in the 890th Battalion more than a decade
earlier.

In fact, when Yoni invited me to join the Unit, my role in the
civilian world was as financial coordinator of my kibbutz, Maoz
Haim. I didn't have a clue about the Unit. All I knew was that some
of the guys from Maoz Haim had served there, but the unwritten rule
was: ask no questions, expect no information. I came with a mindset
open to surprises. And a lot of surprises there were, too, as well as a
lot of hard work.

About a year later, just past mid-June 1976, my service with the
Unit was to have ended, but Yoni asked me to sign an extension. I
was 35, married, and a father of three children. My situation was
different from that of the other soldiers, who were mostly 18 to 20
years old, or at the most 25, and of course Yoni was fully aware of
that. His suggestion was to give me another day off at home
midweek. But I didn't want special treatment, I enjoyed my service in
the Unit, and, assuming that the kibbutz would approve the extension, I had but one request. "I know which operations I can participate in and which I can't," I said to him, "but on those I can join, I
just want you to promise that you'll slot me in." He promised, the
kibbutz authorized my request, and a week later, Entebbe....

Sunday, 27 June 1976: The Air France Airbus is Hijacked

I left the kibbutz and reached the Unit's base at 8 AM. Some of its members were down south in the Sinai with Yoni, and those who weren't, were called in for a 10 AM meeting at the airport. As soon as precise details about the hijacked plane came in, we started preparing and allocating equipment for a takeover should the plane land in Lod, the location of Israel's Ben Gurion International Airport, as had happened in 1972 when the Belgian, Sabena Airlines flight landed in Israel. Waiting at the airport were Shimon Peres in his role as Minister of Defense, and Kuti Adam, head of the IDF Operations Directorate. Both wanted to see firsthand how we were preparing the assault on the ostensibly incoming airplane. In the afternoon, once it became clear that the jet wasn't going to be diverted to Israel, we were released back to our base.

Monday and Tuesday, 28-29 June

We didn't do anything that related to Entebbe. We were busy with other things, and since we didn't read the papers, watch TV, or listen to the radio, we had no idea about the pressure that the families of the captive travelers were putting on the political decision makers. We did sense "background noise," though. I knew someone was collecting intelligence; I knew Ehud Barak, Amiram Levin, and Muki Betser were meeting with people from Israel's largest construction company, Solel Boneh, which had built the old airport terminal in Uganda, and with Israel Air Force pilots who'd landed there and were familiar with the tarmacs and the prevailing wind patterns. These meetings were possibly held in the IDF's main HQ or some bureau or another, or perhaps in a private home, but definitely not in the Unit.

Wednesday, 30 June

An ongoing General Staff exercise reached its end. Kuti Adam invited all units relevant to an Entebbe terminal takeover to the underground bunker at the IDF HQ: representatives from the Unit, the Naval Commandos, the Golani Brigade's recon unit, the Para- troops, the Air Force… and at the end of the discussion of the recently completed exercise, the issue of Entebbe came up. The guys asked who was handling the matter of the hijacked plane and where the situation stood in general. People said that if the Operations Directorate didn't take command, they were going to resign. We all sat there together in that hall, on swivel chairs, with a different map taped to each of the four walls: an IAF map, a world map…

At the end of the discussion, the Military Intelligence Directorate and the Operations Directorate shared all the information they had available and Kuti said that now each unit would go back to its base and draw up a plan of action. When we left the hall, we promised each other that no matter whose plan would be chosen, we were all in, all the units involved, and no one would leave anyone else out. The truth, though, was that we couldn't believe the government would approve an operation of any sort to free the hostages at Entebbe.

Thursday, 1 July 1976

The terrorists began releasing non-Jewish hostages. Amiram Levin was sent to Paris to interrogate the released passengers.

That afternoon, Yoni returned from Sinai. Dan Shomron, asked us to come to Beit HaTzanchan in Ramat Gan, central Israel, and we set out in two cars. Riding in Yoni's Israeli-made Carmel Ducas were: Yoni, me, and Rami Sherman, the operations officer; in the other car sat Avi Weiss, the intelligence officer, Tamir Pardo the radio and communications officer, and perhaps also Muki Betser. There at the offices, without wasting any time, Dan Shomron dived in. "I'm tasking you with this. You're the force that will break into the terminal." We asked questions, some of which were answered, some of which weren't, and we returned to the Unit's base.

Then, and only then, in the Unit, in Yoni's offices, did the detailed planning begin.

Information began flowing in from Amiram in Paris, allowing the planning of the operation. Amiram has a very fertile mind: I don't know of many others as creative as his. He knew what to ask, and what to conclude from the answers, he knew what to send and what not to bother with, so as to avoid wasting time. Now, at least, we knew how many terrorists there were, where they were positioned, where they resided, which of the terminal's rooms they occupied, the total number of rooms, and the distribution of the hostages among them. Additionally, he provided us with a sense of the size of the Ugandan force deployed there; where it was located and what was happening in the control tower.

We started building a model of the airport. We brought in all the equipment, from jute sacks to "Czech hedgehogs" and metal angles, and built a model of the old Entebbe terminal based on the data we had, including entrances into the passenger lounges, the plaza fronting the terminal, and the control tower.

The Unit operators and officers were completely isolated for the purpose of complete secrecy. No one came, no one left. And it was made impossible to place an outgoing call. All phone lines had been disconnected. My wife Talma tried to get hold of me and every time, she was told, "He's not available right now," "he's in a meeting," "He's busy."

That night she did manage to get hold of me in my apartment in Petah Tikva and asked when I'd be back home. "Only when it's all over," I answered. I didn't say what, but the news was full of Entebbe and the idea that we'd be deployed there scared her. She told me that she went to see her father, a former Palmach deputy commander, and he calmed her down, saying there was no way we'd go to Entebbe because we had no planes that could make it all the way there.

Friday, 2 July 1976

At 7 AM a bunch of orders came through, requiring tons of coordination. We started hunting for a Mercedes. We found one, but it was white. We'd need to paint it black to make it look as close as possible to the one used by Idi Amin, which meant getting hold of Ugandan flags too. We needed strong weapons for the BTR-40 APCs (armored personnel carriers) which meant hunting around the lots of the Ordnance Corps.

Every so often when there was a moment to think in more general

terms, we'd encourage each other. "We CAN do this, wherever, whatever the weather, but the government won't approve it…."

Meanwhile, Ehud Barak was sent to Kenya to coordinate the
possibility of our landing there to refuel. Nairobi was a 40-minute
flight from Entebbe and we had good relations with the Kenyans. A
second option was to take over the fuel tanks at the Entebbe airport,
but that would be more problematic. The fuel nozzle spout doesn't
always match a plane's fuel tank, and if that happened, there was no
way to refuel. The air force found a solution. We could refuel in
Entebbe but it would cost us time and would be dangerous.

As evening fell, the IDF Chief of Staff Motta Gur flew to Sharm
el-Sheikh with the Hercules pilots to ensure that they could, in fact,
land in the dark. When he saw that it was possible, he told [Prime
Minister] Rabin that he would sign off on the plan.

That night we conducted a model exercise in Sirkin, with the
planes and pilots. We loaded the vehicles onto the planes, two APCs
to each plane, and clamped them down to prevent them from moving
around during the flight. Then we released the cables and offloaded
them. It all took time. The vehicles had to be directed down the ramp
to avoid damaging the plane doors. We repeated it over and over until
we got our completion times down and our execution perfect, earning
Yoni's approval. Then we spread out on the model's area, each of us
storming the location assigned to us.

Once the model exercise was over, Motta Gur noted that the jeeps
were overloaded and several soldiers would have to be removed.
Everyone wanted to be a part of the mission: not only did we view it
as a privilege, but we felt it our duty. I remember thinking that if I'm
taken off the APC and deemed unnecessary for this operation, I'll
walk home and never come back to the Unit. Thankfully, and on
account of Yoni's promise, there was no need for such action.

Saturday, 3 July 1976

A Mossad agent, who flew on Friday morning to Entebbe,
managed to take photographs of the old terminal. I have no idea what

he told the Ugandan flight controllers, but he had his story and clearly it worked. He sent the negatives back to Israel, and Avi Weiss, our intelligence officer, drove on Saturday to collect them from where they were being developed.

That afternoon, on the way to Ben Gurion Airport, we saw some of the guys who'd been removed from the operation. They were walking away from the Unit. What a shame, I thought. I really had pity on them. They must have felt dreadful.

We were already on the plane and about to take off for Sharm when Avi showed up with the photos. I remember he left his car engine running and made a mad dash to the plane. It was really the last second. The Hercules' engines were revving and ready, but those photos were an ace in the hole, and in his last briefing, Yoni used them.

The take off from Ben Gurion Airport was tough. It was very hot, the planes were heavy, and the pilots needed to fly at "grass-skimming height" so as not to be spotted by external radar. I remember how, while flying over Kibbutz Mashabei Sadeh, I thought that if my sister, who lived there, happened to be passing by, we were so low that we could have shaken hands. Because of the heat and the ridiculously low flight altitude, the plane bounced and danced around throughout. One of our operators couldn't endure any more: he disembarked in Sharm el-Sheikh and from there made his way back home.

In Sharm, before getting back on the plane, Yoni gave us our last briefing. I will never forget it. Its impression is seared in my mind and heart. He gave us a rousing speech, persuasive, and not just for the information he had gleaned from the photos, but for its clarity on the mental level. He spoke directly to each operator's heart, and exuded faith in our ability to carry out this tremendous mission.

We reboarded. I was in the second Hercules, in an APC with Mofaz, who at the time was Yoni's deputy. The tension was so high that I couldn't fall asleep. As we approached Entebbe, a serious sand storm accompanied by lightning and thunder whipped up. On one hand, a stunning scene; on the other, extremely frightening, but our pilots, true heroes, managed to catch the right angle despite the storm and land on schedule.

When we landed, the tarmac lights were still on but as we taxied along the runway they went out. Since this possibility had been taken into account, the paratroopers, riding with Matan Vilnai in the first plane, had already set up improvised flares in tins down the length of the tarmac so that planes three and four would have an illuminated landing strip.

Entebbe in 54 minutes

We're off the planes. There's a 1.5-kilometer ride ahead of us. I put on my night vision glasses so that I can direct the driver. Only when we're moving forward and in control on the tarmac, do I start preparing the MAG, because machine guns can't be readied on the plane for safety reasons: one stray bullet and we could all be goners.

The forces in the four APCs are responsible for securing the perimeter of the terminal, but at some stage it becomes clear that the Ugandan fire from the control tower isn't letting up and our suppressive fire force isn't able to silence it. We set out in the APC for the terminal's front plaza. On the way Mofaz is informed via radio that Yoni's been wounded. We reach the plaza and start shooting in both directions, towards the control tower and the terminal rooftop, preventing the dozens of Ugandan soldiers in those two locations from disrupting our forces fighting below. I shoot full, 250-bullet belts from the MAG, one belt at the control tower, one at the roof, alternating between them. When the MAG overheats and the barrel whitens, I let it rest for a moment and take up the Kalashnikov. From our position we can see Yoni, wounded, and the doctor treating him.

From a distance we hear shooting from the second APC at the Ugandan MiGs and catch sight of them for barely a couple of seconds before they go up in flames.

Fire from the control tower stops. The terminal has been cleansed. Now the order is given to get the hostages out of the waiting lounges. Our Land Rovers were already in the plaza and hostages were starting to come out and board the vehicles. It was clear to us that they were in a panic, scared that something could go wrong. I can hear voices: "Get on," "Get off." I can see how some hostages are being removed from the Land Rovers which couldn't carry so many people at once. Those hostages start walking to Hercules 4 which has drawn closer to the old terminal.

At this stage the old terminal, being the military terminal, was neutralized. Not a single Ugandan dared move in there. The international terminal was also incapacitated. Paratroopers from the 35th Brigade had taken control of it right from the outset. On the other side of the terminal was Lake Victoria: clearly no one would be coming from that direction. The only exposed angle was the side facing the town of Entebbe. We make sure the Ugandans aren't getting any reinforcements from that direction.

With all the hostages evacuated, our APC leaves. Not far from the 4th Hercules we get an update that some hostages are missing and we're told to head back to the Airbus and check if they're there. As we reach it, we see a convoy of vehicles coming down from the town of Entebbe towards it. Some of the guys have jumped up on the wings of the Airbus. The rest are firing at the convoy, primarily as deterrence.

We go back to the Hercules. Three of our aircrafts have already taken off. We're the last plane. We disarm. This is a really dangerous moment because if anyone turns up with a Bazooka or machine gun, we won't be able to return fire. We strap down the vehicles and the plane is off and away to Nairobi.

In Nairobi I get off and go looking for Ehud Barak. I need to know what's happening with Yoni. I find Ehud and he tells me that Yoni has been killed.

The second parabola of my life, which began when I joined the Unit, lasted for some 20 years. I'll never be able to talk about a lot of fateful events from those years but Entebbe is one I can talk about. It's a heritage that is important to preserve and every so often, more details come to light that weren't previously known.

I heard the story of the Mercedes only recently. Colonel (res.) Roded Orian (Oriel), who was personally involved in bringing and returning it, recently sent me this anecdote. Roded is from Kibbutz Maagan Michael and he enlisted in the Unit in 1974. Some months later, during the long course of training in Sayeret Matkal, problems with his back forced him to join the rear-echelon support forces (known by a different name back then). During the operation, Roded was a non-commanding weapons officer, who, for his excellence, received the rank of sergeant personally from Yoni. Since then, his military career has progressed and he completed his service in 2000 at a rank of full colonel.

The Mercedes: Roded Tells What Really Happened

In those days I headed the "kayak" team and was Amitzur Kafri's right hand man for special missions of the "get hold of this…." variety. On Friday afternoon as we prepare for Operation Entebbe, I get a call from Amitzur. He wants to buy all kinds of gear for the forces, such as white hats and tons of black spray paint. I don't ask a thing but instantly get the "engineering" guys in the technological unit on the job: Hanan Pollack, the deputy manager; Aloni, who is responsible for acquisitions; and others who can help out, including Shlomo the tailor, who's Orthodox and needs to get home for Sabbath. I'm insistent, and pretty soon they're all harnessed to the tasks at hand.

We must remember that this is 1976, and on Friday afternoon here in Israel everything in the country is shutting down for the Sabbath. Aloni, as usual, updates me that he's called all the shops and only because the owners all know him, they've agreed to leave their shops open and he's off to collect what we need.

The Mercedes arrives at our base through the connections of Alex Elhanani, a mythological technical officer from the Mossad's Caesarea unit. Here, too, no questions are asked and no explanations are offered. A 7-seater Mercedes. White!

On Friday night we conduct the model exercise in Sirkin and as the hour approaches, I turn up with a "rickshaw" loaded with equipment. After the exercise, the "experts," Amitzur Kafri and Dani Dagan, decide that the tires needed to be changed, including the inner tubes. A way has to be found to obtain four tires and inner tubes on Friday night, and to get them onto the car. What else? The Mercedes is white, so it needs to be painted black.

Amitzur hooks me up with Dani Dagan. Yoav Wachman and I receive a Volkswagen double cabin and off we go. Dani calls Yoav Neta, our contact person in those days at the "Mabat" manufacturing plant in the Israel Aerospace Industries. We set up a meeting with him for 20:00 at the gates of the factory in Yahud. Keep in mind that, in those days, cellphones didn't exist.

So at 8 PM we're telling Yoav Neta of our problems and he, in his typical manner, answers, "No problem." He knows the chairman of the Union of Tire Technicians. He gives him a call from the office at the factory gates and explains that we need four tires and four inner tubes for a Mercedes taxi pronto. No further explanations are added. Simply, we just need it. Tonight.

The guy on the other end of the phone line says, "OK, but…" "What 'but'?" we hurl at him. He explains the 'but.' His store is in the Shalom Commercial Tower and the entire area is shut and he doesn't even have a key and has no idea of the address of the guy in charge and that guy doesn't even have a phone at home! But then he adds the inevitable "but, ok, hang on…" bit: there's a guy who fixes tires in Or Yehuda who owes him a favor. "Contact him. Tell him that I, the Chairman of the Union of Tire Technicians, sent you. Tell him that he should give you whatever you need and direct him to me if he has any questions."

It's already 9 PM. Yoav Wachman and I are on our way to Or Yehuda, to the home of the guy who fixes tires and owes a favor to the Chairman of the Union of Tire Technicians, who is Yoav Neta's friend from "Mabat"…. And this is sounding a bit like "The house that Jack built…" We arrive. Outside, it's a bit dark. The soldiers (us) knock on the door. A child opens and says, "What do you want?" We ask for his father. He explains that his parents have gone out to see a movie and will be back later. To the question of "when?" the answer is "I don't know." We say thanks and decide not to move from the house. We'll wait until they're back.

Around midnight the couple returns. We approach, say "Good evening," (like two kibbutz members behaving as though they're on the kibbutz). The couple looks at us and asks if we're speaking to them. We answer "yes," and explain how we got to their home, and that we need those four tires and inner tubes for a Mercedes taxi. He pauses and thinks for a couple of moments, says "Sure," and doesn't even call his friend to check. He just says that "If the Chairman sent you to me, I'm not asking why." He says we look trustworthy and because it's so late, he won't make the phone call.

His tire-repair shop is at the Paz gas station on Jaffa's Ben Zvi Boulevard. We all hop into our car and head out there. On the way he explains he's not sure he has all four tires but he has a friend and if necessary, we can go there (Oh great, friends bringing in friends... just like in the Unit!) Happily for us, he does have everything we need. Then he asks, "What about payment?"

I explain. "We aren't paying you right now. On Sunday there'll be one of two possibilities. Either you'll get the tires and inner tubes back, or I'll come with a check."

He gazes at us. "I don't believe it," he says. "It's Sabbath, early dawn, two soldiers I don't know turn up, and I'm giving them equipment worth a ton of money and they say they aren't paying me, but I'll get the money next week."

He shakes his head in disbelief and mutters. "It's not because I believe you. It's because I believe my friend who sent you here and to whom I owe so much. (Well, and aren't all the Children of Israel responsible for one another?)

Back in the car. We bring him home and return to the base, drop off the equipment and black spray paint next to the Mercedes, and the Unit's weapons guys take command. By morning, the Mercedes is ready for the operation. In the morning one of those guys says to me that there was barely enough spray but somehow they managed. Next time, though, they prefer not to use spray. (Who cares now about a next time?!)

Later that morning Amitzur's got another item on his wish list: he needs to prepare a Ugandan flag to put at the front of the Mercedes. Oh good…. remember that back in those days there was no internet and where the blazes does one even get hold of a picture of the Ugandan flag? Off we head to Muki Betser, and he explains how it looks and what its colors are. Something very general. Six stripes of black, yellow and red and in the center a white circle with a bird, the crane. (Wikipedia: Six equal horizontal bands of black (top), yellow, red, black, yellow, and red (bottom); black represents the color of African skin; yellow is the searing sun; and red is the color of fraternity among them. A white disc is superimposed at the center on which is depicted the national symbol, a grey crowned crane, facing the hoist side.)

I say I'll handle the task and race off to deal with it. But where does one find a piece of white cloth? I go over to Nir Giladi (currently, Professor Giladi) and say that there's no choice: we've got to use part of his white bedsheet for the "war effort." While he's still thinking (he was professorial already back then) I pick up a pair of scissors and cut a piece of his bedsheet into the designated flag and race off again to the intelligence guys. With their help, and with colored markers and all kinds of coloring pens, we make a flag. Was it an exact replica of the Ugandan flag? Of course not, but similar enough. I show it to Muki. He smiles. To me it seems to be a smile of resignation, an "it's the best we can do right now" kind of smile. Then he says, "It's fine," and the rest is history.

Once the mission is over I help return the car to the garage. The mechanic says, "But it was white…." and then he half-asks half-says, "Ah, I know where it's been." I nod in confirmation and tell him that as far as the color and payment, he should talk to Alex Elhanani. He laughs and I leave. Some time after Operation Yonatan, we need a Mercedes for a weapons department experiment and we contact the same auto repair place. He gives me a white one and half-begs half-demands that I don't bring it back black because last time he had so much trouble with the client. Anyone familiar with the unit's weapons guys know that when I returned it this time around, he had a whole different set of problems!

As for the tire repair guy: I phone him on Sunday and tell him that I'll come with a check on Tuesday. I turn up as planned. He asks me if it was for the Entebbe operation. I confirm and he invites me to join him for a meal and drink, and we part as friends.

This is Roded's story, who meanwhile married Danit and together they have three children: Tal, Gal and Amit.

———

Looking back to so many years ago, the memory of Operation Entebbe has lodged itself so firmly in the Israeli mind and shaped our consciousness so strongly, but often I come against the contradictions between what is told, and what actually happened. For example, for some reason there's a solidly lodged impression that Shimon Peres encouraged the operation whereas Prime Minister Yitzhak Rabin opposed it. That's just not true. Rabin didn't oppose it. He simply told Motta Gur: "Bring me an operational plan that you think is doable, and we'll discuss it. If you don't bring me a plan, I'll have to enter negotiations for the exchange of captives." He did disqualify, and justifiably, all kinds of plans that involved things like parachuting into the killer-crocodile-infested waters of Lake Victoria.

Often, I hear ruminations spoken aloud about how we managed to get organized within less than 48 hours, particularly when it comes to a unit that generally readies itself for many months in advance of every possible type of operation. But for the Unit, it doesn't really matter if the operation is at home at the Ben Gurion Airport or at the Ugandan terminal. The soldiers are the same men, with the same training, the same capabilities, the same motivation. The greatest difficulty, really, is the government, which needed to reach a decision on whether the operation ought to be put into action or to commence prisoner-exchange negotiations with the terrorists.

Once the scope of the success became clear, some tried to "steal" some of the glory, but if there's one thing that can't be doubted, it's that each and every one of us had a role in the operation's success. To me, each of the 200 people who got onto those Hercules C-130s deserves a medal. Same goes for the IAF, and the pilots who carried out an operation of such complex difficulty that words are barely adequate to laud it. And the paratroopers too, who neutralized the Entebbe International Airport; and the Unit forces that stormed into the terminal; and the Golani Brigade commandos who guarded the planes; and the injured, among them our seriously wounded soldier Surin Hershko, and Yoni, who died.

I was back in Entebbe some 20 years ago on the occasion of 25 years since the operation. Several of us from the Unit traveled there together. We were hosted by the Ugandan government and guarded by the Presidential Guard. We wandered around the old terminal, we reconstructed the operation, each of us told the story from his specific perspective. We went up into the control tower, to the Ugandans' lookout point. From there we could see the terminal's roof, the place where the MIGs had been parked, and where we'd been at the outset. We saw the shrapnel and damage to the control tower's walls, and realized why our suppressive fire team there couldn't halt the gunfire coming from the tower: much stronger firearms had been needed, and it should have come from the APC. On the ground where Yoni fell, we held a memorial service. Yiftach Reicher spoke, and we stood there and sang Israel's national anthem, Hatikva.

Yohai Brenner was born on Kibbutz Maoz Haim in the Beit She'an Valley. On completing his paratroopers training track, he opted for officer's training and returned to 890th Battalion as a platoon commander. After the Yom Kippur War, he was recruited to the Unit as Amiram Levin's and the late Yoni Netanyahu's operations direc-

torate officer. His service in the Unit over, he set up the intelligence battalion in the 36th Division and commanded it for three years. For most of his years he worked in agriculture. He traveled for a security role to Buenos Aires, and to Kazakhstan to manage cotton growing projects. He also has held roles in the Prime Minister's Office and the Ministry of Internal Affairs. Currently he lives in Afula with his wife Talma. They have three children and 11 grandchildren.

Master-Sgt. Dani Dagan, Tactical Driving Officer
Driver-operator: Mofaz APC Force

ENTEBBE [EXCERPTED FROM DAGAN'S HEBREW AUTOBIOGRAPHY,
SULAM DANIEL—DIZZY MEMISHMAR HAEMEK]

I was 43, the oldest participant in the mission. I drove a BTR-40 armored personnel carrier, a spoil of war, from which operations officer Yohai Brenner and mobile perimeter force commander and former deputy Unit commander Shaul Mofaz fought. My memories of the operation, and the preparations for it, were written down two years after the fact, and spoken at different debriefings held over the years.

"Last night on TV I saw the movie *Operation Thunderbolt*. It moved me like a kid. I remembered my discussions with Yoni. I remembered our departure for the mission. I remembered standing with my vehicle outside the control tower in Entebbe, with us raining hellfire on that tower, and I remembered Yoni lying 20 meters away, alongside the terminal, while the doctor treated him, and I remembered Muki reporting, 'Yoni's hit, I'm taking command.' For me, Operation Entebbe was different from everything I'd known, and I'd known some wars, and some special and some not-so-special ops, but this was the most moving of all.

It all started on Thursday at two in the morning. The phone rang at home: Dani, come to the base. I didn't know what they wanted, so I asked them to let it wait till morning. I took my daughter to the airport on her way to France.

I got home at 6:30 a.m., organized my gear, which was always on standby, and hustled over to the base. I found it abuzz. From far out I could smell that something was up. One of the officers filled me in. I was happy I hadn't missed it. Still, I knew Yoni was the one who had to make the call about whether I was in or not. My chances were better than ever, since in the Unit I was in charge of a lot of the vehicles that were supposed to be deployed, and I felt that this time they'd ignore my age etc. I walked into Yoni's office. We already had a pretty special bond of friendship by then. Yoni said to me: Dani, you're in charge of the vehicles, prepping them and teaching the drivers. I asked, how much time do we have? He said: around two hours. Before leaving his office, I turned to him and said: Yoni, this is not just a mission for the Unit, but for all the People of Israel, and the guy who knows best how to handle these vehicles should be the guy on the ground. In my opinion, that's me. Then I asked: Am I in? Yoni thought about it for a second and then said: this time, yes. It was very clear to me why he hesitated. He knew my family and he knew my age (43). But I shot out of there like a rocket. I figured the best course of action was to break contact with Yoni before he had the chance to have second thoughts…I checked each vehicle….some folks thought it was unnecessary…I had to scratch two of the vehicles….we replaced whatever was missing. Then we rolled out with the vehicles, us drivers and the back-up drivers, to get familiarized with the Soviet-made armored personnel carriers…I explained the possible technical glitches, we headed back, and each crew started preparing its vehicle.

By the afternoon, everything that had to do with the vehicles— was set. All that was left to do was to take care of the Mercedes-brand jalopy that the Defense Ministry had provided, a sedan in which everything leaked and nothing started and the tires were bald. I let Yoni know. Then I had an idea—we could get a similar car from someone in the civilian world. Specifically, the person I had in mind was Boaz Ben-Zion (one of the people menaced by Dudu Topaz years after the operation), a talent agent from Bimot and a colleague from my old days in the bohemian scene (who knew where I served). I called him at one in the morning, and he said: 'I'm leaving the keys in the gas cap, just make sure it's all covered by the Defense

Ministry.' We drove to Kings of Israel Square and checked out the car. It turned out to be 60 centimeters longer than the Mercedes, and, since the load-up drill had already been done, I decided to drop the idea…later that night I called a friend who had a tire shop and warehouse in Jaffa. At two in the morning we grabbed four new tires, I signed off on them on a paper napkin, promised that I was responsible, and drove off toward the base. We added a few more improvements, then spray painted the white sedan black. In the morning it looked like a zebra. We re-painted it. I said to Amitzur, the Mercedes driver, I think they forgot us behind. We almost missed the flight. We got there a few moments before takeoff and they waved us up onto the plane. I ran for mine….three more minutes and they would have left without us…we took off, landed in Sharm. A short briefing from Yoni, he showed us photos of the hijackers. I parted with Yoni. It was the last time, the last time I saw him alive.

Another driver from our force drove my APC to the airfield. We boarded the plane, second in line in the convoy, and off we went. On the way to Sharm I thought through the possible scenarios. I got my APC ready in the usual way and then added not just spare parts but also some extra fuel. Some simple math made it clear that there was a chance of us getting stuck in Entebbe. In that case, I'd drive to Kenya. I even took a piece of paper and jotted down a map of the route…I shared these thoughts with the Unit's operations officer, Yohai Brenner of Kibbutz Maoz Haim, a true gentleman and the machine-gunner on my APC. After the battle I made sure to note, when telling the story, that this officer didn't even bother to aim his machinegun at the enemy, he just tilted it so that I, Dugen, would get showered with the hot casings…I grabbed him by the 'jewels' and the flow stopped.

On the flight from Sharm to Entebbe, I took a stretcher off my vehicle and asked them to wake me up in four hours. That was the deadline for final authorization of the mission. If it was cancelled, we could still get back. Yohai Brenner woke me up. I realized the mission was on…till then I'd had my doubts…as soon as we were wheels-down in Entebbe, I felt terrific. The amount of training drills made me feel like I'd been there already…I drove with determined precision straight to the old terminal. At the end of the runway we started to hear the gunfire and the explosions. I drove fast and made it to the square outside the terminal, where the hijacked plane was parked off to my right and the hostage-packed terminal to my left and the control tower to my rear. We fired in all directions till the coast seemed clear and then turned around to face the control tower. Whoever was up there didn't stop firing and we focused all our fire on him. While in motion I had the driver's hatch open, but as soon as we stopped, in a spot facing the fire, I shut it. Just then I heard Muki over the radio report that Yoni was hit and he was taking command. I saw the doctor care for a wounded man lying between us and the terminal. I realized I was looking at Yoni. I was fully focused on Yoni, and then I heard Mofaz, our force commander, call out: Dugen, reverse! You sleeping? I stirred and started driving…I saw the stretcher borne on one of the vehicles toward a plane, which had taxied toward the terminal, and that was the last time I saw Yoni, from very far away.

We kept pounding the control tower with fire…the hostages started running towards the hostage-evac plane, two guys boarded our vehicle, asked if we needed assistance. A few minutes later I saw the plane doors close and the aircraft started to taxi. Once it was airborne, I realized that we'd won…we asked over the frequency about further losses and were happy to hear there were none. I asked about Yoni and was told that he was moderately wounded…I under- stood this to be the case…the planes took off one after another and then we rode over to our plane, which was the last one on the runway. Just then we were instructed to head back to the old terminal and to check if by chance someone was left in the hijacked plane. I remember the way back very well, especially as none of us was exactly clear on where we'd left the surprises on the taxiways. We got there, two guys got off the vehicle and boarded the stairs to the plane, until someone said that maybe it was boobytrapped. Dan Shomron, the overall commander of the mission, instructed us not to open the door. When we turned back, the person in the control tower again opened fire even though the whole tower was gripped by flames. We returned fire and headed back to the plane. Suddenly, we saw off to the right a pair of headlights approaching the terminal. We asked permission to take care of the vehicle…we waited till it reached the terminal and opened fire…the flight was smooth…each man to himself…great excitement, and then suddenly fear, what if Yoni wasn't okay, and then I heard a voice behind me: Dugen, don't worry, everything'll be alright.

We landed in Nairobi. The doors opened. We were told not to get out. I got out. All around us were friendly looking African soldiers. I knew that there was an IDF Medical Corps plane and I waited for word about Yoni. Shai Avital came over and said to me: Dani, Yoni's dead. At that moment, all the joy in me died. I walked to the rear of the plane, and I think I cried a little. We waited on the ground for an hour and then took off, yet again trailing behind everyone else. On the way back to Israel, despite the tiredness, I wasn't able to fall asleep…I lay there and thought about Bruria, Yoni's girlfriend, and about my wife, remembering how Yoni and I had prepared a birthday party for her on Friday and then we—and by 'we' I mean Yoni—had told her that it had to be delayed till Sunday or Monday. I envisioned the meeting with Bruria, and got the chills…when I spotted the motion of a hot water kettle and the glow of a cigarette in the cockpit I thought it was a mirage…not a second later I was up there in the cockpit sipping coffee and sucking on a cigarette…up until that moment, for the previous fifteen hours, I hadn't eaten, hadn't drunk, hadn't smoked…sitting up there I found Dan Shomron and a few other guys who'd made the discovery before me…

At around four or five in the morning we heard the news broadcast for the first time. Only then did we realize what was happening in Israel. Hour by hour announcements of joy and festivities, and we the heroes of the party were on the way. We heard the description of the landing and the reception of the first plane at Lod Airport and were moved. We, the classified ones, landed elsewhere so as to be seen by no one. I got off the plane, asked one of my crew to drive the armored vehicle back, and Amitzur and I took the jalopy back to the base. A vehicle with no license plates, banged and dinged on all sides, with two guys in tiger-striped uniforms inside, passing through all the checkpoints, and no one paid us any attention. The police watched us and made a motion for us to hurry up and not block the traffic. During the drive, the crowds on the sides of the road pointed at us and I realized that they had discovered that we were the ones. They started to close in on us. We were nearly choked by their sheer joy. We got out of there by the skin of our teeth and kept going to the base. We got there first.

I met Avraham Arnan, the founder of the Unit and a friend of mine, sitting on a rock. I told him what I knew, went to the medical clinic, Avraham debriefed Hassin the doctor, who'd treated Yoni, asked questions…I called home…my wife asked about Yoni…I told her briefly that he'd been killed. I managed to tell her that I was going to see Bruria and that afterwards I'd come home…I went to see Bruria. I was at her place for two hours. I went back to the base for a debriefing and a summary conducted by a few senior officers. We received official word of the new commander. I went home. Again, I went to see Bruria…"

On Yoni Netanyahu

"…My ties to Yoni were unique. They were forged fast and true. The differences between us—I, a field worker from [Kibbutz] Mishmar HaEmek, a guy who believes no one, an old fox who's seen a lot, and he, in my eyes, a professor, a believer, an innocent, a scholar…the contrast between us led to an outstanding relationship. It started shortly after he was given command of the Unit. He hadn't forged good ties with the officers. It's possible they didn't understand him. It's possible that the move from the armored corps to the Unit wasn't well thought out enough. It's possible that the officer corps at the time was not his cup of tea. Regardless, I was of the mind that he was being treated unfairly and just not right. One Shabbat I decided to talk to him. To this day I don't know why it had to be me, but later on I was happy that I'd acted as I had. I called him up and said there's something I have to say. He asked: is it urgent? I said: I think so. And that's how I found myself in his home, a glass of whiskey on the table…I said I wanted to talk about the situation in the Unit. If that seems inappropriate to you, I said, we drain this glass and I leave. If it seems right, then let's get to it. He was surprised, and also looked very curious. I said it wasn't my place….that one of the officers ought to step forward….he encouraged me to speak. A long conversation ensued, I told him what I would do and how I'd go about doing it…we grew very close…true, Yoni didn't do exactly as I suggested, but what I had to say I said."

The story of the operation, Operation Yonatan, has a continuation. With Entebbe, there's always a continuation.

Since the kids and the school administration asked, I told the Entebbe story. Two-hundred kids sat on the floor, listened to me talk, as I showed them part of the movie about Entebbe. Heavy applause at the end, including from the teachers. I came home satisfied and moved, but that was nothing compared to what happened afterwards. In the evening, the doorbell rang and a delegation from school came to thank me and handed me a paper on which dozens of kids had written, "With thanks to Dani Dagan, with all our hearts." My ability to communicate with people of all ages has served me well and brought me satisfaction throughout my life."

Lt.-Col. (res) Dani Dagan (1933-2020 may he rest in peace) was a founder of Kochav Yair. Married to Irena. "Dizzy" from Mishmar HaEmek, a pioneer in Mizpe Ramon. A bohemian in Tel Aviv. Twenty years in Sayeret Matkal. It's been said of him that he was: "An engineer who didn't study engineering. An educator who didn't study education. A commander without soldiers. The man who re-defined tactical driving in the IDF."

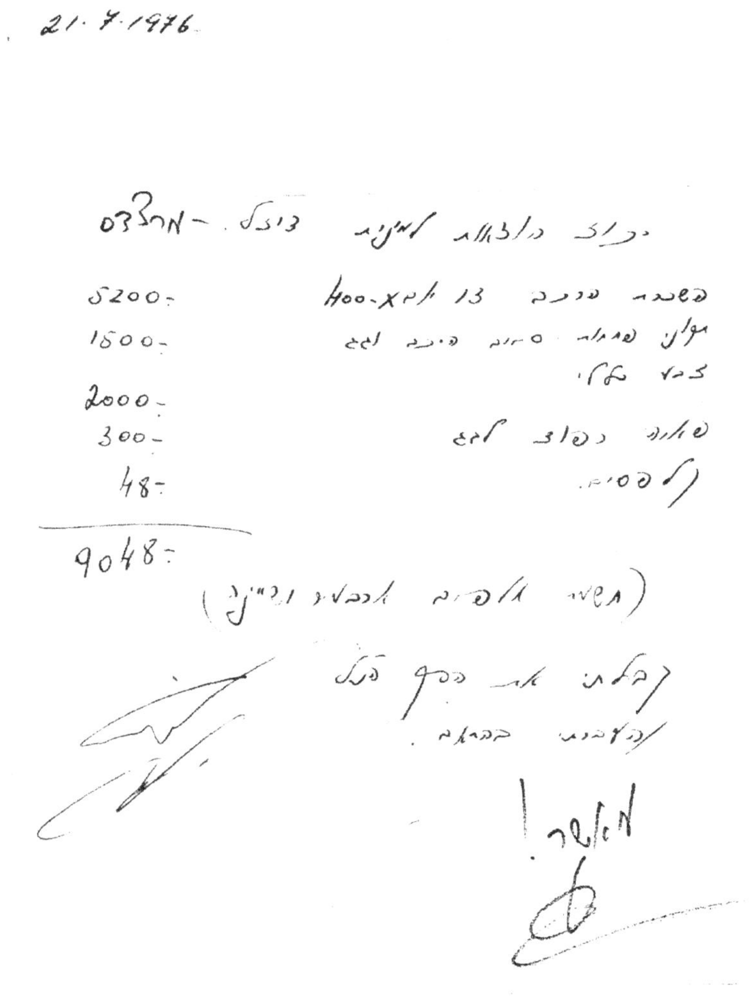

21. 7. 1976

(handwritten Hebrew note)

5200.-
1500.-
2000.-
300.-
48.-
──────
9048.-

The Mercedes was selected and acquired by the Mossad on Thursday night. At the end of the operation, it was returned to the garage from which it was borrowed. The garage owner sent the Mossad's chief weapons innovation officer, Alex, may he rest in peace, a bill for repairs. Alex asked the Unit to foot the bill, but after receiving a polite refusal from Amitzur Kafri, the driver of the vehicle during the operation, he brought the bill to Mike Harari, the commander of the Mossad's operational unit, who authorized the payment. Yet another Mossad contribution to the annals of the operation.

Staff-Sgt. Eldad (Perkal) Dolev, Team Omer Bar Lev
Operator on Mofaz's APC, APC Force

WE WERE THERE

The flight was like a dream. To avoid premature exposure, we were scheduled to fly at a low altitude, which meant a bumpy and rocky flight, so at boarding we received nausea pills and all the heroes fell asleep.

We had to struggle to be included in this rescue operation. When we learned of the kidnapping, we were busy training for another important and silent operation, something we can't talk about to this day. The operation was scheduled for the following month, and we had been training for it for almost a year. In contrast to that mission, the training for the Entebbe raid was like child's play. We did not know much about the conditions and did not have much time to prepare. We practiced storming in and out between burlap sheets that were stretched out overnight as tarpaulins and were supposed to simulate the terminal area and the location of buildings and runways at the Entebbe airport – very amateurish compared to the standards we had become accustomed to. Our professional skills as operators and our capacity for improvisation were supposed to compensate for the missing intel and lack of preparation.

We awoke as we approached our destination. Upon landing, the shooting started immediately. I was in charge of one of the two machine guns that were installed on the BTR under the command of Mofaz. Our first target was the control tower. Later, each lamp or light of an approaching car presented a legitimate target for us. Because of the great distance, there was only a slim chance of hitting these cars, but the light of tracer bullets was a warning and a clear deterrent to anyone thinking about intervening in any way whatsoever—stay away and let us finish our job.

Our two BTRs were positioned just outside the terminal, where the hostages were being kept. Inside the terminal an entirely different battle was taking place – sterile and much more accurate. Outside, it was hard to know what was happening inside, until a long and quiet crowd of people emerged from the terminal. It was surreal and very exciting. In total darkness, a line of people walked, a convoy of survivors. Long and very orderly and peaceful on their way to the Hercules and home. Those of us with a historical memory were reminded of other convoys from other darker times in another period. This time it was a rescue train. A convoy of hope, victory and life.

On the flight home we could not sleep. Beautiful Hebrew songs especially fit for times like these were heard as they issued from the loudspeakers of the plane, and the music reinforced and assured those still in doubt that this was indeed a successful operation. The bad guys were beaten, and our people were on their way back home, alive.

That evening we got leave from the army. The next day was set aside for debriefings and for the procession to Mount Herzl, where Yoni Netanyahu would be laid to rest. I decided to go to Tel Aviv in the evening. The driver who gave me a ride from the intersection near the base could not stop praising "those soldiers", those men who had carried out the mission. We had become the anonymous heroes of the day.

At the time, Dorit worked in a housewares store in Tel Aviv. I was in uniform and wearing my heavy military boots, so I didn't feel right entering the pristine shop where I would probably damage something or ruin the clean, aesthetic atmosphere of the store. I waited outside for Dorit to notice me. Finally, it was the owner of the shop who noticed I was there, and she turned Dorit's attention to the fact that someone was waiting for her outside by saying, "Your soldier's such a hero that he's even too scared to come inside."

So our story is probably not really about heroes. Since all went

well and the operation was managed successfully
need heroic stories. And if there is someone wor
personal courage should be celebrated, it is the m
favor of and gave his authorization for the oper;
failed, he would probably have been left standing,
Prime Minister Yitzhak Rabin.

Decades later, I visited Uganda as part of my work as an expert in
agricultural and irrigation systems design. With me were two
colleagues from the American John Deere corporation. After about a
week in the country and with the completion of our work, we were
invited to a meeting with local church leaders, who supported and
had initiated the project. They were interested in who we were and
where we were from, and whether it was my first visit to their country. I replied that it was my first visit in which a passport was
required. They continued to ask questions. I told them about the raid
from my perspective as an Israeli and as a solider. They asked why I
had not told them about it until now, and I said I did not want to
insult or upset them. After all, not only had we arrived uninvited and
not only had we refrained from asking the Ugandans for permission
to visit and to land, but we had also left destruction and damage to
property and human life. They laughed and dismissed the remark. For
them anyone who fought against Idi Amin, his army and his people,
were to be considered their partners and their faithful friend. So we
cracked open an additional round of beer.

*Staff-Sgt. (res) Eldad Perkal (Dolev) was drafted and recruited to the
Unit in November 1973. Born in Kibbutz Beit Zera, he today owns a
farm in Moshav Kefar Yedidiya.*

Cpt. Udi Salvi, Discharged Company Commander
APC-Pair Commander; Armored Force

FORTY-FIVE YEARS TO OPERATION YONATAN: RECOLLECTIONS

A few days before the hijacking of the Air France plane to Entebbe, I was discharged from the army (for the second time). This came after more than two challenging and riveting years as commander of the Unit's training company and anti-terror company. On the morning of the hijacking, 27 June 1976, I heard the radio report and then found myself, in that dramatic moment, a discharged officer with no role to play. Happily, a few minutes later I got a call from Rami Sherman, the Unit's operations officer. He informed me that a state of readiness had been declared and that I was to be prepared for an eventuality in which the hijacked plane would be landed in Israel. I was happy for the call and pleased that I was still in the books as someone who ought to be kept in the loop—apparently on account of my last post as commander of the Unit's anti-terror company. Rami asked that I stay near a phone, and be at the ready.

Only on Tuesday, two days after the hijacking, did I get a call from one of the Unit's phone operators, telling me to come in immediately, as per Muki Betser's request. I came straight to the base and was told that a covert hostage-rescue mission was in the works. Armed with that information, I rushed over to the quartermaster's supply store and signed for all the necessary gear (the same gear that I'd given back at the same place a few days earlier…)

At the barracks, I bumped into my younger brother, Omer, who had nearly completed the Unit's training course. He was surprised to see me back on the base and asked what I was doing there; I told him I'd been summoned urgently, but didn't yet know why. His response: "You're probably planning on rescuing the hostages." I smiled and carried on.

My girlfriend, Orly, whom I'd met in the Unit, where she served as a clerk in the operations division and later as secretary to the commander of the Unit, was very happy to see me back on the base and helped me get organized with my gear.

A full operational plan had not yet been assembled, yet Tuesday and Wednesday were filled with preparations. Mostly we focused on personal and platoon-related drills, organizing clips, rifles, battle vests and all the rest of the personal and platoon gear. A brief meeting with Muki revealed that the general plan was to arrive at Entebbe on several C-130s, launch a ground assault on the area where the hostages were being held, free them, and then fly them back to Israel. He was on his way to the Israel Defense Forces' HQ to discuss further.

Later on, I met up with Shaul Mofaz, who had just completed a stint as deputy commander of the Unit and whom I knew from before, when he'd served as the commander of the Paratroop recon unit. During the Yom Kippur War, I'd served as his second-in-command. He exuded a deep calm. With Yoni's arrival on Thursday, we were all called—commanders and team leaders—to the briefing room alongside the intelligence officers' bureau.

Outside the briefing room, Yoni spotted me and I heard him grumble: "What're you doing here?" I figured he was bothered by my presence because, several weeks earlier, I'd participated in a late-night meeting in his office along with several team leaders and other officers and expressed dissatisfaction with his conduct as commander of the Unit.

Muki Betser came to my aid. He told Yoni in a very authoritative voice: "I invited Udi Salvi. He's an excellent officer and operator, and he just finished commanding the anti-terror company. We need him on this mission." Yoni, thankfully, nodded his head and continued filing into the briefing room.

At the briefing, the primary force deployment was unfurled and to be honest I was a bit disappointed: I was not made part of the assault force. Nonetheless, I was happy to have been appointed ground commander of all troops on the third plane and the point man for all communications with the pilots as well as commander of the two teams led by Alon Shemi and Yuval Fein. I held both of those platoon commanders in high regard and made my peace with the assigned role. We were to fly on the third of four planes to Entebbe and to secure the northern side of the old terminal. From there we were to isolate the assault force and provide protection against incoming Ugandan troops, either from the town of Entebbe or the capital city of Kampala. Additionally, we were the backup for the assault force, to be summoned in the event that the force required assistance during its raid on the old terminal, where the hostages were being held.

Immediately after the general briefing, I huddled with Yuval Fein and Alon Shemi and laid out the plan for the rest of the preparations. One problem that presented itself, and which I said I would promptly look into, was our lack of familiarity with the BTR-40 armored personnel carriers, the combat vehicles on which we would be deployed.

In the pre-dawn hours of Friday morning I went to see Yoni in his office. He and Muki were poring over the maps and the plans and I suggested that I call a certain Colonel G.H., the commander of a brigade that used the BTR-40s operationally. Muki knew the colonel well and said he didn't think he could be bothered to assist us. I'd better come up with an alternative source, he said. I asked for permission to invite an officer from outside the Unit to the base, to explain to us the standard operating procedures, the foreseeable problems, the weapons systems, and Yoni immediately granted his authorization.

At around eight in the morning I called the colonel. I told him that it was crucial that he come to the Unit and familiarize us with the BTR-40s. Of course, I didn't mention the nature of the urgency or the planned usage of the battle vehicles, but he didn't even give me the time to explain what I was allowed to say. Instead, he replied: "I'm not going to waste my time with your nonsense," and hung up the phone (just as Muki had predicted). I went straight to Plan B and called a serious and skilled officer whom I knew from my time in the Paratroop recon unit—Akiva Horowitz of Kibbutz Givat Haim.

Happily, after a short explanation of my request, Akiva said: "I'm coming." He arrived at the assembly area outside the base a short while later and gave us a learned and thorough explanation, which helped us throughout the training and the operation itself.

The assembly area and the model simulation were positioned near our base, and so, shortly before noon, we headed over to the model on the far west side of an old runway and ran through a few drills.

Later the heavy C-130s started to land on the runway, which hadn't been in use for years. There were some concerns about maintaining secrecy, as it was hard to predict what the residents of the area might make of the ordinarily dormant runway being used for landings and take-offs on a Friday afternoon, but this concern turned out to be unfounded. No alert citizen or media outlet asked a single question.

In the evening we went to the mess hall, which was festively decorated for a Friday night dinner and took some pleasure in the return to routine. After that, we headed out to the assembly area with all the tactical gear and equipment. The C-130s were already waiting for us, cargo ramps down, and we drilled the loading of the armored vehicles on board and practiced securing and releasing them quickly a few times.

The start of the simulation was delayed on account of the IDF Chief of Staff (who, we later learned, had joined the commander of the Israel Air Force and the commander of the C-130 squadron to witness firsthand the pilots' ability to land the aircraft on a darkened runway). Shortly after 22:00, IDF Chief of Staff Lt.-Gen. Motta Gur arrived and the simulation drill was given a dry run, with no live fire at all.

Positioned in defensive posts with the APCs, I spotted a "suspicious" car approach. It was coming from an area that was supposed to be closed-off and it was heading straight toward us, lights doused. I immediately gave the order to train the heavy machine guns on it and to be ready to open fire (dry fire, of course) on my command. I called over the radio frequency and asked if any of our force members were supposed to be coming from that direction. Having received no adequate response, I was about to give the order to open fire (dry fire), when the driver flipped his lights twice. I immediately recognized the vehicle of the Chief Infantry and Paratroop Officer, Brig. Gen. Dan Shomron, who was coming to see the drill with his mobile command and his staff officers.

During the post-simulation debrief, I stressed to the Chief Infantry and Paratroop Officer that, during a combat operation, I would have opened fire on him and his mobile command. We had to be updated over the radio, I said, or shown some other agreed-upon signal to announce his arrival on the scene. He assured me that would be the case. But to our surprise, he did the exact same thing at Entebbe, where he arrived at the old terminal without advance notice and only by luck was not shot.

Immediately after the debrief, I sat with the team leaders to nail down the remaining details and to run through a few more scenarios and responses.

On Saturday morning 3 July 1976 the armored personnel carriers were loaded onto tank transporters and driven to IAF Airbase 27, home of the C-130 Hercules squadron. Just before 10:00, all of the Unit's force commanders were summoned to a final briefing and meeting. It was led by Muki Betser and took place in the office of the deputy commander, Yiftach Reicher. At around noon, we boarded buses and rode off to the Hercules squadron. There was plenty of commotion on the ground and some of the plane engines were already revving their engines. We confirmed that the APCs were properly ratcheted down and that all the gear was ready to go.

Shortly afterward, we took off for Ophira (Sharm el-Sheik). An hour or so later, we landed and re-grouped for another briefing around one of the underground plane hangars. Surprisingly, a military intelligence officer from the Chief Infantry and Paratroop Officer's bureau (Lt.-Col. Amnon Biran, who had previously served as the Unit's chief intelligence officer) showed us newly taken diagonal aerial photos of the area around the control tower and the old terminal; they were very helpful in navigating from the landing zone to our security post to the north of the terminal.

The briefing itself was more of a speech delivered by Dan Shomron than a true briefing. Most of the operators felt that the oration was directed at other soldiers or perhaps at another audience….and Yoni, who recognized this, convened the soldiers from the Unit around another underground plane hangar, and, amid the roar of the engines, tried to deliver a few words of encouragement and motivation. As far as I was concerned, there was no need for it. I saw clearly how all of the soldiers under my command (15 soldiers and officers) were ready and fully familiarized with the mission and all it entailed.

Time ticked down. It was clear that if we weren't given the green light soon, we wouldn't be able to make the H-hour of 23:00 (Israel time), but then we were told to board the planes and get ready for take-off. Government authorization would either come in mid-flight or we'd turn back.

All of the soldiers boarded the aircraft and I made sure that the whole force was present—the 15 Sayeret Matkal operators under my command and the Golani Brigade troops—and that all of the soldiers were ready to go. I took a seat in the cockpit and donned the internal radio headset. The flight captain, Arie Oz, manned the control wheel on the right side of the cockpit and his co-pilot, Chezi, was on the left side, directly in front of me (a Hercules cockpit is raised above the passenger cabin and if you want to get into the pilots' flight deck you have to climb up a spiral staircase).

The take-off was dicey as the plane was loaded to the max and carrying the outer limit of fuel poundage, but as soon as the wheels came off the ground, the tension in the cockpit eased and we were greeted with the calm, pastoral sight of the Red Sea, its reefs and corals lit by the horizon's sinking sun.

A few minutes after take-off, we were joined by the Golani Brigade commander, Col. Uri Saguy, who said to me that he knew full well that I had been appointed ground commander of the plane and was therefore seated upfront, but that he would, nonetheless, permit himself to come up to the cockpit every now and again for the purpose of regular updates. I, a captain in Sayeret Matkal, felt a bit embarrassed that the commander of the Golani Brigade was sitting in the back with the enlisted men and the junior officers, tucked in somewhere amid the APCs, while I was sitting in the comfort of the cockpit, but alongside that there was also a feeling of pride, because the IDF brass trusted us—the operators and officers of Sayeret Matkal.

The planes started to ascend to a cruising altitude and gathered into a tight formation. The darkness crowded out the light, the sky grew fully dark. The crescent moon had been up before sunset and now cast a pale light across the departing landscape. Based on flight time and the fuel gauges, which were nearing the halfway mark, it was clear that if we didn't soon get government authorization for the mission, the pilots would have to turn around, toward home. The matter was raised several times over the internal frequency, but of course had no effect whatsoever on the execution of the mission itself.

Suddenly, without any preamble, I heard the authorization code-word spoken over the internal frequency. The Government of Israel had authorized the mission!!! Up in the cockpit we exchanged surprised glances and small smiles and I hurried out to give word to the Golani Brigade commander and the team leaders. When the commanders heard of the much-anticipated decision, the expressions on their faces spoke of readiness and conveyed an understanding of the importance of the mission. I felt a great pride to be the commander of such excellent soldiers, with whom any mission could be accomplished for the greater good of Israel.

I climbed back up the stairs to the cockpit and donned the headset again. The pilots took turns with the yoke and tried their best to get some rest. I didn't shut my eyes for a single second during the seven-hour flight. Instead, I continued following the complex and elaborate aerial navigation and ran through the gamut of possible scenarios on the ground. In truth, I was constantly nettled by the feeling that we, the "green army," would get the job done on the ground, but the weakest link, I feared, the most vulnerable part of the operation, was the blue-uniformed airmen and their ability to deliver us safely to the theater of operations. (During the post-op debriefings, the airmen told me that they'd harbored a similar feeling, only in reverse: they were sure of their ability to deliver us safely to the destination, they said, but were unsure of our ability to execute on the ground...)

Time passed and all of a sudden, with no warning at all, the cockpit windshield was lit up by a horizon of lightning bolts, long tendrils of fire and a stack of dark clouds. In an instant we found ourselves jolted up and down and tossed around inside the plane. On my headset I heard the order to break up the formation and the planes spread out so as to avoid a collision due to the awful weather. The soldiers in the passenger cabin were spread out around the vehicles and most of them slept through the turbulence. Only a few of them felt sick and vomited. During the first few moments of the storm it seemed that we might not be able to reach our destination, but thankfully just as the storm suddenly appeared so too did it disappear and once again the moon shone in a rather clear sky.

Several minutes later we were treated to a stunning view: the reflection of the moon as a bright silvery line in the vast waters of a dark lake. "That's Lake Victoria," the captain said and it was clear that we were very close to our destination. As agreed in advance, a bell rang in the passenger cabin and red lights were turned on so that the soldiers could get organized without any of the light leaking out and revealing our presence. I went down to the cabin, confirmed that everyone was alert and ready, and returned to the cockpit.

The lead plane broke off from the formation and began its descent, the runway lights ablaze and visible from afar. The minutes crawled by and we heard the codeword for a successful landing and then the second plane followed.

Our turn arrived and the captain pointed the nose of the plane down toward the runway and descended fast. The wheels were approaching the tarmac…and suddenly the lights went off and an awful darkness filled our line of vision. Oz cursed but kept his calm and continued with his approach (while I was afraid that he would pull up and come around for another pass, as was customary in the air force, but would prevent us from fulfilling our mission as planned) while the co-pilot, Chezi, pressed his face up against the window and tried to see out…then came the thwack of the wheels on the ground and the plane's landing run along what we hoped was the runway. Only once the wheels were on the ground did we see the lights lit by the paratroopers. (According to the plan, as soon as the first plane touched down, a pair of soldiers was to jump out off the cargo ramp at one-hundred-meter intervals and operate the lights along the length of the runway, in case someone cut the ground lights). The pilot guided the plane between those edge lights and said a prayer of thanksgiving to whoever thought of bringing them and especially to the paratroopers who'd lit them.

We reached the disembarkation point. Within seconds the chains fastening the APCs were released and the drivers rode swiftly down the ramp. I yelled a hasty thanks to Oz and the flight crew and then ran down the stairs and out through the rear of the plane, where I mounted the lead APC while in motion and took my position at the commander's station. Yuval Fein, the platoon commander and a good friend, who hadn't seen me hop on from behind, asked worriedly: "Where's Udi?" and I, while sliding into position, calmly intoned, "Fein, I'm right here, at your side as always." A smile crossed his face and I immediately gave Chibutro, the driver, the order to roll out, while making sure that Alon Shemi was in our line of sight and in motion behind us.

We drove at high speed toward the old terminal and the control tower, noting the streams of tracers flying toward the tower and the silhouette of the parked airbus that had been hijacked and taken to Entebbe.

The Shell station was an important trail marker for me. As soon as I saw it, I told the driver to take a left just before it, as planned, but immediately afterward we came face to face with a locked steel gate.

At first I thought I might have missed the turn, or that we simply hadn't seen the gate on the aerial photos, but it was clear we were in the right place and all we had to do was get around the gate. I told Chibutro to head west along the length of the gate and look for an opening. After a few seconds, we realized there was no entrance and I told him to turn around and circle back to the gate. Once we stood facing it, I gave him the order: Go. Chibutro didn't move. He said: "But there's a gate in the way." I yelled: "You're in an APC. Run it down." Chibutro hit the gas, the gate collapsed, and we sped toward our positions.

Alon deployed his platoon's APC at the southwest corner of the square just north of the terminal, and I, with Yuval's platoon, took up a position fifty meters to the north, adjacent to the terminal. While in motion we opened fire with the heavy machineguns on Ugandan soldiers, but only on the ones facing us or coming toward us, not those in the process of fleeing. I ordered Yuval and Alon to send two squads to nearby huts, to ensure that there were no hostages or flight crew being kept inside. The buildings were dark and locked and the soldiers reported that they were uninhabited. The second squad found a hangar alongside the terminal in which several BTR-60s were being kept (Russian-made armored personnel carriers, much like ours, but with four pairs of wheels). I gave the command to shoot the tires so that enemy forces would not be able to pursue us as we retreated.

The supporting element, like us, laid down heavy suppressive fire at the tower. We fired constant bursts with the machineguns to ensure that we wouldn't be sniped at from the dominant post in the region— the control tower.

Raz Gur-Aryeh, a machine-gunner on the APC, spotted a suspicious Ugandan soldier some fifty to sixty meters away. When he started moving in our direction, Raz opened fire with the heavy gun. The Ugandan went down and Raz held his fire. Suddenly the Ugandan started getting back to his feet and Raz shot him again, and again held his fire; this recurred several times until the soldier was finally eliminated.

At this stage, Arnon Epstein's soldiers emerged from the old terminal building, wearing their white identification hats and calling out to me as friendlies. We called back that we were in position and they carried on with their mission.

Once Yoni's and Muki's force had finished loading the hostages on board (at this point we still didn't know that Yoni had been wounded), Mofaz radioed us to join him alongside the control tower. I called Alon's platoon and we left the way we'd come, rumbling back over the trampled gate. We linked up with Mofaz and turned toward the new terminal, where the Hercules planes were waiting, save the fourth plane, which had already departed with the hostages. Mofaz's APCs followed ours, dropping a screen of smoke and a trail of blast-delay explosive blocks to foil any last-ditch efforts to pursue us.

At the airport apron, where the planes were parked, I learned that Yoni had been hit. Shortly afterwards Mofaz was instructed to return to the old terminal and inspect the hijacked Air France plane to make sure that we hadn't mistakenly left behind any hostages or flight crew, because the head count on the fourth plane, he was told, had come to 87 when there should have been 105.

Omer Bar Lev turned to me and asked that we hold off with our departure until they returned, so that they wouldn't be left alone. I promised him we would do just that. As we readied for departure, I returned to the cockpit and was sorry to hear that we hadn't been able to fill up fuel and that we only had enough to make it to Nairobi, where we'd refill.

Just before take-off from Entebbe, while waiting on the runway for the second plane, the pilot turned to me and said he thinks a soldier's been left on the ground, shining a bright green light. We checked again to make sure that all force members were present and were told that everyone was accounted for. Oz, nonetheless, opened the side door for someone to go out and look, and there we saw a spectacular sight: an orb of bright green fireflies (or some other insects) shone as brightly as a torch. The second plane arrived and we took off and headed in an easterly direction toward Nairobi, Kenya.

At the airport in Nairobi, just as we were trying to refuel, Ehud Barak arrived. He patted us on the backs, but said: "We've got to get the refueling done quick and get out of Kenya as soon as possible. The Kenyans have found out that we're post-rescue and not in a pre-operation readiness, as I'd told them."

The flight crew spurred on the fuel handlers (after a specific problem took nearly half an hour to solve) and boarded the aircraft, shut the doors, taxied to the runway, and took off at around 03:00.

The way back was smooth sailing till around five in the morning, when dawn broke and we heard over the radio that either French or English news was reporting the operation, including the fact that the Israeli planes were currently on the way back. This news came when we were still far from home, surrounded by enemy states on either side of our flight path (Sudan and Egypt to the west, Saudi Arabia to the east). The fact that either country could scramble fighter jets to intercept us, forced the pilots to plunge down low over the Red Sea again and fly at a very low altitude, beneath enemy radar. As a passenger, the stunning view of the blue waters and the corals and reefs made the flight seem like a sort of aerial safari…

As time passed, the tension rose. Everyone seated up in the cockpit strained his eyes and moved his gaze across the cockpit windshield to try and spot incoming enemy fighter jets. Suddenly the pilot said: "Fighter jets ahead…" My heart skipped a beat, but within seconds we heard the voice of an Israeli fighter pilot congratulating us on a job well done and informing us that they were here to escort us to safety.

Sure enough, the little black dots we'd seen on the horizon quickly turned into a pair of F-4 Phantoms, carrying the Israeli star of David over their wings. They circled us elegantly and took up positions on either side of our plane and we all felt moved by the projection of Israel's force and by the removal of the threat to our aircraft. The flight continued on for some time and the coast of the Sinai Peninsula came into view and we carried on north toward the center of the country. After passing the port city of Eilat, the pilot announced over the internal frequency that he'd been ordered to land at Tel Nof Airbase and not Airbase 27. Half an hour later, we dipped down and landed at Tel Nof.

Already at this stage I felt my heart swell with pride at the operation, the boldness of it and the significance of what we'd managed to achieve, but we had no way of anticipating the eruption of joy and the festivities that took hold of the country from the moment the hostages landed, alongside the realization, among the public, of the way Israel had managed to stand firm against terror organizations, which sought, time and again, to lash out at us.

Dozens of soldiers received us with an ovation at the airbase, and we, "the Sayeret Matkal operators," were filled with pride but also with the understanding that there was no time for partying. We mounted the APCs and hustled back to the Unit. At the base I was reunited with Orly, my girlfriend at the time (and wife today). We embraced for a long while and she told me, with tears in her eyes, that during the night it was just her and three other girls at the switchboard and several calls had come in from Bruria, Yoni's girlfriend, asking how things were going. By then an update had been patched through, but it was inaccurate and did not provide a full picture of the situation. It reported that all planes were en route back to Israel and that all force members had emerged unscathed….Orly told me that, as promised, she called Bruria, updated her, and advised her to get some sleep. Less than half an hour later, the girls at the switchboard were given word of Yoni's death. Orly felt awful…and was filled with pain for Bruria.

During the post-operation debriefings, each of us relayed the details of the mission, the mistakes made, the successes attained. We were widely praised for the operation. During the debriefing a representative of the military intelligence's internal security department went out of his way to tell us that we were not permitted to mention the Israeli airborne command plane that had flown over Entebbe during the mission so as not to reveal this capacity. Most of us had no idea there had even been such a plane…and we smiled at the unnecessary, if well-meaning, reveal by the officer entrusted to conceal…

The tremendous success of the operation and the reams of congratulations mingled uncomfortably, and for a long while, with the sadness over Yoni's death. Yoni's funeral and the visit to the Netanyahu family home left a searing impression on us, especially when the chief of staff told the family: "Yoni was responsible for his own death." He said this after learning, during the debrief, that Yoni had instructed the stationary force to hold its suppressive fire, in contrast to what he, the chief of staff, had personally told Yoni, ruling that they should open suppressive fire at the control tower immediately upon arrival; this, it turned out, was a first-hand lesson the chief of staff had learned during the Six-Day War, when he, Motta Gur, had served as the commander of the Paratroop Brigade and had seen, during the battle for the Old City of Jerusalem, how susceptible his soldiers were to fire from dominant field positions, just as at Entebbe.

Gur's statement and the competing versions of the lead-up to the operation sparked an unholy fire and a feud over Yoni's role in the planning and execution of the mission, a struggle that has not abated to this day.

Amiram Levin was appointed commander of the Unit and immediately thereafter he asked me to return to service and to participate in some of the special ops that were in the works at the time. With a strong sense of calling regarding my military service, I returned to the Unit and was rewarded with an array of challenging and compelling activity.

A year later I was once again discharged (for the third time) and I embarked on a months-long backpacking trip through South America, and there, as well as in the United States, wherever we went and whenever it was mentioned that I'd taken part in the operation (be it to Israelis or Jews or random unaffiliated people) I got pats on the back and boundless admiration.

Late in 1977, at Muki Betser's behest, I returned to Sayeret Matkal and, along with him, was part of the founding team of Shaldag; in October 1979, once it was separated from Sayeret Matkal and made the commando unit of the Israel Air Force, I was given the opportunity to replace him as commander. In essence, from then on, I continued to serve until I was discharged at long last in 1998 with the rank of Brigadier-General, after serving as the commander of the IDF's 80th Regional Division.

In 1990, after a long stretch of service along Israel's northern border, I was sent to Britain for a year-long course at the Royal College of Defence Studies, the UK's highest-level course in strategic studies. Foreigners from roughly thirty-five different countries and some forty British nationals were enrolled and I felt that many of them sought proximity to me, thirsting for heroic tales from the incredible mission that had found a place of honor around the world. (The interested parties included, to my surprise, the representatives from Arab and Muslim countries such as Egypt, Jordan, Oman, Pakistan, and Malaysia).

The only officers in the course who felt operationally "on par" with me, and who, I felt, were speaking to me out of shared combat experience, were the three British brigade commanders, who had fought against the Argentinians in the Falklands War of 1982. Of course, when asked by the course commander to give a lecture about the operation at Entebbe, I agreed, and all of the course participants and instructors crowded into the hall and cheered loud and long at the close of the lecture.

As the twenty-fifth anniversary of the operation approached, and with the reign of Idi Amin having ended and Uganda having reverted back to a "normal" country, a group of soldiers and officers from the Unit put together a trip to Entebbe. I was hesitant about joining, but my wife Orly, at a surprise fiftieth birthday party, informed me and the guests that the real birthday present was a trip to Entebbe with the guys and that there was little time to waste because it was happening in two days' time…After practically tripping over my own two feet, I got ready quickly. And in fact in mid-January 2002 a group of twelve of us flew off to Entebbe. It was quite moving for me to land on a civilian plane at the airport in Entebbe and the feeling was only intensified when we stepped out of the arrival terminal. Standing outside and waiting for a car to come and pick us up, someone said: "Look, there's the old control tower." He pointed northwest, and in the distance we could see the tower, standing out against the skyline... We knew we would be given an organized tour of the tower and the old terminal, but that didn't stop us from lifting our heads and seeking out the looming tower as we drove out of the airport toward Kampala.

The following morning our Israeli host surprised us. We were taken to the old terminal and the control tower in a black Mercedes, like the one we'd used, but decorated with Israeli and Ugandan flags. The trip back to the airport was rife with a strong sensory feeling of returning to a place where a slice of history, both personal and national, had been made, and when we arrived at the scene I stood there for many long moments and stared at the tower, which now looked far smaller and far more bullet-ridden than it had on 3 July 1976. The terminal itself seemed ancient and abandoned, and tree roots and branches had woven themselves into the walls and floors, and the terminal too seemed old and piteous.

We walked around the terminal for a while and around the area where my APC had been stationed that night, and I was surprised to see that the nearby huts that we'd searched that night were now inhabited by local families, with chickens and other animals wandering around freely. One of the friendly Ugandans accompanying us explained that the area belonged to the military and that the families were the women and children of officers who'd been given authorization to live there.

Later we climbed up the broken stairs to the top of the control tower. The number 3,789 FT was etched onto the outside wall—the altitude. It was made very palpable to us how whoever sat up there had a commanding position over all of the troops situated outside the terminal, and how starkly right the chief of staff had been in ruling that we ought to open fire at the tower immediately upon arrival.

Up high in the tower, on the outside deck, each one of us unpacked the memories that he still had from that night. Afterwards we gathered outside the terminal and spoke to our Ugandan hosts, who mumbled words of praise every few minutes. At one point one of them inquired: "Say, how many of Idi Amin's soldiers did you kill in the operation?" We were hesitant to answer, not wanting to strain our ties with our hosts and speak of the death of their people, but when we said that, to the best of our knowledge, it was around thirty Ugandan soldiers, they looked disappointed. "So few of the criminal Idi Amin's wicked men were killed?" they asked. "We thought it was far more." I smiled to myself about the misunderstanding, and about the extent to which Idi Amin and his men were reviled in Uganda.

The rest of the week in the country was terrific: we boated along Lake Victoria, saw the incredible waterfalls at Jinja, and spent several days on safari in Uganda's gorgeous national parks, enjoying the privilege of seeing up close a great diversity of animal life. The takeoff from Entebbe triggered many thoughts and memories, and we were all delighted, yet again, to be on the way home.

Brig.-Gen. (res) Udi Salvi, a native of Kibbutz Yiftach, lives in the community of Har Adar. He is married and a father of three and a grandfather of two. His military service started in the Paratroop recon unit, where he served as an enlisted man and went on to serve as a platoon commander and as deputy commander of the unit during the Yom Kippur War (XO to Shaul Mofaz). Afterward he was transferred to Sayeret Matkal, where he served as commander of the training company and commander of the anti-terror company. He later served as one of the founders of Shaldag, and as its second commander. He was deputy commander of Brigade 769 and commander of Brigade 300. He was commander of the squad leader school in Yerucham, the deputy commander of the Judea and Samaria Division, and the commander of the 80th Regional Division in the Southern Command. He was discharged from the IDF with the rank of brigadier-general. After completing his service, he was for six years the Deputy CEO of the International Convention Center in Jerusalem. Later he served for nine years as chief of staff to Israel's Minister of Public Security (until August 2015).

Lt. Yuval Fine, Team Leader
Officer-Operator, Salvi's APC, APC Force

Entebbe—A Blend of Dimmed Memories and Mixed Feelings

The thunder of artillery still echoed through the mountains of the Golan Heights overlooking my home, a small Kibbutz built by my parents. The battles were still apparent on every hill and valley of my childhood paradise. The dust had not yet settled from the dreadful rupture of the Yom Kippur War and the War of Attrition; the collapse of faith, the battle wounds, the friends who never returned.

I was a young officer in Sayeret Matkal, striving to get back to routine. Battle-hardened, we were given new strategic, clandestine objectives and a novel kind of thinking was needed. The training through which I put my soldiers was long and arduous. Pain and weakness were seldom discussed. We prepared to operate under extreme conditions. Our planning was precise, no detail left to chance, no room remaining for error. During moonless nights and sweltering days, through rain and snow, we trained and trained. We were a team, the tightest of bonds among men, a brotherhood cast through three strenuous years. I was their commander. I loved and trusted my soldiers. I cared for them and protected them at all costs, knowing full well that only they would be there for me when the bullets started to fly.

Suddenly, a dark new period took us by storm. A wave of hostage-based terror attacks swept the nation. The government had a clear policy: there shall be no negotiations with terrorists, and their solution was us, Sayeret Matkal, "the Unit." We were given a task we had not considered or previously trained for—counter-terrorism. The enemy we faced was relentless; willing to die for the cause. Time after time we were met with failure and agonizing physical and emotional pain. Many hostages were killed, along with our friends and commanders.

The massacre at Kiryat Shmona, in which terrorists, in 1974, went door to door killing civilians, was the first of an onslaught of deadly attacks that became my reality. It was followed by the slaughter at Ma'alot, in which terrorists took over an elementary school and we stormed into a terrible inferno; the terrorists murdered scores of children with grenades and automatic fire while we scrambled to reach them. This was quickly followed by the attack in Beit Shean. Shortly after that came the Savoy Hotel, on the Tel Aviv beachfront, which was seized by terrorists who'd arrived by sea. We stormed the hotel from all entrances; the floor in which the hostages were being held was exploded and dropped on top of us. As I scaled the stairs, the soldier that stood beside me was killed. So was Col. Uzi Yairi, my future father-in-law. Then came the attack at Kfar Yuval, the village adjacent to my Kibbutz: a family was taken captive, only the baby survived, found in the wreckage.

We kept failing. No one was safe. Scores of innocent lives and loved ones were taken with every strike.

Young people don a toughness that cloaks their insecurity and vulnerability. But beneath that cloak I felt like a walking hostage. Whenever and wherever an attack occurred, we were there, putting our lives on the line each and every time. I carried the foreboding knowledge that each attack bears with it another calamity. When, I wondered, would my turn come?

The strategic clandestine operations we kept training for served as an effective distraction, taking our minds off the ceaseless reality of terror attacks. There was a need, an objective, ample intelligence, and a sense of fulfillment in accomplishing those missions.

———

Then a plane was hijacked. Hostages. Entebbe. Uganda. For me there was a sense of relief — no reasonable person would dare fly us there. Every now and again strange ideas cropped up, like parachuting

forces into Lake Victoria and reaching the adjacent airport by boat. I
was calm. Parachuting troops into a crocodile-infested lake didn't
seem like something we were capable of doing. Regardless, we were
in the midst of training for another important operation and it seemed
very unlikely we would be chosen for this mission.

The hostages in Entebbe were not on my daily radar. We
completed a week of training and were released on Thursday for a
long weekend at home. Suddenly, a call from The Unit, we were
being summoned. The base was in an uproar. I came to the startling
realization that the Entebbe idea had not been forgotten. Yet the plan
didn't sound serious, more like something taken from a movie script.
With our lack of success during the previous hostage-rescue
missions, the feeling of fear pulsated through me, flooded me. My
feet felt heavy and my throat was dry. Deep within me, in the secret
corners of my heart, I hoped this was just a theoretical exercise.
Outwardly, I tried to project a sense of enthusiasm to my soldiers and
put all my energy into ensuring my men were included in the force
structure. Raz was in officers' school; I made the decision to summon
him. Chibutro, may he rest in peace, was made an APC driver. I
didn't think about the operation itself, just about my men and their
placement in the force.

───────────

On Saturday morning we headed to the airport. Two of my soldiers
were still not slated to deploy. Despite Yoni Netanyahu's directives, I
included them in the force. I was still hoping we wouldn't actually
take-off. Yoni scolded me for adding my soldiers and they were left
at the airfield. The plane took off while my thoughts stayed with
them. After a short flight, we landed in Sharm al-Sheikh for a final
briefing. A few of the men didn't feel well and Yoni asked if my
soldiers by chance had tagged along…

I boarded the plane with heavy steps. Fear of the unknown
mingled with a bitter sense that I'd been in a similar situation before.

The landing at Entebbe cleared my mind. Everything, I realized, must now be done to mitigate a failure foretold. Just an hour later we were on the plane yet again, Kenya-bound, and the hostages were heading back to Israel.

In Kenya we learnt that Yoni had been killed. Unfathomable. Uzi Yairi at the Savoy and now Yoni! Distress accompanying joy. Before landing, Israeli Phantom fighter jets appeared, escorting us home. I realized something monumental had happened. I feared the illusion of our invincibility.

Major (res) Yuval Fine was born in 1952 on Kibbutz Ma'ayan Baruch to parents who both served in the Palmach. He was drafted into Sayeret Egoz and joined the Unit after the Yom Kippur War. He served as the platoon commander of the August 1974 team and holds an M.A. in architecture. Yuval and his wife, Tal, whom he met in the Unit, have three sons and (so far) two grandchildren. Tal is the daughter of Uzi Yairi, former commander of Sayeret Matkal and the Paratroop Brigade. Uzi gave his life in the Savoy operation while rescuing hostages.

Lt. Alon Shemi, Team Leader
Alon APC Commander, APC Force

RUMINATIONS FORTY-FIVE YEARS AFTER THE RESCUE AT ENTEBBE

Forty-five years since Entebbe. What's that got to do with me, was my first reaction. After all, I wiped it from my mind, erased it as an active ingredient in my own self-image practically upon return. I did not read a single one of the books, did not care about the quarrels over credit, did not take a "roots tour" back to Entebbe many years later…nothing. Several days passed, and suddenly it became clear to me that my reaction today and my recollection of my initial reaction post-mission, the manner in which they were fixed in my consciousness, might be worth elaborating on, as a small contribution to the mosaic of stories and musings collected here. I'll return to these matters later on, but maybe I'll start, despite all, with some flashes of memory that endure, like still photos in the album of my mind:

I served at the time as, what we called in the Unit, a *matsbi*, which is to say the point man of a huge mission that was coming through the pipes. My role, as such, was to serve as both a member of the operational force and head the coordination between the different elements contributing to the mission. Nonetheless, the pursuit of an operational solution to the hostage crisis burned feverishly in the minds of many. I first heard about a rescue plan (roughly in the way it was executed) from Amiram Levin, during a meeting about the other mission. I remember it being difficult for him to concentrate on the matter at hand, and, as a result, he spent most of the time talking about his ideas for a rescue operation, opening it up to discussion and responses, before heading to a planned meeting with the commander of the Israel Air Force. I can't swear that this was how the idea came to be, of course, but fixed in my mind is the notion that the operation was born in that room...

I remember that, on account of the coming operation, Yoni wanted Team Omer and I to sit out the rescue mission. Only intense pressure changed his mind. I was penciled in as one of the APC commanders in Shaul Mofaz's force, along with Omer Bar Lev and Udi Salvi. We were charged with isolating the terminal and barring the arrival of any reinforcement troops. Several images are seared into my mind from the preparations stage: the model drill with IDF Chief of Staff Motta Gur, who wanted to see firsthand the readiness of the assault squads and the ability of the pilots to land on a darkened runway; the endless flight and the thin tension in anticipation; the quiet and the darkness of our landing at the airfield; the drive, in the wake of the strike force, which had apparently already reached the terminal. Like old scenes from an antiquated action movie...

The next significant snapshot etched in my mind is from the pitstop in Nairobi, where Ehud Barak was milling around outside, and only there were we told of Yoni's death. Suddenly the whole operation looked different. A deep sadness descended on me; the surging euphoria and the joy of success dissipated. I had a complex relationship with Yoni, but we had been working together very closely on that upcoming mission and maybe for that reason the sudden slash of his death hit me so hard. From that moment on, it colored everything.

We landed at Tel Nof, having heard on board the plane about the waves of happiness washing through the country. We took a bus back to the base and passed Ben-Gurion Airport, where we saw the celebrators circling the plane that brought the hostages home, and at every intersection and in every town—signs of truly ecstatic joy... And I looked at those scenes with a feeling of pride and serenity, alongside a mounting anger, a real anger, building up inside me on account of the hysteria...both because we were returning home with our dead commander in tow and because of the manic depressive nature of this nation, which would have reacted in a diametrically different manner had the mission ended in partial or total failure.

After all, just the day before the hostages' relatives had protested outside the Prime Minister's Office, demanding a prisoner exchange. My response was so strong that it overshadowed everything else.

We had no time for contemplation or carnivals. On the day after Yoni's funeral, once the debriefings were done, we returned in earnest to the planning of that other mission, for which time was running fast through the hourglass. To the best of my recollection, we moved on quickly and did not belabor the issue and certainly did not attend all sorts of events held around the country in honor of the mission. As though it had been cut from the protocol, erased by the events requiring our full attention and energy.

I was discharged less than a year after the mission. One year after that, I set off to travel around the world. Already toward the end of my service, and later, while traveling, I encountered the theatrical show that happened whenever someone discovered that I'd "been there." Suddenly I was treated differently, sometimes dramatically and ridiculously so. Suddenly, I was seen as a hero, a participant from an otherworldly event. I decided that I was not interested in that, not interested in being honored, not interested in having my esteem, in their eyes and in mine, built on, and influenced by, a single biographical detail from my military service. I didn't want that ridiculous fairy dust of heroism on me. And that's why I erased it from my mind and from the surface of my soul. Whenever Entebbe popped up, I'd make a point of cropping it quick…

The uniqueness of the operation, all across the board, is of course quite clear to me. The real credit for the audacity ought to be given to the military brass who initiated, crafted, and authorized the mission operationally, but even more so to Rabin and Peres, who dared to give the final authorization. Among us troops on the ground, the true credit goes to the small group of guys who burst into the terminal and despite the partial and hasty preparations and the disorder on the ground en route to the terminal and the uncertainty about what was happening within the terminal, did such effective, cool-headed, and necessarily brave work. My role, on the other hand, was minor (though of course necessary from a military perspective). I was there;

I participated; I'm proud of having done that, but nothing more. Feeling that the halo was not good for me and even harmful during my later spiritual quests, I stored the memory of the hostage rescue at Entebbe somewhere deep and dark in the basement…

Lt.-Col. Alon Shemi, born in Kibbutz Kabri, was drafted into the Unit in February 1972, to Team Zvika Livne. He continued to serve as a team leader, a matsbi, *and an operational company commander during the tenure of Giora Zorea, Yoni Netanyahu, and Amiram Levin. He was discharged in 1977 and, along with Muki Betser and other reservists from the Unit, founded the IAF commando unit, Shaldag, where he served in reserves, in a variety of roles, until age fifty. In 1989 he took part in the founding of Kibbutz Neot Semadar in the Negev, where he lives, works, and continues to question, along with his wife, Haidi. They have five grown children.*

Second Lieutenant Eyal Oren, Team Leader
Alon APC Operator, APC Force

My Recollections from Operation Entebbe

The Preparations and Deliberations

July 1976. For roughly a year I'd been commander of a team in the midst of a grueling training schedule. During the training period, I was transferred to the veteran Team Omer for a complex mission. I returned with them from training in the field on Thursday night and heard, for the first time, of the hijacked plane and the preparations being made in the Unit. Silently, to myself, I grumbled when thinking of the other guys on my team—they, having not gone to officers' school, were enjoying some pre-discharge R and R while I, this time with the team under my command, was once again living through the long and fatiguing training period, and subject to frequent, nerve-wracking alerts about hostage-based terror attacks. During our service we'd amassed much experience in anti-terror raids—on buildings, planes, trains, skyscrapers. Lit in my memory forever is the trauma of the terror attack on the school in Ma'alot, the heavy price we paid and the sight of the children tumbling out of the high windows and being executed. A year earlier we'd lost one of our team members during the hostage-rescue operation at the Savoy Hotel. The constant emergency call-ups, triggered by every bit of incoming information, and often cancelled later on, exacted a price and scarred us all.

My physical condition at the time was subpar. A cast that I'd worn for three weeks, after fast-roping too quickly out of a helicopter and onto the rooftop of a building during a training exercise, had only just come off, and my knee, which had been badly bruised, could hardly support my weight. Walking was difficult, running out of the question.

At first, I was not included in the array of forces training for the mission. I don't recall being very disappointed. The likelihood of a rescue operation seemed slim to none. I remember an officers meeting where someone raised the option of parachuting a force into Lake Victoria with rubber boats, and already then it was noted that the lake was filled with crocodiles. In essence, no one really believed that there was a tenable operational plan, one that might be authorized and executed.

On Friday the base was humming with activity. I met up with the guys from my old team. They'd been brought back from R and R and put on the strike force. I promptly decided that there was no way I was going to be left behind, no way I wasn't going to find a spot for myself somewhere on the force, injured or not. I grabbed Yoni for a quick chat, explained to him that as a commander of a young team I could not be left behind, and since there was a vehicular force being deployed, in which running would not be mandatory, I had to be included. It took Yoni a second to agree. That's how I became a member of Mofaz's force, part of the crew of Alon Shemi's APC, along with guys I knew well from Team Alon and Team Omer.

Friday's preparations were devoted to acquiring the necessary gear, outfitting and arming the vehicles, and preparing personal weapons and supplies. A model simulation drill was conducted on a mock terminal made of fence posts and burlap, with the control tower and the approach route marked out. Our force was to secure the perimeter on the rear side of the terminal, eliminating the Ugandan soldiers deployed there and barring the arrival of reinforcements that might arrive from the direction of the city of Entebbe. Blueprints or photos of the airfield were scarce and inadequate. We took comfort in the fact that our primary coordinate was the control tower, which could not be missed, and beneath which we would pass on a service road near the terminal. An escape-and-evasion plan was given scant attention, if at all. There was talk of making it to neighboring Kenya, should the need arise, but we were equipped only with the location of the state and its general direction relative to us. We took comfort in the fact that, at least, we weren't on foot. Another concern that came up was jet fuel. The planes couldn't carry enough for the roundtrip. Fuel pumps were loaded up on board and the plan was to refuel at the airport in Uganda.

Our Hercules C-130 was to be the third plane to land. Amongst ourselves we traded macabre jokes about the dwindling chances of the second and third plane to land in one piece. By the time we came in for a landing, we moaned, the element of surprise would be long gone, the runways would be dark, and a few bursts of direct fire could well terminate our visit before we'd even been given the chance to set foot on Ugandan soil. The preparations and drills continued all through the night, without sleep.

Stepping Up a Level

On Saturday morning I led the APC convoy to Lod, where the vehicles could be watched over without suspicion in advance of take-off. A short while later the forces arrived. We boarded the plane along with the Golani Brigade soldiers. The first stop was Sharm el-Sheikh for an additional refueling and a final briefing. The flight to the Sinai Peninsula took roughly an hour, but at low altitude and amid strong turbulence. We suffered from nausea and grew concerned that a few more hours of this and we'd not be operating at our peak.

Yoni delivered a moving address at the airfield in Sharm. Around us there was excitement and swirling bets about whether or not the mission would be aborted in mid-flight. The window of opportunity, during which the mission could be called off, was slim, and beyond that there was no turning back.

Yoni's briefing focused on cultivating in us a fighting spirit, a faith and confidence in our strength and skill and in our ability to accomplish the mission, and a reiteration that the People of Israel were behind us. Yoni, as I knew him, from the point of view of a young team leader, was the responsible adult; the experienced, level-headed officer who exuded confidence. We pored over photos taken by a Mossad combatant who'd landed at Entebbe the day before and managed to deliver up-to-date information that dovetailed with what we knew. After the briefing, anti-nausea pills were shoved into our hands and we were told to take them on the plane, to prevent a redux of the first leg.

En Route to the Mission

We're in the air. Darkness. Trying to find a place to rest and sleep amid the vehicles. I don't really fall asleep, maybe on account of the thoughts and the excitement, and then at some point the information is conveyed: the mission's been authorized by the government. We carry on. I toss a glance at the window: dark and serene all around. The landing hour is near, a red light comes on in the cabin, the signal to organize personal gear and board the vehicles. Suddenly I see flashes of light and the plane shudders. Have we been spotted? Are we taking incoming fire from the ground? The pilot soothes us. A lightning storm over Lake Victoria. We start coming in for a landing, the lights on the ground visible and getting closer, the edge lights on the runway glowing brightly. An encouraging sign. It means the element of surprise is still intact. The first plane must have landed. Any moment now the wheels will hit the tarmac. A chill passes through me. Here's hoping the plan works. Seconds before the wheels strike the runway, the lights are extinguished; a moment later, the torches lit by the paratroopers mark the path. The plane manages to land and taxis to the disembarkation point.

Galloping Ahead

The rear ramp of the Hercules opens. The APCs roll down and we head out full speed ahead toward the terminal where the hostages are being kept. Darkness, clear skies, stars above, warm air washing our faces. We gallop toward the looming control tower. The gunfire that we hear raises questions for which there are no immediate answers. There's still fire from the control tower. The APCs return fire in an upward trajectory; we continue on toward the base of the tower, along the left side of the terminal. The service road is dark, as is the rear side of the terminal. Up ahead a group of Ugandan soldiers cross the dark road, moving toward the overgrowth on the left side of the lane; we open fire and hear only the grunts and screams that soon fall silent. Ahead of us there's a gas station and a row of rooms in a long hut. We spray whatever looks like soldiers' quarters; no one emerges. Shadmi, one of the operators on the assault force, comes out of the back door of the terminal and updates us that the evacuation of the hostages is starting. We wait, primed and ready, to see if a convoy of Ugandan backup will approach, but aside from the faraway lights of the city there is no vehicular traffic coming our way.

A short while later we regroup at the square in front of the terminal. The bonfire of the Ugandan Air Force fighter jets, lit by ordnance from Omer's APC, is visible. I spot the hijacked Air France plane deserted on the runway. We wait in formation, providing perimeter security for the forces heading back to their planes. There are rumors of wounded, but no word yet of Yoni being hit.

The Long Way Back

We takeoff for home. The mystery of how we'll make it back has not been solved; that said, I recall no concern. The feeling of success spreads fast, the adrenalin floods through my body and I glue my face to the window and watch the wheels rise up off the ground. A short flight—we land in Nairobi, where we meet Shai Avital and Ehud Barak. We are updated about the refueling and about Yoni's death. The euphoric feeling is immediately diluted by a sense of loss and sadness. There's no time. We're being spurred to depart, hurrying back up onto the plane for takeoff. Seven hours pass like an eternity in full wakefulness and in the hope that we'll arrive safely. In the early morning, with first light over the blue waters of the Red Sea, the pilot announces that Israeli radio is reporting news of the operation. We listen to the Voice of Israel update, which is piped into the cabin. There's still a lot of time before landing and I'm concerned that we may be discovered by Egyptian or Saudi radar and attacked in midair. Two hours later we land in Israel. A reception, speeches, festivities and joy, but for me and my friends it's mixed with sadness and loss.

Back at the base, Yael, the devoted bureau clerk comes running toward me and tells me that she's called my girlfriend, (and later my wife) Malki, to let her know that I've returned unharmed. Time is nipping at our heels; there's no orderly and rigorous debriefing, a large crowd is gathered at the base and they're thirsting for stories and for release from the stress. I return to the routine of training with my team.

In Conclusion

After the operation we quickly resumed our routine and, as we were accustomed during our service in the Unit, managed to lock up the feelings and emotions. Over the years, and on account of the way the mission has resonated, I realized how fine the line was between dizzying success and reverberating failure. The brave leadership, headed by Prime Minister Yitzhak Rabin, Defense Minister Shimon Peres, IDF Chief of Staff Motta Gur and others inculcated in us the faith and the confidence that we could go to the end of the earth to free Israeli hostages. The message was contagious and it spread through the ranks, to soldiers and commanders alike. Despite the dearth of intelligence data and the rushed preparations, despite the immense risks and the uncertainty during the lead-up and execution, the pervasive can-do spirit within the Unit and elsewhere was, we must note, guided, with confidence and leadership, by Yoni Netanyahu, may he rest in peace. Determination, daring, and devotion, we were taught, can make the impossible possible.

Lt. (res.) Eyal Oren grew up in Hadar Ramatayim, which has since become Hod HaSharon. He went to the Katzenelson High School in Kfar Saba, where he was a fixture on the ball courts. A javelin thrower both in the fields and for Hapoel Kfar Saba, he starred at the national youth championships. In 1973 he was drafted into the Unit, to Team Amnon, and then moved to Gvaot Kola, which imprinted itself on his very soul and body. In 1975 he was sent to IDF Officers

School and returned to the Unit as a team leader. Eyal is married and has three children and six grandchildren. A specialist in orthodontics and dentofacial orthopedics, he studied dentistry at Tel Aviv University and continues to practice to this day, relishing the opportunity to help kids and adults smile freely and openly.

Lt. Yoni Raz, Team Leader
Officer-Operator on Omer's APC, Armored Force

MEMORIES FROM AFRICA; OR HOW I CAME BACK FROM ENTEBBE WITH A CLEAN GUN

Some Personal Background:

I was sent to an abbreviated officers' candidate course during the summer of 1974. Once commissioned, I started the training period with my team. This began, as in the tradition in the Unit, with a 120-km march, early in the winter of 1975.

Pre-Hijacking and Planning for the Mission

Late in June 1976, the team under my command was at the beginning of the advanced training stage of its service. The first week was conducted in the northern Negev, practicing off-road operational driving skills and wheeled combat maneuvers in the desert.

On Sunday June 26, 1976 the Air France plane was hijacked and we were put on alert, along with all the other operational teams, and sent to the northern sector of the runways at Ben Gurion International Airport, where we drilled the takeover of a hijacked plane. This was not our first time practicing for such a mission. The airplane on which we trained for the takeover had already seen plenty of action. At noon, once it became clear that the hijacked flight was well on its way to central Africa (with a pitstop in Libya), we received an order to carry on with our week of training. The senior officers, in the meanwhile, started planning what would become known as a most complex and unprecedented operation. We headed down to the small desert town of Yerucham, resuming our week of field maneuvers: operational driving and mobile live-fire drills. Every evening, after completing the day's training, I drove to a nearby army base and put in a phone call to make sure that they hadn't left without us. I had a deep conviction that this hijacking was an act that must be countered by the IDF, and in this case, it seemed, the IDF was us.

Late on Thursday night, July 1, we completed the week of training. We returned to our base and found the place humming. The operational teams were in mid-preparations, as were some of the Unit's reservists, who'd materialized from who knows where. My main, vital role: to make it to the office of the Unit commander and ensure that my team was slated to take part. A few sorties later, the situation was clear: my team would not be deployed as a team. Some of the operators would be dispersed among the forces, and some would not be participating at all. A difficult and unpleasant development, and a trying chore indeed to speak to those who were not included.

I was made the radio operator in Omer's APC (the operational teams, including Omer's, were "reserved" for a different mission and therefore kept in a more peripheral role and not part of the assault force). Other members of my team were scattered throughout the fighting force.

On Friday evening, July 2nd, a "model" drill was conducted at our base. The old terminal at Entebbe was constructed out of metal poles and jute sheets, with the walls and doors erected on a 1:1 scale so that each and every one of the operators would know precisely where he was supposed to be and what he was supposed to do during the raid. Even though we had plenty of experience in this sort of combat, the feeling this time was different, strange, and it stood alongside a deep understanding that the operation was fast becoming real.

Heading Out

Saturday, late morning, July 3: pre-op equipment adjustments, a final set of detailed instructions delivered at the Unit briefing hall. I won't soon forget the escape and evasion instructions: "If you lose your squad, head towards Lake Victoria." I don't remember if we were told what we were to do once there—carry on or stay put and wait. And if so, for whom? It was quite clear we were being issued a one-way ticket.

Noon: We drove a short distance to the Air Force base, where the planes were ready and waiting. We loaded the vehicles onto the Hercules C-130s (those planes are called "Rhinoceroses" in Hebrew) and flew to Sharm el-Sheikh, the southernmost point in the Sinai desert, which at the time was a part of Israel.

On the ground in Sinai, there was a very last commander's briefing. We were told that the government of Israel was convened to discuss the approval of the operation. They had until 8 PM. We would take off in few minutes, knowing that if the pilots kept flying in the same direction after eight in the evening, it meant we had the government's authorization to carry out the mission. I was not endowed with a "historical feeling." Instead, I was alert and clung firmly to the notion that the operation simply must succeed. We had no other option.

Entebbe Airport, On the Runways

As far as I remember we were on the last plane that landed. We rolled out, started driving. All around us was a deep, sticky dark. No sign of Polaris in the sky, no stars at all. Orientation conducted only by compass, or what you remember from the maps and photos we studied during the preparations. Team Omer's mission was to block the old terminal from the east, where the Ugandan Air force base was located. We had to prevent the local army from intervening and to allow our forces freedom of action in and around the old terminal.

Driving along, we cruised past the control tower. From time to time we heard the semi-automatic pop of the "Uzi" light submachine guns. I saw Eyal Yardenay aim an RPG rocket launcher at the control tower. After a slight malfunction, he launched a rocket. The shooting from the tower stopped immediately.

We arrived at our position and turned the vehicle toward the terminal building. We were in a position with a good line of sight to the terminal. I could clearly see operators from Team Dani Arditi approaching the terminal doors and at that very moment I heard a call over the radio (I do not remember if it was Tamir Pardo, our chief communications officer, or Muki Betser, Yoni's second in command) announcing: "Yoni's injured, Muki's taking command."

Within our APC there was talk: "The operation is almost over, and our weapons are still clean." This was promptly followed by a command from Omer: "Open fire at the jets."

Those MiG fighter jets were parked right opposite us and quite close. It was very easy to light them up from our position. The wave of fire was quite long. Immediately afterwards the jets started burning and lit up the whole vicinity. Since I was sitting at the front of the APC, facing the terminal, and enough people from the team were shooting like hell, I thought that there was no point in joining the orchestra of shooting. My gun stayed clean. I shot not a single bullet.

After a while we were ordered to pack it in. We were the last vehicle on the ground at Entebbe, the last to leave the field of battle. On our way back to the plane, we left detonation devices with a delay mechanism, to waylay any force that might try to chase us.

On the taxiway, heading toward our plane, we passed the hijacked Air France aircraft. I thought: Maybe someone was forgotten inside? Why was that not taken into account? Why is no one searching it?"

I looked at my watch: 00:25. It was Sunday already. July 4th. My birthday. Definitely a special event to mark my special day.

The Flight Home

We took off in the same darkness in which we'd landed. A certain feeling of relief. At dawn, we touched down in Nairobi, Kenya, for refueling. The sun rose. I did not know of any other casualty aside from Yoni.

We took off for home. As we approached Israel, the plane's PA system started patching Israeli Independence Day songs into the cabin. I felt very strange: "What, in total, had happened? Why the great celebration? All we'd done is our job! Just another successful operation." I thought: For our teams the distance from Israel was insignificant. The real heroes are the pilots, the intelligence officers, who provided the crucial, updated information. Only years later did I realize that the bigger heroes were the decision makers, those who approved this operation at the upper echelons of the IDF and within the government.

Pre-Epilogue

During the winter of 2002, 25 years after the operation, a group of veteran operators went on a "roots trip" to Entebbe. The guided tour was organized by Amitzur Kafri, the officer who drove the black Mercedes sedan during the actual operation. Fortunately, it fell on the same year that my youngest son had his bar mitzvah. I thought it would be a unique and very special opportunity to provide him with some educational heritage.

The group included eight veteran operators and some of their families. Fifteen men and women all told.

Luckily, this group consisted of soldiers from nearly all of the different forces and squads. We visited the old terminal and its surroundings. We held an emotional memorial ceremony at the foot of the control tower, then followed the trail of the battle step by step. At each point, the operator who was directly involved in that stage told his story and we tried together to recreate a full and authentic rendition of the battle. Climbing to the control tower to check on the effect of Eyal Yardenay's RPG round, we found that the missile had hit the tin roof of the tower and had not damaged the walls, but it had done enough to quell the shooting from there. I consider this recreation of the battle to be the most thorough debriefing and investigation of the raid at Entebbe.

My main insight from that debriefing was encapsulated in Shlomi Reisman's words: "Everyone performed in an exemplary way, but the maestra of the event was Lady Luck, who worked overtime here."

Epilogue and Lessons

Who dares (and prepares very well) – wins. Best with a dash of luck.

My life lesson is: Prepare yourself in the most detailed way, but remember that reality will always be otherwise and full of surprises.

Luck visits those who aid her arrival, but not always. There are exceptions (I have evidence.)

———

Maj. Yoni (Jonathan) Raz was born in Kvutzat Geva, 1953. Recruited to the IDF in August 1972, he was drafted to Team Gidoni Avidov. He fought in the 1973 Yom Kippur War on the northern front, where, in the Nafah region of the Golan Heights, Gidoni was killed. He fought in a combined mission force of soldiers from the Training Company and operators from the Reserves Company. The force was led by Muki Betser (the Training Company commander) and Yoni Netanyahu. Toward the end of the war, he fought as a member of Team Galili (who replaced Gidoni as the team commander) and participated in the conquering of the peak of Mount Hermon (April 1974) and the anti-terror raid at Maalot, in which the Unit attempted to rescue a group of hostage school children. Many of the hostages were killed and the strike was considered a failure in the Unit. But it led to the acquisition of some very important lessons and the formation of a combat doctrine that has made the Unit the best anti-terror force around The proof came to light in Entebbe.

Staff-Sgt. Yossi Shak
Operator on Team Omer, Omer's APC

SHARDS OF MEMORY AND IMAGES FROM OPERATION ENTEBBE

Forty-five years have passed since Operation Entebbe and when thinking of the operation I'm flooded with shards of memory that are not easily assembled into a single, whole story.

Not long ago, my daughter, Lior, gave me the book *Entebbe 1976* by Sara Davidson, one of the hostages held at Entebbe along with her husband and two sons. I read it eagerly, both as a former soldier who participated in the hostage-rescue mission who has since felt that our fates are forever linked, and in solidarity with them, as part of an attempt to understand the plight of the people who were thrust into such a lowly situation: far from home, dependent, kept in captivity.

The sight of the convoy of hostages walking together in the dark, from the old terminal to the Hercules planes, is imprinted indelibly in my mind. Survivors marching in a long, jostling line. I saw them from up close and could not help but think for a fraction of a second of the Holocaust and the dread of those forced marches. Maybe because I'm the son of two Holocaust survivors. My father was imprisoned in a German labor camp, and my mother pretended to be Christian and lived on a remote farm before fleeing and finding refuge in the forests.

There's no doubt in my mind that the rescue of the hostages and their liberation from dread and despair, dependency and captivity, is the beating heart of Operation Entebbe, the human significance of the rescue. Happily, and despite the risks inherent in the action, I was given the chance to participate along with my team members and friends from the Unit in a mission that succeeded beyond what anyone thought might be feasible.

The operation is considered a great success story, both in Israel and abroad. The media, cultural, and political resonance of the operation was immense; it became a national ethos. In the ensuing forty-five years a fixed narrative has emerged: flying-fighting-rescuing-returning. It is composed of heroic superlatives: good vs. evil, David vs. Goliath. And yet, in my mind, the reality of that mission is more complex than the offerings of that imagery, and is, in many ways, from my perspective as a soldier and a human being, far simpler. To a large extent, its dimensions in my eyes are different.

My Entebbe story starts with induction into the IDF after the Yom Kippur War, a stark line that divides my childhood in Kibbutz Ein HaMifratz from my service, starting in November 1973, as a soldier and operator on Team Omer Bar Lev.

As a junior team in the Unit we went through a complex and grueling training process that included long weeks of hard drills in the field and little by little the team was whittled down to less than half of its original number. We learned to operate an array of weapons; we navigated by day and by night, in the hills and in the deserts; we endured difficult marches and acquired professional skills; with time, we became operators. Once we'd made it to a certain benchmark in our training, we participated in the Unit's operational activity, including the hostage rescue operations that were all too common at the time—in Nahariya, in Beit Shean, and in the heart of Tel Aviv at the Savoy Hotel. I remember waiting for hours outside the Savoy while negotiations with the terrorists continued on until we heard the awful explosion that killed some of the hostages. During the assault stage, much to our sorrow, two of our men were killed— Col. Uzi Yairi, a former commander of the Unit, and Itamar Ben-David, who was an operator on Team Amnon and a good friend to us all.

In my military experience there are three circles. The first circle is the individual. Here you tackle significant physical and mental hurdles; you grapple with yourself and you operate alone; you recognize that all is possible. Your capabilities, your physical and mental stamina, and your self-esteem are fortified, while, at the same time, the Unit's code of modesty and secrecy is absorbed and fixed within you.

The second circle is the team. Here you act as a single part, a component within a larger group in which each individual has his role and his realm of responsibility, both personal and collective. My fellow team members are, in effect, my closest friends to this very day and we know each other so well, and rely so fully on one another, that often there's no need even for words.

The third circle is the Unit at large, the many teams and team leaders. Each team has its own assignment and together the teams work like a well-oiled machine. The familiarity and skill are such that, even during complex and dangerous missions, in which situations shift and require quick responses and physical and emotional stamina of the first order, you know your role and your place and are capable of acting accordingly in any situation. The keys are confidence in yourself and in your mates, a sharp vigilance and awareness, and the ability to prepare and execute at the highest level.

As opposed to what many believe, hostage-rescue and counter-terror battles were not part of our routine. Utterly different operations occupied most of the space on the Unit's schedule, grueling operations that could take several long days and nights to execute and a training period of weeks if not months. Operations that cannot be spoken of to this day.

The hostage rescue and the battle against the terrorists in Entebbe was, for me, and to the best of my recollection, similar to a stop on a train ride to another destination; we hopped off and deftly did what had to be done, re-boarded, and continued to prepare for the next mission. I did not feel like I was part of a group of heroes. We did what was required of us and we did it in the best, most professional way we could; an expression of a soldierly approach and an upholding of a longstanding norm and operational legacy of the Unit.

The danger level and complexity of Operation Entebbe was clearly a lot like other hostage-rescue operations: triggered without warning, in a civilian environment, facing armed terrorists willing to go all the way. For this reason, our training track included many different counter-terror scenarios and responses, including copious selective-fire drills, which taught us to open our eyes wide and find the bad guys and spare the good guys. The constant drilling and the steady state of alert gave us the skills and the confidence to be calm and serene. The fundamental difference between Operation Entebbe and the hostage-rescue missions for which we were called up in Israel, was that Entebbe, near the shores of Lake Victoria, was thousands of kilometers away.

On Sunday June 27, 1976, when the Air France plane was hijacked, our team was engaged in training for a large and very important mission that was to be launched several weeks later. It nearly came to us being told that as a team we were too important to risk and so, in order to protect the other mission, we would not participate in Operation Entebbe. But Omer, our team leader, stood firm and didn't back down and fought for our right to take part in the mission. He apparently recognized the significance and the enormity of the opportunity.

As soldiers we were not aware of the raging political dilemmas and the military decisions that had to be made regarding the feasibility and success of the mission. We only learnt of that after the fact. What we knew, and what we were told was discussed, were creative ideas such as landing us on rubber rafts in Lake Victoria along with the guys from the Naval Commandos. The concept—landing on water if the target can't be reached by land— was not novel, but the idea was shelved once it became clear that the lake was filled with crocodiles.

If my memory serves, mission orders were issued only on Friday morning, July 2nd. The different Unit forces were delineated and each team received its objective. Our team, one of the most experienced teams in the Unit, was to approach the southeast corner of the old terminal, where the hostages were being held, as part of a combined thrust that was to complete and assist the strike force storming the terminal. We readied our firearms, stuffed our battle vests with magazines, and acquired other equipment. We were to approach the terminal on armored vehicles, with the chosen model being a rickety, Russian, wheeled APC. During the day there were many briefings and drills, logistical liaisons and strike simulations, conducted under the gaze of the IDF Chief of Staff Lt.-Gen. Motta Gur, on the runway of an old airport on a model that was meant to mimic the old terminal at Entebbe.

Like other Unit missions, here, too, there were many variables during the preparation stage. For instance, up until the last minute it was not clear how many terrorists were present in the passenger hall and how many Ugandan soldiers were securing the terminal. We knew that the planes could carry fuel for only one leg of the journey. We did not know that there were plans for a pitstop in Nairobi. We were told that if there was no other option, the planes would be refueled at Entebbe and we would have to assist the maintenance crew with that mission. We received largescale evasion-and-escape maps so that if the planes were harmed and we were unable to takeoff, we'd know where we were and where we had to go. Since navigation and orienteering were brought to a phenomenal level in the Unit, maps, like weapons, felt like a part of our bodies, and the matter of escape and evasion did not weigh heavily on us. We had faith in ourselves. We were determined and poised to act, devoid of stress or pressure.

Additionally, up until the last minute there were changes to the plans and changes in the briefings. Up-to-date photos of the terminal, taken by a Mossad operative the day before the mission and arriving on the morning of the mission, dictated several changes to our overall plan. And above all of that hovered a cloud of uncertainty—the Government of Israel had yet to authorize the mission. But we were accustomed to that too. Changes to the plan and doubts about the actuality of a pending mission were part and parcel of many of our other operations.

The first part of the mission was the very-low-altitude flight to the airfield at Sharm al-Sheikh. Once there, all the teams and forces assembled at the airfield in Sharm and Yoni Netanyahu, the commander of the Unit, delivered a final briefing. We sat on the ground on the edge of the runway, in a semi-circle, and listened to his strong words. It was a final, summarizing briefing before taking off for distant Entebbe, and we all knew what was expected of us. I remember the briefing well and the way Yoni seemed tense; he seemed to me to be very concerned, his face grayer and different than usual. He looked like someone who hadn't slept for many days, someone aware of the weight of responsibility on his shoulders. As soldiers, we all knew Yoni. He was considered a brave commander and ever since he'd replaced Giora Zore'a at the helm, he often joined us during training drills and on missions.

After the short layover, we boarded the Hercules C-130s and headed out. My team boarded planes two and three. The Hercules C-130 was heavy and filled with gear and a pair of APCs, and as loud as ever, but I remember the flight as something serene. It was my first time flying abroad. All of a sudden, I felt a bit like a casual tourist. Once I confirmed that all my gear was with me on board, I tucked myself into a corner, lit the gas burner that I'd brought, and brewed up a pot of good coffee. I looked out the window, searched for the bays of Sinai and the jungles of Africa…at some point, of course, I fell asleep. At long last, there was time to sleep.

I awoke with preparation for landing. The flight maintenance crew skipped into action and skillfully freed the APCs from their chains, so that we could disembark quickly. Riding out of the plane and into the darkness, we saw the lights of the city of Entebbe on the hill and were smacked by the special smell of the lush parts of Africa; a tropical scent that I'd never before encountered, carried on the winds from Lake Victoria. Pulling away from the plane, we were enveloped in a quiet that was soon violated as we approached the terminal.

From afar we saw the headlights of approaching Ugandan troops coming from the direction of Entebbe. We fired effectively in their direction; some were hit, the rest fled. I remember well the large square outside the passenger hall, the doors leading inside, and the relatively high control tower, from which the gunfire—in bursts of tracers—did not stop. Later we learnt that one of those bullets fatally wounded Yoni. There was incessant fire flying through the air, really much like an action movie. One of the operators shot an RPG missile up at the control tower and silenced it with a single blow. Once the terrorists were eliminated and the battle had died down, we turned to the Ugandan MiG fighter jets, which glistening like statues on the edge of the runway. The missile I fired at one of the jets missed the mark; I remember the feeling of frustration...but nonetheless our machinegun and rifle fire set the MiGs aflame. The jets were parked in a line and one ignited the other. Everything was burning and popping and for a moment we were seized, like children, with the happy, celebratory sight of Lag BaOmer bonfires.

Once all of the hostages had been evacuated to the first plane for takeoff, our team, the sweep force, boarded the fourth and final plane. An operator in our APC placed delay-action explosive blocks on the runway and taxiways; they were to explode every quarter of an hour, further confusing the enemy. Those moments were slightly worrying as I was concerned that the blocks might explode in his hands. We checked everyone was present and then took off for home.

Much like the landing, the takeoff was aggressive and loud. Forty minutes later we landed in Nairobi to refuel. Ehud Barak came aboard the plane to say hi. A rumor circulated that Yoni had been killed in battle.

––––––––––

We landed at Tel Nof Airbase and continued from there straight to the Unit. There was no orderly debrief as was customary after missions. There was a sort of summing up in the briefing room. During the conversation in the room, I remember that each team leader reported what had happened and Amiram Levin announced that he would be replacing Yoni as commander of the Unit. We got the night off, went home, came back, and attended Yoni's funeral. Immediately afterwards, we transitioned back to training and preparing for that other upcoming mission. There was no time to grieve or digest what had happened. We most certainly did not participate in the festivities and feasts held across the country. The whole "festival" was far removed from our world.

They say that failure is an orphan and that success has many fathers. There's no doubt that Operation Entebbe was a success and no doubt that those who bore ultimate responsibility—Prime Minister Yitzhak Rabin, Defense Minister Shimon Peres, and Chief of Staff Motta Gur—faced a unique and complex dilemma in advance of the operation. Luckily, the operation was a success. Clearly, it all could have ended differently. And yet there is a wide gap between the way the operation is publicly perceived and the way that I and most of my friends relate to it.

The operation is seen as lightning fast and clean; we flew-fought-rescued-returned mostly unscathed. But just as open-heart surgery is an expression of the long medical training of the surgeon, so too is this operation an expression of our training in the Unit. At times we are treated as heroes, and I am most uncomfortable with that. In my mind, heroes are, for example, the warriors of the Warsaw Ghetto Uprising, the foot soldiers of the War of Independence or the largely anonymous armored corps soldiers who fought tank battles on the blackened fields of destruction during the Yom Kippur War, those who blocked, with their bodies and their fighting spirit, the advancing Syrian tanks from rolling into the southern Golan and the Hula Valley. Those are the true heroes; the soldiers and commanders who were not given the skill set and the training, even mentally, that was afforded to us, and yet were forced to contend with consecutive days and nights of battle, in difficult combat conditions and without a steady supply of ammunition, and further hampered by hunger, fatigue, uncertainty and fear; and even as commanders and friends fell around them, they did not give up and fought to the very last bullet.

While traveling far and wide through Israel I have made a habit of stopping among the monuments to the fallen. A personal curiosity of sorts. I read the brief text. Not so much for the story of battle, but for the loss, the terrible price paid, the personal tragedy of family and friends. A soldier falls in battle, and what remains? A cairn of stones, a pair of trees, a dry bouquet of flowers and a sign. How saddening that he, as far as most of the public is concerned, remains anonymous.

Staff-Sgt. (res) Yossi Shak was born and raised on Kibbutz Ein HaMifratz. He was drafted to the Unit in November 1973 and became an operator on Team Omer Bar Lev. He served in the Unit during the tenures of commanders Giora Zorea, Yoni Netanyahu, and Amiram Levin. A former employee of the Society for the Protection of Nature in Israel, Shak has a masters in life sciences and biochemistry from the Hebrew University and a masters in urban and regional planning from the Technion: Israel Technological Institute's Department of Architecture and Town Planning. He works for a private architectural firm as an urban planner and lives in Moshav Amikam. He is married and a father of three.

Cpt. Dr. Arik Shalev, Unit Doctor
Doctor-Operator in Omer's APC, APC Force

MY ENTEBBE

It all started on Friday at seven a.m. I could tell in advance that it was an ill-fated Friday: a second-year resident at the time, I was supposed to start a 48-hour rotation at Gehah psychiatric hospital. Already not awesome. But the craziness that commenced that day really caught me by surprise. "Yoni wants you here on the base ASAP," a female clerk said over the phone.

This was not completely new. Ever since I'd finished my tour of service as the Unit's resident doctor, I'd been called up repeatedly and had spent a large part of my psychiatric residency in live-fire drills, pre-operation drills, cross-border rescues, field navigation drills—all the things that a doctor with a healthy back and a pair of working legs is subjected to when in uniform. Those adventures have certainly left gaps in my professional knowledge, which I'm not sure I've ever filled. All in an all, however, I enjoyed serving in the Unit, and suffered in silence, like everyone. One night, as we lay in a narrow ravine near the Dead Sea, I mentioned that it was my 30th birthday. A much younger operator turned to me and sanely uttered: "Doc, I really don't get you." But who cared about being sane in those days.

An urgent summons on a Friday morning had to be something special. Something that would save me from the tedium of a double shift in a hospital for the insane. Like a kid being called home from school, I was both nervous and happy, and had a feeling that I knew what was going on: I connected the dots and figured that we were going to be dispatched to pick up the freed hostages from a remote airport, as we'd done, in a previous hostage-exchange deal months earlier. For some reason I had it in my mind that the exchange would

take place in South Africa. They always take a doctor to these operations, because if the doc vomits in the plane then it's perfectly fine
for others to barf and the Unit's spirit is not broken.

I notified the hospital that I was (yet again) off to save the
country and that someone else should take my double-shift. I also had
an agreement with my wife Vered that, without divulging the
specifics, whenever I left home with the Unit I would tell her if it was
'for real' or just a training exercise, so that she could sleep soundly
most of the time. I mumbled something—I can't remember if I said
the words duty free—and left. We lived a fifteen-minute drive from
the base, so it didn't take long before I was in Yoni's office, where I
saw, on the wall, an aerial of an airport under the headline "Entebbe
—Uganda." I forgot about tax-free shopping.

It was a chaotic day, full of drills amid burlap structures meant to
mimic buildings. Vehicles were loaded up onto a plane that landed in
our airfield. Generals. Briefings. Role assignments. Outside the
armory they spread an array of personal weapons on a plastic sheet
for each of us to pick. I thought of maybe swapping my AK-47 to
something lighter that would allow me, as a doctor, to have my hands
free, but it wasn't meant to be. Our alternative evacuation plan (driving along Lake Victoria in the event that the planes weren't able to
takeoff) was so insane that I opted to take a proper rifle; my very
personal weapon, which I'd "acquired" during the Yom Kippur War,
when we'd gone up to the northern front without a weapon, and
which I gave away just a year before writing these lines.

Toward evening, after the briefings, I decided that the whole
thing wasn't exactly to my liking. Worse, the girls—Orly and others
—stopped by the medical clinic and beseeched me to bring everyone
back safe. I promised that I would. I then retreated from the general
tumult and started my own drill—going over medical gear, picking
surgical kits and bandaging supplies. I tried to guess what might
happen and what had to be immediately available. I peeled off unnecessary packaging to save seconds in response time and to ensure that
no Hebrew-marked gear would be left behind. I practiced finding
every single piece of medical equipment in my pack by touch and

made sure I got it right every time. Later in the evening I rounded up some victims -- soldiers who were not slated to participate in the mission, and practiced inserting IV lines with and without light. It went great!!! From that point on I felt complete serenity and a clear sense that the operation would succeed: The training was already a success! How little one requires to convince oneself one way or the other.

I slept at home, and slept well, safe in the knowledge that everything was under control. All we needed was the green light. In the morning I headed off to the base and from there to Lod airport and to the plane. I cursed myself for yet again forgetting that he who boards the plane first gets the best place to recline for the duration of the flight—on the hood of a jeep for example. I tucked myself into a corner, and shortly thereafter the most difficult medical ordeal began: We flew to Sharm at zero altitude and with extreme turbulence, which left everyone green and sick and whatnot. At Sharm I discovered that we had seven more hours of flight time. I figured that conditions on the second leg wouldn't be any better, which meant that after seven hours of motion sickness and vomiting, we'd all be useless. I checked the duration of action of Dramamine, the IDF-dispensed anti-emetic drug—and found, alongside warnings not to operate any machinery or engage in any actions that require alertness, that it was six hours. Barring any mishaps, therefore, the operators would be fresh and timely ready for action if each of them took one pill before departure. I found the drug in the Sharm airbase clinic and distributed it to all. And once again I forgot the speed with which our hallowed warriors snag every spot fit for human repose in an airplane's belly and entered last. We took off. Turned out we flew at a cruising altitude, with zero turbulence, and with sweet dreams.

On the armored personnel carrier in Entebbe airfield I was yet again awarded an opportunity to shield our warriors from harm. We patrolled around the front of the terminal and created a "screen of fire" by shooting in every direction—including with a grenade launcher. The burning hot casings of newly released rounds fell straight into the driver's open shirt - Yoav Wachman, I think, - and he hollered! Seven years of intense medical studies prepared me for just that moment: I freed the searing metal casings from the space between his shirt and his bare back, wondering if a doctor with charred fingers is still fit for practicing medicine.

The brilliant glare of the terminal's fluorescent lights allowed us to see the operation unfold as a movie in shadow. I thought I saw someone fall. I distinctly remember the gunfire from the control tower and the return fire from the ground up until all was quiet— around a minute. It wasn't clear to me if I ought to disembark from the vehicle and help [Dr.] David Hassin inside the terminal. Turned out there was no need.

Without meaning to ignite it, and without knowing about a squadron of Ugandan MiGs on the ground, one of the fighter jets in our field of fire sprung a leak and caught fire, and the flames shot up in a vertical column. We poured more fire on the fighter jets. Then we saw the large crowd walk out of the terminal, headed for the IDF Medical Corps evacuation plane, and our hearts got a little lighter.

Like all carefully planned missions, though, there was a moment in which everything almost went bust. As the force sweep, the last ones to depart (or, God forbid, embark on a long journey around Lake Victoria), we left blast-delayed explosive blocks and smoke grenades behind us, apparently to stymie any tactical enemy assaults. And just as we'd finished littering the field with explosives, the commanders inquired about the head count—there were people unaccounted for— maybe hostages (Dora Bloch, may she rest in peace) and perhaps members of the flight crew. They asked us to turn around and check the [Air France] plane. I remember approaching in the direction of the cockpit, which seemed incredibly high as we drove back through the smoke, and calculating, or at least trying to calculate, how much time was left before the explosives would go off. It's a known medical question: "Doc, how much time I got left to live?" Some- how, somewhere, someone, must have convinced Dan Shomron to call off that strange maneuver; I remember well the short discussion over the radio about whether "the plane is booby-trapped or not" and the brave decision to abort mission and get us back home in one piece. We left with the vehicles in tow and without encountering Lake Victoria's crocodiles, or the mosquitoes on the road encircling it, which would have surely presented interesting preventative medicine challenges. All told, I clocked fifty minutes on the ground.

In Nairobi we learned that Yoni had been killed. Two other operators sustained light shrapnel wounds and I bandaged them. Back in Israel I thought that Dr. David Hassin, who had tried to resuscitate Yoni, should go and examine Yoni's body in the morgue. That's what I'd done after Itamar Ben-David had died in my hands at the Savoy March 5 1975 hostage rescue attempt: it spares you a lifetime of doubt and piercing feeling that you could have done better. I wasn't able to convince David. Ehud Barak arrived at the Unit and together we looked at Yoni's battle vest. The right breast pocket had a mini-frag grenade with a bullet stuck inside it; the trajectory of the bullet was downward. At the time I interpreted that to mean that he was hit by gunfire coming from the control tower, but this was after the fact and not all that important. We won, we lost, we soldiered on with it all embedded in our hearts.

I thought there was some historic justice in the fact that Team Amnon, which had lost Itamar during the raid on the Savoy, had been at the center of this operation. We became very close friends. For years I didn't think about Entebbe. Most important: on the way back from Entebbe I found a place to sprawl out in the plane, which shows that old dogs do learn new tricks.

At Geha hospital I was offered a five-year post as a senior doctor —an indication that, truly, I had let myself get way behind in my studies. Vered is still with me but I no longer head out on missions at nights.

Epilogue

For doctors, military ops don't end when the action stops.

Wounded soldiers, hospitals, families…

And true to form, two days after our return I got a call from a friend who told me that one of the teenage hostages in Entebbe was responding badly to the ordeal, not sleeping at nights and in distress.

I asked to meet him and he told me that during the rescue he'd laid down behind a wall that had shielded him, but heard the wild bursts of fire and saw the bullets slam into the wall. He'd figured that the terrorists were about to finish them off and that soon they would reach him. In captivity he'd also befriended Jean-Jacques Meimoni, a hostage who was killed during the raid. The most difficult part had been to lie there, paralyzed, as the bullets zinged past, and to feel that soon he would be found and killed. I thought that he deserved some sort of counterweight to that experience, got authorization, and took him and my ever-ready Kalashnikov to a shooting range alongside the Unit.

A barely grown kid— I had no idea how he'd respond to the fire and so I wrapped him up in my arms and started shooting myself, single shots first and then bursts of fire. He immediately recognized the sound and especially the smell. I suggested that he try squeezing the trigger himself but continued to circle him with my arms. I added: "You're in control now, and not captive to the fire."

Interesting.

He started with single bullets and shortly switched to bursts of automatic fire.

Magazine after magazine.

In fury and fervor.

Had I brought enough magazines, we'd still be shooting to this very day, in a liberating bliss.

The circle, for him, was closed. I later heard that he was doing well and continued to thrive.

Who would believe it: a Kalashnikov as a therapeutic tool!

Not sure it will be included in the national healthcare's medical devices' list, but useful all the same.

Lt.-Col. (res) Dr. Arik Shalev arrived at the Unit shortly after the Yom Kippur War, in which he served as a doctor in the Paratroop's Northern Brigade. He was deployed to Mount Hermon and there he saw a band of handsome Sayeret Matkal operators heading out on a mission. He wanted to get a cool battle vest like theirs, so he hid the fact of his corrective eyeglasses and was accepted to the Unit, where he served for years. Later he continued to serve with the same operators in the IAF's commando unit, Shaldag, which didn't really improve his vision. He completed his residency in psychiatry and transferred to Hadassah Medical Center, where he served as the chairman of the department until his retirement. He continues to conduct research in the field of traumatic stress and post-traumatic disorder. He's married to Vered and a father to Tali and Anat, and a grandfather to Noga, Rotem, Stav, and Uri.

Recently he returned to the high ridge of Mount Hermon to visit the friends who never returned and found it hard to comprehend the insane amount of strength and bravery needed to climb up that steep mountain under fire, and recapture the outpost at the summit. Youth's madness.

Lt. Omer Bar Lev, Team Leader
Omer APC Commander; APC Force

"Go For It"

OR

To Entebbe and Back in 48 Hours

On the eve of Operation Entebbe, I was the commander of the most veteran team in the Unit. Team Amnon, known as "August 73," was technically still in service but was on its end-of-service leave. My Team, "November 73," was training for a classified major operation scheduled for September 1976 and, during that specific week, on routine alert at the base, maintaining a state of readiness for a hostile, terrorist attack. Most of the week was relatively quiet. The junior teams of the Training Company were off the base, evidently conducting exercises, and the rest of the Operational Company (excluding my team) was taking part in an operation in the Sinai, led by Yoni Netanyahu. Muki Betser was the on-duty "chief commander" at the base.

Although an Air France plane that took off from Ben Gurion Airport at the beginning of the week had been hijacked, after a layover in Greece, the atmosphere in our base was tranquil. We had no sense that the hijacking had anything to do with us. On Wednesday, however, Muki came to me, and told me to pick five soldiers from my team who "know how to swim" because we were about to take part in an operation to save the hostages, which required us to parachute into Lake Victoria. From my point of view, this option was off the table pretty much as quickly as it came up. I didn't make any special preparations and didn't choose any proficient swimmers from among my soldiers. As I always recount in my military heritage stories about the operation, they had evidently forgotten that there were crocodiles in the lake. Once they realized this, the plan was cancelled. I later learned that there had been such a plan and several attempts had been made to drop Zodiac rubber boats from a Hercules C-130 aircraft, but the rafts shattered on contact with the water.

On Thursday Yoni and the rest of the operational company came back from the south and the hustle and bustle of the Unit returned to normal. Knowing all was okay, I decided to take an "after" (a short "after duty") and drop in on my girlfriend. It was easy to find someone to replace me on call and I left in the evening. I grabbed a Jeep and made some space for Maxie Katzir (an officer in the Unit who was assigned to my team for the September operation) and headed out. I dropped him off at his flat in Tzahala and proceeded to Neve Magen where I lived, to meet my girlfriend.

Towards midnight, I got a call from the Unit to come back immediately. It was clear to me that the reason was Entebbe. I jumped into the Jeep and headed for Tzahala to pick up Maxie. He was waiting for me on a street corner, dressed in "civvies," wearing a suit and carrying luggage. Surprised, I asked him, "Maxie, why are you wearing a suit and what's the suitcase for?" He looked at me in wonder and replied, "It's clear that we're flying to Entebbe to rescue the hostages, and how are we going to get there? The only way, obviously, is as civilians on an international flight." What's interesting about my reaction is that it wasn't, "What are you, nuts?" or anything of the sort, but just the opposite. "How could I not have thought of that? It's obvious that we ought to fly to Entebbe as civilians on an international flight." This was exactly 48 hours before landing in Entebbe.

We arrived at the Unit around midnight and were informed that Yoni was on his way from Beit HaTzanchan. When he arrived, he gathered all of us team commanders in the office and described the operation in general. The next day, Friday – equipment organization and briefings; Friday night— "dry run" asserting control over the terrorists and rescuing the hostages ; Saturday morning— off to Ben Gurion Airport to begin the long flight south, stopping in Sharm el-

Sheikh in the southern part of Sinai for final refueling and then on to Entebbe.

Friday was a day of organizing the teams, stocking up on gear, and sitting for briefings. At the time, a command force that I headed, and which included my team and Yuval Fine's, was in the midst of an intensive training regimen that had been ongoing for several months, preparing for a highly classified operation that could well be termed "historic." It did, in fact, take place a few months later. Given the situation, and contrary to the Unit's tradition, by which the senior team is assigned the primary task, which in this case was bursting into the terminal building and rescuing the hostages, the mission we were given was to secure and isolate the old terminal. After the operation, I learned that Chief of Staff Motta Gur had instructed Yoni that "Omer and his team will not participate in the (Entebbe) operation," because of the special-op for which we were training. I don't know if those were his exact words to Yoni, or if he just wanted to make sure that my team and I wouldn't constitute the first breakthrough force. In any event, when I asked Yoni on Friday why my team was not leading the assault force, he explained to me what the Chief of Staff had said and stated that he was therefore giving me the responsibility of "sealing off the area of operations" and not the honor of manning the lead strike force. Having no choice in the matter, I accepted the decree.

As mentioned above, Friday was a day of organizing the teams, stocking up on gear, and sitting for briefings. The force that was supposed to isolate the operations area included four groups, each on a BTR, a type of Russian light armored wheeled military vehicle. In the lead pair of APCs, Mofaz commanded the first and I the second. In the second pair, Udi Salvi commanded the first and Alon Shemi the second. Our job was to isolate the old terminal from the rest of the airport on one side and for Udi and Alon to do so on the other. The specific staffing of the BTR force changed throughout the day. Typically, in such situations, in which the number of soldiers that can participate is limited, each team commander does his utmost to make sure that as many of his men will participate as possible. Almost inevitably, a sort of "struggle" develops between the team commanders as to who will have more of his soldiers in the operation. Thanks to my seniority in the Unit and our operational experience, I had priority in choosing. So, in the "first round" I managed to get in ten of the twelve operators on my team, but two were still left out. All day I lay in wait for Yoni, waiting for the right opportunity to approach, and successfully convinced him to add Uri Ben Ner as the driver of the Land Rover which shadowed the Mercedes, and, also my last soldier.

Throughout the day, from briefing to briefing, the plan was formulated. In the late afternoon, after one of the briefings, I was really shaken, even horrified. Why? Because the plan looked to me like Swiss cheese, filled with gaping holes. I had made quite a few comments during the briefings, some of which were critical. For instance, there was a command to Yiftach Reicher and his force that, while charging through the upper floor of the old terminal, they were to open fire only if fired upon. About a year earlier, during the Savoy Hotel counter-terror raid, in which I was one of the team commanders leading the charge, Uzi Yairi and Itamar Ben David were killed by a terrorist who had been hit during our initial assault. The wounded terrorist crawled into one of the rooms, where, after some time, he recovered and then opened fire almost randomly, hitting and killing Uzi and Itamar. When I heard that hold-fire order issued to Yiftach, I couldn't help but visualize a situation in which we had burst into the old terminal, rescued the hostages, and then, while taking them out to the Hercules, a Ugandan soldier, who had hidden on the top floor, came out to the balcony and started shooting at the hostages, injuring and killing some of them. I got up in the middle of the briefing and said that I thought the order "to open fire **only** if fired upon" was dangerous and mistaken. I remember that after the briefing I was restless and said to Yiftach that he must "clean out" the entire top floor with live fire. Another example was the directive issued regarding the return trip, after freeing the hostages. According to that battle order, once all troops had returned to their plane and once that plane was ready for takeoff, it should depart without waiting for the other planes. Whether it was because, according to the plan, I was slated to be the last Israeli soldier on Ugandan soil to get on the last Hercules, or if it was more on account of my insights into the nature of operations, I again stood up and stated that this decision too was wrong. For the first two Hercules, the decision made sense, but the third one must wait on the runway for the fourth, and only when it was ready should they take off together, in tandem, to make their way home. Otherwise, a situation could develop in which the third plane takes off and leaves the last one on the ground and Ugandan forces attack, rendering the plane incapable of departure and stranding its crew and all of us on the ground, in the hands of the Ugandans. In light of my comments, the orders were changed. I should have been pleased that my opinion prevailed, but, in fact, I felt just the opposite. "How is it possible that such a basic principle, and such a simple issue, hadn't been considered by Yoni and the rest of the 'wise men' of the Air Force?"

In the evening, we went out for a "dry run" on the runways. I note "dry run" in quotations as our feeling was that the drill was closer to a joke than the kind of practice exercise we were familiar with. The training company had evidently set up some metal stakes on which they stretched canvas tarps—in order to resemble the old terminal at the airport. We manned the light armor, went around the planned course, fired a few muffled blanks and "all forces safely returned to their base." The Chief of Staff had come to the exercise and we were later told that he was impressed with our performance. That just added fuel to the fire we felt within us regarding the loose nature of the preparations, and the very plan itself.

On Friday night after the "dry run," I went to the office of the Deputy Commander of the Unit. We were a few team commanders and staff officers who sat down to talk. The feeling was pretty dismal. As far as we were concerned, the plan was not as tight as we were used to and the "dry run" had been a joke (to say the least!), even though the Chief of Staff had been impressed. I felt that the officers around the table were putting pressure on me to inform my father that there was a huge gap between the level of readiness that had likely been presented to the government and the reality. I debated hard and struggled with myself over what I should do. At this point the dilemma was mine alone—to involve him or not?

My father, the late Haim Bar Lev, by virtue of being a Cabinet member and earlier the IDF's Chief of Staff, of course knew that I was part of the force headed to Entebbe. He was accustomed to such situations. I remember him telling me that after the battle for the peak of Mt. Hermon in Syria following the Yom Kippur War in 1974, he had heard on the radio that the IDF had about 12 casualties. Based on his military experience, he knew that when the number of casualties is announced, with no mention of fatalities, it usually means that a third of the casualties are, in fact, fatalities. He waited three days for my call after I got off the mountain to hear that I was not among the casualties. And a year later, when terrorists took over the Savoy Hotel in the heart of Tel Aviv, he went to IDF Headquarters where he sat in the war room next to Motta, the Chief of Staff, and listened to the conversations on the military communications network, including to "Team Omer." But this time it was different. The unwritten task being placed on my shoulders by my brothers in arms, and the decision I had to make was much harder. Should I tell Dad? After much deliberation, I decided it was my obligation to accept the "mission." I would update him. Never in my five years in the Unit as a team commander and then commander of operations for three years, had I come close to such a conversation with my father.

And yet, in that way, I found myself on Friday night heading out in a D-200 pickup truck for Neve Magen, to talk with Dad. While riding along, right after Sirkin Junction, the hood of the pickup truch popped open, covering the entire windshield and blocking my field of vision. I stopped immediately, closed the hood, started the car up again, turned around, and headed back to the base.

More than once I have wondered what would have happened if the hood hadn't suddenly popped open? What exactly would I have told Dad? What would he have done? Each time I've come to the same conclusion—he would have listened, asked some questions and, maybe, tried to assure me that the situation was not so dire, and I would have returned to the base because the next day was Shabbat and we were leaving for Entebbe. And Dad, what would he have done with the heavy weight I had dropped on him? He would undoubtedly have taken a deep breath, bitten his lips hard, buried the information deep inside and kept his fingers crossed until I returned.

The preparations and plans for Operation Entebbe were vastly different from what we, the operational commanders and the staff officers, were accustomed to. We had only 24 hours, midnight Thursday to midnight Friday, to do everything: formulate the basic plan; get acquainted with some equipment for the first time (like the light armored vehicles and the grenade launchers which were installed in each armored vehicle and which we had never seen or used before and which did not work during the raid); briefings; dry runs, and final equipment details. One could say that the hasty nature of the preparations undermined all we had previously known. It came as no surprise that the mood of the team commanders and staff officers was grim indeed that Friday night. We were young, determined, and confident in ourselves as only young people (or aging fanatics) are, and we were immersed in a world where everything is either black or white and from our point of view what we saw was black! Although I can still understand the root of that sentiment, looking at it today, with the perspective I have gained from my professional and military experience, I recognize and understand that we were close-minded in our thinking and that we were wrong.

The next day, Saturday morning, we finished the very last preparations and set off to the Israel Air Force site at Ben Gurion Airport. Right before we left, I made sure to put in the right pocket of my pants a map on a scale of 1:1,000,000 or maybe even larger, which showed the network of roads from the airport in Entebbe to the Kenyan border. If it turned out that I had to scramble out of the airport in a way other than by plane, I would need to seize some vehicle and drive to Kenya. Whatever will be—put a map in your pocket. What's sure is sure!

The loading of the armored vehicles into the belly of the Hercules was done by in-flight mechanics who wouldn't let us get anywhere near to help. We wondered why they insisted on securing the vehicles themselves and wouldn't even let us approach the iron chains. Why were they making such a fuss? We were trained and experienced, even beyond enemy lines, in securing vehicles in helicopters using ratchets to tie them down – so why were these guys making such a stink about securing equipment in the Hercules? Only when we landed in Entebbe and the plane braked with incredible force did I fully understand the rationale for the iron chains.

We boarded the four Hercules C-130s. My team and I were on the second plane and took off for the last refueling station at Ofira airport in Sharm el-Sheik. We landed, fueled-up, and gathered for a final briefing with Yoni. I believe that at that point we saw the latest photos of the airport in Entebbe, and primarily of the old terminal. A Mossad operative had sent them from Entebbe just a few hours earlier. At the end of the short briefing, I went to Yoni to confirm again that I was permitted to shoot at the Ugandan MiGs once I was in the right position. His answer was perfectly clear -YES! I make a point of this because the day after the operation, Giora Sussmann, my company commander, said that were Yoni still alive he would oust me from my position in the Unit as team commander, since he had given an explicit order that no one, and I was no exception, was to shoot at the Ugandan planes. Sussmann's comment is as strange to me today as it was then.

The flight from Ofira to Entebbe was calm and even pleasant. As usual, the soldiers fell asleep immediately while Alon Shemi and I stayed up most of the flight. The bad feelings we had the previous evening flipped 180 degrees while in transit.

July 1976 came, for us, at the end of two difficult years, during which we were called to respond to quite a few "extortionist terrorist attacks," in which terrorists penetrated into Israel and took hostages as bargaining chips. In one case they took over a school, in another a hotel, and we were sent in to rescue the hostages. We didn't always get the chance to participate in the actual rescue operation, but we were always called in. In each situation, the other side, the terrorists, were the initiators. They dictated the timing and the location of the attack and we were suddenly called into action—usually in the middle of the night, often while asleep. No matter the location of the takeover, even if it was in the middle of Tel Aviv, in those critical moments when we were awakened from deep sleep and taken by helicopter or truck to the scene, the place felt strange and dark. And now, on our way to Entebbe, both Alon and I felt confident, even good. Although this time we had to go far away, we were the initiators and the enemy was in for a surprise.

Along with our sense of confidence, we felt that we were on the cusp of a historic moment. As teenagers we had lived through the IDF's raid on the Beirut Airport and then the raid against the terrorist leaders in Beirut. On this flight to Entebbe, we felt we were about to take part in an operation as historically important as those had been.

Then came the landing. We landed seven minutes after the first plane carrying Yoni and the force under his command. Their "excuse" to the air traffic controllers was that they needed to make an emergency landing due to mechanical problems with the plane. As the wheels of our plane hit the ground, all the lights on the runways went out. The pilot braked hard and I immediately realized why we'd needed the iron chains to secure the armor.

We quickly emerged from the belly of the Hercules, with Mofaz and his crew leading and me and mine following. We charged toward the old terminal, gunshots audible along the way. Apparently, those were the bursts of fire that had killed the Ugandan sentries at an improvised blockade set up to separate the runway and the arrivals hall of the old terminal, where the hostages were being held.

And now: a "time out." One of the most poignant disputes that arose after the operation was between Muki Betser and the late Yoni Netanyahu, or rather by others in his name, and it revolved around this: What was the right way to respond to that blockade? Muki's claim was, and remains, based on his familiarity with the Ugandan army. He saw it as a standard act of saluting a VIP upon arrival. When they saw a black Mercedes approaching, they assumed it was Idi Amin and fired their guns over the car in salute. From his point of view, they had no intention of opening hostile fire. When Yoni saw them aiming their weapons in the direction of the Mercedes, he gave the order to shoot them with muffled ammunition. Shots were fired but the targets were not hit. Realizing what had happened, the machine-gunner in the Land Rover trailing the Mercedes, shot and killed the Ugandan soldiers.

In a later debriefing, Muki claimed that Yoni's decision to open fire at the Ugandans led to "un-muffled shooting" which undermined the element of surprise and could have damaged the entire success of the Operation. After the fact it turned out that when the terrorists in the old terminal heard the shooting, they told the hostages that the Ugandan soldiers were acting out of control and were firing wildly and that they should all "keep down." Years later when I was the commander of the Unit, and ever since then, when I tell the story of Operation Yonatan, I describe the dilemma Yoni faced in those seconds – should he have relied on Muki's statement, that he knew the Ugandans and that they would not dare to open fire, or should he have given the order to open fire and kill them? Unquestionably, if I was in Yoni's place, I would have behaved exactly as he did, ordering my troops to open fire at the guards. I explain that although such an order may partially compromise the element of surprise, and despite the customary practice of the Ugandans, the chance that one or more of them would decide to fire at the Mercedes at such an early stage was too great a risk.

As we approached the old terminal, we shaved off some of the seven or eight-minute gap between us and the Mercedes and the two Land Rovers. Mofaz, who arrived at the old terminal plaza shortly after the Ugandan soldiers in the control tower opened fire on Yoni's forces, joined in and returned fire at the tower.

According to the pre-mission planning, I was supposed to go to the terminal plaza to check with Yoni if he needed me for the ground operation. If not, I was to move east and hunker down in one spot. I got to the plaza shortly after Mofaz and called Yoni on the radio but got no answer. While we were under fire, Mofaz notified me that he would stay where he was and ordered me to continue east towards the area where I was to block reinforcements that might possibly come from the area of the military base. I left him there and moved on to my appointed destination.

I had a strong spotlight on my armored vehicle and while standing still, I aimed the light in the direction of where I believed the MiGs ought to be. And there they were, two rows, side-by-side, one with five MiG-21s and the other with three MiG-17s. The troops wanted to open fire immediately, but I waited until the takeover of the terminal was complete. There was incessant fire coming from the terminal, and in such situations every second feels like an hour. We heard more and more shots fired and then, after what seemed like an eternity, silence. It stretched on and our tension increased. We needed to see or hear what had happened with the hostages.

During the briefings we had been told that there could be a state of hysteria and a mass exodus of hostages running out of the old terminal. That didn't happen. Eventually, one of my team members said something like, "they're not there." He and some of the rest of us didn't feel hysteria, but silence, and momentarily felt that something might have gone wrong. And then they began to come out in an orderly, controlled manner as they walked toward the Hercules approaching the old terminal.

At that point, I called Mofaz and asked permission to open fire at the MiGs. He didn't answer, so I tried again. And then I put in a call to Yoni, but he didn't answer either. There I was, a soldier alone in the field, who had to make his own decision. It was a situation where you say to yourself, "You are now the Chief of Staff on the ground, you are alone, and you have to make a decision." At that moment I instructed one of my team members to get off the armored vehicle and fire a LAW missile at the MiGs. He got down, shot, and missed! I instructed Yaakov, who was on the grenade launcher (which he'd never fired before), to open fire but he succeeded in firing only one or two grenades before the launcher jammed. At this point, I was manning the machine gun at the turret of the APC, above the driver's head, and I opened fire at the fighter planes. Very quickly, one of them (which evidently had been fueled up) broke out in ironically beautiful flames which spread to the sky and to the other planes, torching them all.

In retrospect, it became clear that Deputy Chief of Staff Maj.-Gen. Kuti Adam, who was in the air command room aboard a Boeing plane orbiting over Uganda, had ordered Dan Shomron, at roughly the same time, to instruct me to blow up the MiGs. But just as my attempts to get approval for my intention to blow up the fighter jets hadn't succeeded, so too did Kuti's order never arrive and I blew them up on my own initiative.

Only 40 years later did I hear the full story from Amos Eran, the Director General of the Prime Minister's office during the ceremony commemorating 40 years since Operation Yonatan, which took place at the Rabin Center. The C-130's didn't have enough fuel to fly home from Entebbe and needed to refuel on their way back in Nairobi. Col. Ehud Barak had been dispatched to Kenya in advance to take care of the refueling of the Hercules C-130s for the return trip. To avoid information leaks, it had been decided not to inform Kenya in advance about the operation, or the need to stop at the Nairobi airport to refuel. The decision was based on the belief that the good relations between Kenya and Israel would lead them to agree even if they were notified in the middle of the night and only after the hostages were released. Around midnight, Col. Barak phoned Kenya's President, woke him up, and informed him of the operation. The President's first reply was "No way! Tomorrow Ugandan fighters will attack and bomb Nairobi's airport." After a while he relented, but only on condition that the Israeli commandos blow up the Ugandan MIGs in Entebbe Airport. The rest is history.

After the hostages boarded the Hercules airplanes and departed with the rescue force, I was left quite alone to secure their getaway. Then I received an order to start moving towards the main runway – a relatively long distance. The concern was that Ugandan reinforcements would show up and attack our remaining planes before takeoff. It was my responsibility to delay them. At one point, we stopped about 200 meters from an elevated, ball-shaped fuel tank. Today I can't remember if my soldiers suggested we blow up the tank or if I debated internally about doing so. The tank was just "crying out" and pleading for us to blast it with a LAW missile. It was an easy target and I could imagine the powerful explosion which would light up the entire airport area. I felt somewhere between being an actor in a Hollywood movie featuring a raid on an airport and a participant in the descriptions relayed in Virginia Cowles' biography of David Stirling, "The Phantom Major," in which the commander of what would become the SAS describes the British commando teams attacking German airports in North Africa during World War II. The scene of us blowing up the giant fuel tank fit right into the script.

It was a long, difficult moment. In the excitement, clutched by the swirling impulses of enthusiasm and adrenaline, I had to decide whether to blow up the tank or not. This was precisely one of those situations where, in a split second, you make a decision that might for some unknown reason, however low the probability, cause enormous damage. The question for you as a commander at that instant is whether you realize that this is one of those moments. Could the explosion be so massive that some of the burning fuel might be blown hundreds of meters and damage your armored transport? I bit my lips and left the fuel tank whole.

Let's go back to the "reverse getaway" on the runway. At the briefings, one way discussed to delay the arrival of reinforcement enemy troops was for us to move forward to the main runway in quick dashes, dispersing blast-delay explosive blocks with timers which would blow up a few minutes later. This would delay and deter the Ugandans from approaching the planes. I ordered one of my soldiers who was responsible for the explosive devices to prepare the "bricks" for operation. Each one must be attached to an accelerator, the accelerator to a detonator and a latency fuse, which is activated as soon as you want to set off the charge. Connecting all this takes several minutes and he had begun to assemble the system when I was instructed by Mofaz to move out with the armored vehicle. I notified him to dismantle the operating chain, he did, and we took off. We moved to a new position and I ordered him to put the chain together again, but this time more quickly. He was busy doing that but in a

split of a second another order arrived from Mofaz: Move on. Again,
I stopped him. This hectic scenario repeated itself at least three times
until he finally managed to connect the explosive chain, pull the detonator's latency fuse, activate it, and throw the brick into the darkness.
With that, we moved out, pulling further away.

At this point, a commotion ensued regarding the counting of the
hostages. In the first count, while loading them onto the Hercules
aircraft, the number of hostages was two or three more than anticipated. On a recount, it became clear that one hostage, Mrs. Dora
Bloch, was missing. Not a young woman, she had been moved out of
the old terminal a few days earlier, feeling unwell. When this became
clear, Mofaz called and told me to go back to the area of the old
terminal to see if, by chance, she had been put in the Air France
Airbus which was parked nearby. In situations like this, you of course
don't ask whether it is logical that she be there alone in the empty
plane, so I prepared to backtrack to see if she was on the plane. But I
realized with alarm, that only a few minutes earlier we had finally
been able to place one of the explosive devices somewhere on the
dark runway between us and the Air France plane. But an order is an
order. We retraced our tracks to the plane, trying to guess where we
had thrown the explosive, in order to avoid it.

We successfully got to the plane and Mofaz lit up the area. My
soldiers and I circled the plane to inspect it. As far as we could tell, it
was pitch black and totally still. Do we go up and walk into the plane
to look around? Not a very enticing prospect. Some of our troops had
already taken off for home and others, who were about a kilometer
from us, were approaching the last plane, which was revving its
engines and getting ready for takeoff. While deliberating with myself,
a radio message came through saying that the plane may be booby-
trapped and we should not board but only have a look around it. We
completed the scan and began to advance towards the end of the new
runway where the Hercules was standing by when, suddenly, the
sabotage brick that was supposed to hold back the Ugandan reinforcement forces finally exploded, managing only to waylay us.

Then, as foreseen during expected according to the "Incidents and

Reactions" possibilities we discussed prior to the raid, reinforcements of Ugandan vehicles with lit headlights arrived from the airport's administrative entrance area. We opened fire on them, the lights went out; they were stopped and maybe even hit. Within a few minutes we received the final order to head for the Hercules which was waiting at the edge of the runway. The rest of the forces, including Mofaz's armored vehicle, were already secured inside the plane. We got off our BTR, Yoav Wachman our driver drove it up the cargo ramp, the troops boarded, and I walked in—the last Israeli soldier on Ugandan soil that night. I peeked at my watch – exactly an hour and a half on the ground in Uganda. It was a bit after midnight, and we were already on our way home.

My sense is that on the way to Nairobi we were informed that Yoni was wounded, maybe seriously so. Only when we landed to refuel did we learn from Shai Avital[1] and his men that Yoni had been killed. The feeling was mixed. On one hand, an adrenaline rush from the excitement of the operation's success, to a great extent beyond our expectations, but, on the other, Yoni Netanyahu, our commander, the Unit commander, was dead. These feelings escalated as we made the flight to Israel, particularly during the hours before landing when the pilots connected the plane's PA system to the radio in Israel, turning up the speakers for us to hear. A sort of a celebration was audible over the airwaves, perhaps best called mass hysteria, yet we didn't feel comfortable with that. Yes, we had taken part in a bold operation, and, yes, we had succeeded, but we were returning with the body of the Unit commander. We honestly felt that we just did what was expected of us. What's the big deal?

To this day, the operation to free the hostages from Entebbe symbolizes to me an effort that succeeded thanks primarily to the initiative of the individual soldier and less to the team and platoon commanders. What do I mean?

Usually, in terrorist attacks of this sort, and certainly in all those in which we took part during the two years before and after Entebbe, it was often the team commanders who led and fought at the front of the action. This was true two years earlier in the attacks on the Savoy

Hotel, in Beit She'an, in the takeover of the kindergarten in Misgav-
Am and at the time of the hijacking of Bus 300. In most of those
events, those who fought were the commanders, one or two junior
officers leading their troops behind them. In Operation Entebbe, it
was different. Those who improvised, took initiative, advanced, and
fought were mostly individual soldiers. Even the team commanders
largely acted as individuals. Not because it was planned that way,
but, on the contrary, because there had been limited intelligence and
imperfect planning.

As for the planning of the operation itself – Operation Entebbe
was extraordinarily complex and complicated. In "normal" times we
would have trained for such an operation for weeks and maybe even
months. Here we had 24 hours. Forty-eight hours elapsed between
midnight Thursday, when we were summoned by Yoni to headquarters to receive our first orders, and midnight Saturday, when the last
plane from Entebbe took off for home. Unbelievable!

I mentioned earlier that on the eve of the takeoff, there was a
grim feeling among the Unit's operational team commanders and
staff officers. At the time we were critical, as we were accustomed to
a different standard of detailed planning prior to going out on an
exercise, not to mention an actual operation. The likeness of certain
deficiencies in the plan to the large holes in Swiss cheese was absolutely accurate! But, given the schedule we had to contend with, the
achievement was enormous. On the macro level, the IDF succeeded,
and from our narrower perspective, we, the troops, were able to
successfully carry out the operation despite the limitations. This was
possible thanks to the infrastructure of a daring Unit commander,
excellent team commanders, and soldiers who were ready to "go for
it" with resourcefulness and determination! Finding a good balance
between long, orderly, detailed planning and good sense, intuition
and initiative is the basis for real strength at a moment of truth. This
insight accompanied me for many years in my service within the Unit
and, later, as its commander.

Prior to Operation Entebbe, I was with Yoni under fire at least
once. His courage impressed me. Even in Entebbe, when the takeover

force disembarked from the vehicles, staying as close as possible to the side of the old terminal building as they moved along under his guidance, he stood firmly on the open runway, easily seen, commanding the forces. This truly was the best place for him to be. Had he been close to the building, his field of vision would have been blocked and his ability to command compromised. The mere seconds involved in this type of situation can lead to success or failure. It was Yoni's quickness and agility that motivated the forces. But Yoni's fortitude was truly revealed perhaps all the more starkly in those relatively quiet moments that I, and most of us, did not share with him. In the 24 hours before the operation, I imagine he stood in front of the Chief of Staff and likely the defense minister and prime minister and said confidently, without hesitation, "we can do it!" Years later as a commander of the Unit myself, I was present in those quiet rooms, faced with similar issues. In those critical times when everyone's eyes are focused on you, you are alone, and it is just your voice that will determine the outcome. The weight of responsibility is massive, as you understand that in the event of failure, there could be a disaster and it will be you alone in command. It's not just bearing the burden of responsibility, which will later be brought to the fore, but the responsibility to deal with the moments of chaos and to bring your troops home - alive, wounded, or dead. Since Operation Entebbe, particularly during the years in which Gilad Shalit was held in Hamas captivity, I have been asked more than once if today's State of Israel is capable of carrying out an operation like Operation Yonatan; and more specifically—would today's national and IDF leadership be able to do so? My immediate response was always "Yes!" but over the past two years my belief in our current capacity has been weakened. I am no longer so sure. Why? Certainly not because of the fighting forces, but because an overweight, large army, as the IDF is today[2], often favors "quantity" over "quality and guts," and it may therefore find itself incapable of carrying out such an operation, despite its desire to do so.

There is a fine line, and a need for balance, between detailed planning and initiative and intuition, between quantifying and daring.

It cannot be taken for granted that this balance is achieved in all situations. Such a reality is fraught with risk. An army that believes the answer to risk is quantitative may cross these fine lines and lose its ability to perform.

Col. Omer Bar Lev (res) was a team commander in the Unit's Operational Company during the Entebbe Operation in July 1976; the Commander of Sayeret Matkal from 1984-1987; established and led the "Acharei!" ("Follow Me") movement for fifteen years; a former high-tech entrepreneur; served as a Member of the 19th Knesset on behalf of the Labor Party in 2013-2014. A Member of the 20th Knesset on behalf of the Zionist Union in 2015-2019, a member of the 21st and 22nd Knesset on behalf of the Labor Party, and currently (2021) a member of the 24th Knesset on behalf of the Labor Party.

Notes

1. Avital at that time was already a reservist of the Unit and had been sent to Nairobi several weeks earlier to train the Kenyan president's personal guard.
2. These lines were written just after Operation Protective Edge in autumn 2014 when I was a member of the Security and Foreign Affairs committee of the Knesset.

Offloading the Mercedes back in Israel. Muki Betser, standing, is to the right of the vehicle. Dani Arditi, turning his back to the camera, is on the left.
Photo: IDF Spokesperson's Unit

Offloading the Mercedes back in Israel. Pinchas Buchris, getting off the cargo ramp, is to the right of the vehicle; Alex Davidi, standing, is to the left. Seated from right to left are Arnon Epstein and Gal Raif.
Photo: IDF Spokesperson's Unit.

The Mercedes backing off the plane. Seated, from right to left, are Arnon Epstein and Gal Raif. Photo: IDF Spokesperson's Unit

Prime Minister Yitzhak Rabin (white shirt) and Defense Minister Shimon Peres congratulating the operators, with their backs turned to the camera, upon return.
Photo: IDF Spokesperson's Unit

Operation Yonatan:

List of Operators and Authors
(roles and positions of those deployed)

Operator	Rank	Unit post at time of operation: assignment and position during operation
		Assault Force
Yoni Netanyahu	Lt.-Col.	Unit commander: commander of all Unit forces: Assault Force, Suppressive Fire Force, APC Force. Commander of Assault Force - Mercedes.
Alik Ron	Maj.	Former commander of Unit Anti-Terror Company: member of Yoni's command squad—Land Rover 2
Tamir Pardo	Lt.	Unit communications officer: Yoni's command squad—Land Rover 2
Dr. David Hassin	Cpt.	Unit doctor: Yoni's command squad—Land Rover 2
Muki Betser	Maj.	Unit reserves forces commander: deputy force commander, squad commander, hostage hall, left door-Mercedes
Alex Davidi	Staff-Sgt.	Operator Team Amnon Peled: Muki's squad—Mercedes
Gadi Ilan	Staff-Sgt.	Operator Team Amnon Peled: Muki's squad—Mercedes
Amos Goren	Staff-Sgt.	Operator Team Omer Bar Lev: Muki's squad—Mercedes
Amnon Peled	Cpt.	Operational Company team leader: squad commander, hostage hall, right door-Land Rover 2
Shlomi Reisman	Staff-Sgt.	Operator Team Amnon Peled: Amnon's squad—Land Rover 2
Ilan Blumer	Staff-Sgt.	Operator Team Amnon Peled: Amnon's squad—Land Rover 2
Amir Ofer	Staff-Sgt.	Operator Team Amnon Peled: Amnon's squad—Land Rover 2
Amos Ben Avraham	2nd-Lt.	Training Company team leader: commander of Amnon's auxiliary squad (hostage hall, right door)—Land Rover 1
Gal Raif	Sgt.	Operator Team Dani Arditi: Amos' squad—Land Rover 1
Dani Fredkin	Sgt.	Operator Team Dani Arditi: Amos' squad—Land Rover 1

Operator	Rank	Unit post at time of operation: assignment and position during operation
		Assault Force
Giora Sussmann	Cpt.	Operational Company commander: squad leader, small hall, terrorists' quarters—Mercedes
Adam Kolman	Sgt.	Operator Team Dani Arditi: Sussmann's squad—Mercedes
Yoram Rubin	Sgt.	Operator Team Dani Arditi: Sussmann's squad—Mercedes
Amnon Ben-Ami	Sgt.	Operator Team Dani Arditi: Sussmann's squad—Mercedes
Yiftach Reicher Atir	Cpt.	Training Company commander, deputy commander of the Unit: commander of customs hall and second floor squads—Land Rover 1
Rani Cohen	2nd-Lt.	Training Company team leader: Yiftach's squad—Land Rover 1
Amir Shadmi	Lt.	Training Company team leader: Yiftach's squad—Land Rover 1
Arnon Epstein	2nd-Lt.	Operational Company team leader: commander of Yiftach's auxiliary squad—Land Rover 2
Udi Bloch	Cpl.	Operator Team Yoni Raz: Arnon's squad—Land Rover 2
Yonatan Gilad	Sgt.	Operator Team Dani Arditi: Arnon's squad—Land Rover 2
Pinchas Buchris	Cpl.	Operator Team Arnon Epstein: Arnon's squad—Land Rover 2
Dani Arditi	Lt.	Operational Company team leader: squad leader, VIP rooms—Land Rover 1
Aharoni Berkowitz	Sgt.	Operator Team Dani Arditi: Dani's squad—Land Rover 1
Amir Drori	Sgt.	Operator Team Dani Arditi: Dani's squad—Land Rover 1

Operator	Rank	Unit post at time of operation: assignment and position during operation
Wheeled Mobile and Suppressive Fire Force		
Rami Sherman	Lt.	Unit operations officer: commander of Wheeled Mobile and Suppressive Fire Force—Land Rover 1
Amitzur Kafri	2nd-Lt.	Unit weapons innovation officer: Mercedes driver, Rami's squad—Mercedes
Eyal Yardenay	Sgt.	Operator Team Dani Arditi: driver Land Rover 1, Rami's squad—Land Rover 1
Uri Ben-Ner	Staff-Sgt.	Operator Team Omer Bar Lev: driver Land Rover 2, Rami's squad—Land Rover 2

Operator	Rank	Unit post at time of operation: assignment and position during operation
APC Force		
Shaul Mofaz	Maj.	Outgoing Unit deputy commander APC Force—APC 1
Yohai Brenner	Maj.	GHQ Operations Officer: operator—APC 2
Itzik Kirschner	Staff-Sgt.	Operator Team Shai Avital, active reserves: operator—APC 1
Arik Kamus	Staff-Sgt.	Operator Team Omer Bar Lev: operator—APC 1
Eldad Dolev (Perkal)	Staff-Sgt.	Operator Team Omer Bar Lev: operator—APC 1
Yoel Tzibulski	Cpl.	Operator Team Yuval Fine: operator—APC 1
Dani Dagan	Master-Sgt.	Tactical driving officer: driver—APC 1
David Tzfira	Cpl.	Operator Team Yoni Raz: operator—APC 1
Omer Bar Lev	Lt.	Operational Company team leader: APC commander —APC 2
Yoni Raz	Lt.	Operational Company team leader: deputy commander APC 2

Operator	Rank	Unit post at time of operation: assignment and position during operation
APC Force		
Yoav Eran (Wachman)	Staff-Sgt.	Operator Team Shai Avital, active reserves: APC driver—APC 2
Yaakov Gil (Gilenberg)	Staff-Sgt.	Operator Team Omer Bar Lev: Operator—APC 2
Yossi Shak	Staff-Sgt.	Operator Team Omer Bar Lev: Operator—APC 2
Shauli Ravid	Staff-Sgt.	Operator Team Omer Bar Lev: operator—APC 2
Dr. Arik Shalev	Cpt.	Unit doctor in reserves: force doctor—APC 2
Ron Liberman	Cpl.	Operator Team Yuval Fine: operator—APC 2
Udi Salvi	Cpt.	Outgoing Training Company commander: commander APC 3 and 4
Yuval Fine	Lt.	Operational Company team leader : deputy commander APC 3
Zvi Chibutro	Cpl.	Operator Team Yuval Fine: driver APC 3
Tzachi Fuchs	Cpl.	Operator Team Yoni Raz: operator—APC 3
Uri Steinmitz	Cpl.	Operator Team Yuval Fine: Operator—APC 3
Raz Gur-Arieh	Cadet Officers School	Operator Team Yuval Fine: Operator—APC 3
Maxi Katzir	Lt.	Operator-officer: operator—APC 3
Ron Gal	Cpl.	Operator Team Yoni Raz: operator—APC 3
Alon Shemi	Lt.	Operational Company team leader: commander APC 4
Eyal Oren	2nd-Lt.	Operational Company team leader: deputy commander APC 4
Eyal Shifroni	Sgt.	Operator Team Dani Arditi: operator—APC 4
Asaf Lippman	Staff-Sgt.	Operator Team Omer Bar Lev: Operator—APC 4

Operator	Rank	Unit post at time of operation: assignment and position during operation
APC Force		
Zeev Ronen	Staff-Sgt.	Operator Team Omer Bar Lev: operator—APC 4
Yaron Asaf	Staff-Sgt.	Operator Team Omer Bar Lev: operator—APC 4
Meke Magal	Sgt.	Operator Team Dani Arditi: Driver APC 4
Hilik Glazer	Cpl.	Operator Team Yoni Raz: Operator—APC 4

Operator	Rank	Unit post at time of operation: assignment and position during operation
Staff Officers and NCOs		
Avi Livne (Weiss)	Cpt.	Unit intelligence officer: force intelligence officer — in Israel
Yael Zangen Taterka	Sgt. (res.)	Yoni's administrative bureau chief: on base—in the bureau
Michael Aaronson	Staff-Sgt. (res.)	Operator Team Giora Sussmann: Lake Victoria reconnaissance--Kenya

ACKNOWLEDGMENTS

Thanks to Sayeret Matkal. We served in the Unit, each in turn, each in his or her own role. It may have been difficult and dangerous, but we had an incredible service that will remain in our hearts forever. Today we are part of the Unit's fellowship (Hamisdar) and the Unit's non-profit fellowship is part of us.

Thanks to all of the operators. Including those who opted not to write. You were there, in Entebbe, and thanks to you nearly all of us made it back alive and well. You are part of the history and are present within the pages of this book.

Thanks to those who did write. Thirty-three stories. Thirty-two men and one woman who fretted over keyboards and put to paper their memories from the period and the operation. Well done.

Thanks to the Meir Amit Intelligence and Terrorism Information Center, its directors and managers, and to Effi Melzer (1955-2018, may he rest in peace), who granted us the honor of publishing the Hebrew edition of the book.

Thanks to Dana Elazar-Halevi for her inestimable assistance and her constant professionalism.

And last but not least: Though editors often remain in the background, we can't not thank Aviram Halevi, the man entrusted with the Unit's legacy and the man who supported us and propelled us along during this entire process.

And a great thank you to Shlomi. This book would not have been published without Shlomi Reisman. He is the spirit behind the book. He made contact with the operators, convinced them to write, helped them be precise about details when necessary and helped them strive for brevity where possible. He was the taskmaster and the lube in the chain. A heartfelt thank you.

The steering committee: **Yiftach Reicher Atir**, Avi Livne (Weiss), Amir Ofer, Amnon Peled, Giora Sussmann, Dani Arditi, Yohai Brenner, Amos Goren, Rami Sherman.

Printed in Great Britain
by Amazon

61639745R00234